THE
ORIGINS OF PRUSSIA

THE
ORIGINS OF PRUSSIA

BY

F. L. CARSTEN

Lecturer in History, Westfield College
University of London

OXFORD
AT THE CLARENDON PRESS

Oxford University Press, Ely House, London W.1

GLASGOW   NEW YORK   TORONTO   MELBOURNE   WELLINGTON
CAPE TOWN   SALISBURY   IBADAN   NAIROBI   LUSAKA   ADDIS ABABA
BOMBAY   CALCUTTA   MADRAS   KARACHI   LAHORE   DACCA
KUALA LUMPUR   HONG KONG   TOKYO

FIRST PUBLISHED 1954

REPRINTED LITHOGRAPHICALLY IN GREAT BRITAIN
AT THE UNIVERSITY PRESS, OXFORD
FROM SHEETS OF THE FIRST EDITION
1958, 1964, 1968

PREFACE

THIS volume is not another history of Prussia, but its purpose is to describe the growth and the decline of the classes
and the institutions which formed the basis of the later
Prussian state. For this reason rulers and reigns, foreign and
military events are only mentioned in so far as they are relevant
to this study, and it ends with the late seventeenth century when
the Hohenzollern state had come into being, because this state
remained fundamentally unaltered throughout the eighteenth
century. As there is an enormous wealth of documents and
other material dealing with the subject, my problem throughout has been what to omit and what to select, so that certain
aspects of the history of the territories which became the Prussia
of the eighteenth century had to be disregarded, while at some
points the story had to transcend the geographical boundaries
of these territories.

My thanks are due to many scholars who have shown an
unflagging interest in my work over many years and have helped
me with their advice and encouragement, above all to Professor
Norman H. Baynes, to Sir George Clark, Provost of Oriel
College, to Professor M. M. Postan, and to Dr. Norbert Elias, as
well as to the editors of the *English Historical Review*, Professor
J. G. Edwards and Professor Richard Pares, who have published extracts from my work in the issues of April 1947, April
1950, and April 1951. They and the publishers, Messrs. Long-
mans Green & Co. Ltd., have kindly permitted me to use the
same material in this book. I am indebted to Professor Eleanora
Carus-Wilson for several valuable suggestions. Dr. R. F. Leslie,
Dr. A. Bridbury, and my wife have been good enough to read
through the typescript and to suggest a number of alterations.
Grateful thanks are also due to the institutions which have
helped me by generous grants: Wadham and Magdalen
Colleges, Oxford, and the Central Research Fund of the
University of London.

F.L.C.

LONDON
August, 1953

CONTENTS

I. THE COLONIZATION

II. THE RISE OF THE JUNKERS

III. THE FOUNDATION OF THE HOHENZOLLERN DESPOTISM

I

THE COLONIZATION

I

The Conquest and Conversion of the Slavs and Prussians

IN the earlier Middle Ages the lands to the east of the Elbe
were inhabited by Slavonic tribes. They penetrated into
this area at the time of the Barbaric invasions when the
Germanic tribes pushed westwards and southwards, thus
evacuating the more eastern territories. It has often been asserted
that some Germans remained behind when the great migrations
took place. If that was the case, they were absorbed by the immigrating Slavs: no Germanic traces can be discovered in the
Slavonic districts before the Germans began to move eastwards
across the Elbe. The Slavs in their westward push not only
gained the line of the middle Elbe, but they penetrated across
the river and reached the Saale river and Thuringia in central
Germany. Farther to the north they filled the great eastward
bend of the Elbe north of Magdeburg: to the present day the
district east of Lüneburg, on the left bank of the Elbe, is called
the *Wendland* on account of the Slav origin of its inhabitants.[1]

The frontier running southwards from the Baltic to the
Bohemian mountains which separated Germans from Slavs was
fluid and the areas of settlement were not clearly delimited. The
population on either side was thin and wide stretches of wilderness and primeval forests surrounded the sparse settlements. Yet
military expeditions could penetrate into these solitudes; there
was frequent border warfare between Slav and Teuton as well
as between the different tribes on either side. The German tribes
in their eastward expeditions sought to capture slaves for sale.
Indeed, the earlier documents do not speak of the inhabitants

---

[1] *Wenden* is the German name for the West Slavonic tribes.

of the eastern regions as *Slavi*, but as *Sclavi*.[1] The Slavs in their turn called the Germans *Niemtsi*, people who could not speak, a description which has remained the word for German in the Slav languages. Another serious division appeared with the conversion of the Germanic tribes to the Christian religion from the days of Charlemagne onwards. The latter asserted German power to the east of the Elbe through military expeditions and the creation of frontier marches against the Slavs. The Slavs came to consider Christ the *Teutonicus deus* and Christianity an alien religion brought to them at the point of the sword. To the Germans the looting expeditions against the Slavs assumed the character of a crusade: the gain of material advantages could be combined with the salvation of their souls and deeds perpetrated against the heathen foe would be welcome in the eyes of God. The warfare along the border was exacerbated by the religious element. In the course of two to three centuries the Germans, helped by the missionaries of the Church, succeeded in imposing their religion upon the Slavs. In the region of the middle Elbe, about the middle of the tenth century, the bishoprics of Brandenburg and Havelberg were founded to undertake the mission among the Slavs; they were soon followed by the great archbishopric of Magdeburg. Christianity slowly spread; in the course of the tenth century it was adopted in Bohemia, Silesia, and Poland. From Poland Bishop Adalbert of Prague journeyed northwards to convert the heathen Prussians on the Baltic coast and met a martyr's death at their hands. From Poland another great missionary, Bishop Otto of Bamberg, set out to convert the Pomeranians, farther to the west on the Baltic coast.

Our information about the Slav tribes from the Baltic to the Bohemian mountains is very scanty.[2] There was no political unity among them, and no states had been formed to the west and north of Poland, but there were many principalities. Some of these, for example Pomerania, seem to have been fairly extensive, many others, for example those in Brandenburg, rather small. Everywhere a castle—*grad*—seems to have formed

---

[1] This identification occurs in all western European languages, indicating the main source of the supply of slaves for the west: R. Koebner, in *The Cambridge Economic History of Europe*, i, 1941, p. 52.

[2] Cf. H. Aubin, ibid. i, pp. 361-4.

the centre of a district which in the later documents is called a *terra*. To the castle the inhabitants had to bring their dues; for its erection, maintenance, and defence they had to perform services of various kinds. There was a fairly numerous nobility of different grades and many dynastic families of princely or semi-princely status. The lower classes, fishermen and peasants, had to render services and dues to princes and noblemen, such as the rearing and feeding of their horses and hounds, hunting services and hospitality, ferrying and carrying services, fishing and wood cutting.[1] Owing to the features of the area, with its numerous lakes and rivers, many inhabitants lived from their exploitation, or from that of the forests which covered much of the land. Agriculture was practised, either in the form of cattle rearing or of tillage, but it was of a primitive kind. The villages were small, and the implements used, especially the wooden or 'hooked' plough (*uncus*), permitted only the scratching of the surface and favoured the cultivation of light and sandy soils so that the yields were poor. There were some larger settlements, situated close to the castles and protected by them; at the coast there were a few trading centres visited by foreign merchants, such as Stettin at the mouth of the Oder, but there were hardly any towns. The districts to the east of the Oder were influenced by the more advanced Silesian and Polish principalities which were their neighbours. In general, however, the geographical difficulties of the area, its small population and the paucity of its resources resulted in a general backwardness which could only be altered by outside influences.

In the tenth century the Germans penetrated across the middle Elbe and began to establish their power in what later came to be called the Brandenburg Mark. The foundation of the bishoprics of Brandenburg and Havelberg by King Otto I in 946–9 was a political move asserting German claims to territories on the right bank of the Elbe.[2] If all the lands between the Elbe and the Oder were assigned to Brandenburg as its diocese, this did not indicate that their inhabitants were Christians or under Christian influence. In 983 a great rising of the Slavs,

---

[1] From these and other services Slavonic peasants were freed later: *Riedel*, ii, no. 7, p. 443 (1179); *Fabricius*, iii, no. 447*b* (1297); *Pomm. U.B.* iii, no. 1927, p. 398 (1300); *Riedel*, xii, no. 27, p. 430 (1420); *Landbuch 1375*, pp. 249–50: services of Slavonic fishermen in the Old Mark.

[2] *Riedel*, ii, no. 1, p. 435; viii, no. 2, p. 91.

which was both anti-German and anti-Christian, destroyed whatever advances had been made.[1] Not before 1005 could the two bishops return to their sees, and only after the Slavs had been promised the free exercise of their pagan religion by King Henry II.[2] Until the twelfth century the German hold on the right bank of the Elbe remained very precarious. Even on the left bank, where the North Mark of the Empire had been founded by Otto I, the struggle was not over. A decisive change, however, occurred when, in 1134, Count Albert the Bear, a prince of the house of Anhalt, was enfeoffed with the North Mark by the Emperor Lothar.[3] Albert became the founder of the Ascanian house of margraves which ruled in Brandenburg until 1319. During the following years he extended his power into the Priegnitz on the right bank of the Elbe and incorporated the district of Havelberg with the North Mark.[4] Farther south he established his sway in the Zauche which is said to have been a christening present of the Slav Prince Pribislav of Brandenburg to Albert's eldest son, Otto. When Pribislav died in 1150 without leaving a direct heir, he left his whole principality to Albert, according to the chroniclers. Yet Albert had to conquer the town and castle of Brandenburg and to reconquer them a few years later after a last Slav uprising.[5] It is impossible to say whether the stories of Pribislav's christening present and last will are true.[6] But whether true or not, it is remarkable that the Ascanian margraves thought it necessary to establish a direct link with the Slav rulers and to prove their legitimacy to their new subjects.

Under Albert and his son Otto (1170–84) the Havelland and the Zauche were finally incorporated with the Mark. The two destroyed bishoprics were restored, so that the spread of

[1] 'Thietmari Chronicon', *Mon. Germ. Hist., Script.* iii, p. 764.

[2] Ibid., pp. 799, 812–13.

[3] There is a useful biography of Albert: O. von Heinemann, *Albrecht der Bär*, 1864.

[4] B. Guttmann, 'Die Germanisierung der Slawen in der Mark', *F.B.P.G.* ix, 1897, pp. 422–3; W. von Sommerfeld, *Beiträge zur Verfassungs- und Ständegeschichte der Mark Brandenburg im Mittelalter*, 1904, pp. 6–10.

[5] 'Heinrici de Antwerpe tractatus de captione urbis Brandenburg', *Mon. Germ. Hist., Script.* xxv, pp. 483–4; 'Chronica Principum Saxoniae', ibid., p. 477; 'Chronica Marchionum Brandenburgensium', *F.B.P.G.* i, 1888, p. 117; 'Pulcawa's Böhmische Chronik', *Riedel*, D i, p. 3.

[6] This has always been assumed by German historians, but there is no documentary evidence.

Christianity should reconcile the Slavs with German rule. In the late twelfth and early thirteenth centuries Albert's successors expanded eastwards in the Priegnitz, into the Barnim and the Teltow (to the north and south of Berlin), and into the Ucker Mark which was ceded to them by Duke Barnim of Pomerania.[1] They thus reached the Oder and during the following decades they made further considerable advances.[2] To the east of the Oder, in the *terra* of Lebus, missionary and colonizing activities began before the Ascanian margraves reached the Oder. They partly emanated from Poland, and partly from the archbishopric of Magdeburg which, in 1249, acquired half of the *terra* from Poland.[3] Shortly afterwards, however, the margraves were the owners of part of Lebus, and by 1285 they had supplanted both their rivals.[4] During the second half of the thirteenth century they gained more territory to the east of the Oder from Poland and from Pomerania, reaching the eastern Drage river about 1290, and conquering, during the following decades, the wide wooded country between the rivers Drage, Netze, and Küddow.[5] In the course of two centuries the Ascanians thus established a large and strong principality, which had its centre between the Elbe and the Oder (the 'Middle Mark'), and extended westwards across the Elbe (the 'Old Mark') and eastwards far across the Oder into the valley of the Vistula (the 'New Mark'). In the early fourteenth century they even attempted to conquer Pomerelia (Pomorze) and to reach the mouth of the Vistula; but there they were defeated by a more powerful German rival, the Teutonic Knights.

The Teutonic Knights—the Order of St. Mary's Hospital at Jerusalem—were one of the militant orders founded during the crusades to further the conquest of the Holy Land from the Infidel. In the early thirteenth century the Order was granted

---

[1] 'Chronica Marchionum Brandenburgensium', loc. cit., p. 121; 'Pulcawa's Böhmische Chronik', loc. cit., p. 9; S. Passow, 'Die Occupation und Kolonisierung des Barnim', *F.B.P.G.* xiv, 1901, pp. 1 ff.

[2] *Riedel*, B i, no. 44, p. 31 (1250); *Pomm. U.B.* i, nos. 512–13, pp. 398–9 (1250); vi, no. 3937, p. 332 (1288).

[3] *Riedel*, xxiv, no. 17, p. 336; cf. ibid. xx, no. 2, p. 178 (1226), no. 7, p. 129 (1244).

[4] Ibid. xx, no. 10, p. 183 (1252); H. Krabbo, *Regesten der Markgrafen von Brandenburg aus askanischem Hause*, iii, nos. 741, 761.

[5] G. W. von Raumer, *Die Neumark Brandenburg im Jahre 1337*, 1837, pp. 4–9; P. van Niessen, 'Die Erwerbung der Neumark durch die Askanier', *F.B.P.G.* iv, 1891, pp. 323 ff.

wide uninhabited districts in Transylvania by King Andrew of Hungary to found a frontier march against the heathen Kumans (Turks); but friction soon arose owing to the Order's political aspirations, so that it had to evacuate Transylvania in 1225.[1] At that time a new field of activity was opened to the Teutonic Knights in the lower valley of the Vistula. There the Slav princes of Danzig in the late twelfth century started colonizing activities, founded the Cistercian abbey of Oliva and the town of Danzig, and began the settlement of the low lands in the delta of the Vistula.[2] Farther to the east, however, the Prussians, a tribe akin to the Lithuanians and Latvians, fiercely resisted the spread of Christianity. Against them crusades were proclaimed, and finally Duke Conrad of Masovia called in the Teutonic Knights. His offer of lands around Culm and of far-reaching privileges was eagerly accepted, as the Order sought to find a new dominion after the loss of Transylvania. The Grand Master Hermann von Salza secured further privileges from Pope Gregory IX and the Emperor Frederick II, which granted to the Order full sovereignty over all the land it would conquer from the Prussians, under a nominal suzerainty of the Pope.[3]

Having established their independent position the Teutonic Knights, using the military methods developed in Palestine,[4] began the systematic reduction of the territories to the east of the lower Vistula. With the help of many crusaders, Germans as well as non-Germans, they succeeded in conquering within a comparatively short time the districts of the Culmerland, Pomesanien, Pogesanien, Ermland, Natangen, Samland, and Barten. Everywhere castles were built to hold down the country and German towns were founded under their protection. Yet the resistance of the Prussians continued for over fifty years: rising followed upon rising, embittered and ruthless warfare was carried on by both sides, until in the end the determination

---

[1] H. Prutz, *Preussische Geschichte*, i, 1900, p. 40; R. Kötzschke and W. Ebert, *Geschichte der ostdeutschen Kolonisation*, 1937, p. 96.

[2] Prutz, op. cit. i, p. 42; Kötzschke and Ebert, op. cit., pp. 85–86; E. Keyser, *Die Bevölkerung Danzigs und ihre Herkunft im 13. und 14. Jahrhundert*, 2nd ed., 1928, pp. 2–4.

[3] *Preuss. U.B.* i i, nos. 56, 64, 75, pp. 41–56; no. 108, pp. 83–84; K. Lohmeyer, *Geschichte von Ost- und Westpreussen*, 1908, pp. 171–2; Prutz, op. cit. i, pp. 43–44; Kötzschke and Ebert, op. cit., p. 87.

[4] Prutz, op. cit. i, pp. 46–47; and *Kulturgeschichte der Kreuzzüge*, 1883, pp. 245, 258–9.

and military superiority of the Knights triumphed over their enemies and their new Prussian state became firmly established.[1] After the death of the last Slav duke of Pomerelia in 1294 the succession was disputed between Poland, Brandenburg, and other claimants. Finally, in 1308, the Teutonic Knights, whose help had been invoked against the margraves of Brandenburg, seized Danzig and then conquered the whole province, cutting off Poland from the sea and crushing all resistance. The Brandenburg claims were eventually bought off by the payment of 10,000 marks of silver.[2] Farther to the west, the Order bought the *terrae* of Neuenburg and Bütow from their noble rulers,[3] thus expanding into eastern Pomerania.

In the course of one century the Teutonic Knights established a strong ecclesiastical principality in the south-eastern corner of the Baltic which hitherto had been one of the most backward parts of Europe. Their state was much better administered and considerably more advanced than the contemporary German and Polish principalities. Through its close relations with the Empire of Frederick II in Sicily and the experiences gained in the Near East, Norman, Byzantine, and Italian influences were transmitted to north-eastern Europe.[4] To the present day the vast archives of the Teutonic Order bear witness to its uniform standards of administration, its division of labour among numerous professional officials, its highly centralized organization, its great wealth and financial power. In 1309 the Grand Master transferred his seat to the Marienburg whose massive fortifications were to remain the seat of the Order until its defeat by Poland in the mid-fifteenth century.

In Pomerania, as in some of the other Slav principalities at the coast of the Baltic, there was no conquest. At the beginning of the twelfth century there were two Pomeranian principalities (not counting Pomerelia farther to the east), with Demmin and Stettin as their capitals, and with two branches of the same

[1] Prutz, *Preussische Geschichte*, i, pp. 47–59; Kötzschke and Ebert, op. cit., pp. 87–88; A. Bruce Boswell, in *The Cambridge History of Poland (to 1696)*, 1950, pp. 88–89.
[2] Prutz, op. cit., i, pp. 61–63; Kötzschke and Ebert, op. cit., p. 86; *Preuss. U.B.* i 2, no. 908, p. 570; ii 1, nos. 11, 16, pp. 5, 11; *Riedel*, xvii, no. 2, p. 372; B i, nos. 360, 370, 379, 396, 435, pp. 283–348.
[3] *Preuss. U.B.* ii 1, nos. 94–95, pp. 60–62 (1313); ii 2, no. 665, p. 443 (1329).
[4] Prutz, op. cit. i, pp. 46–47; and *Kulturgeschichte der Kreuzzüge*, pp. 234, 257.

family as their rulers.[1] The neighbouring principality of Rügen was ruled by a family related to the Pomeranian princes; it comprised not only the island of Rügen but also an important stretch of the opposite mainland. In 1120–1 Pomerania was subjugated and made tributary by Duke Boleslav of Poland, and the native princes had to recognize Polish suzerainty. To strengthen his hold over Pomerania and to destroy paganism, Boleslav then employed the services of Bishop Otto of Bamberg, whose journeys to Pomerania he financed and safeguarded. Otto was well received in Pomerania; the conversion of the country, or at least of its upper classes, proceeded quickly.[2] Rügen was converted by force forty years later after its subjugation by King Woldemar of Denmark.[3] Neither Polish nor Danish influences, however, prevailed for long in Pomerania. German power was growing on its western and southern boundaries, and soon Pomerania was cut off from all direct contact with Poland. The dukes of Pomerania were quick to see the advantages to be gained by a closer contact with the Empire. In 1181 Duke Bogislav became the liegeman of Frederick Barbarossa,[4] and Pomerania a principality of the Empire, which it remained until its dissolution. In 1325 Rügen, after the death of the last native prince, was united with Pomerania.

The contrast between events in Prussia and in Pomerania is very striking: in the former the natives were conquered by the sword and for a long time they fiercely resisted an alien yoke; in the latter Christianity and political changes were peacefully accepted by the rulers and their subjects. The same peaceful transformation took place in eastern Mecklenburg and in Silesia: thus in a large part of the colonization area there was no conquest at all. Other territories, such as Brandenburg and Rügen, hold an intermediate position. The same applies to Pomerelia where, in spite of the conquest, the Teutonic Knights respected the existing order and left the native nobility in

---

[1] The family of the *Greifen* which ruled Pomerania until 1637.

[2] The main sources are: 'Herbordi dialogus de Ottone', and 'Ebbonis vita Ottonis', *Mon. Germ. Hist.*, *Script.* xii, pp. 774 ff., 840 ff. See also W. von Sommerfeld, *Geschichte der Germanisierung des Herzogtums Pommern oder Slavien*, 1896, pp. 16–36; H. Lehmann, *Pommern zur Zeit Otto's von Bamberg*, 1878, pp. 24–36; M. Wehrmann, *Geschichte von Pommern*, i, 1904, pp. 61–73.

[3] *Mon. Germ. Hist.*, *Script.* xxix, pp. 121–9, 178, 205; xvi, pp. 193, 403.

[4] 'Ex Saxonis Gestis Danorum', ibid. xxix, p. 152; Bruce Boswell, loc. cit., p. 54.

possession of their lands.[1] Everywhere Christianity triumphed after a longer or shorter struggle. Pagan temples were replaced by churches and pagan rites slowly disappeared. The crusading spirit receded. Upon the period of conquest and conversion there followed a period of peaceful penetration and settlement.

[1] K. Kasiske, *Das deutsche Siedelwerk des Mittelalters in Pommerellen,* 1938, pp. 113, 226–40 and *passim.*

II

The Settlement of Brandenburg and Pomerania

'THE country is excellent, rich in meat, honey, poultry, and flour: therefore come hither, you Saxons and Franconians, men from Lorraine and from Flanders, for both can be obtained here: deeds for the salvation of your souls and settlement on best land'; thus the crusade was preached to the Germans in biblical language in the year 1108.[1] At that time the lands to the east of the Elbe were certainly not a second Canaan where the rivers were flowing with milk and honey. On the contrary, life in the frontier districts was arduous and hazardous. The settlers had to be ready to defend their lives and property against hostile attacks while they were trying to wrest a livelihood from the fields and woods. If the comparison is not too fanciful, their living conditions must have been similar to those of the Boers trekking northwards and of the American backwoodsmen during the great trek towards the Pacific. Indeed, there was the open frontier stretching far into eastern Europe, an abundance of land and a great shortage of tillers and settlers. If these disliked their new surroundings or if they found conditions too difficult, they could at any time move on in search of better circumstances. Very favourable terms had to be offered to attract immigrants into the eastern wilderness. As they expressed it themselves in an ancient Flemish song:

> Naer Oostland wille wij rijden,
> Daer isser een betere stee.[2]

In the twelfth and thirteenth centuries migration to the east was furthered by the conditions prevailing in western Germany and the Low Countries. There the population was growing, the supply of new land was limited, feudal and manorial burdens were often oppressive, serfdom was fairly general, younger sons had to be provided for by members of all classes, famines or floods could endanger the peasants' existence.[3] In general life in the west was narrow; more freedom, more space, and more

---

[1] Quoted by Kötzschke and Ebert, op. cit., p. 38.
[2] Let's ride to eastern lands, There conditions are better.
[3] H. Aubin, loc. cit., p. 365.

wealth might be gained by emigration. All classes participated in this movement, priests and monks, noblemen and servants, burghers and peasants. At first, above all, military services were required, at least in the German principalities, to secure and to hold down the conquered districts. Soon, however, economic activities, the settlement of the land, the clearing of the woods, the draining of the marshes, the building of dikes, roads, and bridges, the laying out of towns and villages, the tilling of the fields, became far more important than military services. The Slavs were soon reconciled to German rule from which they themselves greatly profited; in the Slavonic principalities military considerations never played an important part. Only in Prussia they continued to be of importance in the settlement of the country: native resistance continued for a long time, and later the frontier districts had to supply horsemen for the frequent expeditions against the heathen Lithuanians and had to be guarded against their attacks.

The most prominent part in the colonization and settlement of the country was taken by the Church. Numerous ecclesiastical institutions were founded by the princes and by members of the nobility. These received or bought very extensive lands; for Brandenburg it has been estimated that the Church owned about one-third of the whole country.[1] Its vast but thinly-populated possessions did not yield much revenue; therefore the clerics and monks introduced settlers, cleared the woods, drained the marshes, and started new methods of agriculture. The most important of the ecclesiastical foundations were the bishoprics and their cathedral chapters: those of Brandenburg, Havelberg, and Lebus, of Cammin in Pomerania,[2] and of Culm, Pomesanien, Ermland, and Samland in Prussia.

At its foundation in the tenth century the bishopric of Brandenburg was endowed with half the town of Brandenburg, half the island on which the town stood, half of the appurtenant villages, and two small 'towns' with all their appurtenances.[3] To these possessions the bishops, in course of time, added further considerable property: in the Middle Mark the towns and districts of Blumberg,

---

[1] A. F. Riedel, *Die Mark Brandenburg im Jahre 1250*, ii, 1832, p. 487.

[2] Western Pomerania and Rügen belonged to the dioceses of Schwerin and of Roeskilde and had no bishoprics of their own.

[3] *Riedel*, viii, no. 2, p. 91 (949), and pp. 19–20.

Löwenberg, and Teltow, in Thuringia the castle and town of Querfurt, and near Magdeburg the castle and town of Grabow, all with the villages belonging to them, as well as many scattered villages and holdings in Brandenburg, in Anhalt, and in Magdeburg.[1] Over all these territories the bishops ruled like independent princes, under a very loose suzerainty of the margraves. The cathedral chapter of Brandenburg in 1209 owned 14 villages, 7 parish churches, 100 *Hufen*, and scattered holdings, mills, and rents, a property which was still substantially the same in 1375.[2] The bishops of Havelberg possessed the towns and districts of Havelberg and Wittstock in the Priegnitz; later they acquired the towns and districts of Bellin and Lenzen and the castles of Plattenburg and Zechlin with their villages as well as further districts in the Priegnitz:[3] altogether a very extensive property, mainly situated close to the episcopal see. The bishopric of Lebus, farther east, in 1317 owned 2 small towns and 16 villages there and 3 villages in Silesia,[4] considerably less than the two other Brandenburg bishoprics.

The bishopric of Cammin in Pomerania since the thirteenth century possessed the whole *terra* of Kolberg and the town of that name;[5] in 1274 the bishop invested his nephew with a town and 700 *Hufen*;[6] in the fourteenth century he bought the whole *terra* and town of Cammin for 8,000 marks of silver, and three-quarters of the *terra* and town of Bublitz for 1,850 marks.[7] These transactions give a good indication of the wealth and property of the bishopric. The four Prussian bishoprics received even more extensive lands, probably on account of the ecclesiastical character of the Prussian state. The bishop of Culm was granted 600 *Hufen* and one-third of the *terrae* of Löbau and Sassen.[8] The

---

[1] *Riedel*, viii, pp. 23–27; vii, no. 2, p. 243 (1270); xxiv, nos. 44–45, pp. 348–9 (1305–6); xi, no. 7, p. 208 (1311).

[2] Ibid. viii, no. 40, p. 127; *Landbuch 1375*, pp. 111–14.

[3] *Riedel*, vii, no. 1, p. 85 (1294); ii, nos. 22, 28, pp. 453–9 (1298, 1319); ii, p. 85, no. 14, p. 371 (1319–20); i, no. 10, p. 460 (1430); *von Raumer*, i, no. 71, p. 106 (1438).

[4] *Riedel*, xx, no. 31, p. 201.

[5] *Cod. Pom. Dipl.*, no. 397, pp. 813–14 (1248); *Pomm. U.B.* ii, nos. 1044, 1060, pp. 332–45 (1276–7).

[6] *Pomm. U.B.* ii, no. 983, p. 285.

[7] Ibid. vi, no. 3530, p. 58 (1321); *Oelrichs*, no. 3, p. 77 (1339).

[8] *U.B. Culm*, no. 14, p. 5; no. 151, p. 103; *Preuss. U.B.* i 1, nos. 139, 143–4, 182, pp. 103–33; *Cod. Dipl. Pruss.* i, no. 147, p. 153; ii, no. 45, p. 53.

bishops of Pomesanien, Ermland, and Samland each received one-third of the territory of their dioceses; while one-third of this area was allotted to the cathedral chapter of each bishopric.[1]

The Orders of Knighthood stood next in importance to the bishoprics. Not only the Teutonic Knights, but also the Knights Templars and the Hospitallers took a very active part in the colonization of the east. The Templars especially acquired very extensive property in the disputed border districts between Poland and Pomerania before the Ascanian margraves extended their power across the Oder. In this way the contending powers sought to retain some hold over the area. Thus the Templars were invested by the dukes of Poland and of Pomerania and by the bishop of Lebus with the whole *terrae* of Bahn and Küstrin, all the land between the *terrae* of Bahn and Fiddichow and the town of Königsberg (in the New Mark), 1,000 *Hufen* on the Mietzel river, 200 *Hufen* on the Rörike river, 350 *Hufen* around Lietzen, the town and district of Zielenzig, and many further lands east of the Oder.[2] When Lebus and the New Mark fell into the hands of the Ascanians, the Templars had to cede to them a large part of their vast possessions; they only retained the *curiae* of Quartschen and Rörchen, the district of Zielenzig, and to the west of the Oder the *curia* of Lietzen, all with their villages,[3] as well as the *terra* of Bahn in Pomerania. They remained the property of the Order until its dissolution in 1308, when most of its lands were granted to the Hospitallers.[4] The latter in the early thirteenth century owned three houses with the appurtenant villages in eastern Pomerania.[5] In Brandenburg their possessions were more scattered: a commandery at Werben in the Old Mark, which had been founded by Albert

[1] *Preuss. U.B.* i 1, nos. 233–4, 247, 250, 301–2, pp. 172–224; i 2, nos. 47–48, 372, 481, 540, pp. 46–340; *Cod. Dipl. Pruss.* i, nos. 84–85, 115–16, pp. 79–115; ii, nos. 1, 10, 43, pp. 1–51; iii, nos. 70, 74, 93, pp. 92–123; *U.B. Culm*, nos. 42–43, 120, pp. 29–78; *U.B. Samland*, nos. 52, 57–58, 66, pp. 16–35; *Cod. Dipl. Warm.* i, nos. 26, 31, 78, pp. 47–135.

[2] *Riedel*, xx, nos. 4, 8, pp. 180–2; xix, nos. 1–3, 7, pp. 1–5; nos. 2–3, pp. 124–5; no. 1, p. 173; xxiv, nos. 2, 4, pp. 1–3; *Cod. Pom. Dipl.*, nos. 217, 220, pp. 476–86 (1229–59).

[3] *Riedel*, xix, no. 8, p. 5; no. 4, p. 125; B i, no. 96, p. 70; H. Berghaus, *Landbuch der Mark Brandenburg und des Markgrafthums Nieder-Lausitz in der Mitte des 19. Jahrhunderts*, iii, 1856, pp. 341, 356–7.

[4] Berghaus, op. cit. iii, pp. 174–5, 357; *Cod. Pom. Dipl.*, p. 486; *Pomm. U.B.* v, no. 2722, p. 48; *Riedel*, xix, no. 8, p. 128.

[5] *Cod. Pom. Dipl.*, nos. 177, 247, pp. 406–539; *Pomm. U.B.* i, no. 354, p. 264 (1229–38).

the Bear,[1] and some property in the Priegnitz.[2] In the fourteenth
and fifteenth centuries, however, they acquired, in addition to
many of the Templars' possessions, very extensive lands to the
east of the Oder: five towns, several castles and commanderies,
and numerous villages.[3] Thus the Hospitallers were one of the
most important territorial magnates of the area, enjoying a large
measure of independence which involved them in conflicts with
their liegelords.[4] The Teutonic Knights for obvious reasons confined their activities to Prussia and the countries farther to the
north where they were their own masters.

The most important and most famous abbey of the Brandenburg Mark was the Cistercian monastery of Lehnin, which is
said to have been founded as early as 1180,[5] shortly after the
Zauche had fallen into Ascanian hands. The monastery soon
acquired extensive property in the Middle Mark; in 1375 it
owned there 31 villages (as against 13 in the early thirteenth
century) and a considerable revenue from waters, fishing rights,
and tolls.[6] When the margraves had gained the Ucker Mark
from Pomerania, they called monks from Lehnin to found a
Cistercian monastery there; it was later transferred to an island
in the lake of Chorin and then assumed this name.[7] Endowed
with 5 villages at its foundation, Chorin in 1335 owned 14
villages, 55 scattered *Hufen*, and 6 *curiae seu allodia*, which the
monks could either cultivate themselves or farm out or transform into villages.[8] Another important Cistercian monastery
was founded in the late thirteenth century near the Mecklenburg border, *Coeliporta* or Himmelpfort.[9] In 1342 it owned 12
villages and 2 *curiae seu allodia* under the same conditions as
Chorin;[10] it became one of the richest monasteries of Brandenburg. In the *terra* of Lebus two Silesian Cistercian foundations,

---

[1] *Riedel*, vi, no. 1, p. 9 (1160).

[2] Ibid. vi, no. 2, p. 10; ii, no. 1, p. 202; no. 1, p. 329 (1200–83).

[3] Ibid. xix, nos. 13, 17, 20, 33, 37, pp. 131–48; *von Raumer*, i, no. 73, p. 108 (1347–1430).

[4] *Pomm. U.B.* ii, nos. 891, 914, pp. 218–34; *Riedel*, vi, nos. 16–17, pp. 17–18 (1269–70); xxiv, no. 233, pp. 173–4; *von Raumer*, i, no. 100, pp. 234–5 (1460).

[5] *Riedel*, x, no. 1, p. 182; Berghaus, op. cit. i, 1854, pp. 560–1.

[6] *Riedel*, x, nos. 1–19, pp. 182–91; *Landbuch 1375*, pp. 53, 127–9.

[7] *Riedel*, xiii, nos. 5, 14, 17, pp. 205–16 (1258–73).

[8] Ibid., no. 64, p. 247; *Landbuch 1375*, p. 89.

[9] *Riedel*, xiii, no. 1, p. 8 (1299).

[10] Ibid., no. 32, p. 31.

the monastery of Leubus and the nunnery of Trebnitz, were endowed with 400 *Hufen* in 1224, before this district was incorporated with Brandenburg; they soon founded a town, villages, and granges on this property.[1] Other Cistercian nunneries in Brandenburg were: in the Old Mark, Arendsee, Neuendorf, and Dambeck; in the Priegnitz, Marienfliess and Heiligengrabe; in the Barnim, Friedland; in the Ucker Mark, Marienpforte, Seehausen, and Zehdenick; in the New Mark, Zehden, Bernstein, and Reetz. They all acquired considerable property: thus in 1375 Arendsee owned 13 villages,[2] Dambeck 21 villages,[3] Friedland a small town and 7 villages,[4] Seehausen a small town, 6 villages, and 4 *curiae*,[5] and in 1457 Neuendorf possessed 24 villages,[6] to mention only the more important nunneries.

In Pomerania also the Cistercians were the most prominent monastic order and the most active in the colonization of the country. The first monastery was founded as early as 1172 at Dargun and endowed with large tracts of land in the west of the country.[7] Two years later the monks were permitted to invite and to settle on their lands Germans, Danes, Slavs, or men of any other nation.[8] The first convent, however, left Dargun before the end of the century;[9] in 1216 the monastery was re-established and endowed with more villages and the adjacent wastes.[10] It soon received many more villages and estates in western Pomerania and also in the *terra* of Schlawe far to the east of the Oder,[11] and became one of the leading Pomeranian monasteries. To the east of Stettin a famous Cistercian house was founded only one year later than Dargun, the monastery of Kolbatz, which was inhabited by a Danish convent.[12] Soon it received or bought large possessions in eastern Pomerania.[13] In 1240 it owned 34 villages; by 1282 their number was nearly 50,

---

[1] *Riedel*, xx, nos. 1, 3, 7, 8, pp. 126–30 (1224–45).
[2] *Landbuch 1375*, pp. 182, 187.   [3] Ibid., pp. 176, 179, 190–2.
[4] Ibid., pp. 73–74, 84–85, 87.
[5] Ibid., pp. 136, 160–1, 168–70.
[6] *Riedel*, Supplement, no. 13, p. 366.
[7] *Cod. Pom. Dipl.*, no. 34, pp. 86–87.
[8] Ibid., no. 36, p. 92; but this charter may not be genuine.
[9] *Pomm. U.B.* i, no. 136, p. 103; 'Annales Colbazienses', *Mon. Germ. Hist.*, *Script.* xix, p. 715.
[10] *Cod. Pom. Dipl.*, nos. 105, 109–10, pp. 243–59.
[11] Ibid., nos. 153, 156, 162–3, 294, 310, 355, 390, 393, 424, 471, 473, pp. 362–944.
[12] Ibid., no. 33, p. 84; 'Annales Colbazienses', loc. cit., p. 715.
[13] *Cod. Pom. Dipl.*, nos. 39, 55, 58, 62, 81, 137, 224, 251, pp. 98–546.

and by 1313 it amounted to 53 villages.[1] From Kolbatz, convents went out to found the monastery of Oliva near Danzig, and later two monasteries in the New Mark, *Nemus Sanctae Mariae* or Marienwalde, and *Locus Coeli* or Himmelstädt. Dargun in its turn founded a new monastery at Buckow, in the east of Pomerania; this in 1275 owned 16 villages and other property and became the focus of colonization in this area.[2]

In Rügen the first Cistercian abbey was founded in the early thirteenth century at Eldena and endowed with wide but mainly uninhabited lands; the monks were granted the right to use settlers of any nation.[3] On these deserted possessions they set to work;[4] by 1248 they owned a town and 29 villages, and by the end of the century 33 villages and 7 granges, to which further property was added later,[5] so that Eldena became one of the richest Pomeranian monasteries. The other important foundation in Rügen was Neuenkamp, founded and richly endowed in 1231.[6] It also acquired very extensive property,[7] and founded, in 1296, a new monastery on the island of Hiddensee which became an important house.[8] Eldena and Neuenkamp had the right to transform their villages into *curiae*, and their *curiae* into villages, according to their pleasure,[9] exactly as Chorin and Himmelpfort in the Ucker Mark. Important Cistercian nunneries were founded at Ivenack, in the west of Pomerania, and at Stettin.

The Premonstratensians were almost as prominent as the Cistercians in the settlement of the east. In Pomerania two important Premonstratensian monasteries came into being at Grobe, on the island of Usedom, and at Belbuk in eastern Pomerania. Grobe was founded as early as 1154, but the first convent soon left and a new one was called from Havelberg to

[1] *Cod. Pom. Dipl.*, no. 286, pp. 613–14; *Pomm. U.B.* ii, no. 1232, pp. 471–2; v, no. 2816, pp. 116–21.

[2] *Pomm. U.B.* ii, nos. 875, 935, 987, 1011, pp. 204–307; iii, no. 1477, p. 52.

[3] *Cod. Pom. Dipl.*, nos. 83, 85, 88, pp. 198–210.

[4] 'Animadvertentes labores qui in excolendis ficunt desertis possessionibus et expensis . . .': ibid., no. 304, p. 650 (1241).

[5] Ibid., nos. 400, 472, pp. 826–942; *Pomm. U.B.* ii, nos. 1171, 1221; iii, nos. 1892, 1917, 1956, 1964–5; iv, nos. 2013, 2053, 2132–3; v, nos. 2765, 3436–7.

[6] *Cod. Pom. Dipl.*, no. 188, p. 427.

[7] Ibid., no. 309, p. 659; *Pomm. U.B.* ii, nos. 861, 968, 1016, 1026, 1184, 1195, 1279, 1322, pp. 193–545; iii, no. 1427, p. 13.

[8] *Pomm. U.B.* iii, no. 1764, p. 270; iv, nos. 1996, 2009, 2032, 2036, 2269, 2277, pp. 18–218.   [9] Ibid. iii, no. 1710, p. 228; ii, no. 1322, p. 545 (1285–95).

take its place.[1] The monastery obtained extensive property on Usedom as well as on the opposite mainland and owned many villages.[2] From Belbuk also the first convent emigrated shortly after its arrival; but a new one was installed in 1208 and soon prospered.[3] The monastery bought the town of Treptow and half of the *terra* around it for 240 marks of silver and founded a Premonstratensian nunnery, *Rubus Sanctae Mariae* or Marienbusch, which was endowed with twenty-six villages.[4] Grobe in its turn founded the monastery of Gramzow in the Ucker Mark when this district still belonged to Pomerania.[5] Two other Premonstratensian monasteries in Brandenburg were Leitzkau and Jerichow, both founded in the early twelfth century and situated near the eastern bank of the Elbe. They acquired large possessions: Leitzkau in particular became one of the richest Brandenburg monasteries.[6] The same applied to the Premonstratensian nunnery of Lindow, in the *terra* of Ruppin, founded in the late thirteenth century by its lords, the counts of Lindow.[7] All the other religious orders only had single houses in Brandenburg and Pomerania. None of them could rival the Cistercians and the Premonstratensians, although some of these foundations might locally exercise great influence: for example the Augustinian nunnery of Diesdorf, in the Old Mark, which was one of the richest Brandenburg convents;[8] or the Benedictine nunnery of Spandau which also owned many villages and rights.[9]

Side by side and intermixed with the possessions of the Church lay those of the princes, the members of their families, and those of the nobility. In Brandenburg as well as in Pomerania the nobility had two different constituents: native Slavs and immigrated Germans. In Pomerania German knights appeared comparatively late, many decades after the monasteries. Only from 1235 onwards are there any definite proofs of their presence in

[1] *Pomm. U.B.* i, no. 45, p. 22; *Cod. Pom. Dipl.*, nos. 24, 43, pp. 55, 106.

[2] *Cod. Pom. Dipl.*, nos. 26, 37, 43, 56–57, 65, 271–2, pp. 61–586; *Pomm. U.B.* ii, nos. 596, 620, 630–1, 659, 680, 695, 726, 742, 770, 841, 862, 907.

[3] *Cod. Pom. Dipl.*, nos. 29, 86, pp. 70–206.

[4] Ibid., nos. 148, 164–5, 221, 242, 314, pp. 351–668.

[5] *Riedel*, xiii, nos, 1, 2, 5, pp. 483–7.

[6] Ibid. viii, pp. 21–22; x, nos. 1, 2, 9, 10, pp. 69–76, and p. 64. As to Jerichow, see ibid. iii, nos. 1–3, pp. 79–81.

[7] Ibid. iv, p. 439, no. 13, pp. 453–4; Berghaus, op. cit. i, p. 386; ii, pp. 6–7.

[8] *Riedel*, xxii, no. 304, pp. 274–6 (1458).

[9] *Landbuch 1375*, pp. 51, 53, 65–66, 71–73, 79–80, 84, 87, 95, 97, 99, 106.

the country.[1] As there had been no conquest, there was no dispossession of the native nobility, although there may be some doubts about the *bona voluntate* with which the *heredes* of the *terra* of Bahn ceded their estates to the Knights Templars in 1234, as the charter does not mention any compensation.[2] Intermarriage between the native nobility and the German immigrants soon became very frequent; the two groups quickly amalgamated into one feudal upper class, so much so that it is often impossible to find out whether a certain family is of Slavonic or of German origin.[3]

Exactly the same applied to Brandenburg: those Slav noblemen who refused to submit to German rule and laws and to the Christian religion had to leave the country, but many remained and retained their status and their estates. Many adopted Christian or German names;[4] while Slavonic names recurred frequently in many noble families as late as the fourteenth and fifteenth centuries.[5] This very likely indicates that the family in question was of Slav origin, as a German family would not easily have given Slav names to its children. Apart from this somewhat uncertain fact, it is impossible to say which of the Brandenburg noble families were of Slav, and which of German

[1] *Cod. Pom. Dipl.*, nos. 227–8, 241–2, pp. 501–30; *Pomm. U.B.* i, p. 64 (1235–6): members of the families von Plessen, von Stove, von Badelaken, von Brusewitz, von Walsleben witnessed documents of the duke of Pomerania and of the bishop of Cammin.

[2] *Cod. Pom. Dipl.*, no. 220, p. 483.

[3] Von Sommerfeld, *Geschichte der Germanisierung des Herzogtums Pommern*, pp. 228–9; Wehrmann, op. cit. i, pp. 110–11.

[4] As early as 1208 the 'Sclavi nobiles Heinricus, Prizzlaviz, Pribbezlauz et Andreas fratres' witnessed a charter of the margraves: *Riedel*, iii, no. 11, p. 89.

[5] Thus in the family von dem Knesebeck, the names Yvan and Paridam; in the family von Redigsdorf, the names Prizbur and Yvan; in the family von Wartenberg, the names Yvan, Benesch, Wenzla, Janekow, and Janco; in the family von Wedel, the names Czulz, Czulis or Tzules, Jeszeke, Vyveyanz, and Thyczo; in the family von der Osten, the name Dobergost or Tobirgast, &c.: *Riedel*, xxii, nos. 85, 153, pp. 132–77; i, no. 53, p. 150; no. 16, pp. 486–7; ii, no. 1, p. 262; no. 9, p. 27; xxv, no. 29, p. 21; B i, no. 500, p. 413; iii, no. 10, p. 296; v, no. 130, p. 360; vi, no. 15, p. 408; xix, no. 175, p. 286; B iii, no. 1162, p. 47; xviii, nos. 1, 3, 5, 6, pp. 1–7; no. 59, p. 38; no. 10, p. 67; no. 89, p. 154; nos. 23–24, pp. 293–4; no. 52, p. 309; xix, no. 5, p. 67; no. 1, p. 444; no. 56, p. 482; xxiv, nos. 125, 129, pp. 69–77; B i, nos. 230, 248, 320, pp. 179, 192, 252; *Pomm. U.B.* iv, no. 1999, p. 21; vi, no. 3937, p. 333; *Schoettgen-Kreysig*, iii, no. 157, p. 109; *Regesta Historico-Diplomatica*, ii, nos. 1017, 1171, 1594, 1616, pp. 122, 140, 185–8. Guttmann, loc. cit., p. 453, n. 3, thinks that the Christian name Zabel which recurs in many Brandenburg noble families is Slavonic.

origin, the best proof of the complete amalgamation which took place soon after the conquest.[1] There are indications that in certain districts, for example in the Priegnitz, the New Mark, or eastern Pomerania, the Slav component was particularly strong, and that Slav institutions continued there for a considerable time. But that is almost all that can be said with reasonable certainty.

If there was no distinction with regard to the 'racial' origin of the different noble families, there certainly was a sharp distinction between the higher and the lower nobility. The difference between *nobiles* and *ministeriales* soon disappeared completely;[2] but a few families of the high nobility continued to stand out above the ranks of the nobility as a whole. They possessed whole districts, had numerous vassals owing military services to them, and enjoyed all the prerogatives of princes.[3] It is not known how these families acquired their rights and possessions; but at least in one case, that of the lords of Friesack, it can be proved that they were Slav dynasts closely related to the ruling families of Mecklenburg and Pomerania.[4] In 1287 the lords of Friesack and Pribislav, prince of Belgard, were jointly invested with three *terrae* in Pomerania by the margraves 'sicut moris est nobilium et baronum suscipere bona sua . . .'.[5] Soon afterwards this family seems to have died out.[6]

Two other families of the high nobility, although enumerated among the margraves' *ministeriales*,[7] held very large territories in the Priegnitz: the lords of Plotho the *terrae* of Kyritz and Wusterhausen,[8] and the Gans von Putlitz the *terrae* of Grabow, Perleberg, Putlitz, and Wittenberge, and perhaps also that of Pritzwalk.[9] In peace treaties the Gans von Putlitz were especially

[1] Riedel, op. cit. ii, p. 39; Guttmann, loc. cit., p. 455; von Sommerfeld, *Beiträge zur Verfassungs- und Ständegeschichte der Mark Brandenburg*, pp. 45–46.
[2] Von Sommerfeld, op. cit., pp. 146, 158. The *ministeriales* were originally unfree, but this was of no practical importance in the colonial area.
[3] *Riedel*, i, pp. 268–9.
[4] Ibid., p. 269; vii, p. 42; Riedel, op. cit. i, pp. 369–72.
[5] *Riedel*, B i, no. 244, p. 189.
[6] Ibid. vii, no. 2, p. 48 (1290) seems to be their last document.
[7] 'Johannes de Plote' in 1196 and 'Johannes Gans' in 1269: *Riedel*, C i, no. 2, p. 3; B i, no. 135, p. 101.
[8] Ibid. iv, p. 385; i, p. 270, nos. 2–3, pp. 366–7; iii, no. 7, p. 341.
[9] Ibid. i, p. 270; nos. 2–3, p. 242; nos. 1–2, pp. 122–3; A. Ernst, 'Kritische Bemerkungen zur Siedlungskunde des deutschen Ostens', *F.B.P.G.* xxiii, 1910, pp. 336–7.

enumerated as participants, an honour otherwise conceded only to members of ruling houses, and their possessions were always recognized as a separate dominion by the margraves.[1] In the course of the thirteenth century, however, the *terrae* of Kyritz, Wusterhausen, Grabow, and Perleberg came into the hands of the margraves. The von Plotho almost disappeared from the ranks of the Brandenburg nobility; while the Gans von Putlitz lost their pre-eminent position: through sales and partitions of property and through matrimonial links with other noble families their status approximated more and more to that of the nobility in general.[2] In view of the very large territories owned by these two families and their great prerogatives, contrasting with their classification as *ministeriales*, it seems likely that they also were Slav dynasts whose rights were more ancient than those of the margraves.[3] The latter made comparatively few changes in the Priegnitz after its acquisition.

Two other families of the high nobility were of German origin: the burgraves of Brandenburg, a family which immigrated from Saxony but disappeared again soon after,[4] and the counts of Lindow and Ruppin. They were descendants of the Edle von Arnstein who originally came from Swabia. Gebhard von Arnstein, a great-grandson of Albert the Bear, conquered the *terra* of Ruppin, to the north of the Middle Mark, and established himself there like an independent ruler.[5] His successor Gunther married a daughter of Prince Jaromar of Rügen. In practice the counts of Lindow and Ruppin were almost sovereigns. They continued to hold a position far above that of the other noble families, into which they did not marry, until the last count died in 1524; then the county was amalgamated with Brandenburg.[6] Equally loose was the relationship of the margraves with the von Strele who owned the *terrae* of Beeskow and Storkow, in

[1] *Riedel*, i, p. 271; Berghaus, op. cit. i, p. 656.

[2] *Riedel*, iv, no. 1, p. 392; i, pp. 270, 274–5; iv, pp. 18, 386; Berghaus, op. cit. i, pp. 656–7.

[3] Thus G. W. von Raumer, 'Der Senioriatslehnhof der Freiherren Edlen von Plotho', *Allgemeines Archiv für die Geschichtskunde des Preussischen Staates*, ix, 1832, pp. 290–4, and Berghaus, op. cit. i, pp. 655–6; against this opinion *Riedel*, i, p. 277, and von Sommerfeld, op. cit., p. 23.

[4] *Riedel*, i, p. 269; Riedel, op. cit. i, pp. 332–5; von Sommerfeld, op. cit., pp. 138–9.

[5] P. Meyer, 'Die Begründung der Herrschaft Ruppin', *F.B.P.G.* xxxix, 1927, pp. 281–4; *Riedel*, iv, pp. 3, 18.

[6] *Riedel*, i, p. 270; iv, pp. 4, 14, 18, 22–23, 30–31.

Lusatia, as well as large estates in the *terra* of Lebus on both banks of the Oder.[1] In general, however, the few families of the high nobility were pushed aside by the rise of the *ministeriales* and soon ceased to play an important part in Brandenburg affairs.[2]

In the New Mark, to the east of the Oder, and especially in its most eastern parts close to Pomerania and to Poland, the power of the margraves was rivalled by that of their great vassals who settled there before the Ascanians crossed the Oder. The first colonizing activities came from Poland and Silesia;[3] under the Ascanians the Slav system of castellanies as administrative units remained intact;[4] the Slav noblemen remained in the country, and immigration of German noblemen seems to have been negligible.[5] Three families especially held very large estates in the most eastern parts of Brandenburg and in the adjoining districts of Pomerania. The most important were the von Wedel. They were first mentioned in Pomerania in 1269, and about twelve years later they appeared as liegemen of the margraves.[6] Apparently they became the successors of the Slav princes of Belgard and of the Slav nobleman Dubislav von Wödtke, but it is not known how this succession was accomplished.[7] Within their territories the von Wedel founded towns and granted privileges without ever mentioning the consent of the margraves. In 1374–5 they owned in Brandenburg 7 towns, 15 castles, all with their appurtenant villages, and as many as 5,000 *Hufen* of open country and heath to the east of the Drage river,[8] as well as extensive lands in Pomerania.[9] In 1388 they undertook to support the Teutonic Knights in expeditions against Poland with the large force of 100 well-armed knights and squires, 100 archers, and 400 horses.[10]

The two other families with very large possessions in the

[1] *Riedel*, xx, no. 1, p. 340; nos. 23–24, pp. 195–6; Berghaus, op. cit. ii, p. 562; iii, pp. 571, 607.   [2] Von Sommerfeld, op. cit., pp. 134–54.

[3] See above, pp. 5, 13.

[4] *Von Raumer*, ii, p. 117; *Landbuch 1337, p.* 52.

[5] Guttmann, loc. cit., p. 495; P. von Niessen, *Geschichte der Neumark im Zeitalter ihrer Entstehung und Besiedlung*, 1905, p. 391.

[6] *Pomm. U.B.* ii, nos. 891, 914 (1269–70); *Riedel*, xviii, no. 1, p. 2; xxiv, no. 8, p. 6; B i, no. 198, p. 150 (1281–2).

[7] *Pomm. U.B.* ii, nos. 1069, 1312, pp. 354, 536; *Landbuch 1337*, pp. 40–41.

[8] *Riedel*, xviii, nos. 84–85, pp. 148–50; *Landbuch 1375*, pp. 32, 37.

[9] *Pomm. U.B.* ii, no. 1312; iii, no. 1804; v, nos. 2792, 3232, 3279; vi, nos. 3750, 4106; *Oelrichs*, 1339, no. 3, p. 77; 1346, no. 6 *b*, p. 84.

[10] *Riedel*, xviii, no. 87, pp. 151–2.

eastern New Mark were the von Güntersberg and the von Liebenow. The former derived their rights from the Polish family von Kenstel whose large estates were first mentioned in 1286.[1] About the same time the von Liebenow were invested by Duke Premislav of Poland with more than 1,000 *Hufen*, to which they added another 400 when the margraves advanced across the Drage river.[2] In 1337 they held two independent *terrae* in the east of the New Mark with thirty-six villages, a large territory stretching towards the Polish frontier.[3] There are no parallels of such extensive possessions from any other part of the colonization area. It is not known how these three families acquired their estates. They certainly did not appear in the east as followers of the Ascanians, but before them.[4] The von Güntersberg were identical with a Polish noble family, the von Wedel were the successors of Slav princes. In this family Slav names occurred very often; when all its members were listed in 1374 and in 1388, one-quarter of them had Slav names.[5] It thus seems very likely that these families were not German immigrants who had started from very small beginnings,[6] but Slav dynastic families which remained in the country.

Certainly Slav were several great landed families in the same area: the von Borke whose wide estates in eastern Pomerania were confirmed to them by the margraves in 1297 as they had held them of old;[7] the counts of Neuenburg, the counts of Schlawe, and the von Rügenwalde, who owned the *terrae* of Schlawe and Rügenwalde and other large property in eastern Pomerania;[8] the princes of Belgard who, in 1287, were enfeoffed

---

[1] Von Niessen, op. cit., pp. 313, 468.

[2] *Preuss. U.B.* i 2, no. 558, pp. 348–9; von Niessen, op. cit., pp. 335–6.

[3] *Landbuch 1337*, pp. 105–7; P. J. van Niessen, *Zur Entstehung des Grossgrundbesitzes und der Gutsherrschaft in der Neumark*, Programm 1903, p. 17.

[4] The von Liebenow were mentioned in Pomerania from 1261 onwards, even earlier than the von Wedel: *Pomm. U.B.* ii, nos. 698, 700, 710, 734, 737, 740, 750, 757, 761, 770, 775, 782, 810, 818, 826–7, 849, 882, &c.

[5] 6 out of 25 in 1374, and 5 out of 20 in 1388: *Regesta Historico-Diplomatica*, ii, nos. 1017, 1171, pp. 122, 140; see also above, p. 18, n. 5.

[6] This is assumed by von Raumer, in *Landbuch 1337*, p. 9; Berghaus, op. cit. iii, pp. 342–3, and van Niessen, op. cit., p. 17, but without any evidence.

[7] *Riedel*, xviii, no. 1, p. 100; *Pomm. U.B.* ii, nos. 1044, 1259, 1365; iii, nos. 1454, 1730, 1737, 1789, 1821.

[8] *Pomm. U.B.* iii, nos. 1761, 1814; iv, no. 2395; v, nos. 2726, 2783, 2961; vi, nos. 3547–8; vii, nos. 4497–8, 4558; *Oelrichs*, 1333, nos. 1, 10 i, pp. 69–70; F. W. Barthold, *Geschichte von Rügen und Pommern*, iii, 1842, pp. 113–14, 308, n. 1.

with the *terrae* of Belgard, Daber, and Welsenburg by the margraves and continued to hold their ancient possessions until
most of them were acquired by the von Wedel.[1]

Thus feudal law and custom spread to the easternmost districts
of Brandenburg and of Pomerania. Soon German towns and
villages sprang up there as they had done farther west. The
political authority of the margraves over these frontier areas
remained weak; it was rivalled by that of the dukes of Pomerania
and of other rulers, as well as by that of the great families,
whether Slav or German. These continued to rule their hereditary domains almost like princes in their own right; they
formally recognized the suzerainty of the prince who held the
strongest power at the time, and the latter had to be content
with this formal allegiance. It is significant that all the above
examples concern frontier regions which frequently changed
hands. Such conditions favoured local independence and
baronial power; but they were in no way typical of the interior
of the countries concerned. There noble rights and possessions
were much smaller, and the ruler's powers were considerably
greater.

Unfortunately, the size of the estates granted to immigrating
German noblemen in Brandenburg and in Pomerania is not
known. It seems likely that there was no uniform pattern, but
that the size varied according to the status of the family in question, its wealth, the services it had rendered or was expected to
render to the ruler, and its usefulness from the point of view of
colonization. As land was cheap and the population thin, probably fairly large estates were granted in the early stages; but
this very likely changed later when the value of land rose with
the quick development of the country. Many of those who at the
outset received large estates would be unable to make use of
them and would have to assign sections to other noblemen or to
entrepreneurs for purposes of settlement. These lesser owners in
their turn might break up their possessions, so that soon the
interwoven pattern of land-holding characteristic of any feudal
society came into being. Frequent sales, divisions among heirs,
pious endowments, political and economic difficulties were
further causes of the break-up of the large estates which can be

[1] *Pomm. U.B.* ii, no. 1355; iii, nos. 1431, 1489, 1504, 1592; they are only mentioned until 1292: ibid. iii, no. 1611.

traced in many instances. Indeed pieces of land changed hands so often, even several times within a few years, that it is quite impossible to reconstruct from the surveys of the fourteenth century a picture of the likely state of affairs at the time of the conquest and colonization. There are, however, other sources which give an indication of the estates held by noblemen at a comparatively early time.

Soon after the beginning of the colonization some liegemen of the margraves were able to endow an ecclesiastical foundation with a whole village,[1] which presumably was not their only possession, or to found a monastery on their estates.[2] In 1276 the von Kerkow were enfeoffed with a castle and ten villages in the Ucker Mark by the margraves.[3] In the same district and at about the same time the Slav villages as a rule had one *dominus*.[4] On the other hand, at an equally early time other liegemen of the margraves merely owned scattered *Hufen*. Thus in a Havelland village four noblemen had possessions in 1204: one von Plotho held it in fee from the margraves, but other knights held 2, 6, and 8 *Hufen* respectively.[5] In another village forty years later a knight and his sons had a fief of only 7 *Hufen*.[6] In the late thirteenth century both forms of possession existed side by side and little distinction was made between them: a treaty of 1283 between the margraves and their subjects stipulated that, if there was a *dominus* to a village, he was responsible for the collection of the tax due to the ruler, the *Bede*; if there was no *dominus*, this was the task of the village mayor; where the liegemen only held scattered possessions, they were nevertheless responsible for the tax from them.[7] The same treaty further stipulated that, as a reward for the military services which they

---

[1] Before 1164 in the Havelland, before 1184 and before 1196 in the Zauche, before 1204 in the Havelland, in 1241–2 in the Barnim: *Riedel*, viii, no. 18, p. 106, no. 40, p. 127, no. 38, p. 125; x, no. 8, p. 185, nos. 35–36, p. 200.

[2] In 1269 in the Ucker Mark: *Riedel*, xxi, no. 1, p. 1.

[3] *Riedel*, xiii, no. 13, p. 318.

[4] 'Propter clamorem dominorum slavicarum villarum, praecipue in novellis plantationibus . . .': *Riedel*, xiii, no. 18, p. 217 (1274?).

[5] *Riedel*, x, no. 14, p. 188.

[6] Ibid., no. 40, p. 202.

[7] 'Dominus vero bonorum debet hunc censum praesentare nuntio nostro, et si dominus ibidem non fuerit, ex tunc sculthetus sive villicus dictum censum tenebitur praesentare. . . . Item ubi dicti vasalli nostri tenuerint sigillatim et sparsim bona eorum, licite nobis assignabunt dictum censum recipiendum de bonis eorum . . .': *Riedel*, C i, no. 9, p. 11.

had to render, a knight was permitted a demesne of 6 *Hufen* free from taxation, and a squire a demesne of 4 *Hufen*: if they had more *Hufen* under their plough, those were to be taxable.[1] The treaty thus gave no indication of the actual size of the demesnes, and it is possible that some were larger than 4 or 6 *Hufen*, as an ordinary peasant farm had 2 to 4 *Hufen*. Nevertheless the treaty does indicate a certain norm, which was apparently considered a fair reward for the feudal obligations of the margraves' vassals. Demesne farming by noblemen does not seem to have been very extensive at that time.

In Pomerania also some immigrating noblemen, Germans as well as Slavs, received large estates in the early stages of the colonization. Thus the *terra* of Loitz, in western Pomerania, after 1235 came into the hands of Detlev von Gadebusch, a relative of the Slav princes of Rügen.[2] He and his son were active in colonizing the district and seem to have been independent of any ruler.[3] The *terra* of Gützkow, farther east, was acquired at about the same time by Jaczo von Salzwedel, a Slav nobleman who immigrated from the Old Mark and married a sister of Duke Barnim of Pomerania.[4] Farther south the brothers von Stove were granted such extensive lands that they could found a town and a nunnery on their estates about the middle of the thirteenth century.[5] At the same time another immigrating nobleman, Burchard von Vehlefanz, received the *terra* of Fiddichow, near the Oder,[6] and a member of the family von Behr the *terra* of Zehden, in what later became the New Mark.[7] In eastern Pomerania Count Otto von Eberstein, a nephew of the bishop of Cammin, was invested, in 1274, with the castle and town of Naugard and 700 *Hufen*.[8] A few years later the heirs of the Knight Raven von Brusewitz were able to sell 400 *Hufen* in

---

[1] 'Miles sub aratro suo habebit sex mansos, famulus vero quatuor, et hii erunt penitus liberi, et si plures quidem habuerint, de his dabunt censum praelibatum...': *Riedel*, C i, no. 9, p. 11.

[2] *Cod. Pom. Dipl.*, p. 533; von Sommerfeld, *Geschichte der Germanisierung* ..., pp. 159, 194; C. G. von Platen, 'Ursprung und Nachkommenschaft des rügenschen Königshauses', *Baltische Studien, Neue Folge*, xxxi, 1929, pp. 42–43.

[3] *Cod. Pom. Dipl.*, nos. 307, 426, pp. 654, 879 (1242–9).

[4] Klempin, in *Pomm. U.B.* i, pp. 260–1; *Riedel*, xxii, no. 6, p. 5; no. 17, p. 95.

[5] *Pomm. U.B.* i, no. 553, p. 432; iii, no. 1947, p. 413.

[6] *Cod. Pom. Dipl.*, no. 364, p. 747; *Pom. U.B.* i, nos. 554–5, pp. 433–5.

[7] Von Sommerfeld, op. cit., p. 179.

[8] *Pomm. U.B.* ii, no. 983, p. 285.

the *terra* of Daber to a monastery;[1] and the von Bartuscovitz, in 1342, were enfeoffed with 500 *Hufen* in the *terra* of Bublitz, close to Pomerelia.[2] These were the most conspicuous instances of noblemen receiving large estates, usually situated in border districts.

Most grants of land were undoubtedly much smaller. To the east of Stettin, in the *terra* of Stargard, five German noblemen in 1248 endowed the nunnery of Marienfliess with 40, 50, 60, 150, and 200 *Hufen* respectively.[3] At that time German noblemen had just begun to immigrate into Pomerania, so that their endowments may have comprised all their lands in this area; this seems likely, as only one of these families—the one with the smallest share—was ever again mentioned in Pomerania. Some noblemen owned whole villages: a *magister* Ivanus, in 1242, sold two and bought four villages with over 200 *Hufen*;[4] Knight Tammo held five villages in 1254,[5] *dominus* Rudolf von Nienkerken had four in 1288,[6] and another knight gave five villages to a monastery in the late thirteenth century.[7] In other villages, however, several noblemen merely possessed scattered *Hufen*. Thus in western Pomerania one Eizo in 1278 held 10 *Hufen* from the nunnery of Verchen; in 1301 the same nunnery received 2 *Hufen* in the same village from a knight and 22½ *Hufen* from Duke Otto; some years later two noble brothers had a fief of 13 *Hufen* there, and another knight resigned his fief to the nunnery.[8]

Many of the very large properties of the early colonization period did not survive for long. The von Stove and the von Vehlefanz lost their estates shortly after their acquisition: after 1252 neither family was mentioned in any Pomeranian document. The same applied to four of the five noblemen who endowed the nunnery of Marienfliess. The family of the von Gadebusch died out in 1275, that of the counts of Gützkow in 1357, so that the *terra* of Loitz was amalgamated with Rügen,[9] and the

---

[1] *Pomm. U.B.* ii, no. 1300, p. 525 (before 1284).

[2] *Oelrichs*, 1342, nos. 1–2, p. 80.

[3] *Cod. Pom. Dipl.*, no. 398, p. 818; *Pomm. U.B.* i, no. 476, p. 369.

[4] *Cod. Pom. Dipl.*, nos. 309, 315, pp. 660, 671–2.

[5] *Pomm. U.B.* ii, no. 596, p. 11.   [6] Ibid. iii, no. 1487, p. 59.

[7] Ibid. ii, no. 1025; iii, no. 1447; iv, no. 2005 (1276–1301).

[8] Ibid. ii, no. 1094; iv, nos. 1976, 2001; v, nos. 3364–6; vii, nos. 4468–9 (1278–1329).

[9] *Cod. Pom. Dipl.*, p. 533; *Fabricius* (text), iii, p. 45; iv 1, p. 84.

terra of Gützkow with Pomerania.[1] The von Behr lost the *terra* of Zehden when the New Mark was conquered by the Ascanians. In general, pieces of land and estates were sold so frequently, given away, or divided between heirs, that most large properties were split up within a comparatively short time. As the value of land rose, it was no longer necessary to grant hundreds of *Hufen* to a nobleman to establish a livelihood in accordance with his status. Only in the far east of Pomerania Slav noblemen continued to rule over their hereditary domains in very much the same way as their ancestors, for this area was much less affected by the social changes than the districts farther to the west. There the process of settlement was practically the same as in Brandenburg.

[1] Thomas Kantzow, *Chronik von Pommern in hochdeutscher Mundart*, ed. G. Gaebel, 1897–8, i, p. 214; ii, p. 137.

III

The German and Slav Peasants and their Rights

THE rulers of the principalities, the bishops and abbots, and
the German and Slav noblemen soon tried to increase their
revenues and to make use of their large but thinly populated
estates by the foundation of villages and towns. By offering very
favourable conditions they tried to attract German peasants,
artisans, and burghers. If some immigrants had actual experience in the diking of rivers and the draining of marshes their
skill would be particularly welcome. Helmold, the chronicler,
relates, although not from his personal knowledge, how Margrave Albert the Bear, soon after the conquest of Brandenburg,
sent to Utrecht and to places lying on the Rhine, to those, moreover, who live by the ocean and suffer the violence of the sea—to wit
Hollanders, Zeelanders, Flemings—and he brought large numbers
of them and had them live in the strongholds and villages of the
Slavs. The bishopric of Brandenburg, and likewise that of Havelberg,
was greatly strengthened by the coming of foreigners. . . .[1]

This report need not be taken literally, but Flemings were in
fact settled near the Elbe at the time of Albert the Bear. In 1159
a village near the Havel river was given by Archbishop Wichmann of Magdeburg to the *locator* Henry and to other Flemings.
They had to pay the tithes to the Church and a yearly due of
two shillings from each *Hufe*; Henry was granted a fief of 4 *Hufen*
free from the tithes and any charge; he and his heirs were to be
the judges in all the peasants' affairs and legal cases and were
to receive one-third of the proceeds of the village court, the
remaining two-thirds going to the archbishop; and no count or
advocatus was to have any rights over the peasants.[2] This is the

---

[1] 'Helmoldi Chronica Slavorum', *Mon. Germ. Hist., Script.* xxi, p. 81; *The Chronicle of the Slavs*, transl. by F. J. Tschan, 1935, p. 235. Cf. T. Rudolph, *Die nieder-
ländischen Kolonien der Altmark im XII. Jahrhundert*, 1889, pp. 24–36.

[2] 'Est etiam hoc firmatum ut praeter eundem Heinricum neque comitem super
se habeant neque advocatum. Ipse vero Heinricus vel suus heres omnes causas
eorum et negotia diiudicet et quidquid jure placitandi conquisierit duae portiones
in usum archiepiscopalem cedant, tertia vero sit judicis. Cultores etiam agrorum
pro quolibet manso annuatim solvant duos solidos in festo beati Martini et prae-
terea omnium rerum decimandarum plenam decimationem . . .': von Heinemann,
op. cit., no. 41, pp. 470–1. The *Hufe*, like the English hide, was a variable measure
of land, supposedly sufficient to maintain a peasant family, so that there is no
modern equivalent: but see p. 53, n. 9, below.

only charter referring to a Brandenburg village which has been preserved; but there are similar charters of the same archbishop and other ecclesiastics by which they granted to immigrants villages on either bank of the Elbe and stipulated the conditions of the *locatio*.[1]

In the part of the *terra* of Lebus which belonged to the archbishopric of Magdeburg the *mansus flamingus* was the agrarian unit in 1252;[2] and to the present day the chain of hills in the south of the Middle Mark, where the archbishopric then held large possessions, is called the 'Fläming', thus indicating the origin of many of the early settlers. From Brandenburg itself there is less evidence of Dutch settlements. In 1170 Hollanders lived in the Old Mark above the bank of the Elbe on land of the margrave;[3] and *Hufen* measured according to the Hollanders' customs were mentioned in the same district.[4] There is no further evidence about Hollanders or Flemings, and indeed very few charters of newly founded villages have survived. About the same time that Archbishop Wichmann founded Flemish villages near the Elbe, Margrave Albert the Bear established a market in his village of Stendal, in the Old Mark, which was to become the leading town of medieval Brandenburg. The inhabitants received their holdings with the right of selling and bequeathing them and could dispose of them at their pleasure; their yearly dues amounted to four pennies each; they were freed from all tolls inside Brandenburg; Albert's liegeman Otto was appointed judge and mayor: he and his heirs were to receive one-third of the proceeds of the jurisdiction, the other two-thirds going to the margrave.[5] In the same district the *cives* of the village of Rohrberg bought another village for thirty-six marks of silver with hereditary rights; its pastures and woods were to be used by rich and poor alike.[6] In this contract no dues at all were stipulated by the nobleman who effected the sale: the peasants seem to have acquired free property.

In Pomerania a German knight in 1262 invested three *locatores* with an inclosure near the mouth of the Oder. The *cives*

---

[1] Von Heinemann, op. cit., nos. 39–40, pp. 468–70 (1159).
[2] *Riedel*, xx, no. 10, p. 183.
[3] Ibid. ii, no. 6, p. 441.
[4] *Riedel*, vi, no. 1, p. 10; von Heinemann, op. cit., no. 49, p. 482 (1160–78).
[5] *Riedel*, xv, no. 3, p. 6; *Krabbo*, i, no. 386, p. 74 (between 1150 and 1170).
[6] *Riedel*, v, no. 2, p. 303 (1212).

who were to inhabit the new village were to pay one shilling from each *Hufe* and the tithes from the fields as well as the small tithes; these dues were to be shared equally by the knight and the *locatores*, who also received free *Hufen* for themselves; the peasants could freely brew, bake, and slaughter and could freely sell their produce; they could seek their rights outside the estate wherever they would obtain them properly and conveniently.[1] It seems that the knight had nothing to do with the jurisdiction over the peasants and did not even receive a share of its proceeds as was usually stipulated. This last charter shows that peasants settled on the private estates of a nobleman received the same privileges and favourable conditions as those living under the Church or under the ruler.

Throughout the colonization area it was the function of the *locator* to procure the settlers for the new villages and towns, to lead them from their place of origin into the new territories, to allocate their holdings to them and to measure the village fields. As a reward he became the hereditary mayor (*scultetus, villicus, praefectus*) and was enfeoffed with a number of free *Hufen*.[2] He exercised the lower jurisdiction and normally received one-third of its proceeds, while the other two-thirds went to the landlord. The highest jurisdiction, touching life and limb, was in the hands of the ruler; he appointed the *advocatus* who presided in the high court, the *Landding*. For this purpose the peasants three times a year had to attend the general assizes of their district where the *advocatus* sat in judgement assisted by a jury. In Brandenburg this jury was composed of seven *scabini terrae* or *Landschöffen*; they owned large farms of 2, 4, and even 6 *Hufen* which were either entirely free from dues or less burdened than the peasant holdings.[3] Even the ecclesiastical foundations at the outset stood under the *advocatia* of the margrave. Thus in 1162 Albert the Bear appointed one of his *ministeriales* to be the *advocatus* of the monastery of Leitzkau which had been founded and endowed by the bishops of Brandenburg. The *advocatus* was to preside three times a year over the general assizes, the *placitum generale*, and to pass judgement in cases of homicide, theft,

---

[1] *Pomm. U.B.* ii, no. 720, p. 96.
[2] *Riedel*, xix, no. 1, p. 1; no. 1, p. 124; xxiv, no. 4, p. 3 (1232–43).
[3] *Landbuch 1375*, pp. 75, 98, 100, 105, 135–6, 141–2, 169–70, 262, 264, 268, 272, 280, 285–6, 318.

hostile assault in the house, rape, bloodshed caused by use of arms, and rioting; all other cases were to be settled peacefully by the *nuntius* of the monastery.[1] The *advocatus*, like the village mayor, received one-third of the proceeds of his court, the remainder going to the ruler or to those invested by him with the *advocatia*; while the peasants had to give to the *advocatus* some dues in money and in kind.[2]

The owner of the land, whether he was a nobleman or an ecclesiastic, could employ a *locator* to undertake the settlement of a new village, and this probably was the rule. In that case the landlord's interest was merely financial, as his revenues from the land would increase considerably with the settlement; or it could be military, as the *locator* might have to render him military services. Thus in 1313 Ludolf von Wedel granted 64 *Hufen* of heath to two *locatores*: if the land was inhabited and farmed, they should receive all the peasants' dues but should render him a knight's service.[3] Although the landlord usually had a share in the proceeds of the jurisdiction, at least on the lower level, there was no manorial jurisdiction, for the lower jurisdiction was exercised by the village mayors. Indeed, there was no manor in the western sense of the term: the peasants' sole obligation towards their landlord was the payment of the stipulated dues. The landlord probably as a rule had a small demesne in the village, the strips of which were lying intermixed with those of the peasants; he was, in a famous phrase, 'the peasant's neighbour,'[4] and not his lord.

The relationship was somewhat different if a nobleman himself became the *locator* of a village and thus the village mayor. There is no evidence of this from Brandenburg, but there are some instances from Pomerania. In two cases a knight was invested with a village by an ecclesiastical foundation: the knight was to settle the village, receiving for his services in the first case

---

[1] 'Dignum quoque duximus annotare de qualibus habeat judicare, videlicet de homicidio, furto, si quis inimico in domo assultum fuerit, quod nostri Hussvoconge dicunt, de violento raptu feminarum, quod Noden dicitur, de sanguinis vi armorum effusione, de consueta vulgi conclamatione. Cetera minora nuntius ecclesiae in hoc ipsum destinatus consilio praepositi tractet et in pace componat . . .': *Riedel*, xxiv, no. 2, p. 323.

[2] *Riedel*, x, no. 12, pp. 80–1 (1211), also referring to the monastery of Leitzkau.

[3] *Pomm. U.B.* v, no. 2792, p. 99.

[4] G. F. Knapp, *Die Bauernbefreiung und der Ursprung der Landarbeiter in den älteren Theilen Preussens*, 1887, i, p. 31.

the dues from every third *Hufe* and half the proceeds of the lower jurisdiction;[1] in the second case, the village was to revert to the ecclesiastical foundation after the knight's death, but his heirs were to retain the 2 *Hufen* of the village mayor.[2] In both instances the revenues of the lower jurisdiction partly seem to have accrued to the knight and his heirs. This certainly was the case in a third village, also belonging to a religious foundation, where a knight in 1277 had a *curia villicationis* with 6 *Hufen*.[3] In general it seems that in Pomerania landlords quite often and quite early bought the free *Hufen* of the village mayors which were an attractive investment: this was considered a likely contingency in the agreement over the payment of the tithes between Duke Barnim and the bishop of Cammin as early as 1273.[4] This does not necessarily imply that the landlords themselves then exercised the lower jurisdiction,[5] as they could appoint a mayor for this purpose. Wherever the *dominus* of a village became the village mayor, he would hold a position of vantage in case of any future deterioration in the situation of the peasantry, rather than be able to influence that situation immediately. As there was a surplus of land and a shortage of settlers, they could at any time move to a different village if their landlord wronged or burdened them. These conditions ensured a fairly uniform status of the peasantry in the whole area of colonization.

These conditions had another and far more important result. As it was impossible to procure German peasants in numbers sufficient to till the large tracts of land granted to the monasteries and other landlords, Slav peasants were soon used for that purpose. From the point of view of the Church they only had to fulfil two conditions: they had to be Christians, and that applied soon practically everywhere; and they had to become economically efficient so that they would be able to pay the same dues as the Germans. If the Slavs refused to accept the new religion or the new economic methods, they might be dispossessed. Thus as late as 1235 the peasants of four villages

[1] *Pomm. U.B.* ii, no. 718, p. 94 (1262).
[2] Ibid. iv, nos. 2279–80, pp. 219–20 (1306).
[3] Ibid. ii, no. 1071, p. 356.
[4] 'Si dominus villae mansos villicationis emerit vel quocunque modo ad eum devoluti fuerint, de ipsis sicut villicus respondebit . . .': ibid., nos. 975–6, pp. 277–9.
[5] In a few Brandenburg villages this was the case in 1375, but it certainly was not the rule then: *Landbuch 1375*, pp. 78, 82, 86, 108.

belonging to the nunnery of Diesdorf, in the west of the
Old Mark, still adhered to pagan rites; ten years later it was
announced that German Catholic peasants would take their
places if the Slavs would not renounce their religion.[1] It is not
known whether they complied under the threat of expulsion or
whether they were in fact expelled. Many decades before, the
prior of the monastery of Hamersleben approached the margrave
and begged him to remove Slav peasants from the monastic
estates because they neglected them and to replace them by
Germans who would prove their usefulness to the monastery
under the Christian religion: the margrave granted the request
and invested the monastery with the tithes from these lands.[2] In
this case the motive was the economic inefficiency of the Slavs.
It seems that the monastery required a permit from the margrave before the Slavs could be expropriated. The monks of
Chorin, in the Ucker Mark, removed the inhabitants of a
Slavonic village in order to build a monastery there and to
establish a demesne; but these peasants were resettled elsewhere
by the monks, as were those of another village.[3]

The same may safely be assumed of the great Cistercian
houses in Pomerania which were granted the privilege to convert their villages into *curiae* or *grangiae*, and vice versa.[4] It is
impossible to say to what extent they made use of this right. It
seems likely that their demesne farming mainly served the
monks' own needs, as there were no large towns in the neighbourhood where their produce could have been sold. Probably
they used this right only if they wanted to add a village to their
demesne or to establish a new convent. There is only one recorded example from Pomerania where a *grangia* took the place
of a Slav village:[5] it does not seem to have occurred frequently.

[1] 'Si autem praedicti homines, Slavi scilicet, suis ritibus renuntiare noluerint,
Teutonici catholicae fidei cultores substituantur eisdem . . .': *Riedel*, xvi, nos.
11–13, pp. 400–2.
[2] *Cod. Dipl. Anhaltinus*, v, no. 553 *a*, p. 297 (1177).
[3] *Riedel*, xiii, nos. 17–18, 24–25, pp. 216–21 (1273–7); Riedel, op. cit. ii, p. 195;
Guttmann, loc. cit., p. 430; Ernst, loc. cit., p. 334.
[4] Eldena and Neuenkamp, both in Rügen: see above, p. 16.
[5] 'Kusiz et iterum Kusiz quae villae redactae sunt in grangiam Kusiz nomina-
tam . . .': confirmation for the Cistercian monastery of Dargun of 1282: *Pomm. U.B.*
ii, no. 1233, p. 473. Another example is mentioned by C. J. Fuchs, *Der Untergang
des Bauernstandes und das Aufkommen der Gutsherrschaften nach archivalischen Quellen aus
Neu-Vorpommern und Rügen*, 1888, p. 22, n. 2: *Pomm. U.B.* ii, no. 906, p. 228: but this
is a forgery.

These are all the known instances of a removal of Slavonic peasants. The Cistercians were the only order which undertook demesne farming on a larger scale. The seven *grangiae* of Eldena and the six of Chorin were the highest figures mentioned in any documents.[1] All other houses only had a few *curiae* and seem to have been much more interested in the foundation of new villages which would guarantee them a steady and safe return. Little is known about the size of these *curiae*. Those of two Cistercian houses in the *terra* of Lebus had 15 *Hufen* each; those of two Brandenburg Cistercian nunneries comprised 12 and 20 *Hufen* respectively; while a *curia* of the Knights Templars near Berlin apparently had 25 *Hufen*.[2] This corresponded to about four to eight average peasant farms: none seems to have been very large.

Comparatively early the great Cistercian houses in Pomerania were granted another important privilege: to settle on their estates Germans and Danes as well as Slavs.[3] Somewhat later the monastery of Kolbatz, in eastern Pomerania, was granted the right of receiving any Slavs, whether from ducal or from private villages, if they intended to settle permanently under the abbot and assured him of this intention through guarantors.[4] These monasteries soon used Slavs as settlers in newly founded villages. If they lived in the same village with Germans, their Germanization would advance quickly; they would receive their strips in the open fields and would soon adapt themselves to German methods of cultivation, to crop rotation and the iron plough. If they lived in separate Slav villages, their constitution would be modelled on that of the German villages, with a village mayor and jurymen and the open field system. In either case, they would come under the jurisdiction of the monastery and

---

[1] *Pomm. U.B.* ii, nos. 1171, 1221, pp. 430–63; *Riedel*, xiii, no. 64, p. 247 (1280–1335).

[2] *Riedel*, xx, no. 8, p. 130 (1245); Krabbo, in *F.B.P.G.*, xxv, 1912, no. 14, p. 17 (1306); *Riedel*, xxi, no. 24, p. 15 (1317); Supplement, no. 27, p. 238 (1360).

[3] Privileges for Dargun of 1174, for Eldena of 1209, for Neuenkamp of 1231: *Cod. Pom. Dipl.*, no. 36, p. 92; no. 88, p. 210; no. 188, p. 427.

[4] 'Slavi in dominio nostro constituti, sive in nostris, sive in vasallorum nostrorum villis manentes, si ad praedictum abbatem et conventum causa manendi in villis eorum transferre se voluerint . . . postquam saepedictis abbati et conventui fidejussores certos posuerint quod ad villas eorum venire velint et debeant ad manendum . . . libere ad praedictos abbatem et conventum et ad villas eorum transibunt . . .': *Pomm. U.B.* ii, no. 963, p. 268 (1272).

would have to give approximately the same dues as the Germans. Thus in the new Slav villages of the bishopric of Cammin the peasants, instead of the full tithes paid by the old Slav villages, had to give a fixed money due from each *Hufe*, as the German peasants did, and of approximately the same amount.[1] The same applied in Brandenburg: from 1267 every *Hufe* in the *terra* of Pritzwalk, whether German or Slav, had to give four pennies to the bishop of Havelberg instead of the tithes.[2] The Germans in the New Mark indeed considered the giving of the full tithes a Polish custom: it was soon replaced by a corn due which, so it was stated, would facilitate the settlement of hitherto uncultivated land.[3] In the diocese of Brandenburg this due was fixed at three pennies from each *Hufe* in the *novae terrae* as early as 1237,[4] without any distinction between German and Slavonic holdings.

Only in some early documents were any specifically Slavonic dues mentioned. Thus in the *terra* of Tribsees, in western Pomerania, after 1221 the Slavs who lived in German villages gave the tithes like the Germans; but those who inhabited Slav villages gave the *Biscopounizha* to the bishop of Schwerin.[5] In one village of the monastery of Leitzkau in 1187 the peasants gave a corn due, the *Wozop*, to the bishop of Brandenburg, as it seems in addition to the tithes.[6] In the Old Mark also the corn due of the *Wszop* was mentioned in 1208, but seems to have been given to the margrave.[7] In the course of the thirteenth century, however, these Slav dues and their very names disappeared; they were replaced by the ordinary German dues which, in the Latin documents, were called *pactus* or *census* and varied greatly from village to village. The same applied to the jurisdiction. The peasants of the monastery of Eldena, for example, after 1248 came under the jurisdiction of the *advocatus* of the monastery; they could defend themselves in court according to their own law, but if they lived in the village of a different nation, they had to adopt its law: a Slav German, and a German Slav law.[8]

---

[1] Ibid., no. 976, p. 279 (1273?). [2] *Riedel*, ii, no. 15, p. 449.
[3] Ibid. xx, no. 5, p. 181; xix, no. 1, p. 124; xxiv, no. 4, p. 3 (1236–43).
[4] Ibid. viii, no. 67, p. 152. [5] *Cod. Pom. Dipl.*, no. 134, p. 310.
[6] *Riedel*, x, no. 10, p. 76. [7] Ibid. xvii, no. 2, p. 2.
[8] 'Cunctis etiam hominibus et colonis . . . concedimus in causarum agendis jure proprio se tueri. . . . Si quis vero in villis gentis nationis alterius, ut verbi gratia Danus vel Slavus inter Theotonicos et e converso, elegerit habitare, volumus ut

In the previous year, however, the *jus teuthonicum* was bestowed upon all the peasants of the Pomeranian monastery of Kolbatz,[1] and thus the separate laws disappeared. In Brandenburg the peasants of a new Slav village—specifically called *cives*—had to attend the *communia civilia placita*, the *Landding*, together with the German peasants and were like them fined for absence.[2] The new Slavonic villages soon had village mayors. Thus in 1226 *Heinricus Slavus* was the *magister civium* of a Havelland village;[3] sixty years later the *villicus sive burmester* of a Pomeranian village bore the Slav name Bratus;[4] and in 1327 one Pryszlaw was the mayor of Schillersdorf which may even have been a German village.[5] In 1296 Slav peasants of an east Pomeranian village were apparently acting as assessors in a village court which was presided over by their *villicus* Volzeko.[6] Thus the German forms of jurisdiction and self-government on the village level were gradually extended to the Slavs.

It is very difficult to say whether German and Slav peasants as a rule lived in the same or in separate villages, and whether the so-called 'German' villages were occupied, entirely or partially, by Germanized Slavs. It has been assumed that on the island of Rügen Germans and Slavs as a rule lived side by side;[7] that this was not unusual on the mainland of Pomerania is confirmed by the documents of 1221 and 1248 quoted above.[8] In eastern Pomerania it proved so difficult to procure German settlers that it was stipulated in 1273 that a village was exempted from the payment of the full tithes if two-thirds of its inhabitants were Germans.[9] It has been assumed that the *hagen* villages were purely German;[10] but in 1327 three peasants of Stoltenhagen were classified as Slavs.[11] In Brandenburg also, in the fourteenth

---

illorum jure utatur quorum contubernium approbavit, nisi forte abbas . . . aliter inter eos duxerit ordinandum . . .': *Cod. Pom. Dipl.*, no. 400, p. 827.

[1] Ibid., no. 368, p. 755 (1247).

[2] *Riedel*, iii, no. 15, p. 93 (1275). This and the following example show that Fuchs, op. cit., p. 32, n. 1, and von Sommerfeld, *Geschichte der Germanisierung . . .*, p. 194, n. 1, are wrong in assuming that *cives* was a title only given to German peasants.

[3] *Riedel*, viii, no. 53, p. 140. For another example, see xvi, no. 26, p. 19 (1375).

[4] *Pomm. U.B.* ii, no. 1387, p. 599.   [5] Ibid. vii, no. 4262, p. 87.

[6] Ibid. iii, no. 1751, p. 259.   [7] Fuchs, op. cit., p. 25.

[8] See above, p. 35.   [9] *Pomm. U.B.* ii, nos. 975–6, pp. 277–9.

[10] *Hagen* villages are those whose names end in *hagen*, meaning to 'hedge in', to enclose, thus indicating a foundation on cleared land.

[11] *Pomm. U.B.* vii, no. 4291, p. 119.

century, Slavs lived in German villages;[1] but it is impossible to say how frequently this occurred. It may have been more frequent in Pomerania and especially in Rügen. By the fourteenth century the Germanized Slavs, that is the large majority, were apparently no longer called Slavs, so that the cognomen *Slavus* indicated a non-Germanized Slav: a peasant who adhered to Slav methods of cultivation and was economically less efficient than the other peasants. It is certain that many a 'German' village was, at least partially, inhabited by Germanized Slavs. In the New Mark, as late as 1354, two villages were expressly called *villae theutunicales*;[2] thus they must have been comparatively rare to the east of the Oder where Slav influences remained very strong.

Most German villages seem to have been founded on uncultivated soil, 'from wild root' as it was called at the time. Sometimes this was expressly stated in the charters when monasteries were endowed with wide solitudes, woods and heaths which lacked cultivators.[3] Sometimes the monks' labours in settling their empty possessions were praised.[4] In the *terra* of Lebus those who cultivated untilled soil were granted 'free years' during which they had to pay no dues whatever.[5] In the New Mark also the settlers were usually granted a term of 'free years',[6] which indicates that they received uncultivated land; while in the one Pomeranian charter of location which has been preserved ten free years were granted to the peasants.[7] In a treaty of 1221 between the prince of Rügen and the bishop of Schwerin it was envisaged that forests and solitudes, where previously no village had been, would be turned over to agriculture through the cutting of trees and the extirpation of brambles.[8] In Rügen, indeed, about 140 'hagen' villages were founded in

[1] *Riedel*, xxiv, no. 38, p. 344; xvi, no. 77, p. 438; ii, no. 15, p. 31 (1302–67). For the New Mark, see von Raumer, in *Landbuch 1337*, p. 61; von Niessen, op. cit., p. 152, and van Niessen, op. cit., p. 19.   [2] *Riedel*, xviii, no. 32, p. 81.

[3] *Cod. Pom. Dipl.*, nos. 39, 60, 83, 85, 88, 188, 390, 393, pp. 98–803 (1176–1248).

[4] Ibid., no. 304, p. 650 (1241).

[5] 'Quam diu durabit gratia libertatis quam habebunt illi qui recipient se sub nobis et terram incultam perducent ad fructum . . .': *Riedel*, xx, no. 10, p. 183 (1252).

[6] *Riedel*, xix, no. 1, p. 1; xxiv, no. 7, p. 5 (1232–61): 'retroacto libertatis termino quam colonis ratione locationis consuetudo perdocuit indulgeri . . .'.

[7] *Pomm. U.B.* ii, no. 720, p. 96 (1262): see above, p. 30.

[8] 'Si silvae et locus vastae solitudinis, ubi prius nulla villa sita fuit, precisis arboribus atque rubis extirpatis ad agriculturam devertae fuerint . . .': *Cod. Pom. Dipl.*, no. 134, p. 310.

a comparatively small area;[1] and they can be found all along the Baltic coast to the far east of Pomerania, but less so in the interior, especially farther east. In Brandenburg to the east of the Elbe there are over 60 'hagen' villages, and more than 100 with names ending in 'walde', 'holz', or 'horst', indicating that they were founded in the woods. Most of these new villages were comparatively large, comprising 50 or more and often 64 *Hufen*, or about 20 to 30 peasant farms, in contrast with the smaller Slav villages.

The Slav peasants by preference cultivated light and sandy soils which were better suited to their implements. The immigrants with their iron plough began to break up the heavy soil on which the wooden plough of the Slavs could not produce sufficient yields.[2] They began to dike the rivers, to drain the marshes, and to clear the woods and thus created new arable land to feed the growing population. The fact that the German villages as a rule were founded 'from wild root' explained, in the opinion of a legal commentator of the early fourteenth century, that the peasants had better rights in Brandenburg than they had in Saxony, that they could freely sell and leave their farms, that they had a 'heritage' which was better than a leasehold, as they had improved their holdings with their own work.[3] Thus the medieval lawyer recognized the difference between the older settlements and the colonization area. In the east the peasants held their farms with a right of perpetual possession as long as they paid the dues stipulated once and for all at the time of the *locatio*; as a rule they did not acquire a free property or a freehold but had a landlord who received their dues.

The Slav peasants, especially in the new villages, quickly benefited from this favourable legal position. In Pomerania and in Rügen it was the custom to re-survey from time to time the fields of the villages so as to increase the dues if the arable had been extended.[4] From the mid-thirteenth century onwards non-

[1] Barthold, op. cit. iii, p. 312; Fuchs, op. cit., p. 18, n. 1.

[2] See the interesting study by M. Bolle, 'Beiträge zur Siedlungskunde des Havelwinkels', *Archiv für Landes- und Volkskunde der Provinz Sachsen*, xix, 1909; xx, 1910; xxi, 1911; and W. Gley, *Die Besiedelung der Mittelmark von der slawischen Einwanderung bis 1624*, 1926, pp. 15, 65–67.

[3] Gloss of Johann von Buch, a nobleman from the Old Mark, to *Sachsenspiegel*, lib. ii, art. 59, para. 1: Augsburg, 1516, fol. 114.

[4] *Cod. Pom. Dipl.*, no. 439, p. 894; *Pomm. U.B.* ii, no. 616, p. 27 (1250–5): resurveys of the *terra* of Pyritz in Pomerania and of the *terra* of Tribsees in Rügen. For

monastic Slav villages in Rügen bought themselves free from such re-surveys and were then granted the 'heritage' of their *Hufen* in perpetuity, although in some instances they were using the small Slav unit, the *uncus*.[1] The peasants' dues were fixed once and for all, and their freedom to sell and bequeath their holdings was guaranteed. Simultaneously they were exempted from specific Slavonic burdens which they had had to perform, such as carrying services and the entertainment of the prince and his officials,[2] the duty of rearing their lord's horses and hounds, and the obligation to seek his permission for a marriage.[3] Only one of all these charters, the latest of all, stipulated labour services, at the low level of six days in the year;[4] apparently the other villages did not have to render any. It seems likely that in the Slav villages founded by the monasteries the peasants either from the outset enjoyed the German right of possession, or after the *jus teuthonicum* had been bestowed upon them. Wherever Slavs lived with Germans in one village, it would certainly be difficult to maintain two different rights, as the peasants would intermarry and all distinctions would soon disappear. After the middle of the fourteenth century there are no longer any traceable differences in the right of possession between German and Slav villages; the economic and legal Germanization of the Slavs had been completed.

Originally all the peasants, whether Slav or German, had to render certain public services to their ruler, exactly as they gave to him the general tax, the *Bede*, in common with the other inhabitants of the country. They had to render carrying and relay services, to help in the chase, to extend hospitality to the prince and his suite, to help building and repairing the castles, towns, bridges, dams, and dikes in the neighbourhood of their village, and to render military services in case of war. All these

---

re-surveys of Brandenburg districts which had formerly belonged to Pomerania, see *Riedel*, xii, no. 1, p. 263; xiii, no. 26, p. 221; no. 16, p. 319; xxi, nos. 6–8, pp. 5–6 (1281–93).

[1] Charters of 1255–6, 1276, 1280, 1288, 1290–1, 1294, 1296–7, 1300, 1307, 1324, and 1330: *Pomm. U.B.* ii, nos. 616, 633, 1027, 1173, 1181; iii, nos. 1479–80, 1542, 1574, 1670, 1766–7, 1788, 1795, 1927; iv, no. 2351; vi, no. 3799; vii, no. 4592; *Fabricius*, iii, no. 447*b*.

[2] *Pomm. U.B.* iii, no. 1542; vi, no. 3799; *Fabricius*, iii, no. 447*b* (1290, 1297, 1324).

[3] *Pomm. U.B.* iii, no. 1927, p. 398 (1300).

[4] Ibid. vii, no. 4592, p. 371 (1330).

services were due to the prince, not to any private lord, and were by nature unlimited, as they had to be performed whenever required; but with the exception of the military services they were only due within the district where the peasants lived. It seems unlikely that they were very onerous, as they would be shared among a comparatively large number of people: no complaints on that account are recorded. In course of time, the peasants who did not live directly under the ruler were exempted from most of the public services. The ecclesiastical foundations which were anxious to secure complete immunity from outside interference led the way, and they were soon followed by secular lords who wanted to secure the same privileged position, especially if they belonged to the higher nobility. Thus the peasants were gradually freed from every *servitium* and every *exactio*; or more specifically from the *angaria et perangaria*, the *servitus rustica vel urbana*; from every *servitium reale et personale*, or *commune ac privatum*; from the *urbanum opus*, the *constructio urbium, pontium seu munitionum*; or the *constructio castrorum seu pontium seu restauratio eorundem*; from the *reparatio viae quae dam dicitur et pontis ejusdem constructio seu conservatio*; from the *hospitia, albergaria*, or *herbergaria*; and from the obligation to participate in military expeditions outside the country, the *expeditio* or *herschilt*. The wording of the numerous charters of exemption varied considerably, but the result was that the peasants, from the fourteenth century onwards, were only obliged to render some public services, and those only rarely.

What remained were, above all, some military services. The peasants of Pomerania and Rügen, in case of a hostile invasion, had to provide 1 armed man and 1 horse from every 6 *Hufen*, or about 2 to 3 farms, exactly as the inhabitants of the adjoining principalities.[1] In Brandenburg a village, or several villages together, had to supply one waggon with driver and horses in case of war;[2] in case of invasion the peasants were obliged to participate in the defence of the country.[3] Only a minority of the villages in the fourteenth century had still to render the

---

[1] *Pomm. U.B.* ii, no. 1266, p. 499: the so-called *Rostocker Landfriede* of 1283.

[2] *Riedel*, vii, no. 20, p. 58; x, no. 209, p. 299; xi, no. 114, p. 369; xiii, no. 143, p. 303; xvii, no. 179, p. 160; xviii, no. 42, p. 468; xx, no. 115, p. 106; *von Raumer*, i, no. 95, p. 230 (1353–1541).

[3] *Riedel*, ii, no. 6, p. 441; iii, no. 12, p. 90; viii, no. 40, p. 127; C i, no. 9, p. 12 (1170–1283).

servitium curruum to the margrave.[1] The villages of the district of Salzwedel, in the Old Mark, paid a special due in commutation of the margrave's right to hospitality, unless they owed him real hospitality.[2] Until the sixteenth century the peasants of the monastery of Lehnin had to rear hounds for the margraves and to lodge and feed their hunters and hounds.[3] From other villages also hunting services were due to them.[4] The other public services were no longer mentioned.

It is possible but by no means certain that the peasants, having been freed from most public services, thereafter had to render labour services to their landlords: yet none of the thirteenth-century documents stipulated such services.[5] Demesne farming cannot have been very extensive at this early time, so that there was probably not much demand for labour services. The Cistercians' *grangiae* were administered by a *grangiarius* and were farmed by the monks and nuns themselves, with the help of lay brothers and others who were dedicated to their service, all being obliged to work with their own hands. In 1250 men came to serve the monastery of Eldena who could not easily reach their own confessor:[6] they probably belonged to one of the latter categories. The first charter stipulating labour services characteristically enough also comes from Eldena, which owned the largest recorded number of *grangiae* of all religious houses.[7] In 1306 two peasants were given one *uncus* each, and a third peasant half an *uncus* in the *slavica villa* of the monastery: the village had no other name and seems to have been the only one which was still completely Slav. The peasants had to pay comparatively high dues; they further had to serve the monks 4 days a week during the harvest, 2 for mowing and 2 for binding, and the possessor of the half *uncus* 2 days a week; but the number of weeks was not stated.[8] These were Slav peasants receiving Slav

---

[1] Only sixty-five villages in the whole Old and Middle Marks according to the *Landbuch* of 1375. [2] *Riedel*, C iii, no. 76, pp. 94–96 (mid-fifteenth century).

[3] Ibid. x, nos. 254, 257, pp. 355, 360 (1509–15).

[4] *Von Raumer*, i, no. 95, p. 231 (1464).

[5] Indeed, some alleged thirteenth-century charters mentioning the *aratura* are later forgeries, e.g. *Cod. Pom. Dipl.*, no. 172, p. 393; *Pomm. U.B.* i, no. 251, p. 202; ii, no. 894, p. 221.

[6] 'Hominum ad vestrum servitium commorantium qui non possunt de facili suorum habere copiam sacerdotum . . .': *Cod. Pom. Dipl.*, no. 436, p. 891.

[7] See above, p. 34.

[8] 'Qualibet septimana in messe duobus diebus quilibet ipsorum metet et totidem

holdings in a Slav village, and the charter seems to be only a confirmation of an older one.[1] No general conclusions can be drawn from this isolated example. On the estates of the bishop of Roeskilde on the island of Rügen the peasants of only one village had to render labour services in 1318, amounting to only 3 days in the year.[2] This also may have been an ancient obligation, as few changes had been introduced on the island, which was mainly inhabited by Slavs. In 1330 the Slav peasants of Muckrau had to serve 6 days a year for the von Putbus who were relatives of the princes of Rügen.[3] No labour services of German peasants are recorded from this early period. Their position was uniformly favourable throughout the colonization area.

diebus manipulos ligare nullatenus denegabit. Qui vero dimidium uncum supra-dictum colit . . . unum diem quando et alii duos nobis in messe laborabit . . .': *Fabricius*, iv, no. 551.

[1] 'Confirmare cupientes nostrorum facta praedecessorum . . .': ibid.
[2] *Pomm U.B.* v, no. 3234, p. 408.
[3] Ibid. vii, no. 4592, p. 371.

IV

The Towns and their Privileges

IN Brandenburg and in Pomerania, but not in Prussia, towns existed before the beginning of the colonization. With the exception of Stettin, however, they were very small and had little trade; they had no self-government and no privileges; they were fortified settlements offering protection to the population of the district rather than independent communities. They were dominated by the prince and his officials who had their seat in the town and by the castle under whose protection the inhabitants lived. With the progress of the colonization German merchants, burghers, and artisans migrated eastwards. The rulers, whether German or Slav, found it to their advantage to found numerous towns under German law, to attract trade and wealth, to become the economic and military centres for the new villages in their neighbourhood, and, as free cities, to regulate their own affairs. Duke Barnim of Pomerania clearly expressed it at the foundation of the town of Prenzlau, in the Ucker Mark, that the foundation of free cities was to his benefit and advantage.[1]

Until the end of the thirteenth century more than a hundred German towns were founded in Brandenburg, Pomerania, and Rügen. In contrast with the majority of the German villages, most towns were not founded 'from wild root', but usually old Slav settlements were enlarged, invested with urban rights and privileges, and thus elevated to the rank of a German town. To the present day the majority of these towns reveal their origin by their Slavonic names, and even German names often are an adaptation or translation of an ancient Slav name. Other towns received the names of western towns, perhaps indicating the origin of their founders, e.g. Frankfurt on Oder and Cölln on Spree, the sister town of Berlin. The majority of the towns and all the important ones stood directly under the ruler who granted them their privileges. Only the important town of Greifswald, in western Pomerania, was founded by the abbot of Eldena; but

---

[1] 'Nostris volentes utilitatibus et comodis providere . . . in terra nostra civitates liberas decrevimus instaurare . . .': *Cod. Pom. Dipl.*, no. 219, p. 479 (1235).

shortly afterwards he ceded it to the duke, and gradually all its links with the monastery disappeared.[1]

Many other ecclesiastics as well as great noblemen had received such extensive estates that they could found towns on them. Thus Bishop Hermann of Cammin founded the towns of Köslin and Massow, in eastern Pomerania, with 110 and 130 *Hufen* respectively and granted the law of Lübeck to Köslin and that of Magdeburg to Massow.[2] Farther east, Slav noblemen founded German towns: Dubislav von Wödtke the town of Plathe, the von Borke the towns of Regenwalde and Labes, the von Rügenwalde the town of that name.[3] In the eastern New Mark the von Wedel on their enormous possessions founded the towns of Neu-Friedland, Neu-Freienwalde, and Falkenburg.[4] These towns stood under the jurisdiction of the *praefectus* of the von Wedel. The burghers of Neu-Freienwalde were to be tried before him and their own *scabini* or jurymen, and were never to appear before any court outside the town.[5] Not even the consent of the margraves was mentioned in these privileges, which were granted by the von Wedel as if they were entirely independent and almost a ruling house. In a similar way the von Arnstein granted the law of Stendal to their town of Neu-Ruppin, in the north of the Middle Mark, so that they could freely elect their aldermen.[6] In the Priegnitz the von Plotho founded the towns of Kyritz and Wusterhausen, and the Gans von Putlitz the towns of Perleberg, Putlitz, and Wittenberge as German towns.[7] In western Pomerania the noble Detlev von Gadebusch granted the law of Lübeck to his town of Loitz, so that it should become the key of his territory, and freed its arable from all dues and tithes.[8] Before the *terra* of Lebus fell into the hands of the margraves the Cistercians of Leubus founded a town there upon

---

[1] *Cod. Pom. Dipl.*, no. 414, pp. 862–3 (1249).

[2] *Pomm. U.B.* ii, nos. 802, 1093, pp. 149, 369 (1266–78).

[3] Ibid., no. 1069, p. 354; iii, nos. 1454, 1730, pp. 35, 247; v, no. 2726, p. 51 (1277–1312).

[4] *Riedel*, xviii, nos. 5, 22, pp. 102–11; xxiv, no. 28, p. 17 (1314–38). Cf. above, p. 21.

[5] Ibid. xviii, no. 22, p. 111 (1338).

[6] Ibid. iv, no. 2, pp. 282–3 (1256). Cf. above, p. 20.

[7] Ibid. iii, no. 7, p. 341; iv, no. 2, p. 392; i, p. 270; iv, p. 385.

[8] 'Nos dilectam civitatem nostram Lositz eo quod clavis sit nostri territorii speciali dono libertatis confovere volentes civibus ... jus Lubecense concedimus ...': *Cod. Pom. Dipl.*, no. 307, p. 654 (1242).

which German law was bestowed by Duke Boleslav of Silesia, with market rights and 110 *Hufen*, 12 of which were given to the 2 *locatores*.[1] All the towns, however, which were founded by private landlords remained rather small and unimportant.

The method of foundation was essentially the same as that of the German villages.[2] One or several *locatores* were entrusted with the laying out of the town and all other arrangements; they were invested with free *Hufen* and one-third of the municipal revenues from land, houses, mills, and markets and of the proceeds of the municipal court: they became the hereditary mayors who exercised the lower jurisdiction. Each town was given more than 100 *Hufen* of arable and 50 or more of pasture: for the time being farming would be the burghers' main livelihood. Indeed, the large majority of the new towns remained country towns and the burghers' occupation hardly differed from that of the peasants. Everywhere *consules* or aldermen were installed to regulate the affairs of the town and to act as judges in the municipal court; but at the outset the *advocatus* of the ruler presided in this court and received two-thirds of its proceeds.[3] The aldermen appointed their own successors, gave permission for the formation of guilds and nominated their wardens and other officials.[4] Stettin, the leading town of Pomerania, in 1243 was granted the status of a German town and soon after it received the *Inninge*, the right to form guilds of artisans.[5] This was later extended to other towns in Pomerania.[6]

In Brandenburg as well as in Pomerania, the most important towns were situated in the west of the country where the colonization had started: Stendal and Salzwedel in the Old Mark, to the west of the Elbe; Stralsund and Greifswald, near the coast

[1] *Riedel*, xx, nos. 1, 3, 8, pp. 126–30 (1224–45): the town was called Möncheberg (monk's mountain).

[2] None of the earliest foundation charters have survived. Those from Brandenburg which have all show the same characteristics: charters for Lychen of 1248, for Frankfurt on Oder of 1253, for Landsberg of 1257, for Berlinchen of 1278, for Freienstein of 1287, for Dramburg of 1297, for Kalies of 1303: *Riedel*, xiii, no. 11, p. 316; xxiii, no. 1, p. 1; xviii, no 1, p. 369; no. 4, p. 63; ii, no. 2, p. 262; xviii, no. 4, p. 215; *von Raumer*, i, no. 32, p. 24.

[3] This was still the case, at least in principle, in 1375: *Landbuch 1375*, p. 32.

[4] *Riedel*, xxiii, no. 3, p. 4: letter from Berlin to Frankfurt, communicating the principles of Brandenburg law to the new town.

[5] *Cod. Pom. Dipl.*, nos. 324, 366, pp. 691, 751.

[6] *Pomm. U.B.* ii, nos. 864, 944, pp. 196, 255: grant of the *Inninge* to the towns of Gollnow and Greifenhagen, after the example of Stettin (1268–71).

of western Pomerania; these soon outdistanced Stettin and became leading members of the League of the Wendish towns. None of the towns to the east of the Oder achieved more than local influence; this reflected the general backwardness of the country which became more pronounced farther to the east. All the towns of eastern Germany, founded many centuries after those of the west, lagged behind them in their development; only a few coastal towns—Lübeck and Danzig—could ever rival them in their wealth and enterprise. Only Lübeck became a free city of the Empire, while all the other towns remained under their territorial princes and to some extent dependent upon them.[1]

The leading towns of Brandenburg, in the course of the thirteenth century, succeeded in gaining further political and judicial privileges from the margraves. As early as 1215 the burghers of Stendal, which had been a village sixty years earlier,[2] were exempted from the obligation of attending the court of the *burcgravius* and of receiving their verdicts from this official of the margrave.[3] The Neustadt of Salzwedel, in 1247, was granted the privilege that the margraves' *advocatus* who presided in court should pronounce sentence according to the decision of the aldermen; all the inhabitants of this town, whether Slavs or Germans, should answer before the town judge and should attend his court.[4] As the Neustadt of Salzwedel received the same rights which the Altstadt already possessed, it seems likely that there also Germans and Slavs enjoyed the same legal status and were judged in the same court. As early as 1233 one *Wilhelmus Sclavus* was an alderman of Stendal;[5] in 1272 *Jacobus*

---

[1] They were nevertheless called 'immediate' towns; but this did not mean that they stood directly under the Empire but directly under their ruler, in contrast with the 'mediate' towns which were under a private landlord.

[2] See above, p. 29.

[3] 'Gravamen quod idem Stendalenses per importunitatem burcgravii quem habere consueverunt penitus relaxavimus, statuentes ut in civitate sua deinceps placito et juri non teneantur stare burcgravii . . .': *Riedel*, xv, no. 5, p. 7; von Sommerfeld, *Verfassungs- und Ständegeschichte . . .*, pp. 127-8.

[4] 'Advocatus noster, quem ipsi civitati pro tempore statuerimus, quando judicio praesidebit secundum quod a consulibus ejusdem civitatis sententiatum fuerit judicabit,easdem sententias omnimodis prosequendo. Ad haec volumus ut quicunque ad ipsam novam civitatem confluxerint, rustici teutonici sive sclavi, sub nobis vel sub quocunque manentes, coram judice civitatis ejusdem astent judicio coram eo de hiis quibus incusati fuerint responsuri . . .': *Riedel*, xiv, no. 5, p. 3.

[5] *Riedel*, xv, no. 9, p. 10.

Slavus was a juryman there, an alderman in 1285, and again in 1301 and 1307;[1] while *Johannes Slavus* and *Conradus Slavus* were members of the aristocratic guild of the clothdealers.[2] Thus Germans and Slavs peacefully intermingled in the Brandenburg towns and Slav burghers filled the most important offices; soon all traces of a different origin disappeared.

Before 1278 Stendal and Gardelegen, in the Old Mark, were granted Magdeburg law, according to which any case occurring within their boundaries was to be judged *omni jure plenario*. In that year the same privilege was extended to the town of Prenzlau, in the Ucker Mark which had recently been acquired from Pomerania.[3] By this time other towns had received the same right, either in the direct form of Magdeburg law, or in the indirect form of Stendal or of Brandenburg law, which seems to have been more usual.[4]

As long as the towns were dominated by the princely castle they were controlled by it and could assert their independence only at their peril. Comparatively early they attempted to secure the destruction of the castle and guarantees against its reconstruction, a matter of primary importance for the towns. In the thirteenth and fourteenth centuries they were largely successful in asserting these claims; but in the fifteenth century the rulers succeeded in reimposing their will upon the towns and in erecting a new castle, after a series of heavy conflicts which were to have fatal consequences for the towns. In 1249 Duke Barnim of Pomerania destroyed his castle at Stettin at the burghers' request; he promised never to erect a new one and forbade his vassals to build any fortifications near Stettin.[5] This prohibition was, in 1294, extended to cover the whole area to the mouth of the Oder on which Stettin's wealth depended.[6] The ducal castle at Gartz was pulled down in 1259, and the fields and meadows near the town, hitherto held by noble servants of the duke, were given to the burghers.[7] The town of Greifswald, in 1264, was

---

[1] Ibid., nos. 27, 41, 62, 69, pp. 20–54. [2] Ibid., no. 112, p. 82 (1266–87).

[3] 'Ut judicent tam in campis metarum civitatis suae quam in foro, vicis, teatro et plateis omni jure plenario quemadmodum Burgenses nostri civitatis Stendaliensis et Gardelegensis more Magdeburgensi consueverunt sua judicia judicare . . .': *Riedel*, xxi, no. 8, pp. 93–94 (1278).

[4] *Riedel*, xxiii, no. 3, p. 3; iv, no. 2, p. 282 (after 1253–6).

[5] *Cod. Pom. Dipl.*, no. 420, p. 872.

[6] *Pomm. U.B.* iii, nos. 1672, 1676, pp. 196, 200.

[7] Ibid. ii, no. 663, p. 56; Kantzow, *Pomerania*, ed. Gaebel, 1908, i, p. 218.

assured by the duke that nobody was to build a castle or forti-
fication within its district and that there was to be but one law
and one court in the town.[1] In 1296 the prohibition of fortifications was extended to cover the whole area between the Peene
river and the sea.[2] The town of Stralsund in 1290 was exempted
from the duty of participating in military expeditions outside
the town walls, and its burghers from the obligation of attending any outside court and from all dues and services.[3] In 1319
Prince Wizlav of Rügen undertook to destroy all castles and
fortifications around the town and not to build any new ones.[4]
The town of Anklam after 1312 was entitled to try any ducal
official or any other violator of its rights as a robber.[5]

From the late thirteenth century onwards Stralsund, Greifswald, Anklam, Demmin, and Stettin were members of the
League of the Wendish towns.[6] Stralsund especially soon played
an important part in its councils. As early as 1278 the town
was visited by English ships.[7] In the late thirteenth century the
Stralsunders regularly sailed to England.[8] When in 1293 the
towns of Lübeck, Rostock, Wismar, Stralsund, and Greifswald
concluded an alliance for the preservation of peace and the
safety of their merchants, Stralsund's armed strength was estimated at half that of Lübeck, Greifswald's at more than one-
third of Lübeck's.[9] Thus the towns of Pomerania soon became
a strong force in the country. The towns to the east of the Oder,
however, failed to acquire these far-reaching privileges and
hardly shared in the general development.

The towns of Brandenburg also succeeded in strengthening
their position and in wringing important concessions from the
margraves, but their power never equalled that of the west
Pomeranian towns. As early as 1262 the burghers of Salzwedel
enjoyed favourable treatment in the Hamburg customs for the
linen which they sent to Flanders, and in the following year the

---

[1] *Pomm. U.B.* ii, no. 757, p. 119.   [2] Ibid. iii, no. 1783, p. 289.
[3] Ibid., no. 1541, pp. 101–2.   [4] Ibid. v, no. 3244, pp. 423–4.
[5] Ibid., no. 2707, p. 37.
[6] *Hans. U.B.* i, nos. 917, 925, 938, 954–6, 970, pp. 313–32 (1283–5).
[7] *Pomm. U.B.* ii, no. 1091, p. 367.
[8] *H.R. 1256–1430*, i, no. 28, p. 18; *Hans. U.B.* i, nos. 1204, 1207, p. 410; p. 443,
n. 2.
[9] In case of need Lübeck was to provide 100 armed men, Rostock 70, Stralsund
50, Greifswald and Wismar 38 each, or proportionately more: *Hans. U.B.* i, no.
1129, p. 390; *Pomm. U.B.* iii, no. 1779, pp. 285–7.

town was admitted into the partnership of the Hanse at Visby on Gotland.[1] In 1280 the aldermen and commons of Stendal declared their agreement to the transfer of the staple from Bruges.[2] Two years later the town's annual tax was fixed at a hundred marks of silver, and twice that amount if the margrave was taken prisoner; if their ruler ever infringed this treaty the burghers were entitled to place themselves under another ruler until the wrong had been righted, together with the burghers of Osterburg and Tangermünde and the surrounding districts.[3] In the early fourteenth century Stendal was exempted from all military services outside a small part of the Old Mark; later the burghers' obligation to serve outside the town walls was rescinded completely.[4] In 1295 the margraves undertook to destroy their castle near Rathenow and not to build a new one in or near the town.[5] In 1319 the town of Brietzen received the site on which the princely castle had stood and the promise that none would ever be erected within the town.[6] About that time the burghers of Prenzlau, Brandenburg, Berlin and Cölln, Frankfurt, Spandau, Landsberg, and Brietzen were granted the privilege that their burghers were to be tried exclusively by their own mayors and jurymen and were not to be summoned to attend any outside court or the general assizes.[7] This the towns rightly considered one of their most important privileges so that it had to be confirmed by every new ruler.

From the later thirteenth century onwards corn was exported from Brandenburg. As early as 1262 special customs arrangements were made at Hamburg for ships bringing corn from the Mark.[8] In 1292 the town of Königsberg, in the New Mark, was granted the privilege of free corn exports on the Oder to Stettin.[9] The burghers of Berlin and Cölln, in 1317, were permitted to

[1] *Riedel*, B i, no. 106, p. 80; xiv, no. 13, p. 9; *Hans. U.B.* i, nos. 573, 593, pp. 203–8.

[2] *Riedel*, xv, no. 35, p. 24; *Hans. U.B.* i, no. 865, p. 299.

[3] 'Si quicquam de omnibus praemissis infringeremus . . . ex tunc dicti Burgenses . . . libere se divertere poterunt ad alium dominum . . . donec talis injuria et violentia . . . fuerit ex integro retractata . . .': *Riedel*, xv, no. 38, pp. 26–27.

[4] Ibid., nos. 66, 79, pp. 51, 62 (1305–14).

[5] Ibid. vii, no. 4, p. 410.

[6] Ibid. ix, no. 11, p. 357.

[7] Ibid. xxi, no. 22, p. 104; ix, no. 17, p. 12; xii, no. 1, p. 350; xxiii, no. 17, p. 14; xi, no. 32, p. 23; xviii, no. 9, p. 375; ix, no. 11, p. 357 (1305–19).

[8] Ibid. B i, no. 106, p. 80; *Hans. U.B.* i, no. 573, p. 204.

[9] *Riedel*, xxiv, no. 11, p. 8.

export corn in good years; two years later it was stipulated that rich and poor alike had the right to ship corn to Hamburg or other places; and the town of Spandau received the same right.[1] In 1321 the town of Prenzlau, in the Ucker Mark, was assured of its right of free exports of corn and merchandise,[2] and other towns soon followed suit. Nothing is known about the size of these exports. It seems probable that Pomerania, owing to its better soil and its better geographical position, exported more corn than Brandenburg, and that both were outdistanced by Prussia in the fourteenth century.

The towns of Brandenburg and Pomerania were soon overshadowed by Danzig which came into being in the late twelfth century as a settlement and market of German merchants, above all from Lübeck. About 1225 the town was endowed with German law and the rights of self-government and jurisdiction by Duke Swantapolk of Pomerelia. Soon its commercial relations reached from Bruges and England to Novgorod. Its position at the mouth of the Vistula made it the natural outlet for the export trade of its wide hinterland, stretching far into Poland and eastern Europe. In 1263 Danzig received Lübeck law.[3] The other towns along the lower reaches of the Vistula and along the Prussian coast were founded by the Teutonic Knights; they granted urban rights and privileges to Thorn, Culm, Marienwerder, Elbing, Braunsberg, Memel, and Königsberg. None of these towns was ever able to equal Danzig, which was the oldest foundation and had come into being independently of the Teutonic Order. It was the only town of true international importance, inhabited not only by German burghers, but also by Flemings and Dutchmen, Englishmen and Scandinavians, Poles, Bohemians, Moravians, and Hungarians.[4] None of the Prussian towns acquired the far-reaching political privileges which were enjoyed by the Pomeranian and Brandenburg towns, for these powers remained in the hands of the Teutonic Order.

Throughout eastern Germany and beyond, in the course of

---

[1] *Riedel*, xii, no. 1, p. 350; xi, no. 35, p. 26; E. Fidicin, *Historisch-diplomatische Beiträge zur Geschichte der Stadt Berlin*, 1837–42, i, p. 57; ii, no. 14, p. 19.

[2] *Riedel*, xxi, no. 48, p. 125.

[3] E. Keyser, *Die Bevölkerung Danzigs und ihre Herkunft im 13. und 14. Jahrhundert*, 1928, pp. 4–6; and *Geschichte der Stadt Danzig*, 1951, pp. 6–7.

[4] Keyser, *Die Bevölkerung Danzigs und ihre Herkunft im 13. und 14. Jahrhundert*, pp. 8, 23–24, 42–45.

the thirteenth century, vigorous towns sprang up whose wealth and power were growing apace. A completely new force in society had come into being, a factor to be reckoned with, and a balance to the weight of the nobility and the other landed classes. The question was how long this balance could be maintained: would it eventually, as in western Europe, tip in favour of the rising towns and the middle classes, or would it, in territories still very largely agricultural, tip in favour of the nobility?

V

The Teutonic Knights and the Settlement of Prussia

THE evidence available for the settlement of Prussia is much more detailed than it is for any other part of the colonization area.[1] The archives of the Teutonic Order have preserved a wealth of records, charters, contracts, and accounts. Its standards were much more uniform than those of the other rulers, and it retained control over the whole process of settlement in its own hands. The numerous *Handfesten* issued to landlords and to villages provide evidence of its advanced technique and careful planning; its financial strength allowed it to exercise a close supervision over the great landlords. As the colonization of Prussia started comparatively late, the Teutonic Knights could use their own experiences, gained in Palestine and in Transylvania, and equally those made in other districts; even some of the *locatores* and entrepreneurs had been active in the same capacity in lands farther west.

During the first decades of their rule in Prussia the Teutonic Knights as well as the Prussian bishops granted to immigrating German landlords very large estates, always situated near the eastern boundary of the area under their control at that time. Their own forces were insufficient to cope with the conquest, defence, and settlement of such large areas: in this way the responsibility could be divided, and additional forces could be mobilized to help them with these tasks. Land was almost valueless, and if good men were to be secured they had to be offered large awards, as there were many other fields of activity for them farther to the west.

By far the most extensive property was acquired by the family

[1] The subject of this chapter has been studied in much greater detail than any of those treated above. Particularly valuable are: L. Weber, *Preussen vor 500 Jahren*, 1878; H. Plehn, 'Zur Geschichte der Agrarverfassung von Ost- und Westpreussen', *F.B.P.G.* xvii, 1904, pp. 383 ff., xviii, 1905, pp. 61 ff.; G. Aubin, *Zur Geschichte des gutsherrlich-bäuerlichen Verhältnisses in Ostpreussen*, 1911; C. Krollmann, 'Die Besiedlung Ostpreussens durch den Deutschen Orden', *Vierteljahrschrift für Sozial- und Wirtschaftsgeschichte*, xxi, 1928, pp. 280 ff.; K. Kasiske, *Die Siedlungstätigkeit des Deutschen Ordens im östlichen Preussen*, 1934; and *Das deutsche Siedelwerk des Mittelalters in Pommerellen*, 1938.

of the Stanges who were engaged as contractors on a large scale in the settlement of Moravia.[1] In 1285 Dietrich Stange resigned to the bishop of Pomesanien the estates and rights which had been granted to his father, among them the castle and town of Marienwerder, and received instead 1,200 *Hufen*, 200 of which he gave to the monastery of Garnsee, thus retaining 1,000 *Hufen* or 65 square miles for himself.[2] From the Teutonic Order he received, in the same year, the castle of Stangenberg with 100 *Hufen*;[3] eleven years later these were exchanged for two villages, and it was stipulated that he and his family were to take their residence in Prussia within three years.[4] In 1293 the Stanges' possessions in the bishopric of Pomesanien were finally limited to 665 *Hufen*, of which Dietrich held 276, his brother 250, and his nephew 139 *Hufen*.[5] In this way their vast estates were gradually reduced. The same happened in the case of the noble Dietrich von Tiefenau: in 1236 he was invested by the Order with a castle and 300 *Hufen*, three years later with 22 *Hufen*, and another three years later with nine Prussian villages, altogether with about 450 *Hufen*,[6] or nearly 30 square miles. Before the end of the century, however, the heirs of Dietrich's son sold the estates at Tiefenau to Dietrich Stange.[7] These two were certainly exceptional cases, even for the early period of colonization. Dietrich Stange probably acquired part of his extensive property through marrying into a Prussian noble family; while the Tiefenaus were the only family belonging to the high nobility which had to be provided on an adequate scale.[8]

The other grants of land, even at the beginning of the colonization, seldom exceeded 100 *Hufen*;[9] the larger grants can be

[1] C. Krollmann, 'Die Herkunft der deutschen Ansiedler in Preussen', *Zeitschrift des Westpreussischen Geschichtsvereins*, liv, 1912, pp. 24–26, 29–30; Kötzschke and Ebert, op. cit., p. 64.

[2] *Cod. Dipl. Pruss.* ii, no. 8, p. 10; *Preuss. U.B.* i 2, no. 462, p. 297.

[3] *Cod. Dipl. Warm.* ii, no. 542, p. 571.

[4] *Preuss. U.B.* i 2, no. 654, p. 413.

[5] *Cod. Dipl. Pruss.* ii, no. 29, p. 34.

[6] Ibid. i, nos. 46, 50, 54, pp. 45–51; Plehn, loc. cit. xvii, p. 391; Krollmann, 'Die Besiedlung Ostpreussens durch den Deutschen Orden', loc. cit., p. 289.

[7] *Cod. Dipl. Warm.* ii, no. 542, p. 573.

[8] Krollmann, loc. cit., p. 289.

[9] A hundred Prussian *Hufen* is estimated equal to 1,680 hectar or 4,090 acres and was thus an estate of a very substantial size. Only in Prussia a standard *Hufe* was used, so that it is possible to give the modern equivalents. Examples of large grants

explained by the noble status of the grantee or by his family relationship with the grantor. In the eastern parts of the Culmerland and of Pomesanien and in the districts farther east where the Prussian population remained, even grants of 40 *Hufen* were an exception.[1] According to the *Culmische Handfeste* of 1233, which laid down the principles of Prussian law, the owner of 40 or more *Hufen* had to render a heavy knight's service with armour and several horses; while the owner of less land had to serve with light arms and one horse.[2] Both kinds of service were needed by the Teutonic Knights at the time of the conquest, and accordingly large as well as small estates were created: those of 40 *Hufen* or more belonged to the larger kind and seem to have been a standard measure, separating the knight from the ordinary horseman.[3] Only about 100 knightly families received estates from the Order during its first 50 years in Prussia.[4] Their fiefs were no larger than those of noble families in Brandenburg or in Pomerania. In Prussia nobody holding land from the Order was allowed to buy more than one estate.[5] It seems likely that the larger possessions were Prussian estates which had been expropriated or had become ownerless during the fighting;[6] for wherever there lived a more numerous native population the estates were considerably smaller.

During the settlement of Prussia in the fourteenth century no large estates were granted in the interior of the country. Because of the complete subjugation of the Prussians the Order's military requirements receded into the background, with the exception of the frontier districts. It now preferred the dues of peasant villages to knights' services and equally wanted to prevent the rise of a powerful class of landlords which might challenge its supremacy.[7] Therefore fiefs of 10, 8, 6, 4, and even fewer *Hufen*

---

may be found in *Preuss. U.B.* i 2, no. 514, pp. 323–4; *Cod. Dipl. Pruss.* ii, no. 18, p. 21; *Cod. Dipl. Warm.* i, nos. 79–83, 96, 102, 157, pp. 136–273; G. Aubin, op. cit., p. 10, n. 3 (all from the second half of the thirteenth century).

[1] Krollmann, loc. cit., pp. 289–90.
[2] Point 17 of the *Culmische Handfeste*: *Preuss. U.B.* i 1, nos. 105, 252, pp. 80, 189.
[3] Cf. ibid. i 2, no. 135, p. 112, for the standard measures used in Livonia.
[4] Krollmann, loc. cit., p. 288.
[5] Point 16 of the *Culmische Handfeste*: *Preuss. U.B.* i 1, nos. 105, 252, pp. 80, 189.
[6] Krollmann, loc. cit., p. 288, therefore calls them 'claims'.
[7] G. Aubin, op. cit., p. 19; Krollmann, loc. cit., p. 291; E. Wilke, 'Die Ursachen der preussischen Bauern- und Bürgerunruhen 1525', *Altpreussische Forschungen*, vii, 1930, p. 36.

were created in the fourteenth century.[1] At the same time the very large estates of the earlier period were broken up into many parts through sales, divisions among heirs, separations among joint owners, or the giving up of claims.[2] Thus the vast possessions of Dietrich Stange were split into many parts already in the next generation;[3] perhaps they had only been granted for the purpose of subdivision. No single landlord could make use of such large tracts of land.[4]

In the 'wilderness' of eastern Prussia, however, the Order continued its practice of granting large estates to noblemen and others. The best-known example of this kind was the investment, in 1321, of three noblemen 'and some of their friends' with as many as 1,440 *Hufen* in the south-east of the *terra* of Sassen,[5] at the edge of the area then colonized. Six heavy knight's services had to be rendered from 80 *Hufen* each, and 24 light horseman's services from 40 *Hufen* each,[5] indicating the way in which the tract was to be subdivided. Later 29 independent villages and estates came into being on this large property.[6] In the same district, in 1325, another nobleman 'and his friends' were granted 400 *Hufen*: of these the principal grantee received 80 plus 40 *Hufen* for himself and was obliged to render one heavy and one light knight's service.[7] In the same year he founded on this property a German village with 40 *Hufen*:[8] its mayor took over the obligation of the light service. The remaining 280 *Hufen* were shared out among 6 knights, one receiving 80, and the others 40 *Hufen* each.[7] During the following years the settlement of the *terra* of Sassen proceeded according to the same plan: a heavy service from each estate of 80, and a light service from each of 40 to 50 *Hufen*.[9] In the 'wilderness', where clearing had to be carried out before any yields could be expected, 80 *Hufen*

---

[1] Plehn, loc. cit. xvii, p. 392.
[2] Weber, op. cit., pp. 252–3, 255, n. 1; G. Aubin, op. cit., pp. 18–19; Krollmann, oc. cit., p. 289.
[3] K. Lohmeyer, *Geschichte von Ost- und Westpreussen*, 1908, p. 193; Krollmann, loc. cit., p. 291.
[4] Plehn, loc. cit. xvii, p. 391.
[5] *Preuss. U.B.* ii 1, no. 363, pp. 270–1; *Cod. Dipl. Pruss.* ii, no. 98, pp. 123–5.
[6] Plehn, loc cit. xvii, p. 392; Kasiske, *Die Siedlungstätigkeit . . .*, p. 77.
[7] *Preuss. U.B.* ii 2, no. 534, pp. 359–60.
[8] Ibid., no. 522, p. 353.
[9] Ibid., nos. 608, 620–2, 624, 715, 718–19, 722, 724; ii 3, nos. 749, 782, 858–9, 867, 873; *U.B. Culm*, no. 260, p. 197.

(or 3,275 acres), instead of 40 as stipulated in the *Culmische Handfeste*, were the basis of a knight's service. The grants of hundreds of *Hufen* were collective assignments comprised into one charter,[1] thus relieving the Order of the duty of subdivision and demarcation between the group of 'friends' or entrepreneurs. Estates of this large size would have been quite impracticable for the 'wilderness' and under the economic conditions of the time.[2]

The same principles were applied during the further settlement of the eastern 'wilderness', although grants of hundreds of *Hufen* did not recur. In the area of Gerdauen 30 *Hufen* were the basis of a light horseman's service: there 120 *Hufen* were granted against 4 services in 1376 and in 1406, 150 *Hufen* in 1399, 60 *Hufen* against 2 services in 1400, and 110 *Hufen* against as many as 7 services in 1379.[3] The same applied farther south in the area of Bischofsburg: there a Prussian nobleman and his four sons in 1373 received 120 *Hufen* against 4 services; 2 brothers von Uelsen in 1379 were given 150 *Hufen* against 5 services, and 2 other brothers of the same family another 150 under the same obligation;[4] while the von Wildenau received 250 *Hufen* against 7, and 350 *Hufen* against 9 light services in 1388.[5] In the lake district, farther to the east, 60 *Hufen* were given out against 2 services in 1392 and in 1400, 120 *Hufen* against 3 services in 1397 and against 4 services in 1406.[6] In Nadrauen, in the northeast of Prussia, a Prussian family in 1404 held 300 *Hufen* against 12 light services, and 2 years later 2 brothers of the same family were invested with $62\frac{1}{2}$ *Hufen* against $2\frac{1}{2}$ services. There 25 *Hufen* were the basis of a light service, and the estates either had that size, or they comprised 50 *Hufen* against 2 services, and in one instance 100 *Hufen* against 4 services; the latter had 4 owners,

---

[1] Krollmann, loc. cit., p. 297; Kasiske, op. cit., p. 77.

[2] H. Aubin, loc. cit. i, p. 373, wrongly assumes that the 1,440 *Hufen* formed one estate.

[3] M. Rousselle, 'Das Siedlungswerk des Deutschen Ordens im Lande Gerdauen', *Altpreussische Forschungen*, vi, 1929, pp. 236, 247; Kasiske, op. cit., pp. 110–11; H. and G. Mortensen, *Die Besiedlung des nordöstlichen Ostpreussens bis zum Beginn des 17. Jahrhunderts*, i, 1937, pp. 189, 202.

[4] M. Töppen, *Geschichte Masurens*, 1870, pp. 100–1; Kasiske, op. cit., p. 125.

[5] *Cod. Dipl. Warm.* iii, no. 226, p. 185; C. Krollmann, 'Zur Besiedlungs-Geschichte und Nationalitätenmischung in den Komtureien Christburg, Osterode und Elbing', *Zeitschrift des Westpreussischen Geschichtsvereins*, lxiv, 1923, pp. 26, 40; Kasiske, op. cit., pp. 84, 125.

[6] Töppen, op. cit., p. 111; Kasiske, op. cit., pp. 128–30.

and the estates of 50 *Hufen* usually 2 owners.[1] With the progress of the colonization eastwards the basis of a light service changed: from 40 *Hufen* in the *terra* of Sassen in the earlier fourteenth century, to 30 *Hufen* around Gerdauen and Bischofsburg, and to 25 *Hufen* in Nadrauen. In Masuren, which was colonized in the fifteenth century, only 10 *Hufen* were the basis of a light service in the western, and 10 to 15 *Hufen* in the eastern part.[2] In Gerdauen most estates were no larger than 10 to 12 *Hufen*, in Seehesten and Ortelsburg, in the south, they had merely 10 *Hufen*, and the same applied to other parts of the 'wilderness'.[3] The grant of large estates was the exception and not the rule: the Order obviously preferred small estates.

The large estates in the 'wilderness', moreover, were allocations or claims which were not always taken up by the grantees. Sometimes the grants were later repeated on a smaller scale; other estates remained unoccupied or 'wood' for a long time. Even if the landlords realized their claims, they did not, as a rule, preserve them as compact units or farm them themselves. Many of them, alone or in company, used them for a peculiar speculation in real estate. By parcelling out their estates or founding villages on them they succeeded in transferring their military obligations towards the Order to the owners of the smaller estates or to the mayors of the new villages who then had to render the military services stipulated in the original charter; while the first landlord's estate was reduced in size but became free from any burden. Those on whom the military services had devolved, on the other hand, entered into direct relations with the Order, so that their possessions later were enumerated among the villages and estates belonging to the Order, and every link with the original landlord had apparently disappeared.[4] This type of speculation also seems the most plausible explanation for the issue of one charter to several knights as collective contractors,[5] and equally for the origin

---

[1] 25 *Hufen* twice in 1376, in 1387, 1394, 1404; 50 *Hufen* in 1376, twice in 1384 and in 1394; 100 in 1394: Weber, op. cit., pp. 530–2; Kasiske, op. cit., pp. 134–6; Mortensen, op. cit. i, pp. 173, 187, 192, 202.

[2] Töppen, op. cit., pp. 93–94, 100, 105–6.

[3] Kasiske, op. cit., pp. 105–6, 107–8, 110–11, 116, 122–4; Mortensen, op. cit. i, pp. 7, 68, both with many details.

[4] Mortensen, op. cit. i, pp. 65–68, 94, 112–13, 134, quoting in the notes to these pages and in the *Ortsverzeichnis* several examples of these transactions.

[5] Ibid. i, p. 112, and notes 417, 420.

of 29 independent villages and estates on the 1,440 *Hufen* in Sassen.[1]

Outside the 'wilderness' the estates which were liable to render knight's services were very small in the fourteenth century. In the Culmerland, which had been colonized first, their size varied from 2 to 40 *Hufen*: most comprised about 10 *Hufen*, ten estates had between 10 and 20, and one each 30, 39, and 40 *Hufen*.[2] Only these last can be classified as substantial estates. Farther north, in the commandery of Elbing, the average size of such estates amounted to only 6 *Hufen*, in the commandery of Christburg it varied between 5 and 10 *Hufen*.[3] In these two districts the estates were smaller than in the Culmerland where the average size was 12 *Hufen*.[2] In the Prussian bishoprics these estates were even smaller than they were in the territory of the Order, as military considerations played a less important part in them.[4] In the bishopric of Culm knight's services had to be rendered from estates of only 3 and 4 *Hufen*.[5] Parallel with the rising value of land and the settlement of peasants, the break-up of the large estates had progressed very far, for obvious reasons in the interior further than in the frontier districts; but even there few large estates existed in the later fourteenth century.

The tendency towards the splitting-up of the large estates existed in spite of the fact that Prussia undoubtedly exported corn in considerable quantities. As early as 1287 a burgher of Elbing was granted the special privilege to send the corn which he produced on his 12 *Hufen* anywhere by land or by sea.[6] In 1330 the peasants of a village near Marienburg were permitted to ship their corn and other produce to Elbing for sale.[7] The Teutonic Knights themselves undertook demesne farming on a fairly large scale. Their manors were distributed over the whole country and excelled in their management and their yields.[8] Some of their demesnes were no larger than a peasant farm, others were of a medium size, and a few were very large. From

---

[1] See above, p. 55.

[2] Weber, op. cit., p. 253; cf. *Acten der Ständetage Preussens*, ii, no. 30, p. 41: noble estates of 2 and 4 *Hufen* in the Culmerland in 1437.

[3] Weber, op. cit., pp. 253, 453, 458–67; G. Aubin, op. cit., p. 25.

[4] Weber, op. cit., p. 255; Aubin, op. cit., p. 26.

[5] *U.B. Culm*, nos. 279, 347, pp. 210, 267 (1343–77).

[6] *Cod. Dipl. Warm.* i, no. 75, p. 129.   [7] *Preuss. U.B.* ii 2, no. 678, p. 448.

[8] G. Aubin, op. cit., pp. 23, 38; W. Naudé, *Die Getreidehandelspolitik der europäischen Staaten vom 13. bis zum 18. Jahrhundert* (*Acta Borussica*), i, 1896, p. 255.

the quantity of seed-corn used on four of these manors the size of the area cultivated, including the fallow, has been estimated as about 10, 15, 23, and 84 *Hufen*, or between 410 and 3,500 acres.[1] The last example was an exception, concerning as it did the manor of Marienburg, the Order's centre and seat of administration. There is, however, very little evidence of private demesne farming in the fourteenth century, and even less of sales for export by private landlords. Most private estates were too small to produce a marketable surplus. An estate of 10 *Hufen* could provide a nobleman with the means of living suitable to his status, but could not produce a substantial surplus. Most of the larger estates were situated in the 'wilderness' and consisted largely of wood, waste, and meadows.[2] But there were some larger estates in the interior, and these may have produced corn for the market. They undoubtedly did so in the fifteenth century, and there is no reason for doubting that the same was the case in the fourteenth.[3] Production for the market, however, seems to have been the exception, and not the rule. The manors of the Order may have been 'agricultural factories' or 'large farms'; but this certainly did not apply to the large majority of the private estates in the thirteenth and fourteenth centuries.[4] Moreover, the corn exports were handled by the Order and by the towns, and not by the landlords.

About 1280, after the final subjugation of the Prussians, there began the systematic colonization of the country and the immigration of German peasants. Within a few decades hundreds of German villages were founded by the Teutonic Knights as well as the bishops and the cathedral chapters. In contrast with Brandenburg and Pomerania, comparatively few villages were founded on the estates of private landlords, for these were usually too small to separate from them 25 to 30 *Hufen* for a village with only ten peasant farms.[5] Furthermore, as shown above, many a village founded by a private landlord later appeared as standing directly under the Order: its conditions would in no way be different from those obtaining in villages founded by the Teutonic

---

[1] Aubin, op. cit., p. 24.   [2] Ibid., p. 28; Mortensen, op. cit. i, p. 65.
[3] Aubin, op. cit., p. 65.
[4] This against the opinion held by W. von Brünneck, in *Jahrbücher für National-ökonomie und Statistik*, i, 1888, p. 370; Plehn, loc. cit. xvii, p. 425; W. zur Ungnad, *Deutsche Freibauern, Kölmer und Kolonisten*, 1932, p. 149.
[5] Aubin, op. cit., p. 17.

Knights themselves. In general the private landlords had to use the same standards as the Order, otherwise they could never have secured the required peasants.[1] The same applied to the bishops and the cathedral chapters. Uniformity of their standards with those of the Order was ensured by the fact that the bishops and canons were members of the Order, with the only exception of the canons of the Ermland.[2] There the bishops and the cathedral chapter were particularly active in promoting peasant settlement: between them they colonized more than 3,000 *Hufen*, or about 200 square miles. The commander of Elbing alone within four decades settled about 1,200 *Hufen* with peasants.[3] Over 750 German villages came into being in western Prussia, and nearly half that number each in Pomerelia and in eastern Prussia: a total of over 1,400 villages with about 60,000 *Hufen*.[4] In the east, however, they were more thinly distributed, and few were to be found in the 'wilderness' which covered much of eastern Prussia.

The revenues from German villages, either in kind or in money, were so attractive that the Order distinctly preferred them to the granting of estates against military services which had lost their value. Only in the eastern frontier districts bordering upon Lithuania new estates of this type were still created. Furthermore, the Teutonic Knights reduced the estates granted during the earlier period by settling members of noble families in the 'wilderness' and by exchanging estates in the west for such in the east of the country.[5] In Pomerelia, acquired in the early fourteenth century, military necessities played no part, as the neighbouring districts had been secured before. The Order therefore bought out many estates of Slav noblemen as well as of Germans and used them and escheated fiefs for purposes of peasant settlement.[6] Even in the eastern commandery of Oste-

---

[1] Aubin, op. cit., pp. 17–18; E. Wilke, loc. cit., pp. 43–44; R. Kötzschke, *Grundzüge der deutschen Wirtschaftsgeschichte bis zum 17. Jahrhundert*, 2nd ed., 1921, pp. 148, 151–2.

[2] Aubin, op. cit., p. 17; Kasiske, op. cit., pp. 153–4.

[3] H. Witte, *Besiedlung des Ostens und Hanse*, Pfingstblätter des Hansischen Geschichtsvereins, 1914, p. 27.

[4] Weber, op. cit., p. 318: 753 villages in western Prussia, 342 in Pomerelia, and 313 in eastern Prussia.

[5] Examples may be found in Krollmann, 'Die Herkunft der deutschen Ansiedler in Preussen', loc. cit., pp. 65, 67–68, and Kasiske, op. cit., pp. 21, 78, 141–2, 144.

[6] *Preuss. U.B.* ii. 1, nos. 78, 96, 120; ii 2, nos. 656, 667; *Urkunden der Komturei Tuchel*, no. 101; *Handfesten der Komturei Schlochau*, nos. 158, 167; F. Mager, *Geschichte*

rode noble estates were bought out in the late fourteenth century.[1] These measures were not only economically advantageous, but they also prevented the rise of a powerful nobility. There is no parallel for such a policy from any other eastern principality, for no other ruler was financially strong enough to carry it out. For the time being it achieved its object: the rise of the nobility was, if not prevented, at least considerably delayed. In the fifteenth century, however, this policy led to sharp conflicts between the nobility and the Teutonic Knights: it was one of the causes of the great revolt of the Prussians against their rule, which ended with their defeat and the cession of western Prussia to Poland.[2]

The easy revenues to be gained from peasant settlement also seem to have caused a tendency towards less demesne farming, at least as far as the ecclesiastical foundations were concerned. As early as 1326 the Ermland cathedral chapter used 18 *Hufen* of an *allodium* of 30 to found a village on them.[3] Towards the end of the century the bishop of Ermland founded villages of 26 and 50 *Hufen* on his *allodia*.[4] Other *allodia* were sold to burghers of the towns of Heilsberg, Wartenberg, and Braunsberg; but in the last instance the bishop retained 5 *Hufen* and a wood for himself.[5] All these examples came from the Ermland where peasant settlement was particularly strong; but the Teutonic Knights also sold two demesnes of 6 *Hufen* each to peasants in the commandery of Schlochau and transformed one *allodium* there into a village.[6] These changes seem the more remarkable as the later fourteenth century was a time of growing corn exports. There is no evidence that the same tendency also affected the private estates. It has often been assumed that the landlords' demesne farming became more prominent at this time; but a parallel development on ecclesiastical and private estates seems

der Landeskultur Westpreussens und des Netzebezirks, 1936, pp. 28, 30; Kasiske, *Das deutsche Siedelwerk des Mittelalters in Pommerellen*, pp. 145, 182, 190–1.

[1] *Das grosse Ämterbuch des Deutschen Ordens*, ed. W. Ziesemer, 1921, pp. 323–4; Krollmann, 'Zur Besiedlungs-Geschichte und Nationalitätenmischung...', loc. cit., pp. 23–24.

[2] *Acten der Ständetage Preussens*, i, no. 487, p. 629; ii, nos. 30, 150, pp. 34, 219–20; iii, no. 68, p. 141; iv, no. 23, p. 42; Plehn, loc. cit. xvii, p. 418.

[3] *Cod. Dipl. Warm.* i, no. 226, p. 381.

[4] Ibid. iii, nos. 125, 205, pp. 91, 164 (1381–6).

[5] Ibid. iii, nos. 310, 422, 456, pp. 283, 418, 458 (1396–1410).

[6] *Handfesten der Komturei Schlochau*, nos. 31, 133, 164, pp. 45, 144, 171 (1350–1412).

the more likely, as the examples of the Order and the bishops would carry great weight in a country where they owned most of the land. The buying out of estates in the west, where most demesnes were concentrated, and the transfer of noble landlords to the east seem to point in the same direction. Nothing more definite, however, can be said until more evidence has come to light.

The actual foundation of a village was, as in the other parts of the colonization area, undertaken by a *locator* who became the village mayor, exercised the lower jurisdiction, usually up to the sum of four shillings, and received one-third of the revenues of the village court.[1] The remaining two-thirds and the higher jurisdiction were as a rule reserved to the Order; its *advocati* presided in the high courts competent to judge crimes. The village mayor generally received one-tenth of the village land, free from all dues, that is a holding of 3 to 6 *Hufen*. His only obligation was service as a horseman in the defence of the country and on military expeditions. The same obligation was performed by the peasants. Gradually, however, the military services lost their importance in the interior, so that the peasants merely had to provide a waggon with horses and provisions from a number of *Hufen* if they were called out to take part in an expedition.[2] The other military service they had to render, that of guarding the frontier in the east, in course of time was commuted into a quit-rent, the *Wartgeld*, which had to be given by every landowner, exactly as a corn due for the provisioning of the fortifications in the east.[3] Another corn due given by every landowner was the *Pflugkorn* which took the place of the tithes and was early fixed at the very low level of one *modius* of wheat and one of rye from each German plough, or from about 3 or 4 *Hufen*.[4]

All these dues were given to the Teutonic Knights and were

---

[1] In some instances the village mayor was even granted the higher jurisdiction: *Preuss. U.B.* ii 1, nos. 194, 366; ii 2, nos. 490, 538, 604; ii 3, nos. 759, 790, 793; *Cod. Dipl. Warm.* i, no. 187; *U.B. Samland*, no. 256; *Handfesten der Komturei Schlochau*, no. 85 (1317–66).

[2] *Preuss. U.B.* ii 3, nos. 769, 868, pp. 510–86; M. Töppen, 'Die Zins-Verfassung Preussens unter der Herrschaft des Deutschen Ordens', *Zeitschrift für preussische Geschichte und Landeskunde*, iv, 1867, p. 345; Weber, op. cit., p. 324; G. Aubin, op. cit., pp. 17, 29.

[3] Töppen, loc. cit., pp. 351–6; Lohmeyer, op. cit., pp. 190–1; Aubin, op. cit., p. 30.

[4] *Preuss. U.B.* i 1, nos. 105, 252, pp. 80, 191; Töppen, loc. cit., p. 222; Lohmeyer, op. cit., p. 190.

comparatively small. The main due of the peasants, but not of the other landholders, was the *census* which had to be paid to their landlord. Its level was fixed once and for all at the foundation of the village and was the same for each *Hufe*; if the village was founded on uncultivated soil, which seems to have been the rule, its payment only began after 10, 12, 15, or even more 'free years'.[1] Usually the *census* amounted to half a mark and two chickens from the *Hufe*; often it was less, sometimes more.[2] That the *census* was fixed in money did not mean that it was always given in this form; but any rise in the price of corn, as it undoubtedly occurred in the fourteenth century, would thus benefit the peasants. Their holdings usually comprised 2 or 3 *Hufen*, sometimes 4, or between 80 and 160 acres.[3] They received them under the favourable conditions laid down in the *Culmische Handfeste* which did not stipulate any restrictions of their right to leave freely.[4]

The earlier *Handfesten* granted to the German villages merely stipulated the dues and the public services which the peasants had to render: up to about 1320 these were their only obligations. There is only one exception: in 1290 20 *Hufen* were given to the peasants of the village outside the castle of Roggenhausen, and they had to render labour services of eight days in the year.[5] This seems to have been a native village which was enlarged at the time of its transformation into a German one; for the village existed before the charter was granted, and no *locator* was mentioned in it. After 1320 the stipulation of labour services was the exception and not the rule. Of the many village *Handfesten* issued between 1320 and 1341, only eleven stipulated labour services: they also may concern transformed, and not newly-founded, villages, as seven of them were situated in the delta of the Vistula, on old Slav and not on Prussian soil. In three instances

[1] Kasiske, *Die Siedlungstätigkeit des Deutschen Ordens* . . ., p. 4; Mortensen, op. cit. i, p. 107.

[2] Töppen, loc. cit., pp. 221, 618, 752; Lohmeyer, op. cit., p. 194; Aubin, op. cit., p. 31; Mortensen, op. cit. i, p. 98, n. 369.

[3] Weber, op. cit., p. 319; Plehn, loc. cit. xvii, p. 394; Aubin, op. cit., p. 22; E. Wilke, loc. cit., p. 45; Mortensen, op. cit. i, p. 106.

[4] H. Aubin, loc. cit. i, p. 378. Plehn, loc. cit. xvii, pp. 438–9, and G. Aubin, op. cit. pp. 86–89, are of a different opinion, but the document the latter quotes as evidence (*Cod. Dipl. Warm.* i, no. 61, p. 107) does not state or imply that the peasant required a permit if he wanted to leave.

[5] *Preuss. U.B.* i 2, nos. 569, 729, pp. 357, 453.

the peasants had to serve 2 days in the year, in seven 6 days, and in the eleventh case only 1 day.[1]

In the second half of the fourteenth century such services became more customary, although peasants might, as a special favour, be exempted from them, or might pay a quit-rent instead.[2] Up to the early fifteenth century the services amounted to no more than 2 to 4, or at most 6 days in the year, usually during the hay harvest.[3] They were required by the Order to provide the fodder for its large herds of horses and cattle.[4] Thus an ancient Prusso-Polish law quite generally stipulated three days of hay-making a year for men and women alike.[5] When the peasants of an episcopal village in the Ermland in 1389 disputed their obligation to render labour services, the arbiters decided that they were a custom of the country, especially the carting of corn, hay, wood, fish, and stones.[6] In several *Handfesten* it was then merely stipulated that the peasants of the new village had to serve like those of the neighbouring villages.[7] By that time this was a general custom which need not be specified. These labour services had to be rendered instead of the public services which were no longer required by the Order. From the peasants' point of view this was no aggravation, as the labour services were fixed at a low level, while the public services by their nature had been unlimited.

Peasants living under a private landlord might equally have to render him labour services if he required them for his demesne. Thus peasants of one private village in the commandery of Tuchel had to serve one day, and those of another village two days in the year, exactly the same as the peasants under the Order.[8]

---

[1] *Preuss. U.B.* ii 1, nos. 317, 359, 407; ii 2, no. 516; ii 3, nos. 794, 827–9; iii 1, nos. 278, 366, 411. The first is almost certainly a transformation of a Polish village.

[2] *Urkunden der Komturei Tuchel*, nos. 10, 21, 34, 56; *Handfesten der Komturei Schlochau*, no. 28; Töppen, loc. cit., pp. 232, 618, 753; and *Geschichte Masurens*, p. 127.

[3] Töppen, loc. cit., pp. 231–2; Weber, op. cit., p. 562; G. Aubin, op. cit., pp. 41–43. In the western commanderies of Schlochau and Tuchel labour services of one to three days were customary.

[4] Weber, op. cit., pp. 249, 562; Aubin, op. cit., p. 43.

[5] A. Z. Helcel, *Starodawne Prawa Polskiego Pomniki*, Cracow, 1870, ii, p. 33.

[6] *Cod. Dipl. Warm.* iii, nos. 231, 253, pp. 191–3, 226; *Cod. Dipl. Pruss.* iv, nos. 68, 99, pp. 95, 142.

[7] Töppen, loc. cit., p. 232; and *Geschichte Masurens*, p. 127; Rousselle, loc. cit., p. 250; Ungnad, op. cit., p. 165.

[8] *Urkunden der Komturei Tuchel*, nos. 44, 80, pp. 50, 83 (1354–78). Cf. above, n. 3.

Two *Handfesten* of private villages from the later fourteenth
century, however, stipulated unlimited labour services, in
addition to the usual *census*; one of them comes from the
Ermland and the other from eastern Prussia, and they may concern transformed Prussian villages.[1] This would seem the most
natural explanation of these exceptional cases, as the Prussians'
services were not limited.[2] As long as the demesne farming of
private landlords was inconsiderable, such unlimited services
need not have been a heavy burden. Nevertheless, these two
charters indicate a rather precarious position of the peasants:
they had no defence if the demands of their lord grew. No
general conclusions can be drawn from these two isolated instances. As long as the number of German villages under private
landlords remained small, such examples could not exercise any
influence on the situation of the peasantry as a whole. This
remained very favourable throughout the fourteenth century.

As in the other districts of the colonization area, it is by no
means certain that all the 'German' villages were inhabited by
German peasants. In a 'German' village the peasants used the
German plough, and not the 'hook', the arable was subdivided
into *Hufen*, the open field system was used, and there was a
village mayor and a village court; but its inhabitants might be
Poles or Prussians, provided they were economically efficient
and paid the dues stipulated. Although the opposite has been
asserted recently,[3] nothing was further from the Teutonic
Knights than a policy of racial or national victimization; their
standards were those of expediency, and not those of modern
nationalism. As they could not obtain German peasants in
sufficient numbers for their vast projects of settlement, they soon
had to use non-Germans. Especially against the Polish population in the south and west of the country the Order had fewer
political and economic prejudices than against the Prussians
who were more backward and more inclined to revolt. As early
as 1285 the *domina* Kunegundis was granted the privilege of
founding new villages *jure Culmensi vel Polonicali* on her lands.[4]
From the late thirteenth century onwards Polish villages were

---

[1] *Cod. Dipl. Warm.* ii, no. 476, p. 483; *Regesta Historico-Diplomatica*, ii, no.
1191, p. 143 (1373–89). The latter seems to be a *Handfeste* of a transformed Prussian village.   [2] See below, p. 68.

[3] By M. Z. Jedlicki, in *The Cambridge History of Poland (to 1696)*, pp. 140–7.

[4] *U.B. Culm*, no. 110, p. 71.

transformed into German ones and received German law and institutions, so that the Order or the bishop, who effected the change, might benefit.[1] In this way most of the Polish villages in Pomerelia and the Culmerland received German law, although they often retained the 'hook' as their economic unit.[2]

With regard to the native Prussian population the Order made a political and not a racial distinction, dividing those who had remained loyal during the last great revolt of 1261–75 from those who had rebelled. The former were tied to the Order by very real bonds and became an elevated class, the 'Prussian freemen', while the latter were made serfs. Those noble families which had remained loyal retained their extensive lands, were put on an equal legal and economic footing with the German nobility, and became quickly Germanized.[3] Many of these families, in the fourteenth century, received estates in the 'wilderness' and took a prominent part in its settlement; no distinction whatever was made between them and the German noblemen used for the same purpose.[4] The 'Prussian freemen' were either granted the Culmic law which put them on the same legal footing as the Germans, or the Prussian law of succession under which fewer people could succeed to the estate and the obligations were somewhat higher.[5] The freemen were in general treated like Germans and soon became economically Germanized. Frequently they were invested not with 'hooks', but with *Hufen*. In the bishopric of Ermland, as early as 1287, freemen were treated as *Theutonici feodales;*[6] and in the bishopric of Samland later other freemen were called *Theutonici rustici*, although they were given 'hooks', and not *Hufen*.[7]

The size of the estates of the Prussian freemen varied con-

[1] *Preuss. U.B.* i 2, nos. 700, 801, pp. 436–98; ii 1, nos. 73–74, 317, pp. 47, 234; *Cod. Dipl. Warm.* i, no. 137; *U.B. Culm*, no. 247; *Urkunden der Komturei Tuchel*, nos. 81–82, 87–88; Kasiske, op. cit., pp. 22–23, 157.

[2] Jedlicki, loc. cit., pp. 144–5; Kasiske, *Das deutsche Siedelwerk des Mittelalters . . .*, pp. 147–9, 150–1, 266–7. In the area of Danzig the 'hook' was twice as large as the *Hufe*: ibid., p. 147.

[3] Plehn, loc. cit. xvii, p. 399; H. Harmjanz, *Volkskunde und Siedlungsgeschichte Altpreussens*, 1936, pp. 14–15.

[4] Kasiske, *Die Siedlungstätigkeit des Deutschen Ordens . . .*, p. 146; Mortensen, op. cit. i, pp. 63–64.

[5] Töppen, loc. cit., pp. 216–17; Plehn, loc. cit. xvii, p. 400; Lohmeyer, op. cit., pp. 196–7; Harmjanz, op. cit., p. 15.

[6] *Cod. Dipl. Warm.* i, no. 77, p. 131.

[7] *U.B. Samland*, nos. 302, 308, pp. 225–8 (1338–9).

siderably. Many had small estates of 2 to 3 *Hufen* or even less, no more than the German peasants; more substantial freemen would own 6 *Hufen*, and some had up to 30 to 40 *Hufen*.[1] The freemen did not live in a village community, were not answerable to a village mayor, and did not farm according to the open field system. Their dues and services were not those of the peasants but those of the Germans who had to serve as horsemen; they formed the light cavalry which the Order needed for the border warfare.[2] They were by preference settled in the 'wilderness' and along the frontiers. They were also obliged to build and to repair the Order's castles whenever required to do so, as it was repeated again and again in their *Handfesten*. They were, as a rule, exempted from all labour services; but in the bishopric of Ermland some freemen had to render services of four days in the year like the German peasants.[3] The freemen stood under the direct jurisdiction of the Order.[4] They formed a separate class, between the landlords and the German peasants, and enjoyed a privileged position which was guaranteed to each of them by the *Handfeste* which he received.

The lowest class of the population were the Prussian serfs. They were either peasants farming their own holdings, or cottagers—in Prussia called 'gardeners'—with small plots of land, or servants without any land. The Teutonic Knights, with their many castles and manors, concentrated as many Prussians as possible there to employ them as servants and labourers; but they were also to be found on private estates.[5] The serfs had to render the same public services as the other inhabitants. In the thirteenth century they had to take part in military expeditions and in the defence of the country.[6] In the fourteenth century they probably accompanied the army with horses and waggons to carry its supplies.[7] Like the freemen they had to help to build and to repair the Order's castles and to construct dikes and

---

[1] Weber, op. cit., pp. 452, 469, 501, 505, 522–9, 532, 537; Aubin, op. cit., pp. 13, 26–27; Rousselle, loc. cit., p. 242; Mortensen, op. cit. i, pp. 132–4.

[2] Weber, op. cit., p. 139; Aubin, op. cit., p. 13; Kasiske, op. cit., p. 113.

[3] *Cod. Dipl. Warm.* i, no. 268, p. 444; ii, no. 435, p. 436 (1334–69).

[4] Plehn, loc. cit. xvii, p. 412.

[5] Aubin, op. cit., pp. 14–15.

[6] *Cod. Dipl. Pruss.* i, nos. 117, 137; *U.B. Samland*, nos. 59–60, 72–73; *Preuss. U.B.* i 2, nos. 138, 145, 148, 155, 173–4, 262–3, 294–5, 314, 319, 322, 331, 362–3, 485, 859.

[7] Weber, op. cit., p. 326; Aubin, op. cit., p. 29.

canals whenever they were required to do so; and these services
might take them far away from their domicile to the east of
Prussia and might prove very onerous on account of the extensive military and building activities of the Order.[1] The serfs
furthermore had to render labour services to their lord, such as
haymaking, corn mowing, woodcutting, carting, 'and the like':[2]
these seem to have been their typical services, while ploughing
services were not enumerated. Neither was it stipulated that
their services were limited in time: it seems that they had to be
rendered whenever their lord required them.[3] The main due of
the serfs was the tithe which was fixed and had to be given to
their landlord in kind, from each 'hook' at least one *modius* of
wheat, rye, barley, and oats.[4] The serfs' holdings were considerably smaller than those of the German peasants: on an average
they possessed only one 'hook' and a half, equivalent to about
1 *Hufe* or 40 acres.[5]

From the outset the Prussian serfs were not tied to the soil. In
the 1260's it was stipulated that they could leave freely and
settle under another lord on payment of the comparatively
small sum of a quarter of a mark;[6] and in one instance complete
freedom of movement was granted to them without any payment or other condition.[7] In practice their holdings were hereditary; but when there was no son, the Order entered upon the
inheritance, unless it had ceded this right to the lord of the serfs
in question.[8] The serfs certainly could freely own and bequeath
movable property.[9] These facts indicate that they had quite
clearly circumscribed rights and duties, even in the thirteenth

---

[1] Aubin, op. cit., p. 29; *Acten der Ständetage Preussens*, i, nos. 391, 398, pp. 519,
533 (1429-30).

[2] *Preuss. U.B.* i 2, nos. 329, 343, 347, 350, pp. 223-37 (1275-6).

[3] Weber, op. cit., p. 325; Lohmeyer, op. cit., p. 196; Plehn, loc. cit. xvii, p. 452;
Aubin, op. cit., p. 39; Harmjanz, op. cit., p. 15, n. 14.

[4] Töppen, loc. cit., pp. 212-13; Weber, op. cit., p. 561; Aubin, op. cit.,
pp. 31-32.

[5] Weber, op. cit., pp. 326-7; Mortensen, op. cit. i, pp. 33-34, 142; Lohmeyer,
op. cit., p. 196.

[6] *Preuss. U.B.* i 2, nos. 262-3, 353, 381, pp. 189-260; ii 3, no. 732, p. 485;
Weber, op. cit., p. 328 (1267-80).

[7] *Preuss. U.B.* i, 2, no. 204, p. 158 (1263).

[8] Thus ibid., nos. 262-3, 353, 381, 471-2; ii i, nos. 85, 129-30, 134-5, 164, 333,
351, 361. The custom of Prussia is stated ibid. i 2, no. 366, p. 250 (1278).

[9] Lohmeyer, op. cit., p. 196; Plehn, loc. cit. xvii, pp. 434-5; Aubin, op. cit.,
p. 14; E. Wilke, loc. cit., p. 41; Harmjanz, op. cit., p. 17.

century. At the end of this century, however, their economic Germanization began, and therewith their gradual assimilation to the social and legal position of the German peasants, which proceeded throughout the fourteenth century. First in the west of Prussia, and later also in the east, villages were granted to Prussian mayors for settlement.[1] Probably these were not new villages to be founded, but old villages to be transformed: their inhabitants were to pay the *census* and to enjoy in every respect the status of German peasants, while the distinctive marks of serfdom disappeared.

Especially in the bishopric of Ermland, where a very large part of the population were Prussians, their share in the colonization was very important. At least fifty villages were given to Prussian mayors for settlement, usually under Culmic or German law.[2] As many Prussians by the fourteenth century had adopted German or Christian names, presumably many more village mayors were of Prussian origin. Prussian freemen also were granted as many free *Hufen* as they had possessed 'hooks' in or near a newly-founded village, were made subject to the jurisdiction of the village mayor, and were admitted into the village community.[3] The same applied to Prussian peasants who also remained on their holdings when a German village was founded.[4] Later whole Prussian villages were allowed the benefits of Culmic law.[5] In the bishopric of Samland, which also had a large Prussian population, Germans and Prussians lived side by side in the same village: only that the jurisdiction over the Prussians was exercised by the Order's *advocatus*, and not by the village mayor.[6] In 1326, however, German law was bestowed upon the peasants of one village: Germans and Prussians alike were to come under the jurisdiction of the village mayor.[7] In

---

[1] *Preuss. U.B.* i 2, no. 650, p. 411; ii 1, no. 7, p. 4; ii 2, no. 604, p. 398; *U.B. Samland*, no. 242, p. 162; Kasiske, op. cit., pp. 52, 72, 93, 99, 118, 124.

[2] *Cod. Dipl. Warm.* i, nos. 277, 283, 288, 290, 292, 297, 299, 302; ii, nos. 2–3, 7, 19, 22–23, 50, 68, 85, 89, 97, 99, 101, 103, 106, 127, 133, 148, 159, 165, 187, 217, 247, 262, 279–80, 320, 337, 348, 361, 369, 435, 476, 487 b; iii, nos. 48, 102, 167, 191, 311, 477.

[3] Ibid. ii, nos. 138–9, 156, 207–8, 280, 318, 383, 435; iii, nos. 58, 402, 412 (1349–1405).

[4] Ibid. i, nos. 175, 194, 197, 267; ii, nos. 147, 223 (1315–55).

[5] Ibid. iii, nos. 69, 245, 247 (1379–90):

[6] *U.B. Samland*, nos. 244–5, 256, 286 (1326–35).

[7] Ibid., no. 243, p. 163.

the next year Culmic law was granted to the Prussians who wished to acquire a heritage in another village; but first they had to present themselves to the bishop,[1] presumably so that he could reject unsuitable candidates. According to these *Handfesten*, the German and the Prussian peasants had to give the same dues from each *Hufe* and the Prussians were treated like German peasants.

The Teutonic Knights themselves at first only founded villages under Prussian law and granted others to Prussian mayors for settlement or transformation.[2] Later, however, they also permitted Germans and Prussians to live in the same village,[3] if the latter adopted the German plough and thus became economically efficient. From the 1370's onwards they even had to admit non-Germanized Prussians, who still used the 'hook', into German villages: after the Black Death the many peasants required for their villages could apparently not be obtained unless this concession was made. The only condition then stipulated was that these Prussians had to pay the same dues from their 'hook' which the Germans gave from their plough,[4] so that the Order's income would not suffer, while previously the dues from the 'hook' were about half those from the German plough.[5] Prussian peasants also could rise to the status of freemen,[6] which again facilitated their Germanization, as the freemen were soon treated like Germans. Among the 'German' peasants of the fifteenth and sixteenth centuries there was presumably a very large number of Germanized Prussians.

Comparatively few German villages were founded 'from wild root' in the districts with a strong native population. In Pomesanien, Pogesanien, Ermland, Natangen, Barten, Nadrauen, and especially in the Samland, the Prussians were much more

[1] *U.B. Samland*, no. 259, p. 177 (1327).
[2] Instances of presumable transformations: *Preuss. U.B.* ii 1, no. 382, p. 280; *Cod. Dipl. Pruss.* iii, no. 56, p. 79; Kasiske, op. cit., pp. 72, 85, 118; Rousselle, loc. cit., pp. 229, 244; and 'Die Besiedlung des Kreises Preussisch-Eylau', *Altpreussische Forschungen*, iii 2, 1926, pp. 21–22.
[3] Cf. a *Handfeste* of the 1330's excluding Prussians from the new village: *Preuss. U.B.* iii 1, no. 130, p. 94, as an example of the earlier practice.
[4] Thus the *Handfesten* of ten villages from the years 1370 ff., quoted by Kasiske, op. cit., pp. 71, 73, 118; Mortensen, op. cit. i, pp. 95, 97; Rousselle, 'Das Siedlungswerk...', *Altpreuss. Forschungen*, vi, 1929, p. 228.
[5] *Preuss. U.B.* iii 1, nos. 116, 178–82, 239, 248, 256, 258, 266, 273, 288, 296, 298, 304, 318, 330, 332, 364–5, 374 (1337–41).
[6] Mortensen, op. cit. i, pp. 3–4, 141–4, with many details.

numerous than the German immigrants;[1] while in Pomerelia
and in the south the Polish element predominated. It thus seems
quite likely that in the country as a whole the German immigrants were a minority. Before the end of the Middle Ages,
however, the Prussians had become more or less Germanized.[2]
Only in the Samland, where few Germans had immigrated, did
the Prussian language and customs survive until the seventeenth
century.[3] There too they then disappeared, as they had already
done in the other districts. Pomerelia, on the other hand, only
remained under German rule for a century and a half: there
the process of Germanization was halted when the country
reverted to Poland in the mid-fifteenth century.

While the colonization and settlement of Brandenburg and
Pomerania were more or less haphazard and varied greatly
from one district to the other, the settlement of Prussia proceeded along well-defined lines. The direction of policy throughout remained in the hands of the Teutonic Knights; private
landlords only played a comparatively unimportant part, and
that only within the general framework of the policy laid down
by the Order. The administration of the country was undertaken by the commanderies of the Order, each of which comprised a large district. These were subdivided into smaller
districts, the *Kammerämter* and *Waldämter* of the Order. These
offices were responsible for the settlement of the districts allocated
to them; they saw to it that the general principles adopted for
military or economic reasons were observed, that uniform standards were maintained, that the settlers were directed to the
places where they were most needed, and that their dues and
services were fixed according to the Order's requirements.[4] In
its own brothers the Order possessed an efficient professional
bureaucracy which could carry out these tasks. All these factors
gave to the colonization of Prussia a character quite distinct
from that of other areas and made the state of the Teutonic

---

[1] Lohmeyer, op. cit., pp. 115, 141, 200; Plehn, loc. cit. xvii, p. 396; Krollmann,
'Zur Besiedlungs-Geschichte und Nationalitätenmischung . . .', loc. cit., p. 34; and
'Die Besiedlung Ostpreussens durch den Deutschen Orden', loc. cit., pp. 286, 290,
294; Rousselle, 'Die Besiedlung des Kreises Preussisch-Eylau', loc. cit., pp. 14–15,
34–35; Kasiske, op. cit., pp. 16, 41, 53, 60, 74; Harmjanz, op. cit., pp. 16, 29, 31.
[2] Plehn, loc. cit. xvii, p. 401; Kasiske, op. cit., p. 158.
[3] E. Weise, *Die alten Preussen*, 1936, pp. 22, 34–37.
[4] Kötzschke and Ebert, op. cit., p. 89; Jedlicki, loc. cit., pp. 144–5.

Knights stronger and more advanced than the neighbouring principalities. These factors also had other consequences: Prussia became a country of peasants and small landowners, a country in which the nobility was less important and less elevated above the rest of the population than it was elsewhere; a country in which the rural population did not only consist of landlords and tenants, but in which there were strong groups between the nobility and the peasantry, freeholders of German as well as of Prussian origin, and in which the large majority of the population lived directly under the ruler and not under private landlords.

VI

Medieval Colonial Society at its Prime

IN Prussia the strength of the Teutonic Order in the fourteenth century prevented the rise of a powerful nobility. In
Brandenburg and in Pomerania, on the other hand, the
territorial princes had to sell or to pawn most of their lands and
rights which were acquired by private landlords: the ecclesiastical foundations, the members of the nobility, and the burghers
of the rising towns. Thus the nobility was by no means the only
landowning class. This distribution of wealth and power among
different groups was only changed in the sixteenth century,
through the dissolution of the monasteries and the decline of the
towns: until it was finally laid down that only a nobleman was
entitled to hold an estate and that what once had been noble
land was to remain noble land, a notion alien to the Middle
Ages.

In the fourteenth century the power of the nobility was also
balanced in a different way: although its members owned much
land, they only controlled a small part of it directly, for most of
the *Hufen* in the villages were farmed by peasants who merely
owed dues to their landlords. The *Landbuch* of 1375 clearly distinguished between noble land and peasant land in Brandenburg.
The land farmed by the peasants was classified as theirs, and
not their landlord's, unless the *Hufen* in question belonged
directly to a landlord's *curia*. Such *curiae* only existed in a minority
of the villages: a very small minority in the Old Mark, to the
west of the Elbe, where only 39 out of a total of 317 villages had
one or several *curiae*, while all the others were peasant villages.
In the Ucker Mark, on the other hand, 73 out of a total of 150
villages had such *curiae*. The Middle Mark held an intermediate
position: 129 of its 444 villages possessed one or several *curiae*.[1]
These *curiae* were comparatively small. In the Old Mark their
average size was 3·7 *Hufen*, that is less than stipulated in the
treaty of 1283,[2] and hardly more than a large peasant farm; the

---

[1] C. J. Fuchs, 'Zur Geschichte des gutsherrlich-bäuerlichen Verhältnisses in der
Mark Brandenburg', *Zeitschrift der Savigny-Stiftung für Rechtsgeschichte, Germanist.
Abteilung*, xii, 1891, p. 21, gives the number of villages which had *curiae*, but not of
those which had none.   [2] See above, p. 25.

total number of *curiae* there was only 72, and only 5 of these
were larger than 6 *Hufen*.[1] In the Middle Mark there were 207,
and in the Ucker Mark 169 *curiae*, and their average size was
considerably larger: it amounted to 7·6 and 6·2 *Hufen* respectively, or about two to three peasant farms.[2] Even in these
districts, however, the land belonging to the *curiae* amounted to
much less than the land held by the peasants. In the Middle
Mark peasants possessed more than eight times the amount of
land occupied by *curiae*, and in the Ucker Mark more than five
times that amount.[2] The land directly under the nobility was a
small proportion of the total, and the individual noble estate
was not particularly large. In most villages there was no noble
curia; in the others the existence of several *curiae* was more usual
than that of one. The nobleman was still 'the peasant's neighbour',[3] and his *Hufen* were lying in intermixed strips with those
of the peasants.

Even if only one nobleman lived in a village, others usually
had rights and revenues in the same village and were the landlords of some peasants there. Only some noble families owned
numerous villages: in the Zauche the von Rochow 20 villages;
in the Old Mark the von Bismarck 14, the von Bartensleben 8,
the von der Schulenburg 7, and the von dem Knesebeck 6 villages; in the Teltow the von Gröben 5. Most noble families,
however, only had scattered rights and holdings. The great
Cistercian houses alone owned much more landed property than
the leading noble families: Lehnin 31 villages, Dambeck and
Neuendorf more than 20 each, Chorin over 14, Arendsee 13,
Himmelpfort well over 10, and Zinna 10 villages, to mention
only the more important houses.[4] In general, the *Landbuch* of
1375 showed a complex picture of overlapping rights and sub-
infeudations, of fractions of knights' services, of leases and sub-
leases, of small, medium, and large estates. It certainly did not
show any more the agrarian conditions of the time of the
colonization when land was cheap and returns were low, but a
more highly developed society in which the break-up of many

[1] Fuchs, loc. cit., p. 21.
[2] F. Grossmann, *Über die gutsherrlich-bäuerlichen Rechtsverhältnisse in der Mark
Brandenburg vom 16. bis 18. Jahrhundert*, 1890, p. 7; H. Aubin, loc. cit. i, p. 388.
[3] Knapp, op. cit. i, p. 31. Cf. above, p. 31.
[4] *Landbuch 1375*, pp. 53, 74–75, 89–90, 127–9, 176, 179, 182, 187, 190–2; cf.
above, pp. 14–15.

larger units had progressed very far: much farther in the Old Mark which was settled in the twelfth century and before than in the east Elbian lands which were conquered in the thirteenth century and settled later. This explains the striking difference between the number and the size of the *curiae* to the west and to the east of the Elbe, far better than any alleged difference in the national or 'racial' composition of the inhabitants.[1]

The neighbourhood of important towns provided a further stimulus for the break-up of the larger estates, as the towns bought the peasants' produce, and as their burghers invested money in real estate. In Brandenburg, however, only the Old Mark towns, Berlin and Cölln, Frankfurt, and Prenzlau were of any importance; they were outdistanced by the coastal towns of Pomerania and of Prussia. The *Landbuch* shows how many burghers of the Brandenburg towns possessed villages, farms, and rents from land. In the Old Mark as many as 30 villages were owned by burghers, as against 62 belonging to noblemen and 69 belonging to the church.[2] Burghers of Berlin owned demesnes of 8, 10, and $12\frac{1}{2}$ free *Hufen*, while others had substantial holdings and many more possessed rents and rights in the villages around Berlin.[3] One burgher in 1344 bought the office of the village mayor with 14 *Hufen* and was granted the right to buy and to farm any more *Hufen* which might become deserted in that village.[4] In 1315 the burghers of Salzwedel received the privilege of buying 60 *Hufen* and of farming them either directly or from their *curiae*.[5] In 1351 the widow of a burgher of Seehausen, also in the Old Mark, possessed a *curia* and the jurisdiction in a village which she exercised through her own judge.[6] In the fifteenth century one burgher family of Frankfurt owned as many as seven villages.[7] Thus the burghers invested their money in real estate and became the equals of the other landlords.

The growth of towns and of money economy seems to have caused a decline of demesne farming. As most of our records

[1] This against Fuchs, loc. cit., p. 22: it is true that Dutchmen were settled in the Old Mark, but so they were elsewhere; and it seems that the Slav share of the population was larger there than it was in the Middle Mark.
[2] Fuchs, loc. cit., p. 24.   [3] *Landbuch 1375*, pp. 45, 50, 64.
[4] *Riedel*, xi, no. 14, p. 308.   [5] Ibid. xiv, no. 72, p. 56.
[6] Ibid. xxii, no. 92, p. 57.
[7] Ibid. xxiii, nos. 265, 325, pp. 215, 263 (1441–72).

are of monastic origin, there is much more information about monastic demesne farming in the thirteenth century than about demesnes of lay landlords, and equally more evidence for the decline of monastic demesne farming in the fourteenth century. From 1326 onwards at least four *curiae* of the monastery of Eldena, near the town of Greifswald, were transformed into villages.[1] In the short space between 1347 and 1360 six *grangiae* of another great Cistercian house in Pomerania, Kolbatz, were equally converted.[2] A few years before two Cistercian monasteries in the Ucker Mark, Chorin and Himmelpfort, were granted the right to lease their *curiae* or to transform them into villages;[3] but we do not know whether they actually did so. In Brandenburg also monastic demesnes developed into villages: thus the *grangia* of the monastery of Leubus in the *terra* of Lebus,[4] a *curia* of the nunnery of Spandau,[5] and a *curia* of the Knights Hospitallers near Berlin which was transformed into a village in 1360.[6] The reasons for these transformations are unknown. Perhaps the steady revenues of peasant villages were more attractive than the efforts of demesne farming with its risks. Perhaps it was difficult to get the necessary labour, especially after the Black Death and at a time when the colonization was still proceeding apace farther east and attracting many people. If so, both considerations would also apply to lay demesne farming.

The *Landbuch* of 1375, indeed, mentioned in four or five instances that the *Hufen* belonging to a noble *curia* were leased to a peasant.[7] But this seems to have been rather exceptional. On the other hand, in only forty-two cases was it expressly stated that the noble owner of the *curia* farmed its *Hufen* himself.[8] Unfortunately, the *Landbuch* does not say how the large majority of the noble *curiae* were farmed. If they were farmed by the

---

[1] *Pomm. U.B.* vii, nos. 4152, 4162, pp. 8, 16; *Oelrichs*, 1407, no. 6, p. 113; Fuchs, op. cit., pp. 19, n. 1, 287, 303, 309 (1326–1407).

[2] 'Annales Colbazienses', *Mon. Germ. Hist., Script.* xix, p. 718 (a mutilated note *ad annum* 1347); *Oelrichs*, 1356, no. 12, p. 91; 1360, no. 14, p. 93.

[3] *Riedel*, xiii, no. 64, p. 247; no. 32, p. 31 (1335–42).

[4] Gley, op. cit., p. 110.

[5] *Landbuch 1375*, p. 51: 'quondam fuit curia'.

[6] *Riedel*, Supplement, no. 27, p. 238.

[7] *Landbuch 1375*, pp. 46, 96, 121, 135–6.

[8] *Colit per se* or *sub aratro suo*: only five of these *curiae* had more than 8 *Hufen*; the majority were no larger than a peasant farm.

owner himself or by a steward on his behalf,[1] then it is not clear why forty-two cases should have been singled out in which this was said unequivocally, while in all others it was merely noted that there was a *curia* with so and so many free *Hufen*. It must be remembered, however, that the *Landbuch* was compiled for precisely one purpose: to establish how many *Hufen* existed in each village, what dues they gave and to whom, and how many free *Hufen* there were. Once this was established the clerks and officials who compiled the survey were not really interested whether the *Hufen* were farmed by the nobleman himself or not, so that they may easily have omitted to give further details. By 1375 the old system, according to which a knight was entitled to only 6 free *Hufen* in demesne as a compensation for his military obligations,[2] was defunct. There were many demesnes of a larger size, and the *Hufen* belonging to a *curia* were tax-free even if the owner did not farm them himself.[3] In Wilmersdorf, near Berlin, there were three *curiae*, of 3, 8, and 10 *Hufen* respectively, from which only one-eighth of a knight's service had to be rendered.[4] Such fractions of services occurred frequently, and there were many free *Hufen* from which no feudal services at all were due.[5] It thus seems quite likely that the majority of the free *Hufen* lying *ad curiam* were held in demesne, even if the noble owner did not reside in the village but at a court or in one of the princely castles. Probably only the poorer noblemen lived in the villages side by side with the peasants;[6] while the wealthier ones would often be absentee landlords and would prefer revenues to farming on their own.

That demesne farming was by no means preponderant is confirmed by our information about labour services. In 1345 the Old Mark nunnery of Diesdorf acquired 3 peasants who had to serve once a year and another peasant who had to serve, as it seems, 4 times a year.[7] The peasants of the new village of

---

[1] That the latter was often the case is assumed by J. Schultze, the editor of the latest edition of the *Landbuch,* 1940, p. xviii.

[2] See above, p. 25.

[3] *Landbuch 1375*, pp. 46, 121, 135–6, 156, 196.

[4] Ibid., p. 57.

[5] Many examples may be found in A. Ernst, *F.B.P.G.*, xxii, 1909, pp. 517–18.

[6] Such cases are occasionally mentioned in the *Landbuch*: pp. 191, 196, 204–5, 216, 220, 236, and thus seem to have been rather rare.

[7] *Riedel*, xvi, no. 52, p. 423: 'unum colonum . . . servitium eidem claustro temporibus annuis facientem . . .'.

the Knights Hospitallers near Berlin in 1360 had to render ploughing services of 3 days in the year to the Commander at Tempelhof, an obligation which was still the same in 1375.[1] Curiously enough, this is the only clear example of labour services mentioned in the whole *Landbuch*, and no more were enumerated in the other fourteenth-century records from Brandenburg: they seem to have been very rare at that time. In 1403 peasants of the Ucker Mark monastery of Himmelpfort had to serve the abbot 4 days in the year.[2] In the New Mark peasants of the von Uchtenhagen had to serve 3 days yearly in 1412.[3] In the Old Mark peasants of a village near Stendal in 1433 had to serve a burgher of that town 2 days in the year, but only when it was convenient and he required it.[4] Even these few services the peasants had apparently refused to render, for an arbitration had to establish their obligation. In the *terra* of Lebus ploughing services of 3 to 4 days in the year were customary in the fifteenth century, while such of 6 to 7 days were exceptional.[5] At the end of the fifteenth century ploughing services of 4 days yearly were still rendered in different parts of Brandenburg,[6] in one instance in addition to 2 days' service with horse and cart.[7] In 1471 the peasants of the monastery of Zinna, in the Barnim, only had to plough on 3 half-days for the abbot.[8] Thus the labour services were very limited, and mainly confined to ploughing: no more were required for the small demesnes of that time.

Not even these limited labour services were always used. Especially in the Old Mark, with its important towns, quit-rents were frequently paid by the peasants instead of the services. Up to 1370 the peasants of 2 villages of the nunnery of Diesdorf rendered services, but then they were commuted into a money due.[9] In 1375 5 other villages in the Old Mark and 6 in the Ucker Mark paid quit-rents.[10] Quit-rents were frequently

[1] *Riedel*, Supplement, no. 27, p. 239; *Landbuch 1375*, p. 54. Tempelhof to the present day bears the name of its founders, the Templars, whose heirs the Hospitallers had become.

[2] *Riedel*, xiii, no. 49, p. 45.   [3] Ibid. C.i, no. 52, p. 49.

[4] Ibid. v, no. 312, p. 201.   [5] Riedel, op. cit. ii, p. 234.

[6] *Riedel*, xx, no. 85, p. 77; no. 92, p. 86; xiii, nos. 113, 153, 188, pp. 388, 415, 441 (1471–98).

[7] Ibid. xiii, no. 131, p. 292 (1473).   [8] Grossmann, op. cit., p. 12.

[9] *Riedel*, xxii, nos. 177, 179, pp. 192–4.

[10] *Landbuch 1375*, pp. 135, 142–3, 155–6, 158, 226–7, 233–4, 236–8.

mentioned in the documents, sometimes as late as the sixteenth century.[1] Until that time the demand for labour services was not very great.

As labour services only played a subsidiary part in the management of the demesnes, their regular supply of labour had to come from different sources. There were free labourers and servants, perhaps peasants' children whose labour was not required at home, perhaps migratory labour. There were, above all, the cottagers, a numerous class of smallholders whose holdings were not sufficient for their maintenance, and who therefore had to seek work on peasant farms or demesnes. They lived either in separate villages,[2] or more commonly in ordinary villages. In that case, their holdings were either separated from the village *Hufen*,[3] or they consisted of some ordinary *Hufen* in the open fields, only that the individual cottager's holding was but a fraction of a *Hufe*.[4] The dues of a cottagers' *Hufe* were usually the same as those of a peasant *Hufe* in the same village.[5] Cottagers could even own free *Hufen*,[6] and could be elevated to the status of the peasants.[7] Both groups appeared together as witnesses in the village court and participated in sales and other village affairs.[8] The cottagers' legal position seems to have been the same as that of the peasants.

The cottagers worked as free agricultural labourers, not because of any servile obligation; their labour services were no heavier than those of the peasants. In a Havelland village the cottagers and peasants had the same obligation towards the knight who owned the jurisdiction.[9] The cottagers of the newly

[1] *Riedel*, v, nos. 353, 361, 387, 393–4, pp. 480–97; vi, nos. 435, 454, pp. 259–75; x, no. 256, p. 358; xii, no. 67, p. 113; no. 46, p. 184; xvi, nos. 626, 650–1, pp. 182, 276–8; xvii, no. 239, p. 207; nos. 142–4, pp. 315–18; xxi, no. 64, p. 515; xxii, nos. 177, 179, pp. 192–4; no. 13, p. 495; xxiii, no. 417, p. 404; xxv, no. 182, p. 148; no. 394, p. 471; Supplement, no. 32, p. 380: the majority of these are from the Old Mark.
[2] *Landbuch 1375*, pp. 90, 127: cottagers' villages of the monasteries of Lehnin and Chorin. The Teutonic Knights in particular founded many gardeners' villages.
[3] *Landbuch 1375*, pp. 158, 162.
[4] Ibid., pp. 138–40, 142, 144–5, 147, 150, 168; *Riedel*, v, no. 31, p. 36; xx, no. 92, p. 86.
[5] *Landbuch 1375*, pp. 138–40, 145; *Riedel*, v, no. 31, p. 36 (1247).
[6] *Riedel*, xvii, no. 19, p. 239 (1340).
[7] Ibid. i, no. 24, p. 46 (1470).
[8] Ibid. v, no. 81, p. 337; xiii, no. 85, p. 77 (1362–1409).
[9] Ibid. x, no. 23 a, p. 463 (1335).

founded village of the Knights Hospitallers near Berlin had to
serve 3 days yearly like the peasants.[1] In the *terra* of Lebus, about
1400, the cottagers had to serve 4 days in the year, exactly as
the peasants.[2] In 2 New Mark villages of the monastery of
Chorin peasants and cottagers alike had to serve 6 days yearly
during which the cottagers were to receive free food.[3] In other
instances their services were fixed at the low level of 2 or 4 days
in the year.[4] In one case only, and that from the late fifteenth
century, the cottagers of a Lebus village had to serve 6 days,
against the peasants' 4 days.[5] The *Landbuch* of 1375, however,
recorded one example of unlimited services: 8 cottagers of an
Old Mark village had to serve their noble master whenever he
demanded it.[6] Like similar examples from Pomerania,[7] these
may have been non-Germanized Slavs. Definitely Slavs were
the fishermen of Sceldorp who had to cut wood for the margrave, and those of Colbu, both also in the Old Mark, who had
to ferry the margrave and his suite across the Elbe whenever
requested to do so and to bring wood for the margrave's castle
across the river, their only reward being free food and drink.[8]
It is impossible to say whether these were heavy burdens; no
general conclusions can be drawn from such isolated examples
coming from surviving Slav pockets. Neither is it certain that
most cottagers were Slavs.

The general position of the Brandenburg peasants, whether
German or Slav, remained very favourable during the fourteenth and fifteenth centuries. Their dues and services could
not be altered, their legal position remained the same, and they
benefited from the general economic development. The Black
Death and the many other outbreaks of plague strengthened
the peasants' position, as the survivors became all the more
valuable to the landlords. There was a surplus of land, and if
they disliked the conditions in their village they could move
elsewhere. In that case their only obligation towards their land-

[1] *Riedel*, Supplement, no. 27, p. 239 (1360).

[2] Riedel, op. cit. ii, p. 261.

[3] *Riedel*, xiii, no. 131, p. 292 (1473).

[4] *Riedel*, v, no. 299, p. 454; xi, no. 215, pp. 429–30; xxii, no. 289, p. 264 (1439–85).

[5] *Riedel*, xx, no. 92, p. 86 (1485).

[6] *Landbuch 1375*, p. 206: 'viii cossati Alberto pro servitio quamdiu vult . . .'.

[7] See above, pp. 41–42.

[8] *Landbuch 1375*, pp. 249–50.

lord was to pay him the rent due and to plough and sow the fields of their farm. Then the peasant could sell it and leave with his goods and chattels.[1] If he could not find a buyer, he could leave nevertheless, even if the landlord refused to take over; then the peasant could announce this to the village mayor and the other peasants and depart freely. This was the legal opinion of the noble *advocatus* of the Ucker Mark, a district with a strong Slav population, and of the noblemen and burghers who were his assessors in 1383.[2] The transfer of land or rents from peasant holdings took place, according to the local custom, solemnly in the village court before the village community, the seller handing a twig to the village mayor and the latter to the buyer, symbolizing the transfer of rights, and without any participation of the landlord.[3] Six villages of the monastery of Lehnin kept a book in which such transfers were recorded, and the same applied to other monastic villages.[4] The ordinary peasant holding was a hereditary leasehold; but some peasants were freeholders; others bought 'property' and were enfeoffed with free *Hufen*,[5] a right usually reserved to village mayors and noblemen.

The village mayors, in the German as well as in the Slavonic villages, held several free *Hufen* in fee. These freeholds were especially attractive to noblemen who wanted to enlarge their holdings or to provide for members of their families. If the village mayor was willing to sell or if he died without leaving an heir, a new mayor could be appointed who might only receive part of his predecessor's holding, or a peasant could be entrusted with the office.[6] The *Landbuch* mentioned that in a Barnim village two noblemen had the mayor's office, and that in three other villages noblemen or their widows owned *Hufen*

[1] Glosses to *Sachsenspiegel*, lib. ii, art. 59, para. 1, and lib. iii, art. 79, para. 1: Augsburg, 1516, fols. 114, 189.

[2] Quoted by L. Korn, 'Geschichte der bäuerlichen Rechtsverhältnisse in der Mark Brandenburg', *Zeitschrift für Rechtsgeschichte*, xi, 1873, p. 5, n. 8; and W. von Brünneck, 'Die Aufhebung der Leibeigenschaft. . .', *Zeitschrift der Savigny-Stiftung für Rechtsgeschichte*, x, 1889, p. 41, n. 2.

[3] *Riedel*, vi, nos. 32, 54, 64, 68, pp. 363–83; viii, no. 402, p. 375; xvii, no. 77, p. 87; gloss of Johann von Buch to *Sachsenspiegel*, lib. i, art. 34, para. 1: Augsburg, 1516, fol. 34.

[4] *Riedel*, x, no. 230, p. 326; no. 242, p. 341 (1470–6).

[5] *Landbuch 1375*, p. 178; *Fidicin*, i, p. 36; *Riedel*, xxv, nos. 228, 300, 363, pp. 342–450 (1375–1494), mainly from the Old Mark.

[6] Grossmann, op. cit., p. 8. Cf. above, p. 32.

which had once belonged to the mayor.[1] In 1388 a burgess of Frankfurt acquired a *curia* and the right to appoint the mayor and the jurymen in that village.[2] Such 'appointed' mayors were mentioned elsewhere.[3] They were obviously more dependent on the landlord than the hereditary and 'enfeoffed' mayors of the other villages.

The jurisdiction of the village mayor usually covered claims, suits, and most misdemeanours, up to the value of half a shilling, and in certain cases up to three shillings.[4] Crimes involving the *poenam sanguinis* were judged by seven peasant jurymen in the margrave's high court in which his *advocatus* presided.[5] Even noblemen stood under this system of jurisdiction which embraced the whole country. In a Havelland village in 1335 the mayor could judge the noble squire and his sons if they committed an offence, while the squire had no jurisdiction in the village.[6] In Salzwedel also, after 1343, noblemen could be tried in the town court.[7] These may have been exceptional cases; but the commentator of the *Sachsenspiegel*, a Brandenburg nobleman, also wondered why in Brandenburg noblemen could be tried by commoners. According to some people's opinion—which he did not share—this was because the country was freer than others and the noblemen had only gradually migrated thither; yet he emphasized that the proper court for noblemen was that of the margrave, and that only if they sought justice elsewhere, then they had to accept that court's verdict.[8] Thus the greater freedom existing in the colonial area was clearly perceived in the fourteenth century.

Where the *advocatia* and the highest jurisdiction had passed into the hands of an ecclesiastical foundation or of a noble

---

[1] *Landbuch 1375*, pp. 78, 82, 86, 108.

[2] *Riedel*, xxiii, no. 175, p. 124.

[3] Ibid. xxii, no. 92, p. 57; vi, no. 89, p. 63; *von Raumer*, ii, no. 28, p. 136 (1351–1471).

[4] *Sachsenspiegel*, lib. iii, art. 64, para. 11: ed. Homeyer, 1861, pp. 361–2.

[5] *Landbuch 1375*, p. 32.

[6] *Riedel*, x, no. 23a, p. 463.

[7] See below, p. 92.

[8] Gloss of Johann von Buch to *Sachsenspiegel*, lib. ii, art. 12, para. 3: Augsburg, 1516, fol. 73: 'warumme is dit dat dy in der marcke ordel lyden van orem ungenoten. Ethlike spreken yd sy darumme dat de landt vryer sin unde dy guderhande lüde almestich in komen syn, desse van Svaven, yenne van me Rhyne. Mer dit seggen dy sick nicht vorstan . . .'. Yet it seems that these people were right and that von Buch was wrong: he was, after all, a partisan.

family, the peasants no longer stood under the jurisdiction of the margrave's high court and no longer had to attend the general assizes of the district, but the private assizes of the owner of the *advocatia*. This, however, did not imply a change for the worse. In the private assizes also the cases were judged by peasant jurymen, and the customs and procedure corresponded to those of the general assizes.[1] As late as 1497 the von Alvensleben who owned large estates in the Old Mark held their high court four times a year as it had been held of old; their *advocatus* presided, the most experienced village mayors and peasants acted as jurymen, and the peasants had to attend on payment of a fine.[2] The noblemen themselves took no part in the proceedings, but only received part of the revenue. Another well-known Old Mark family, the von der Schulenburg, as late as the sixteenth century also held their private assizes in which peasants acted as jurymen and which protected the peasants' rights.[3]

In Pomerania the peasants, whether Germans or Slavs, enjoyed the same favourable position. Peasants of the monastery of Eldena sold meadows to burghers of Greifswald, and the village mayor transferred them to the buyers, apparently without obtaining the abbot's consent.[4] Peasants gave their assent when their landlord sold land close to their village to peasants of other villages.[5] When two noble families quarrelled about their rights in a village, some of the older peasants decided as arbiters between them.[6] When land was sold by one landlord to another it was stipulated that the peasants were to enjoy the same rights and privileges as under the previous owner.[7] Similarly Prince Wizlav of Rügen in his will enjoined his heirs that his Slavs should have the same freedom in everything which they had enjoyed in his lifetime.[8]

The estates of Pomeranian noblemen were not particularly

---

[1] *Riedel*, xviii, no. 5, p. 372 (allegedly of 1300); x, nos. 230, 242, pp. 326–41; *Landbuch 1375*, p. 263 (1450–76).
[2] *Riedel*, xvii, no. 216, p. 190.
[3] Ibid. vi, nos. 436, 446, 486, pp. 260–303 (1518–72).
[4] *Pomm. U.B.* vi, nos. 3492, 3596, pp. 30, 107 (1321–2).
[5] Ibid. v, nos. 3355, 3385, pp. 500–22 (1320).
[6] *Oelrichs*, 1402, no. 9, p. 112.
[7] *Pomm. U.B.* iii, no. 1697, p. 218; iv, no. 2006, p. 26; vi, no. 3506, p. 40; no. 3872, p. 290 (1294–1325).
[8] Ibid. iv, no. 2057, p. 68 (1302).

large. On the island of Rügen in 1314 only six noble demesnes
were listed, varying in size from 1 to 17½ small Slav *Hufen*.[1]
Noble *curiae* on the mainland usually comprised 3 to 8 *Hufen*, and
in one exceptional case 15;[2] on the island of Rügen the estates
comprised between 1 and 44 small Slav *Hufen*.[1] The estates of
the Pomeranian nobility were matched by those of the church
and of the towns and their burghers, especially those of Stralsund and Stettin. Between 1270 and 1325 Stralsund and its
burghers acquired at least 21 villages and scattered holdings in
another 9; Stettin and its burghers at least 8 villages, scattered
holdings in another 12, 2 islands, and 3 Slavonic fishing villages.
Even smaller towns, such as Demmin and Anklam, during the
same period acquired 10 and 8 villages respectively and scattered
property.[3] Even at this early time the amount of land bought
by the towns and burghers was very considerable. Their investment in real estate led to a break-up of the large estates and the
jurisdictional and other rights of the landlords.[4] It also illustrated the growing wealth of the towns and of their patrician
families.

The growth of urban activity and enterprise, above all at
Stralsund, led to another movement of great importance. The
administration and jurisdiction in the towns were exercised by
the aldermen who were not elected but co-opted from the
wealthy merchant and patrician families which intermarried
with the landed nobility and were often themselves of noble
origin.[5] Against their rule the commons and the guilds revolted
frequently trying to replace it by a less aristocratic municipal
constitution. Influenced by a successful uprising against the
aldermen which broke out at Rostock in 1312,[6] similar conflicts
between aldermen and guilds occurred at Stralsund in the
following year. New statutes were drafted by an elected council
of eight whose rulings both sides undertook to accept; from that

[1] *Pomm. U.B.* v, no. 2918, pp. 191–5. In Rügen the 'hooked' Slav *Hufe* was
probably half the size of the German one.
[2] Ibid. iv, no. 2546, p. 375; v, no. 2858, p. 151; no. 2956, p. 223; vi, no. 3804,
p. 243; vii, no. 4597, p. 375; *Riedel*, vii, no. 5, p. 125; xxiv, no. 138, p. 83.
[3] The above figures are minimum figures calculated from the *Pomm. U.B.* and
the selling contracts which have been preserved.
[4] *Fabricius*, iv 2 (text), p. 79.
[5] Barthold, op. cit. iii, pp. 153, 296–7; Wehrmann, op. cit. i, pp. 160–1.
[6] *Fabricius*, iv 2 (text), pp. 69–72; O. Fock, *Rügensch-Pommersche Geschichten aus
sieben Jahrhunderten*, 1861–72, iii, pp. 11–14.

time all important decisions were taken by the aldermen together
with the wardens of the guilds and the burghers' community,
and no longer by the aldermen alone.[1] This settlement, however,
only lasted fifteen years. As the aldermen had been unsuccessful
in the conduct of military operations, a revolutionary group
demanded that the commons should elect the military leaders
and should share with the aldermen in the exercise of their
jurisdiction, and tried to impose their demands by force of arms.
The aldermen succeeded in crushing the revolt. Five bakers
were executed, others were exiled, and the guild wardens lost
their right of participating in the decisions of the council.[2] The
aristocratic government was restored, but at the end of the century a new attempt was made to overthrow it. Opposition grew
against the wealth of the ruling merchant families, the 'Junkers',
who 'went about in short garments reaching only to the thighs,
with long sleeves down to the feet and long peaked shoes'. They
were accused of co-operating with the robber barons outside
the gates; the mayor was asked to give an account of the urban
revenues during the past twenty-eight years. In 1391 the old
statutes were rescinded; a new popular mayor was appointed,
as was a council of twelve guild wardens who were to work side
by side with the aldermen and to exercise joint control over the
budget. The former mayor and his followers escaped from Stralsund, but were restored after only two years, thanks to the intervention of the Hanse and of the duke of Pomerania. The rival
mayor was executed and the new constitution was abolished.[3]
Another conspiracy against the patricians in the following year
led to further executions and the banishment of forty-eight
burghers.[4] Once more the aristocracy was firmly entrenched in
power.

The same was the case in the other Pomeranian towns. In
1323 the aldermen of Greifswald, Anklam, and Demmin imposed the death penalty upon any would-be conspirators or

[1] *Fabricius*, iv 2 (text), pp. 81–82, 89–91; Barthold, op. cit. iii, p. 305; Fock,
op. cit. iii, pp. 20–34.
[2] Fock, op. cit. iii, pp. 74–83, 239–44; Barthold, op. cit. iii, p. 306; Wehrmann,
op. cit. i, p. 161.
[3] *Stralsundische Chroniken*, ed. G. C. F. Mohnike and E. H. Zober, i, 1833, pp.
164–6; Fock, op. cit. iv, pp. 74–101, 229–37; Barthold, op. cit. iii, pp. 532–5;
Kantzow, *Pomerania*, ed. Gaebel, 1908, i, pp. 303–5.
[4] *Stralsundische Chroniken*, i, p. 167; Fock, op. cit. iv, pp. 102–4, 237–9; Barthold,
op. cit. iii, pp. 535–6, 543.

rioters.[1] Perhaps this threat was effective, for only in the second half of the fourteenth century did the guilds of Anklam successfully revolt against the aldermen. A new council was elected and the constitution was altered; but there also the old order was soon restored, as it seems through an intervention of the Hanse.[2] At Kolberg the internal conflicts went parallel with clashes with the nobility: noblemen tried to win influence over the town and its council; they dominated the cathedral chapter and the company which owned the salt pits on which Kolberg's trade depended.[3]

In Brandenburg internal strife occurred most frequently in the leading town, Stendal in the Old Mark. As early as 1285 the margraves were called upon to act as arbiters between the rich and the poor of Stendal; their decision reinforced the aldermen's authority against the guilds and the other inhabitants and reaffirmed the aldermen's right to appoint their own successors and to impose taxes upon rich and poor alike.[4] In 1345 the guilds were more successful: a committee was set up to work out a new constitution; it decided that henceforth the council was to include ten representatives of the guilds and two of the commons. New orders and statutes were to require the assent of the guild wardens and were to be communicated to the burghers' assembly; income and expenditure were to be accounted for every year.[5] The opposition was mainly directed against the privileged position of the rich clothiers' guild which dominated the urban administration. Some of its members were expelled from Stendal and only readmitted in 1350, on the condition that they recognized the constitutional changes and the equal position of their guild with the others.[6] After some years, however, the clothiers succeeded in regaining their predominant influence: after 1365 the majority of the aldermen again came from their ranks.[7] They were allied with the guilds of the merchants and the butchers; these three ruling guilds were opposed

[1] *Pomm. U.B.* vi, no. 3677, p. 165.

[2] Fock, op. cit. iv, pp. 26–32, 209–11; Wehrmann, op. cit. i, p. 162; *Stralsundische Chroniken*, i, p. 5.

[3] Barthold, op. cit. iii, pp. 296–7; G. Kratz, *Die Städte der Provinz Pommern*, 1865, p. 86.

[4] *Riedel*, xv, no. 42, p. 34.

[5] Ibid., nos. 167–8, pp. 123–5.

[6] Ibid., nos. 179–80, pp. 135–6.

[7] L. Götze, *Urkundliche Geschichte der Stadt Stendal*, 1873, pp. 174–5.

by the lower guilds of the tanners, shoemakers, bakers, linen-weavers, furriers, and clothmakers.[1]

At Salzwedel, the other important town of the Old Mark, the guilds and commons about the middle of the fourteenth century gained some influence over the administration.[2] In 1361 they attempted a rising against the aldermen but were crushed: the margrave intervened and restored the authority of the aldermen over the guilds.[3] In many other Brandenburg towns similar conflicts occurred between the aldermen on the one hand and the guilds and commons on the other, but the latter were seldom successful. At Neu-Ruppin in 1315 they were ordered by the counts of Lindow to obey the aldermen.[4] At Pritzwalk, in the Priegnitz, the commons in 1335 succeeded in deposing the council and electing a new one, whereupon the margrave granted the town the privilege that the aldermen should be elected by the burghers, according to the custom of Seehausen and other towns.[5] In the Ucker Mark towns of Prenzlau, Pasewalk, Angermünde, and Templin the aldermen and the guilds and commons took opposite sides in the struggle over the claims of the 'false' Margrave Woldemar.[6] At Berlin lengthy conflicts between the aldermen and the commons occurred in the second half of the fourteenth century, but the former maintained their rule.[7] A new conspiracy against them, in 1412, was equally unsuccessful.[8]

These movements are evidence of vigorous urban life and strong social conflicts. Only in the leading towns, Stralsund and Stendal, were the guilds strong enough to overthrow the rule of the patricians, and even there their success was ephemeral. The Hanseatic League in particular saw to it that the aristocratic form of town government was maintained in all the towns which were its members. As trade was the principal activity of the eastern towns, and as they depended upon their connexions with the Hanse, the guilds were comparatively weak and unable to maintain themselves in power for more than a few years. Yet they presented a challenge to the ruling aristocracies which these could not ignore, as little as the nobility could ignore the

---

[1] *Riedel*, xv, no. 235, p. 182 (1387).   [2] Ibid. xiv, nos. 138–9, pp. 98–99.
[3] Ibid., nos. 175–7, pp. 124–6.   [4] Ibid. iv, no. 4, p. 285.
[5] Ibid. iii, no. 48, p. 367.   [6] Ibid., Supplement, no. 28, p. 26.
[7] *Fidicin*, i, pp. 176–80; iv, no. 48, p. 51.
[8] *Riedel*, Supplement, no. 63, p. 269; *Fidicin*, i, p. 233.

peasants. In town and country alike the lower classes were vigorous and strong, eager to rise and to ameliorate their position.

By the end of the fourteenth century the colonization area was still behind western and southern Germany in its general development. Most towns were small and poor, and the population in general was much thinner than in the west. Yet very much had been accomplished within a short time: towns and villages had sprung up over wide areas where they had hardly existed before the colonization began, vigorous forms of self-government had been introduced, and the general progress made was astonishing. The manorial system proper with its restrictions of freedom and its private jurisdictions had not been transferred to the east, nor had serfdom. The peasants' position was far better than it was in the west, and this included the native population. Class distinctions in the east were less sharp, noblemen moved into the towns and became burghers, while burghers acquired estates and village mayors held fiefs. The whole structure of society, as might be expected of a colonial area, was much freer and looser than it was in western Europe. It only seemed a question of time until the east would no longer be backward but would belong to the most developed parts of Europe. Indeed, this already applied to the Hanseatic towns along the coast of the Baltic, especially to the Wendish towns and to Danzig. Western institutions and customs had spread far into eastern Europe.

THE RISE OF THE JUNKERS

VII

The Weakness of the Territorial Princes

THE fourteenth century was the period of the greatest wealth and the greatest political power of the towns of Pomerania and of Brandenburg. Frequently they succeeded in imposing their will upon their rulers and the country, and even upon foreign princes. Their power was a match for that of the nobility, and the rulers could only try to play off one Estate against the other. When the duchy of Pomerania was to be divided between hostile brothers in 1295, the two Estates carried through the partition; they used this opportunity to have all their rights and privileges confirmed and to be assured the right of resistance in case the princes broke the treaty or wronged them in any other way.[1] About 1320 the Estates of Pomerania, and before long those of Rügen also, gained the important concession that offices and important appointments could only be filled with their approval: those appointed were to be natives of the country.[2]

In 1311 the king of Denmark and many north-German princes concluded an alliance against the towns. The relationship between Prince Wizlav of Rügen and his principal town, Stralsund, worsened in consequence, and the prince complained loudly about the burghers' pride. When war broke out in 1316 the burghers victoriously withstood siege and blockade and routed in a famous battle a hostile army, taking its leader and many knights prisoners.[3] After the dying out of the Rugian

---

[1] *Pomm. U.B.* iii, no. 1729, pp. 243–5; Barthold, op. cit. iii, pp. 51–59.

[2] M. Spahn, *Verfassungs- und Wirtschaftsgeschichte des Herzogtums Pommern*, 1896, p. 7.

[3] *Fabricius*, iv, nos. 620 *a–b*, 669, 702–3, 719, 732; *Pomm. U.B.* v, nos. 2908, 2989–90, 3021, 3065; Kantzow, op. cit. i, pp. 247–50; Barthold, op. cit. iii, pp. 108–9, 119–25, 128–30, 133–52; Fock, op. cit. iii, pp. 7–15, 37, 42–58.

princely family a new war, from 1326–8, brought more successes to the towns, especially Stralsund and Greifswald. They took the side of the dukes of Pomerania against those of Mecklenburg who were supported by most of the Pomeranian nobility. At the end of the war the Estates were granted far-reaching privileges: the guardianship over minor dukes, the decision whether new ducal castles should be built or pulled down, the right to choose a new master if ever the duke broke his promises or wronged his subjects.[1] Stralsund and Greifswald took a leading part in the affairs of the Hanse and in its wars against Denmark, which in 1370 ended in complete victory for the League and its establishment as the arbiter of Danish affairs and the holder of the fortresses in Scania. Almost half the military force for the war was furnished by the Pomeranian towns, above all by Stralsund.[2]

Owing to the weakness of the government the towns themselves had to secure the peace and to protect their trade. Repeatedly Stralsund, Greifswald, Anklam, and Demmin concluded alliances for the maintenance of peace and order.[3] From 1321 onwards Greifswald could apprehend and try any criminal and any protector or abettor of a criminal in the whole district between the Peene and Swine rivers.[4] In 1325 Stralsund was granted the right to pursue, arrest, and try criminals within the whole principality of Rügen.[5] Against the robber barons the towns took the law into their own hands. In 1322 the towns of Anklam, Demmin, Greifswald, and Treptow conquered and destroyed the robber castle of Bugewitz; they were then granted by the duke the right to break other castles whether built by natives or by foreigners.[6] In 1331 Greifswald destroyed the castle of Eichberg; its owner had to promise never to rebuild it. Stralsund and Greifswald together broke the castles of Gützkow, Kaiseritz, Usedom, Nustrow, and Düvelsdorf, the last two belonging to the von Behr, one of the leading noble families. The

[1] Barthold, op. cit. iii, pp. 203–22; Fock, op. cit. iii, pp. 68–72; Wehrmann, op. cit. i, pp. 136–7.

[2] Barthold, op. cit. iii, pp. 431–40, 456–66; Fock, op. cit. iii, pp. 137–219; Wehrmann, op. cit. i, pp. 145–50.

[3] Barthold, op. cit. iii, pp. 359, 403, 534, 559, 605; Wehrmann, op. cit. i, p. 175.

[4] *Pomm. U.B.* vi, no. 3496, p. 34.

[5] Ibid., no. 3908, p. 316.

[6] Ibid., nos. 3595, 3605, pp. 107–14.

town of Anklam victoriously fought against the von Schwerin and other robber barons.[1]

The towns of Pomerania thus became the leading group in the country. In the assemblies of the Estates they clearly played a more important part than the nobility.[2] The growing number of robber barons indicates that the nobility was not gaining strength: it was unable to retaliate against the towns with their well-built fortifications and well-trained burghers, and had to suffer punishment at their hands. On the other hand, the uneven development of the towns in western and in eastern Pomerania remained very marked. To the east of the Oder only Kolberg was a town of importance and engaged in overseas trade. Kolberg and Stargard were the only east-Pomeranian towns which contributed contingents to the Hanseatic armaments,[3] although in the late fourteenth century Rügenwalde and Stolp, still farther east, were also direct members of the League.

Surprisingly enough, in land-locked Brandenburg, whose urban development lagged behind that of Pomerania, as many as 14 towns were direct members of the Hanse: 7 in the Old Mark, 4 in the Priegnitz, and 3 in the Middle Mark;[4] but again there were none to the east of the Oder, in the New Mark. The Brandenburg towns, however, played a much less important part in the councils of the League and were unable to participate in any naval expeditions or armaments. But in Brandenburg they exercised great power which was increased by their mutual alliances. Already under the Ascanian margraves they concluded 'unions' to stand by each other and to defend themselves jointly against violence and injustice if any of them were attacked by any potentates,[5] clearly pointing to their rulers as well as to foreign enemies.

The greatest period of the Brandenburg towns came under

[1] A. G. von Schwarz, *Diplomatische Geschichte der Pommersch-Rügischen Städte Schwedischer Hoheit*, 1755, pp. 831–2; Barthold, op. cit. iii, pp. 222, 493–4, 523, 529, 590; iv 1, p. 55; Fock, op. cit. iv, pp. 109, 142–4.

[2] Spahn, op. cit., p. 7; Wehrmann, op. cit. i, p. 152.

[3] In 1364 Kolberg one-quarter and Stargard one-eighth of Stralsund's quota, Kolberg one-half and Stargard one-quarter of those of Greifswald and Stettin, this giving an indication of their relative strength: *H.R. 1256–1430*, i, no. 310, p. 263.

[4] W. Stein, 'Die Hansestädte', *Hansische Geschichtsblätter*, xxi, 1915, pp. 119–24, 135–7.

[5] *Riedel*, ix, nos. 10, 14, pp. 7, 10; xiv, nos. 63–64, 66, pp. 50–52: alliances of 1308 and 1309, only the latter containing the reference to *potentes aliquos*.

the weak foreign rulers who succeeded after the death of the last Ascanian margrave, Woldemar, in 1319. The internal troubles and disputed successions of the time provided many opportunities to wring new concessions from weak margraves whose main interests were in southern Germany. Frequently the towns renewed their 'unions' to assist each other if any of them were attacked: the towns of the New Mark in 1320, those of the Middle Mark, the Old Mark, and Lower Lusatia in 1323, those of the Old Mark in 1334, 1344, 1353, 1369, and 1393, those of the Ucker Mark in 1348, and those of the Middle Mark in 1393 and 1399.[1] Five years after Margrave Woldemar's death the new margrave, Lewis of Wittelsbach, had to recognize the validity of these 'unions'; he also undertook to break, together with the towns, all the castles built after Woldemar's death, and warned the landlords not to exploit their judicial rights and their claims to labour services.[2] Obviously the nobility had used the uncertainties of the political situation to erect new castles and to demand new services, and the towns were resisting these encroachments. The town of Prenzlau was granted the right of breaking all castles erected within a radius of three miles around the town.[3]

The power of the Estates developed parallel with the weakness of the rulers. In 1338 Margrave Lewis gave a guarantee to ask them for financial aid only if he were taken prisoner or lost a major battle, or if the country was invaded with such force that he was unable to resist.[4] Five years later he promised the towns of Salzwedel and Stendal anew that all castles built in the Old Mark since 1319 would be destroyed and that no new ones would be built; in future he would appoint his highest officials, the *advocati*, according to the advice of the towns and the nobility; if a nobleman committed a crime in Salzwedel he was to be tried in the town court.[5] In 1345 the nobility and the towns

---

[1] *Riedel*, xix, no. 21, p. 184; iii, no. 38, p. 361; xv, no. 103, p. 76; xvi, no. 10, p. 8; xiv, no. 124, p. 88; vi, no. 138, p. 100; no. 17, p. 409; xvii, no. 72, p. 501; xxv, no. 146, p. 278; xxi, no. 96, p. 161; xi, no. 95, p. 66; xxiv, no. 96, p. 393. These are all those printed in *Riedel*.

[2] Ibid. xv, nos. 104–5, pp. 77–78; xiv, no. 87, p. 65; xx, no. 34, p. 203; *Fidicin*, ii, no. 22, p. 28 (1324–8).

[3] *Riedel*, xxi, no. 61, p. 134 (1324).   [4] Ibid., C i, no. 18, p. 16.

[5] Ibid. xiv, nos. 116, 118, pp. 83–85; xv, no. 157, p. 118 (1343–4). The last clause is missing in the privilege for Stendal.

combined to resist a new tax demanded by the margrave which they considered unbearable; if anyone should suffer for this action they would stand by each other and fight together.[1] The towns especially were indignant about the policy of the Bavarian margraves, the taxes they extracted from Brandenburg, the rapacious south-German 'guests' who came with them, and the sale of whole districts to foreign rulers.[2]

Therefore nearly all the towns in 1348 took the side of the 'false' Margrave Woldemar against the Bavarian margraves when he appeared in Brandenburg and claimed that he was the last Ascanian margrave returned from a pilgrimage to the Holy Land after an absence of twenty-nine years. The towns remembered the good government and internal peace which had obtained under the Ascanians; many noblemen, on the other hand, remained loyal to the Wittelsbachs. Even small towns used the opportunity of the ensuing war and civil war to destroy noble castles and fortified houses,[3] while noblemen occupied and plundered monastic estates.[4] Through the grant of far-reaching privileges the 'false' Woldemar sought to secure the towns' loyalty: castles and watch-towers were only to be built with their consent; those erected since 1319 were to be destroyed; the towns could choose another ruler if he infringed any of their privileges or wronged them in any way; his servants were to be tried in the town courts for any crimes committed there.[5]

These privileges naturally were not binding on the Bavarian margraves. Yet when they eventually succeeded in reconquering the Mark, they had to fulfil many of the towns' demands. They had to promise not to construct any castles against the towns, not to introduce any military forces into them, and to break all castles built during the war.[6] The Estates finally achieved a decisive point: the 'guests' were to leave Branden-

---

[1] Ibid. iv, no. 23, p. 54.

[2] Ibid. xxiii, no. 65, pp. 45–46; 'Chronik des Franciscaner Lesemeisters Detmar', *Die lübeckischen Chroniken in niederdeutscher Sprache*, ed. F. H. Grautoff, i, 1829, p. 268.

[3] Thus Königsberg and Soldin in the New Mark: *Riedel*, xix, no. 71, p. 215; xviii, no. 25, p. 458.   [4] Ibid. xiii, no. 83, p. 258, referring to Chorin.

[5] Ibid. iii, no. 71, p. 378; ix, no. 68, p. 43; xi, no. 54, p. 37; xvi, no. 17, p. 13; no. 27, p. 328; xxi, no. 100, p. 164; Supplement, no. 19, p. 233.

[6] Ibid. vii, no. 16, p. 416; ix, no. 77, p. 49; no. 87, p. 55; xi, no. 55, p. 38; xv, no. 185, p. 140; xviii, no. 25, p. 458; xix, no. 71, p. 215; B ii, no. 951, p. 329 (1349–65).

burg and were only to be readmitted with the Estates' consent; all fortresses were to be entrusted to native noblemen, and only natives were to be given office, while the Estates could veto all appointments.[1] The town of Stendal was assured that in the Old Mark only natives of that district were to hold office and only if approved by the Old Mark towns.[2] For the New Mark a council of four noblemen and four aldermen was appointed which the margrave undertook to consult in all matters concerning the New Mark.[3] The Estates' power was firmly established.

During the following decades the ruling houses changed, many wars were fought over the possession of Brandenburg, the Pomeranians invaded the country frequently. The rulers had more important interests elsewhere so that their authority sank further and further. The different districts and towns of the Mark were almost independent, and some were pawned to foreign rulers. The towns undoubtedly suffered from the many wars and feuds and the general insecurity which they were unable to check.[4] Some of them were granted the right to apprehend robbers, murderers, and other criminals and to try them themselves: thus Frankfurt for the whole *terra* of Lebus as early as 1318.[5] Later other towns were permitted to pursue, arrest, and try those who had robbed their burghers, but native noblemen had to be handed over to the margrave;[6] other towns were at least allowed to try robbers and their helpers together with the margrave's *advocatus*.[7] In the 1370's this was no longer stipulated, so that the towns could try them on their own.[8] These privileges and those from Pomerania mentioned above[9] illustrated once more the weakness of the rulers and their inability to maintain law and order.

Parallel with the decline of princely authority went an almost

---

[1] *Riedel*, B ii, no. 891, p. 258; xi, no. 55, p. 38; vii, no. 16, p. 416; xiv, nos. 138–9, pp. 98–99; xviii, no. 25, p. 458; xix, no. 71, p. 215; B ii, no. 951, p. 329.

[2] Ibid. xv, nos. 185, 201, pp. 141–54 (1351–60).

[3] Ibid. xviii, no. 63, p. 135 (1354).

[4] See ibid. x, pp. 445–6: opinion of the abbot of Lehnin, early fifteenth century.

[5] Ibid. xxiii, no. 20, p. 16; no. 169, p. 117 (renewal of 1378).

[6] Ibid. xv, no. 164, p. 122: privilege for Stendal, 1345.

[7] Ibid. vi, no. 13, p. 354; xxi, no. 366, p. 409: privileges for Seehausen and the towns of the Ucker Mark, of 1340–8.

[8] Ibid. xi, no. 87, p. 60; C i, no. 46, p. 43: privileges for Spandau and the towns of the New Mark, of 1371–7. Similarly ibid. i, no. 105, p. 188; xix, no. 223, p. 321; xxi, no. 268, p. 313, from the fifteenth century.   [9] See above, p. 90.

complete sale of their rights and estates. As a rule the lands and prerogatives were not sold outright but merely pawned;[1] but as the princes' impecuniousness persisted through centuries, they were hardly ever able to redeem their possessions. The sales, however, only aggravated the problem, for the rulers were deprived of the revenues from the pawned lands, taxes, tolls, and jurisdictions. According to the *Landbuch* of 1375, the urban tax, the *Urbede*, was pawned in most towns, while the revenues from the highest jurisdiction still went to the margrave from about half their number.[2] Often the towns themselves had bought these rights, or a burgher had done so. The *Bede* and the *servitium curruum* had nearly everywhere passed into private hands, as had the margrave's lands; thus the landlords acquired the right to the peasants' services.[3] In the New Mark the von Wedel held twelve *munitiones*, many of which had once belonged to the margrave.[4] In the district of Salzwedel even the high court, the *advocatia*, was pawned to two noblemen; but in 1377 the margrave at least redeemed half of it.[5] This is almost the only example of a redemption mentioned; with the loss of the *advocatia* the last important right of the ruler would have passed into private hands.

As the margraves had no other means to raise money, and as the prices were rising and thus their need for money,[6] the sales of lands and rights continued in the fifteenth century. In 1400 King Sigismund sold to the Teutonic Knights the town and district of Dramburg, in the north of the New Mark.[7] This was followed, in 1402, by the pawning of the New Mark itself; in 1429 it was sold to the Order as a property and not redeemed until 1454.[8] The Teutonic Knights did not experience the difficulties besetting the lay rulers and possessed large funds which they used to expand their dominions westwards. In Branden-

---

[1] The legal term used was 'sale with the right of redemption'. It was a way of circumventing the prohibition of usury.

[2] *Landbuch 1375*, pp. 28–32. The margrave received two-thirds of the revenues of the *judicium supremum* as the liegelord of the urban *praefectus*: ibid., p. 32.

[3] In the Ucker Mark as early as 1320 the *servitium curruum* was completely identified with labour services: *Riedel*, xiii, no. 55, p. 240.

[4] *Landbuch 1375*, p. 37.   [5] Ibid., pp. 27, 30.

[6] J. Schultze, *Das Landbuch der Mark Brandenburg von 1375*, 1940, p. xvi.

[7] *Riedel*, xviii, no. 44, p. 243.

[8] Ibid. xxiv, nos. 170, 177, pp. 109–15; B iii, nos. 1268–70, pp. 153–7; B iv, nos. 1527–9, 1745–8, pp. 103–9, 483–6.

burg many castles and towns, with their appurtenant villages, were pawned by the last margraves of the house of Luxemburg. Nor was there any change when the Mark fell into the hands of the Hohenzollerns. It is true that Frederick, the first Hohenzollern margrave, when he arrived in the Mark in 1412, had comparatively large means at his disposal. With these he redeemed some castles and towns of military importance; he also reduced some castles of robber barons who refused to acknowledge him. His means, however, were insufficient to retain the redeemed possessions, and most of them were pawned anew after a few years. The members of the noble Fronde also had their castles restored to them after some years, or they were given other places instead when they made their peace with the new margrave.[1]

Throughout the fifteenth and early sixteenth centuries the margraves' castles, domains, and towns, with their villages, and all marketable revenues and prerogatives were pawned again and again, usually to native noblemen.[2] Often, after a whole series of such pawnings, the possessions were finally sold and given away as a fief.[3] Noble families, such as the von Alvensleben, von Bredow, von Hake, von Krummensee, von Pfuhl, von Quast, von Rohr, von Saldern, von der Schulenburg, von Sparre, von Uchtenhagen, von Waldow, in this way acquired large new estates. Especially the von Arnim gained extensive property.[4] The wealth of these families must have been much greater than it had been in the fourteenth century; while there are only a few examples of burghers or ecclesiastics buying such lands. Clearly a change was taking place in the relative strength of these groups; but the princes' financial weakness continued.

The sale of the rulers' properties and rights had another effect

---

[1] Reconciliation of Margrave Frederick with Werner von Holzendorf and with Hans von Quitzow in 1420–1: *Riedel*, xii, no. 28, p. 430; *von Raumer*, i, no. 31, p. 71.

[2] A list of these would fill many pages.

[3] *Riedel*, xxiv, no. 126, p. 418; no. 258, p. 203; iii, no. 262, p. 505; vi, no. 177, p. 125; iii, no. 31, p. 105; xiii, no. 141, p. 406; ii, no. 14, p. 111; xviii, no. 98, p. 348; no. 78, p. 424; xiii, no. 25, p. 144; no. 92, p. 375; Berghaus, op. cit. ii, pp. 295, 323–4, 368; iii, pp. 178–9, 358; *von Raumer*, i, nos. 70–71, 73, pp. 106–8: sales of the towns and castles of Alt-Landsberg, Bernstein, Bötzow, Boitzenburg, Dramburg, Freienstein, Fretzdorf, Gardelegen, Hohennauen, Liebenwalde, Löcknitz, Plaue, Schivelbein, Sonnenburg, Tankow, Vierraden, Zantoch, Zehdenick, and Zichow, between 1427 and 1560.

[4] See their *Lehnbriefe* of 1441, 1472, 1486, and 1498: *Riedel*, xii, nos. 8, 10, pp. 212–14; xiii, nos. 153, 188, pp. 414–40.

of far-reaching importance. The margraves' highest jurisdiction, exercised through their *advocati* in the general assizes, dwindled and almost disappeared. At the time of the colonization the *advocatia* and the jurisdiction in life and limb was only granted to some of the ecclesiastical foundations to the east of the Elbe, the bishoprics, the monasteries of Leitzkau and Jerichow, founded before the conquest, and the great Cistercian houses of Lehnin, Chorin, and Himmelpfort.[1] Among laymen, only the members of the high nobility, the von Arnstein, von Plotho, and the lords of Friesack, in the thirteenth century had their own *advocati* who exercised the jurisdiction in life and limb.[2] Already in the fourteenth century, however, one-third of the *advocatiae* to the west of the Oder disappeared in the course of the diminution of the margraves' lands and rights.[3] To the east of that river the great families of the von Wedel and von Güntersberg exercised the *advocatia* as a hereditary right: in 1354 Hasso von Wedel was appointed *advocatus et capitaneus* of all the districts and towns across the Oder, and later the same office was held by other members of his family.[4] Farther east, between the Netze and Drage rivers, the von Güntersberg held the *advocatia* since the days of 'the old margraves', and this right was confirmed to them in 1378 and later.[5] In these eastern districts little was left of the margrave's rights by the end of the fourteenth century; but in the western parts the *Landbuch* of 1375 still considered the jurisdiction in life and limb as in principle belonging to the margrave.[6]

In the fifteenth century the *advocatia* was frequently sold or pawned together with the castle which was the centre of a district: thus with the castles of Arneburg, Gardelegen, and Salzwedel, in the Old Mark, of Lenzen, in the Priegnitz, of Boitzenburg and Strasburg, in the Ucker Mark.[7] Sometimes the

---

[1] *Riedel*, viii, no. 10, p. 100; no. 38, p. 125; ii, nos. 4, 7, pp. 439–43; x, no. 12, p. 80; iii, no. 3, p. 81; x, nos. 5, 15, pp. 408–10; xiii, no. 5, p. 206; nos. 3, 5, pp. 11–13.

[2] Ibid. x, no. 12, p. 80; iii, no. 7, p. 341; vii, no. 1, p. 47 (1211–56).

[3] Eight out of twenty-four *advocatiae* into which Brandenburg was divided: S. Isaacsohn, *Geschichte des preussischen Beamtenthums*, i, 1874, pp. 43–46.

[4] *Riedel*, xviii, no. 63, p. 135; von Raumer, in *Landbuch 1337*, p. 51.

[5] *Riedel*, xxiv, nos. 146, 162, 168, pp. 87–108.

[6] *Landbuch 1375*, p. 32.

[7] *Von Raumer*, ii, no. 15, p. 15; *Riedel*, vi, no. 265, p. 198; nos. 155–6, 167, 171, 177, pp. 111–26; no. 409, p. 246; xiv, nos. 319, 343, pp. 250–69; *von Raumer*, i, no. 31, p. 71; *Riedel*, iii, nos. 201, 242, pp. 461–94; xiii, nos. 50, 58, 63, 91, 156, pp. 342–419; vii, nos. 71–72, pp. 165–7 (1414–86).

advocatia was pawned separately,[1] but that seems to have been an exception. Sometimes it was expressly announced that the nobleman to whom a castle was pawned was to be the *advocatus* of the surrounding district.[2] In general it can safely be assumed that the nobleman who held the castle which was the centre of the district was either himself the *advocatus* who held the high court, or that he could appoint an *advocatus* for this purpose. From the fourteenth century onwards many noble families exercised the jurisdiction in life and limb on their estates:[3] it had passed into their hands with the dissolution of the old judicial system. Thus the margrave's subjects lost all connexions with their ruler whose prerogatives passed into the hands of their landlords. Indeed, after the sale of all the margraves' lands and rights there was no point in keeping alive the old judicial system: the functions of public administration were taken over by private lords, whether lay or ecclesiastical, wherever the ruler ceased to have any property.

Exactly the same happened in Pomerania. To acquire funds and to pay off their debts, the princes of Pomerania and of Rügen were compelled to sell their lands and prerogatives and were only rarely able to redeem them. The land-tax, the *Bede*, which could easily be realized on a cash basis, was sold first, often together with the land from which it was levied. Many noble families bought the *Bede* from their estates.[4] Then the *servitium curruum* was also sold, usually together with the *Bede*,[5] so that the landlords were entitled to the peasants' services. As in Brandenburg, the peasants had to attend the general assizes of the district where the prince's *advocatus* exercised the highest jurisdiction. Thus in 1320 there was still an *advocatus* of the prince of Rügen in the *terra* of Streye, although it had been acquired by Count Jaczo of Gützkow, a member of the high nobility, in the late thirteenth century, and although the counts

---

[1] *Riedel*, xiii, no. 13, p. 186; v, no. 155, p. 375; *von Raumer*, i, nos. 101–2, pp. 130–1 (1409–57).

[2] *Von Raumer*, i, no. 60, p. 202 (1447).

[3] *Riedel*, i, no. 39, p. 328; vi, no. 56, p. 37; x, no. 246, p. 347; xvi, no. 94, p. 450; xviii, no. 42, p. 242; xxii, no. 56, p. 33; no. 219, p. 219 (1329–1498).

[4] *Pomm. U.B.* ii, nos. 1019, 1032; iv, nos. 2372–3, 2448; v, nos. 3020, 3296, 3309, 3418, 3425 (1275–1320).

[5] Ibid. v, nos. 3007, 3163; vi, nos. 3527, 3552, 3671–2; vii, nos. 4194, 4206 (1316–26).

of Gützkow of old had their own *advocatia*.[1] In 1321 not even the
town of Stralsund had the right to hold itself the high court in
its ten villages, but the prince's *advocatus* was to sit in court
together with the aldermen.[2] When selling property the princes
at times expressly reserved the highest jurisdiction to themselves.[3]

The most important Pomeranian monasteries and nunneries,
on the other hand, as early as the thirteenth century, were
exempted from the princely *advocatia* and were granted the exercise of the highest jurisdiction through their own *advocati*.[4] They
thus received complete immunity from the public jurisdiction
much earlier than most religious houses in Brandenburg. In the
later thirteenth century some noblemen also possessed the highest
jurisdiction on their estates,[5] although they were neither members of princely families nor of the high nobility. The towns of
Greifswald and Demmin equally were granted the jurisdiction
in life and limb on their lands.[6] In the early fourteenth century
the highest jurisdiction was often granted to noblemen,[7] as
well as to towns and burghers.[8] Up to 1330 these were exceptions rather than the rule; but the exemptions of many
monasteries, and the later ones of noblemen and towns from
the *advocatia* and the princely jurisdiction paved the way
for an early and complete disintegration of the public
administration.

It was only in the fifteenth century, however, that the rulers'
jurisdiction finally disappeared. In 1409 the town of Stargard
was granted the entire jurisdiction and the *advocatia*.[9] The town
of Stettin did not buy the *advocatia* and the jurisdiction in life
and limb until 1482, even Stralsund not until 1488.[10] The same

---

[1] *Cod. Pom. Dipl.*, no. 493, p. 968; *Pomm. U.B.* iii, no. 1843, p. 334; v, no. 3388,
p. 525; vi, no. 3571, p. 92.   [2] *Pomm. U.B.* vi, no. 3497, p. 35.

[3] Ibid. iv, nos. 2137, 2299–2301; v, nos. 2710, 3306 (1304–19).

[4] Dargun in 1229, Neuenkamp in 1231, Kolbatz in 1240, Eldena in 1248,
Buckow in 1252, Belbuk in 1269, Stolp in 1289, Clatzow in 1245, Bergen in 1296:
Cod. Pom. Dipl., nos. 179, 188, 286, 346, 400, 473, pp. 412–943; *Pomm. U.B.* ii, no.
882, p. 210; iii, nos. 1517, 1765, pp. 84, 272.

[5] *Pomm. U.B.* ii, no. 1095; iii, nos. 1520, 1613, 1634, 1643 (1278–93).

[6] Ibid. iii, nos. 1615, 1783, pp. 154, 290 (1292–6).

[7] Ibid. iv, nos. 2123, 2367, 2545; v, nos. 2783, 2878, 2936, 2956, 3313, 3364,
3369, 3425; vi, no. 3819; vii, no. 4524 (1303–29).

[8] Ibid. iv, nos. 1991, 2088, 2601; v, nos. 2894, 3005–6, 3313, 3356; vi, nos. 3626,
3673, 3712, 3819; vii, nos. 4194, 4337, 4534, 4537 (1301–29).

[9] *Schoettgen-Kreysig*, iii, no. 124, p. 80.   [10] *Kratz*, i, nos. 152, 201, pp. 79, 102.

applied to the estates of noblemen: in 1454 the duke of Pomerania sold his castle of Torgelow with the *advocatia* belonging to it;[1] in 1480 the town of Penkun, and in 1483 the castle and town of Zanow, in both cases with the jurisdiction in life and limb which hitherto had been a ducal right.[2] Not before 1485 did the von Kleist acquire the jurisdiction and the *advocatia* on their estates.[3] In 1452 Duke Wartislav was forced to concede to the Estates that, according to an 'old and laudable custom', whoever held the *Bede* and the minting dues between Stralsund and Greifswald was *eo ipso* entitled to exercise the highest jurisdiction:[4] this clearly shows the interdependence between the various prerogatives which had been sold.

The sale of the rulers' lands and prerogatives and the complete disintegration of public jurisdiction and administration in Brandenburg and in Pomerania formed a striking contrast to the conditions prevailing in Prussia. There the power and wealth of the Teutonic Order in the fourteenth century prevented similar happenings: only with the Order's decline in the fifteenth century did Prussia begin to approximate to its western neighbours. Outside Prussia, the weakness of the rulers and of public authority in general disproves the opinion that the Germans built strong frontier marches against the Slavs: if this had been true at the time of the conquest, it certainly was no longer true in the fourteenth and fifteenth centuries. If there was border warfare, it was much more frequent between Pomeranians and Brandenburgers than against the Slavs. The disintegration of public authority was the precondition of the changes of the fifteenth and sixteenth centuries which were to reverse completely the interrelationship between the social classes; but it did not in itself create these new developments.

[1] *Lisch*, iv, no. 507, p. 60.

[2] *Riedel*, xiii, no. 127, p. 398; *Kratz*, i, no. 160, p. 82.

[3] *Kratz*, i, nos. 169, 192, pp. 86, 98.

[4] Barthold, op. cit. iv 1, p. 171, n. 2; Spahn, op. cit., pp. 7-8; F. von Bilow, *Geschichtliche Entwicklung der Abgabenverhältnisse in Pommern und Rügen*, 1843, p. 110.

VIII

The Agrarian Crisis

URING the period of the colonization thousands of villages were founded in the territories to the east of the Elbe; woods, marshes, and wilderness made room for human habitations; in Prussia this process was still continuing in the late fourteenth and early fifteenth centuries. Simultaneously many towns developed which attracted the population of the countryside. Thus the population was growing, and immigration only accounted for part of this growth: it would have been physically impossible to bring so many immigrants to the east. From the later fourteenth century onwards, however, signs of the reverse process can be traced.

Already the *Landbuch* of the New Mark of 1337 contained the names of eighty completely deserted villages.[1] This is the more remarkable as 1337 was a date before the Black Death. Nothing was said about the causes of this desertion of the land. Presumably the inhabitants had migrated into one of the many small towns which were founded in this area at that time, or into Pomerelia, Prussia, or Poland which were colonized in the fourteenth century. The soil of the New Mark was particularly bad;[2] this may have caused the peasants to give up settlements which had only existed for a few decades.[3] When the soil was exhausted or the yields became disappointing they simply moved to more promising surroundings. According to the *Landbuch* of 1375, which unfortunately does not include the New Mark, the Ucker Mark was in even worse a plight. Only twenty-two of its one hundred and fifty villages were fully occupied; in the other villages nearly half the peasant farms were deserted.[4] The same applied to the cottagers' holdings, and numerous villages had been completely abandoned.[5] In the Middle Mark, on the other

[1] *Landbuch 1337*, pp. 82, 84–86, 88, 99, 101, 103, 105–6.
[2] G. Czybulka, *Die Lage der ländlichen Klassen Ostdeutschlands im 18. Jahrhundert*, 1949, p. 9: in the early eighteenth century the New Mark was considered the least fertile part of the whole Prussian state.
[3] The number of *Hufen* in the deserted villages was usually 64, the standard size of the new villages, or even more.
[4] 2,395 out of a total of 4,930 *Hufen*.
[5] Schultze, op. cit., p. xviii.

hand, comparatively few deserted villages and holdings were listed in 1375.[1] Probably the many feuds and frontier wars between Brandenburg and Pomerania were responsible for the ruinous state of peasant farming in the Ucker Mark where most of the fighting took place.[2] Indeed a charter of the bishop of Havelberg of 1409 attributed the lack of cultivation and the desertion of the land in his diocese and elsewhere to the long-lasting furious wars and robberies which had killed many peasants and had forced many more to leave.[3]

In Prussia there is no evidence of any desertion of the land before the fifteenth century, although immigration from Germany had ceased about 1350 and there was a shortage of settlers. Under the strong and efficient government of the Teutonic Knights no feuds took place and no invasions occurred until 1410. Then, however, matters became much worse than in Brandenburg or in Pomerania. In 1410 the Order was decisively defeated by Poland at Tannenberg, and its strength and wealth declined rapidly. Prussia was repeatedly ravaged by Polish forces in this war, and again in 1414, in 1422, and from 1431 to 1433. In that year the Hussites invaded Prussia, advancing northwards as far as Danzig and putting the country to fire and sword. Thousands of people were killed or dragged away into slavery.[4] In 1419 more than 20 per cent. of the *Hufen* belonging to the Order were deserted. In certain areas, especially southern Pomerelia, the damage was much worse. There over 50 per cent. of the holdings were abandoned in 1437–8, and in the commandery of Schwetz as many as 80 per cent., compared with 50 in 1414.[5] In addition, there were crop failures in 1412, 1415–16, and above all in 1437–9, which has been considered the longest and most severe dearth of the fifteenth century.[6] These and many outbreaks of plague aggravated the plight of Prussia and the depopulation of the country and caused a grave shortage

---

[1] *Landbuch 1375*, pp. 56, 76, 78–82, 90, 98, 106–7, 128.

[2] Schultze, op. cit., p. xviii.

[3] *Riedel*, i, no. 16, p. 39.

[4] Details about the devastations can be found in L. von Baczko, *Geschichte Preussens*, iii, 1794, pp. 101, 124–5; C. Sattler, *Handelsrechnungen des Deutschen Ordens*, 1887, p. 303; G. Aubin, op. cit., pp. 72–75.

[5] Aubin, op. cit., p. 73; Kasiske, *Das deutsche Siedelwerk . . .*, pp. 242, 244.

[6] Johann von Posilge's Chronicle, *Scriptores Rerum Prussicarum*, iii, pp. 332, 358, 360; *H.R. 1431–76*, ii, no. 105, p. 101; p. 198, n. 1; no. 262, p. 203; p. 345, n. 1.

of labour and of draught horses.[1] In 1444 it was stated that wood and bush were occupying the sites of many good villages and the habitations of many.[2]

Significantly, it was immediately after the first war against Poland, in 1412, that the Prussian nobility demanded for the first time that no peasant or cottager should be received in any town who could not prove that he had left with his lord's consent; all those without fixed domicile should be driven out of the towns at harvest time. Their demands were incorporated in the same year into the ordinances issued by the Grand Master Henry von Plauen.[3] Five years later the Grand Master and the Estates agreed that a runaway peasant was to be handed over to his lord; the peasant was only free to leave when he had paid his arrears and had provided a successor to take over the farm.[4] This regulation was incorporated into the ordinances of 1420 and repeated several times during the following years.[5]

Another way to secure the necessary farm-hands at a time of increasing shortage of labour was to stipulate compulsory maximum wage-rates. At the urgent request of the nobility of the Culmerland the first decrees fixing maximum wages for servants and labourers in whole districts were issued about 1407, applying to the Culmerland and the three Werder at the mouth of the Vistula,[6] which were among the chief corn-producing districts of Prussia. These regulations were extended to the whole country in 1417 and then incorporated into the ordinances of 1420.[7] They were binding on employers and employees alike; the landlords were enjoined not to entice away each other's servants, a practice about which there were many complaints.[8] A runaway servant had to be surrendered wherever he was found,

---

[1] The Prussian chroniclers report outbreaks of plague in 1346–9, 1360, 1373, 1382–3, 1398, 1405, 1416, 1450, 1464, 1484, 1494–5: *Scriptores Rerum Prussicarum*, iii, pp. 76 and n. 3, 80, 92, 124, 222, 281, 362, 482; iv, pp. 356, 728, 751, 797; v, pp. 444–5, 621, 631, 633. Cf. *Liv-, Est- und Curländisches Urkundenbuch*, viii, no. 859, p. 505, for an outbreak of plague in Prussia in 1432–4, the shortage of horses, and famine.

[2] *Acten der Ständetage Preussens*, ii, no. 397, p. 636.

[3] Ibid. i, no. 155, p. 199.

[4] Ibid. i, no. 250, p. 308.

[5] Ibid. i, nos. 286, 363, pp. 358, 473; ii, nos. 244, 383, pp. 365, 621 (1420–44).

[6] Ibid. i, nos. 74–75, pp. 105–7.

[7] Ibid. i, nos. 246, 282, 286, pp. 303–59.

[8] Ibid. i, nos. 286, 344, 369, pp. 352, 440, 480; von Baczko, op. cit. iii, pp. 411–12, 416–18; Aubin, op. cit., p. 99.

had to work for one year without pay, and to pay a fine of three marks, almost equivalent to another year's wages. Prussians were not to be received as servants or inhabitants in any town or German village.[1] These and further orders[2] met with little success; servants and labourers profited by the growing shortage of labour. In 1425 the landlords and peasants of the commandery of Balga complained that they had to pay wages which were unheard of, of at least six to nine marks; that they could not get any labourers even at those rates, and that the country would be utterly ruined if the servants thus gained the upper hand.[3] In 1444 two rural districts emphasized their great want of agricultural labour; and the noblemen of another district complained about the rising wages which they attributed to the migration into the towns.[4]

To overcome the shortage of farm-hands on their domains the Teutonic Knights began to increase the peasants' labour services. In 1427 the Grand Master Paul von Rusdorf forbade the commanders of the Order to use carrying services in their forestry and fishery and to demand uncustomary labour services, such as carting of manure, ploughing, and building work, and enjoined them to use hired labour instead.[5] That these prohibitions were justified was proved by the accusations of a Carthusian monk from the same year; he listed among the Order's sins that its officials forced the peasants to cut timber and to bring it into the towns and burdened them with heavy services, while the Prussians were often compelled to work on holy days, not only during the harvest but throughout the year.[6] During the following years there were more complaints about wicked and impossible labour services imposed by the Order.[7] Even the freemen had to cut timber and to do peasants' work: the Grand Master had to assure them that this would cease.[8] About the middle of the fifteenth century the Prussian *Bund*, preparing for revolt against the Order, accused it of demanding from the poor

---

[1] *Acten der Ständetage Preussens*, i, nos. 250, 286, pp. 308–9, 358; Aubin, op. cit., p. 96.

[2] *Acten der Ständetage Preussens*, i, nos. 363, 487, pp. 470–3, 628 (1427–34).

[3] Ibid. i, no. 344, p. 439.

[4] Ibid. ii, nos. 388, 393, 397, pp. 627–36.

[5] Ibid. i, no. 382, p. 499.

[6] *Scriptores Rerum Prussicarum*, iv, pp. 459–61.

[7] *Acten der Ständetage Preussens*, i, no. 487, p. 629; ii, no. 243, p. 361 (1434–41).

[8] Ibid. ii, no. 243, p. 361 (1441).

peasants, contrary to their privileges and to old custom, the work which formerly had been done by its labourers, thus causing the ruin and desertion of the land.[1] The Order required these services because of its mounting financial difficulties; it could impose them as it was the sovereign who wielded the jurisdiction and the prerogatives, which had not yet been transferred into private hands.

That similar methods were used by other landlords was shown by a veritable revolt of the peasants of the Ermland cathedral chapter which broke out in 1440. The canons also demanded new uncustomary labour services: carting and floating of timber, transporting of clay to the brick-kilns, and help with fishing. The peasants refused and threatened to use armed force. Sixteen arbiters appointed by the Estates promised them freedom from uncustomary services; but the rebellion went on and further diets had to discuss the affair. Their apprehension was aroused by the news that the peasants were establishing contacts throughout Prussia, and they feared developments 'like those in Bohemia and other countries where the government, the nobility, and the urban patricians had all been ruined'. Thus finally, in February 1442, they published a new award making further concessions to the peasants, and this was accepted by them.[2] The peasants' legal position, however, continued to deteriorate. The noblemen demanded that they should only be permitted to leave with the written consent of their lord and after having provided a successor.[3] It was then stipulated in the ordinances of 1445 that nobody was to receive a peasant without a 'letter' from his lord; if anyone did so, he was to hand over the peasant and pay his arrears. But the peasant was still free to leave if he provided a successor approved by his master; if the latter then refused to give him the 'letter', the peasant could obtain it from the local official of the Order after due investigation.[4] Yet this stipulation neither prevented the towns from receiving peasants, nor the landlords from filling their deserted holdings at each other's cost. The circumstances which caused the labour shortage and the desertion of the land continued unabated, and the cure

[1] Ibid. iv, no. 23, p. 40.
[2] Ibid. ii, nos. 227, 258–62, pp. 349–401; von Baczko, op. cit. iii, pp. 220–2, 375–80.
[3] *Acten der Ständetage Preussens*, ii, nos. 152, 388, pp. 222, 627 (1440–4).
[4] Ibid. ii, no. 410, p. 666.

proved completely ineffective. As the burdens increased, more and more peasants escaped to seek their fortunes elsewhere.

The Thirteen Years War between Prussia and Poland from 1453 to 1466 brought new and frightful devastation of the country,[1] especially as it was also a civil war in which many noblemen and towns revolted against the Teutonic Order. At the peace of Thorn it lost the Culmerland and Pomerelia, with Danzig and all other important towns, except only Königsberg, and retained only eastern Prussia which was less developed and consisted largely of heath, woods, marshes, and wilderness.[2] The decline of the population and the desertion of the land were aggravated by the war and its consequences.[3] At the end of the fifteenth century, after more than thirty years of peace, the districts of Taplacken and Insterburg, in the east, were still 'almost deserted'.[4] In 1508 over 45 per cent. of the holdings were deserted in three districts near Königsberg,[5] after many years of peace. This state of affairs was reflected in the ordinances of 1494. A runaway peasant had to be handed over to his master who could have him hanged; a runaway servant was to be nailed to the pillory by one ear and to be given a knife to cut himself off; no servant was to go idle for more than a fortnight after the end of his employment, but was to accept new service:[6] all this apparently without any trial or arbitrament. The ordinances of 1503 even stipulated that a servant idle for longer than thirteen days was to be arrested and handed over to his lord who could put him into chains or make him serve one year without pay.[7] In Prussia the position of peasants and labourers alike decisively deteriorated in the course of the fifteenth century.

In the central area of Brandenburg, the Middle Mark, comparatively few villages and holdings had been deserted in 1375. The *Schossregister* of the fifteenth century, however, tell a different story. In 1450 almost 30 per cent. of the holdings in 157 villages were deserted.[8] Many other villages occupied in 1375

[1] For details, see *Thunert*, i, nos. 6, 13, 31, 45, 178, pp. 28–31, 75–76, 155, 170, 405–9 (1467–76); von Baczko, op. cit. iii, pp. 365–6.

[2] Aubin, op. cit., pp. 105–6, 113.

[3] According to Weber, op. cit., p. 124, the population of Prussia declined by over 50 per cent. between 1410 and 1466.   [4] Mortensen, op. cit. i, p. 160.

[5] 1,360 deserted *Hufen* and 1,536 occupied: E. Wilke, loc. cit., p. 54.

[6] *Acten der Ständetage Preussens*, v, nos. 142–3, pp. 413–18.

[7] Ibid. v, no. 168, pp. 478–9.

[8] In these villages 1,953 *Hufen* were deserted and 4,714 occupied.

had become completely deserted by 1450.[1] Matters got worse
during the following decades. In 117 villages, for which we
possess comparative data for 1450 and for 1480, the number
of deserted *Hufen* increased from 945 to 1,145 in the course of
only 30 years, and the number of occupied holdings declined
even more.[2] In the two small districts of Ruppin and Templin,
farther north, more than 100 villages were completely abandoned, i.e. half of all existing settlements.[3] This widespread
desertion of the land was not due to the growth of demesne
farming and the buying out of peasants by noblemen. Of 1,953
deserted *Hufen* listed in 1450, only 337½ had become demesne
land: the others were vacant until peasants could be found to
take them over. There was thus 'a net contraction of the area
under cultivation'.[4] By 1570, however, about half the deserted
holdings were again occupied by peasants:[5] the desertion of
the land was arrested because the peasants and their children
were tied to the soil, and probably more so because the
population was again growing. Thus not even in the sixteenth
century was the tendency towards increased demesne farming so strong that all the deserted holdings were absorbed in
that way.

If it was not the growth of demesne farming which caused the
desertion of the land, it was undoubtedly the desertion of the
land which forced many landlords to take some deserted holdings under their own plough so as to derive at least some benefit
from them. The late fourteenth and the fifteenth centuries were
a period of great difficulties for the nobility, as indicated by the
general insecurity and the many robber barons and feuds and
private wars which figure so prominently in the chronicles.
Rising prices and the debasement of the coinage caused the
landlords' real income to shrink, as it was mainly derived from

[1] *Landbuch 1375*, pp. 49, 51, 61, 92, 115, 326, 329.
[2] From 3,714 to 3,483 *Hufen*. All figures are calculated from the *Schossregister*
which are printed in Fidicin's edition of the *Landbuch 1375*.
[3] W. Sorg, *Wüstungen in den brandenburgischen Kreisen Ruppin und Templin und deren
Ursachen*, 1936, pp. 18–20, 57–62.
[4] As there was in England: M. Postan, 'The Fifteenth Century', *Economic History Review*, ix, 1939, p. 161.
[5] In the 157 villages mentioned above at least 5,670 *Hufen* were occupied, as
against 4,714 in 1450. The figures for 1570 are derived from the *Schossregister* of
1624 which has been printed by Grossmann, op. cit., as an Appendix: it lists
changes made during the preceding fifty years.

money dues. Above all, the desertion of the land and the shortage of labour seriously affected their standard of living. Many noblemen were compelled to farm deserted holdings themselves, at least until new tenants could be found. Thus in 1403 a nobleman was invested with 4 deserted *Hufen*; but if the landlord succeeded in finding new peasants for them, he was to give them up and to receive another 4 deserted *Hufen* in that village.[1] In 1412 two noble brothers held a village with 28 deserted *Hufen* so that they ploughed them themselves.[2] The *Schossregister* of the Middle Mark mentioned many instances of deserted *Hufen* which were farmed by noblemen: thus 6 demesnes of 20 *Hufen* and above had come into being by 1450, in addition to many smaller ones.[3] In 1480 the von Arnim ploughed as many as 72 deserted *Hufen* belonging to the small town of Biesenthal,[4] and also had demesnes in other districts.[5]

In view of these facts it is surprising that there was a slight decrease of demesne farming in those villages of the Middle Mark for which there are comparative data: in 136 villages the demesne lands decreased from 1,419½ to 1,361 *Hufen* between 1375 and 1450, and in another 155 villages there was no demesne in either year. In 38 villages the demesne disappeared; only 98 out of a total of 291 villages had a demesne in 1450: all the others were pure peasant villages.[6] This decline of demesne farming at a time of growing desertion of the land once more shows that the holdings were not vacated to make room for larger demesnes. The *Schossregister* only mentioned one instance where a peasant had been bought out by a nobleman, and that between 1480 and 1481.[7] In the district of Ruppin, as late as 1491, no demesne was larger than 9 *Hufen*, and peasants had leased *Hufen* belonging to noblemen.[8]

In Brandenburg the desertion of the land had the same consequences which it had had in Prussia. There were the same complaints about runaway servants, shortage of labourers, and high wages demanded by them, and the same clamour for the

---

[1] *Riedel*, xiii, no. 49, p. 45.   [2] Ibid., C i, no. 52, p. 51.
[3] *Landbuch 1375*, pp. 268, 270, 285, 295, 299, 301, 308, 333: demesnes of 12, 15½, 20, 25, 31, 33, 36, and 69 *Hufen*.
[4] Ibid., p. 295.
[5] *Riedel*, xii, no. 10, p. 214; xiii, no. 113, p. 388.
[6] For details see *English Historical Review*, lxii, 1947, pp. 170–8.
[7] *Landbuch 1375*, p. 331.   [8] *Riedel*, iv, no. 97, pp. 116–42.

stipulation of maximum wages.[1] To overcome their difficulties the landlords imposed heavier labour services and began to curtail the peasants' freedom of movement. As they had already acquired the jurisdiction and the other prerogatives on their estates, they were in a stronger position than the Prussian nobility, for the owner of the jurisdiction had the right to demand labour services.[2] Before 1423 the von Uchtenhagen were accused of burdening the peasants of two villages so much that they became impoverished.[3] When the castle of Arneburg, in the Old Mark, was pawned to a nobleman in 1435, it was stipulated that he could use the peasants' services for his demesne; they should be announced by an official of the margrave according to his judgement, but the peasants should not be overburdened:[4] yet the services were not limited, and the official might easily be partial. In 1487 it was declared that the two noblemen who owned the jurisdiction in an Old Mark village were entitled to demand labour services: to prevent its desertion the peasants should not be burdened too heavily.[5] Again the amount of the services was not stipulated, so that it seems that the noblemen could impose them at will.

Even the burghers of small towns which had been sold to noblemen were obliged to perform services for their new masters. In 1447 margrave Frederick decided a dispute between the von Buch and the burghers of their town of Stolp, in the Ucker Mark, in favour of the former: henceforth each inhabitant of the town was to serve them three days in the year.[6] In 1487 the burghers of the town of Bernstein, in the New Mark, promised to render their new lords, the von Waldow, services of four days in the year, and also to help them if they wanted to build.[7] In 1492 the burghers of Putlitz, in the Priegnitz, were 'on request'

---

[1] A. von Haxthausen, 'Die patrimoniale Gesetzgebung in der Altmark', *Jahrbücher für die preussische Gesetzgebung, Rechtswissenschaft und Rechtsverwaltung*, xxxix, 1832, no. 1, p. 13; *Riedel*, C ii, no. 245, p. 303 (1472–84); *von Raumer*, ii, no. 16, p. 225 (1518).

[2] The connexion between jurisdiction and labour services emerges clearly from *Riedel*, i, no. 9, p. 459; v, no. 97, p. 69; no. 19, p. 311; x, no. 23*a*, p. 463; xi, no. 219, p. 435; xxii, no. 13, p. 495 (1320–1487).

[3] Ibid. x, p. 446.   [4] Ibid. vi, no. 268, p. 201.

[5] F. Priebatsch, 'Die Hohenzollern und der Adel der Mark', *Historische Zeitschrift*, lxxxviii, 1902, p. 244.

[6] *Riedel*, xiii, no. 86, pp. 370–1.

[7] Ibid. xviii, no. 48, p. 90; xxiv, no. 258, p. 203.

obliged to serve the Gans von Putlitz; the latter promised not to ask them for too many named and unnamed services, but their amount was not stipulated.[1] In 1500 the burghers of the town of Freienstein, in the same district, had to perform considerable ploughing, mowing, and carrying services for the von Rohr who had bought the town a few years earlier.[2]

At the same time the right of the peasants to leave freely which had always been recognized began to be curtailed. In western Pomerania the powerful noble family of the von Schwerin in 1458 demanded that the town of Anklam should hand over one of their peasants who had absconded. When the town declined a veritable war broke out in which first the noblemen and then the burghers were victorious; but the peace concluded after three years provided that fugitive peasants were to be surrendered.[3] In 1481 two noblemen of the same family proudly called themselves the 'peasants' foes'.[4] The von Putbus imprisoned a runaway peasant; but this seems to have been illegal, for in 1472 his two sons renounced all their claims on this account and promised not to seek revenge against the von Putbus.[5] The same occurred in Brandenburg. In 1483 sentence was pronounced against the small town of Köpenick for harbouring a runaway peasant: he was to be handed over with all his goods and chattels, and the punishment of the town was left to the margrave.[6] In the following year the assembly of the lords demanded that nobody should harbour a peasant, cottager, or servant who had left without his master's consent, but should surrender him if required to do so.[7] Still another year later it was ordained in the Old Mark that a peasant had to find a successor before he was permitted to leave,[8] exactly as it had been stipulated in Prussia seventy years earlier. The tying of the peasants to the soil had begun.

We do not know on what grounds the noblemen based their demands for the surrender of runaway peasants and servants.

---

[1] *Riedel*, i, no. 34, p. 322.

[2] Ibid. ii, no. 37, pp. 294–5; iii, no. 262, p. 505.

[3] *Gollmert*, no. 336, pp. 249–50; Kantzow, op. cit. i, pp. 387–8; Barthold, op. cit. iv 1, pp. 244–5, 261–2; Kratz, op. cit., pp. 9–10.

[4] *Gollmert*, no. 379, p. 270.

[5] J. von Bohlen, *Geschichte des adlichen, freiherrlichen und gräflichen Geschlechts von Krassow*, 1853, ii, no. 154, p. 122.

[6] *Von Raumer*, ii, no. 119, pp. 180–1.

[7] *Riedel*, C ii, no. 245, p. 303.   [8] Priebatsch, loc. cit., p. 244.

It may be that the fugitives were indebted to them, or had arrears to make good; it may be that they were accused of a misdeed. The demands were certainly novel and could not have been raised in the fourteenth century. Neither is it clear why the towns did not resist much more vigorously, as their growth and influence depended on the influx of newcomers. The resistance reported emanated from small towns, while the leading towns, apparently not realizing the importance of the issue, did not support them. At the same time a long-drawn-out struggle between the nobility and the towns raged in Livonia over the same problem. The Livonian towns, especially Reval, stoutly resisted the demands of the nobility; in the end their resistance was largely successful and the principle 'town air makes free within a year and a day' was recognized.[1] It seems strange that the burghers of Pomerania and of Prussia, whose power rivalled that of the Livonian towns, were so weak-kneed on this vital issue. In Livonia also it was the depopulation and desertion of the country, as a consequence of plague, dearth, and invasion, which caused the demands for the handing over of fugitive peasants.[2] All over eastern Germany and large parts of eastern Europe the deterioration of the peasants' legal and social position prepared the way for the changes of the sixteenth century.

The many wars and the growing desertion of the land in another way severely affected the strength of the Teutonic Order. Hitherto it had ruled the country with a strong hand; in contrast with the development in the other principalities, it retained the most important prerogatives in its own hands and prevented the rise of a strong nobility. As the Order was by far the largest landlord of Prussia, it could dispose over great quantities of corn, partly from its own demesnes, partly from the dues of its peasants.[3] These it could store and later sell at the most opportune moment, thus profiting from any rise in prices;

---

[1] For details see: *Liv-, Est- und Kurländ. U.B.* II i, nos. 330, 655, pp. 241, 488; II ii, no. 604, p. 479; II iii, nos. 816, 831, pp. 603–13; *Akten und Rezesse der livländ. Ständetage*, iii, nos. 41, 52, 54, 58–64, 66–67, 71–72, 76–78, 88–89, 98, 108, 112–14, 242, 298, 301, 304; V. Niitemaa, *Die Undeutsche Frage in der Politik der livländischen Städte im Mittelalter*, Helsinki, 1949, in particular ch. v.

[2] L. Arbusow, in *Akten und Rezesse der livländ. Ständetage*, i 3, p. 305, n. 3; Niitemaa, op. cit., pp. 77–78, 139. Arbusow wrongly assumes that the development in Livonia was in contrast to that in eastern Germany.

[3] For details see: Weber, op. cit., p. 572; Naudé, op. cit., pp. 256–7; G. Aubin, op. cit., p. 55, n. 4.

it used its sovereign powers to demand from the peasants payment of their dues in kind at a fixed price and to buy up corn
below the market price to resell later at much higher prices.[1]
The Order also engaged in trade on a large scale, especially
with Flanders, and thus benefited from the general economic
development. All this changed in the course of the fifteenth century. Owing to the great cost of the wars and the devastations,
the Order rapidly lost its financial strength and had to debase
the Prussian coinage severely.[2] Its income from peasant dues,
trade, and other enterprises shrank considerably in consequence.

The Thirteen Years War in addition caused revolutionary
changes in the landownership of Prussia. Already during the
war the leaders of mercenaries employed by the Order took
possession of towns and villages as a security for their demands
against the Teutonic Knights. Others were given land as they
could not be paid in cash. After the conclusion of peace these
instances multiplied. To pay off its debts the Order had to sell
or pawn domains, towns, and villages, and was hardly ever able
to redeem them. Many mercenary leaders and many German
noblemen who had fought for the Order received large estates
as payment in kind:[3] thus the von Schlieben the town, castle,
and domain of Gerdauen with large tracts of wilderness, the
town of Neidenburg with 14 villages, and other property;[4] the
brothers von Tettau the castle of Angerburg with its wilderness
and 11 villages;[5] the von Querfurt the town of Passenheim with
3 villages;[6] the von Weyer the castle of Wohnsdorf with 4 villages;[7] the von Löben the town of Gilgenburg with 7 villages
and a demesne.[8] Above all, these noblemen were granted the
public services, the highest jurisdiction, and the other preroga-

---

[1] *Scriptores Rerum Prussicarum*, iv, pp. 458–9; Naudé, op. cit., p. 258; Aubin, op.
cit., p. 55.

[2] In the course of the fifteenth century the silver value of the Prussian Mark was
reduced by over 80 per cent., the sharpest reductions taking place during or after
the wars: F. A. Vossberg, *Geschichte der preussischen Münzen und Siegel*, 1843, pp.
208–10; Aubin, op. cit., pp. 118–19.

[3] Von Baczko, op. cit. iv, p. 57; Aubin, op. cit., pp. 106–7; Mortensen, op. cit.
i, p. 152.

[4] Rousselle, 'Das Siedlungswerk des Deutschen Ordens im Lande Gerdauen',
loc. cit., p. 254; Aubin, op. cit., p. 108, n. 1; Mortensen, op. cit. i, p. 154.

[5] *Regesta Historico-Diplomatica*, ii, no. 3211, p. 357 (1469).

[6] Ibid., nos. 3247–8, p. 362 (1469).

[7] Ibid., nos. 3178, 3372, pp. 354, 374 (1468–75).

[8] Ibid., no. 3376, p. 375 (1475).

tives which had been exercised by the Order.[1] The majority of the peasants as well as of the Prussian freemen became the subjects of private landlords. As the Order's power waned it was no longer able to protect them against the nobility.[2]

Thus a powerful noble class which wielded all the prerogatives came into being. Its backbone were the new immigrants from Germany: nearly all the leading families of the sixteenth and seventeenth centuries were the descendants of mercenary leaders and noblemen who invested their war gains in real estate at the cost of the Order.[3] As nearly all important towns had been ceded to Poland, the nobility soon dominated the assemblies of the Estates,[4] where the one town of Königsberg was unable to balance its influence. The decline of the Order and its later dissolution removed another check on the power of the nobility and made it the sole ruling class. Thus Prussia within a few decades went through the development which in Brandenburg and in Pomerania stretched over several centuries. Many of the differences between Prussia and the other principalities disappeared. The last two Grand Masters, Frederick of Saxony and Albert of Brandenburg, were princes of the Empire. Their policy differed from that of previous Grand Masters, who had been of lesser status, and approximated to that of the other territorial princes,[5] long before the secularization of Prussia and its transformation into a duchy, and quite independently of any religious changes.

The most important cause of the agrarian and the other changes of the fifteenth century was the depopulation of the countryside. In its turn it was caused by wars, feuds, and devastations, by outbreaks of plague, dearth, and famine. If the population did recover from the Black Death of the mid-fourteenth century, it was unable to withstand a whole series of disasters which befell it in the fifteenth century. There also seem

[1] Aubin, op. cit., p. 108; E. Wilke, loc. cit., p. 49; Kasiske, *Das deutsche Siedelwerk* . . ., p. 258.

[2] Aubin, op. cit., pp. 107–8; E. Wilke, loc. cit., p. 187; Mortensen, op. cit. i, p. 152.

[3] Aubin, op. cit., pp. 108–9; K. Breysig, introduction to *Urkunden und Actenstücke*, xv, p. 31.

[4] Aubin, op. cit., p. 109; E. Wilke, loc. cit., p. 51.

[5] This has recently been shown by K. Forstreuter, *Vom Ordensstaat zum Fürstentum: Geistige und politische Wandlungen im Deutschordensstaate Preussen unter den Hochmeistern Friedrich und Albrecht (1498–1525)*, 1951.

to have been other causes. At the time of the colonization many villages were founded on soil which was not fertile enough to permit permanent cultivation, or was endangered by floods, lack of water, or soil erosion.[1] In such a case the peasants could easily move into one of the towns, as long as these were allowed to receive them, or could migrate farther east. The colonization did not proceed simultaneously everywhere, but only started in the more eastern lands after it had been accomplished farther west; in Poland and Prussia it still continued at a much later time.[2] The peasants had few possessions which they could not take with them, and their houses were easily rebuilt elsewhere. It thus seems quite possible that many of the deserted sites in central Germany were caused by the colonization to the east of the Elbe, while many of those in eastern Germany may have been caused by the progress of the colonization still farther to the east. From the names of many of the burghers of Danzig and other eastern towns it is evident that they came from Brandenburg, Saxony, and other east-German countries, and the same no doubt applied to many peasants.

Quite apart from a movement of population eastwards, there also was a genuine decline of the population, the causes of which have been outlined above.[3] In Poland equally there were hundreds of deserted villages and the same depopulation of the country-side.[4] In Brandenburg and elsewhere villages with good soil became deserted side by side with those with poor soil, which indicates a genuine depopulation,[5] and not migration elsewhere.

---

[1] G. Hertel, *Die Wüstungen im Nordthüringgau*, 1899, pp. xviii, xxvi–vii; L. Freiherr von Wintzingeroda-Knorr, *Die Wüstungen des Eichsfeldes*, 1903, p. xxviii; W. Zahn, *Die Wüstungen der Altmark*, 1909, pp. xxi–xxii; E. Blume, 'Beiträge zur Siedlungskunde der Magdeburger Börde', *Archiv für Landes- und Volkskunde der Provinz Sachsen*, xviii, 1908, p. 60; M. Bolle, 'Beiträge zur Siedlungskunde des Havelwinkels', ibid. xix, 1909, pp. 59–62; xx, 1910, pp. 8–9; G. Reischel, 'Die Wüstungen der Provinz Sachsen', *Sachsen und Anhalt, Jahrbuch der Historischen Kommission für die Provinz Sachsen und für Anhalt*, ii, 1926, pp. 251, 278–9, 343–4; Gley, op. cit., p. 117; Sorg, op. cit., p. 21; W. Abel, *Die Wüstungen des ausgehenden Mittelalters*, 1943, pp. 72–74, 77, 162.

[2] E. Schmidt, *Geschichte des Deutschtums im Lande Posen*, 1904, pp. 314–15, 330–9, 404–6.

[3] Abel, op. cit., pp. 77–78. For England, see Postan, loc. cit., p. 166.

[4] Schmidt, op. cit., pp. 278–9; J. Rutkowski, *Histoire Économique de la Pologne*, 1927, p. 107.

[5] Sorg, op. cit., pp. 64–65; Abel, op. cit., pp. 76–77; Zahn, op. cit., p. xxi.

All the changes of the fifteenth century taken together did not create the *Gutsherrschaft* of the sixteenth century: they merely prepared the way for it. In western Germany, and in other countries also, the landlords were hard hit by the debasement of the coinage and the agrarian crisis of the fifteenth century. They therefore reinforced old burdens, revived feudal obligations, enclosed common lands, and in general put the screw on the peasants, events which ultimately led to the Peasants' War and to many similar revolts. The further disintegration of the manorial system was perhaps retarded through these developments; but it had already progressed too far to be reversed entirely, and there is no evidence of increased demesne farming as a result of the crisis. In eastern Germany and Poland, on the other hand, corn had been grown for export since the fourteenth century, so that the gradual increase of demesne farming was a way out of the difficulties besetting the landlords. The consequence of this increase was the imposition of heavier labour services, the tying of the peasants to the soil, and ultimately the introduction of serfdom. Conversely, in England the letting out of the demesne and the change-over from arable to sheep-farming were the result of the same economic difficulties;[1] and as demesne farming declined and sheep-farming became more prominent, the demand for labour services decreased and villeinage gradually and quietly faded out. So it did in western Germany and in western Europe in general in course of time, while it was newly introduced in eastern Europe. In England and elsewhere, the depopulation, the labour shortage, and the absconding of the villeins induced the landlords to make concessions to them;[2] while the opposite happened in the east.

Thus the same causes had entirely different effects in the west and in the east. There the general backwardness and the comparatively short time during which the area had been developed at all facilitated a change-over towards more demesne farming. This became economically possible because in western Europe the demand for imported corn was growing, at least from the late fifteenth century onwards. Above all, it was the long-lasting decline and the subjugation of the eastern towns which

[1] Postan, loc. cit., pp. 161, 166; H. Nabholz, in *The Cambridge Economic History of Europe*, i, pp. 511, 520, 525.
[2] Postan, loc. cit., p. 166; Nabholz, loc. cit., pp. 511, 549.

eliminated all resistance to the rise of the nobility. In some western countries also the growth of the towns was retarded in the fifteenth century; but it was resumed after a comparatively short time. This in itself prevented any development similar to that in the east: it was the rise of the towns which led to the break-up of the manorial system,[1] and it was their decline which led to its revival.

[1] H. Pirenne, *Economic and Social History of Medieval Europe*, 1937, pp. 79, 84.

IX

The Decline of the Hanseatic Towns on the Baltic

UP to the end of the fourteenth century the German towns in the Baltic lands grew and prospered; they profited from the progress of the colonization and extended the radius of their commercial activities. The axis of Hanseatic trade to and from the Baltic was the route from Bruges to Novgorod; this cut across the Jutland peninsula, roughly between Hamburg and Lübeck, and thus guaranteed their predominant position in the Baltic trade.[1] This route made it necessary to trans-ship all goods at least twice on their journey eastwards or westwards: it was suitable for costly merchandise, such as spices, cloth, and furs, but not for bulky and less valuable goods, such as corn and timber.[2] With the growing imports of these by western European countries, the alternative route around Jutland through the Sound became increasingly attractive, to the detriment of Lübeck's preponderant position.[3] At the same time the appearance of Dutch and English competitors in the Baltic began to weaken the monopoly of the Wendish towns in the east–west trade. These competitors made their appearance in the east at the time when western countries began to import eastern corn and timber in larger quantities; they used the route through the Sound in preference to that via Lübeck, which was thus threatened by foreign competition as well as by a change of trade routes. Furthermore, Lübeck possessed a practical monopoly of the sale of Lüneburg salt, significantly called 'Traven' salt in the Baltic area,[4] and Prussia and Livonia depended on its supply.[5] From the later fourteenth century onwards, however, Flemish and Bay salt were imported into the Baltic lands and found a ready sale, although considered inferior

---

[1] F. Vollbehr, *Die Holländer und die deutsche Hanse*, 1930, pp. 19–20; M. Postan, 'The Economic and Political Relations of England and the Hanse', *Studies in English Trade in the Fifteenth Century*, 1933, pp. 91, 93; A. E. Christensen, *Dutch Trade to the Baltic about 1600*, 1941, p. 34; F. Ketner, *Handel en Scheepvaart van Amsterdam in de Vijftiende Eeuw*, 1946, p. 9.

[2] Vollbehr, op. cit., pp. 20–21.

[3] E. Daenell, *Die Blütezeit der deutschen Hanse*, 1905, i, p. 274; Vollbehr, op. cit., p. 23; Postan, loc. cit., p. 95; Christensen, op. cit., p. 34.

[4] The Trave is the river on which Lübeck is situated.

[5] K. Pagel, *Die Hanse*, 1952, pp. 54, 56.

in quality to Lüneburg salt, as both were much cheaper,[1] so that Lübeck's salt trade declined sharply.

If Lübeck and the other Wendish towns were threatened by these changes, the same did not at first apply to the towns of Prussia and of Livonia. They welcomed direct commercial relations with the west which would emancipate them from the control of Lübeck.[2] From the year 1366 comes the first evidence of Dutch trading in Livonia, which did not cause any friction.[3] Danzig especially entered into close relations with Dutch and English merchants. Forty-two Dutch ships visited the town in 1391;[4] and in the following year more than three hundred English ships are said to have arrived to load corn.[5] Dutch and English merchants brought quantities of cloth to Prussia from where it was sold into the German and Polish hinterland.[6] The peace between England and Prussia concluded in 1388 permitted English merchants to enter any Prussian port and to sell their goods to anyone anywhere 'sicut antiquitus et ab antiquo extitit usitatum . . .'. Thereafter Danzig's trade with England grew quickly. English merchants settled there, opened their shops, and were granted full citizen rights. In 1391 an English community was formally recognized, with John Bebys from London as its governor.[7] These friendly relations, however, did not last long. In 1397 English cloth was confiscated at Danzig and Elbing. In the next year the treaty of 1388 was renounced by the Grand Master. In 1402 all married Englishmen were ordered to leave, and the others were forbidden to travel about or to trade with any but burghers of the port where they had landed.[8] Two years later all Englishmen were expelled, and the import of English cloth was forbidden, even if it belonged to Hanseatic merchants.[9] In 1405 Dutch merchants also were banned from Danzig for three years because of an alleged

[1] Vollbehr, op. cit., pp. 25–27. See below, p. 128, and the tables of salt prices in the Appendix.

[2] Daenell, op. cit. i, p. 274, and 'Holland und die Hanse im 15. Jahrhundert', *Hansische Geschichtsblätter*, xi, 1904, p. 16; Vollbehr, op. cit., pp. 21–22.

[3] Vollbehr, op. cit., p. 16.

[4] Daenell, op. cit. i, p. 272; Vollbehr, op. cit., p. 22.

[5] Chronicle of Hans Spatt, quoted by T. Hirsch, *Danzigs Handels- und Gewerbs-geschichte*, 1858, p. 39.   [6] Hirsch, op. cit., p. 129; Vollbehr, op. cit., p. 25.

[7] Hirsch, op. cit., p. 100; Keyser, *Die Bevölkerung Danzigs und ihre Herkunft . . .*, p. 42; Postan, loc. cit., pp. 97, 108.

[8] Hirsch, op. cit., pp. 101–2; Postan, loc. cit., p. 109; *H.R. 1256–1430*, v, no. 101, p. 69.   [9] Hirsch, op. cit., p. 102.

infringement of an urban regulation, after a previous complaint of Danzig that the Dutch were selling cloth in the country.[1] In 1409, however, peace was restored between England and Prussia, and a commercial treaty was signed according to which Englishmen were permitted to trade throughout Prussia and with the members of any nation and of any faith, while similar privileges were granted to Prussian merchants in England.[2]

Thus not only the Wendish towns but the Hanse as a whole had to meet the challenge of trade difficulties and of growing foreign competition in an area where hardly any had existed previously. As early as 1401 the aldermen of the Hanseatic merchants at Novgorod complained bitterly about buying on credit in Flanders which would ruin them utterly if it continued.[3] Clearly more goods arrived in Russia than could be sold at a profit, and the merchants could not wait for prices to rise, as they had to satisfy their creditors. Early in 1410 the German factory at Novgorod declared that the church there was packed with merchandise as never before; matters would get worse with the impending arrival of the summer visitors and the merchants would be completely ruined.[4] As about two hundred *terling* of cloth were lying unsold at Novgorod,[5] the Livonian towns discussed whether the route should be closed altogether.[6] Two years later the Hanse factory at Bruges complained that cloth and other goods were fetching very low prices at Novgorod because such quantities were bought on credit in Livonia that the merchants had to sell at any price offered by the Russians; in addition, many merchants bought furs, wax, and corn in Livonia for which they undertook to pay on arrival in Flanders, so that they had to sell hastily there and spoiled the prices.[7] The close connexion between Bruges and Novgorod emerged clearly.

[1] *H.R. 1256–1430*, viii, no. 1173, p. 750; Hirsch, op. cit., p. 129.

[2] Hirsch, op. cit., p. 103; Daenell, op. cit. ii, p. 1; Postan, loc. cit., p. 111.

[3] *H.R. 1256–1430*, v, no. 9, p. 7.

[4] *Liv-, Est- und Curländ. U.B.* iv, nos. 1822, 1829, cols. 695, 709; vi, no. 2984, col. 365; *H.R. 1256–1430*, v, nos. 665–6, pp. 519–21.

[5] *Liv-, Est- und Curländ. U.B.* iv, no. 1830, col. 711; *H.R. 1256–1430*, v, no. 670, p. 525.

[6] *Liv-, Est- und Curländ. U.B.* iv, no. 1834, col. 717; *H.R. 1256–1430*, v, no. 673, p. 528.

[7] *Liv-, Est- und Curländ. U.B.* iv, no. 1915, col. 810; *H.R. 1256–1430*, vi, no. 58, p. 42.

About the same time the Teutonic Knights, who were the close ally and commercial partner of the Hanse, were decisively defeated by Poland at Tannenberg. The rapid decline of the Order, the many wars and invasions after 1410, the depopulation of the country, the debasement of the coinage, the crisis and general insecurity of the fifteenth century, seriously affected the trade and the wealth of the Baltic towns. They constantly complained about the many robberies and the insecurity of the roads. The income of the landlords and noblemen, the chief buyers of merchandise in the countryside, shrank, as did the rural surplus which could be offered to the towns for sale and the population of the villages. Most of the towns were small and depended on the trade with the surrounding countryside. The decline of the rural population also affected the towns in a different way: they ceased to be the magnets attracting the inhabitants of the country, where a surplus of land and a shortage of tillers made migration unnecessary and, from the landlord's point of view, undesirable. The urban population equally declined owing to war and plague, and its ranks could no longer be replenished. The growth of the Baltic towns came to an end; the merchants could not find compensation for selling less to the countryside by selling more within the towns. All this, and much of the contemporary evidence quoted below, points to a declining volume of trade. The appearance of foreign competitors at a time of trade contraction presented a far more serious danger than it would have been at a time of expansion and prosperity, in which the Hanse and the interlopers might have shared.

From the second decade of the fifteenth century onwards, indeed, there is mounting evidence of a growing crisis in all the leading Hanseatic towns on the Baltic. One merchant reported from Lübeck to Bruges in 1414 that he could sell neither silk nor cloth, and that people had no money for buying.[1] Twenty months later he again wrote that he had been unable to sell white cloth.[2] In 1417 he complained that he could sell neither cloth, nor pepper, nor raisins, that nobody bought any cloth, and that the women did not buy any silk.[3] In the following year another Lübeck merchant confirmed this tale: there was no demand for rice, almonds, or alum; all the goods he had received from

---

[1] *Veckinchusen*, no. 97, p. 116.   [2] Ibid., no. 109, p. 133.
[3] Ibid., no. 166, p. 186.

Flanders were still unsold, and he had no money to pay for them.[1] From Reval a merchant reported in 1416 that trade was poor and that nobody was making a profit; and later that there was no demand for figs, and that quantities of cloth were lying unsold at Reval as well as at Novgorod.[2] The Russians, three other merchants wrote, could pick and choose, as so many people wanted to sell, and as the skippers and sailors were underselling the merchants.[3]

At Danzig trade was equally bad. In 1416 one merchant stressed repeatedly that trade was not what it had been shortly before; he could not sell any cloth, not even on credit; his customers would not make any offers, and at Thorn it was the same: 'I believe the devil is in the cloth.'[4] In 1417 his complaints became much more frequent and vehement: many more merchants imported Flemish cloth than had previously done so; what he had sent to Thorn had come back unsold; there were equally poor sales at Cracow, Brest Litovsk, Nizhni, and Breslau, while hitherto the Breslauers had bought large quantities of cloth; at the Marienburg fair, the best in the country, he had only sold eight half-cloths, and those only on credit; the figs, raisins, pepper, rice, caraway seeds which he had received were mainly unsold as there was no money in the country; all they offered in exchange was copper and furs which it would be impossible to sell at Lübeck at a profit.[5] During the following years there were many reports that cloth was cheaper at Danzig than it was in Flanders, and that it was impossible to sell cloth, figs, raisins, almonds, or alum against cash or to make a profit.[6] In 1420 one merchant wrote from Danzig to his correspondent at Bruges that he wished the latter had bought wine and got drunk, rather than buy alum, raisins, and almonds.[7]

At Bruges there was an equal glut in eastern merchandise. Early in 1422 such quantities of wax and fur were unsold there that the Hanse merchants, to prevent a further drop of prices,

[1] Ibid., no. 185, p. 211.
[2] Ibid., nos. 122, 127, pp. 148–51 (July–Sept. 1416).
[3] Ibid., nos. 440, 443, pp. 443–5 (s.d.).
[4] Ibid., nos. 119, 126, 133–4, pp. 143, 150, 155–6 (June–Dec. 1416).
[5] Ibid., nos. 139, 142, 148–9, 155, 160, 164, 167, 171, 177, pp. 160–2, 168–70, 174–5, 179, 185–6, 189–90, 204 (Jan.–Dec. 1417).
[6] Ibid., nos. 207, 222, 238, 241–3, pp. 231, 246, 261, 263, 266–7 (May 1419–May 1420).
[7] Ibid., no. 238, p. 261.

against their custom permitted sales on credit or commission
of either the merchants' or their friends' goods.[1] In the same year
trade at Lübeck was described as sick; the merchants feared for
their existence; the prices of houses were falling, because many
were offered for sale owing to the war between Denmark and
Holstein.[2] It was impossible to sell cloth either at Lübeck or at
Stralsund.[3] Late in 1425 it was still reported from Lübeck that
trade was sick and that nobody had any surplus.[4] With that
year this correspondence between different Hanseatic merchants
unfortunately comes to an end: from their letters a clearer picture of trade conditions emerges than exists for any other decade
of the fifteenth century.

Significantly, it was during the same decade that the Hanse
took the first strong measures against foreign competitors. Dutch
merchants were penetrating into the hinterland of the Baltic
towns, were buying corn directly from the producers, and were
shipping it from small harbours and through the Sound, by-
passing the Hanse towns.[5] In 1416 the Hanseatic diets discussed
the 'forestalling and loading of corn in unusual towns and harbours' and 'the Dutch buying up of corn and shipping it from
unusual harbours'.[6] In the next year Lübeck proposed not to
accept any Dutchmen as burghers in the Hanse towns, nor to
admit their cloth, nor to allow them to sail where they had not
done so of old.[7] The Hanse, however, only forbade the shipping
of corn through the Sound and the Belt and from unusual harbours; this prohibition was then incorporated into the ordinances
of 1417 and 1418.[8] The Hanse factory at Bruges complained
that Hollanders, Zeelanders, and Campeners daily visited
Livonia and sent their sons and nephews there to learn eastern
languages, and demanded that all non-Hanseatics should be
completely debarred from trading in Livonia and from learning
languages there.[9] Only the last demand was agreed to by the

---

[1] *H.R. 1256–1430*, vii, no. 437, p. 261.
[2] *Veckinchusen*, nos. 331, 337, 357, pp. 348, 352–3, 378 (June 1422–July 1423).
[3] Ibid., nos. 430–2, pp. 435–7 (s.d.).
[4] Ibid., no. 408, p. 418.
[5] W. Stein, *Beiträge zur Geschichte der deutschen Hanse bis um die Mitte des 15. Jahrhunderts*, 1900, pp. 130–1; Vollbehr, op. cit., p. 27.
[6] *H.R. 1256–1430*, vi, nos. 262, 319, pp. 228, 293.
[7] Ibid., no. 396a, p. 367.
[8] Ibid., nos. 397–8, 557, pp. 378–9, 383, 387, 389, 557.
[9] Ibid., no. 400, p. 397.

League, and the activities of foreign merchants were limited to the coastal towns of Livonia.[1] In 1421 Lübeck again demanded that the Livonian towns should prohibit any partnership between Hanseatics and non-Hanseatics.[2] In the following year the Hanse considered it necessary that further measures should be adopted against the Dutch 'who have done severe and manifold damage to the common merchant'.[3]

Early in 1423 the Hanse factory at Bruges almost admitted defeat: 'thus the Flemings have the best ships which sail the seas . . . with which ships they have done much trading, both eastwards and westwards, and have gained much money, and have drawn to themselves the skippers and boatswains'; sales of seaworthy ships to non-Hanseatics and the hiring and loading of non-Hanseatic ships for eastward journeys should be forbidden, 'otherwise they will get the whole trade . . . as we clearly and daily notice and find it'.[4] They accordingly banned all eastward sailings of non-Hanseatics.[5] A few months later the Hanse forbade Dutch trading in Livonia altogether.[6] In 1425 the Bruges ordinance against the hiring and loading of Flemish and Dutch ships for journeys to Livonia was accepted by the Hanse; non-Hanseatics were forbidden to buy new ships and to employ Hanseatics as their representatives in the Hanse towns,[7] so that they could no longer participate in their privileges. Thus the League attempted to exclude competitors by restrictive and protectionist regulations, a difficult undertaking even if there had been complete unity among the Hanse towns: for neither the majority of the small towns nor the rulers and landlords were subject to its jurisdiction. They would continue to welcome the interlopers if they paid well for corn and timber and offered more favourable freight rates and merchandise cheaper than the Hanseatic merchants did. This was pointed out immediately by the Livonian towns: if they banned the Dutch, 'other mighty people' would admit them and the Livonian merchants

---

[1] Ibid., no. 397, p. 383: repeated in 1434, 1443, 1447, and 1470.

[2] *Liv-, Est- und Curländ. U.B.* v, no. 2556, col. 752.

[3] *H.R. 1256–1430*, vii, no. 443, p. 269.

[4] Ibid. vii, no. 576, pp. 382–3; *Liv-, Est- und Curländ. U.B.* v, no. 2702, cols. 978–9.

[5] *Hans. U.B.* vi, no. 489, p. 276.

[6] *Liv-, Est- und Curländ. U.B.* vii, no. 14, p. 8; *H.R. 1256–1430*, vii, no. 609, p. 419: repeated in 1426, 1434, and 1470.

[7] *H.R. 1256–1430*, vii, no. 800, pp. 544, 547.

would suffer severely. They thus refused to apply the ordinance against the Dutch and merely repeated the prohibition of visits to the interior.[1] Lübeck in vain protested against this separatist policy.[2]

The difficulties in Livonia and at Novgorod were not eased by the restrictions but continued unabated. In the spring of 1424 the German factory at Novgorod reported a glut of cloth such as had never existed before, the cloth being disposed of very cheaply.[3] Although all trade was forbidden by the Livonian towns because of political strife with the Russians, such quantities of goods continued to arrive during 1425 that the trade stoppage proved ineffective; salt was sent via Narva to Polotsk, thus by-passing the Livonian towns.[4] In 1426 more and more merchandise arrived at Novgorod, so that the Russians would not make any concessions to the Livonians.[5] Dutch merchants for the first time penetrated to Novgorod itself. One arrived there in 1426: the Livonian towns considered having his goods confiscated.[6] More Dutchmen came in 1432, two of them bringing about twenty-five *lasts* of herring and selling them to the Russians. Again the towns urged their goods to be confiscated, but the endeavours of the German factory to get at them were unsuccessful.[7] Thus North Sea herring made its appearance in the east,[8] at a time when catches in Scania were very disappointing. In 1440 the Livonian towns complained about the abundance of English cloth in Livonia and at Novgorod.[9] By that time the decline of the Novgorod factory had proceeded further. It was no longer able to pay its priest, for 'few merchants are visiting Novgorod and the factory is decaying from year to year'.[10] This plea was accepted as correct by the Livonian towns; they agreed that the priest should be given half-pay, 'consider-

---

[1] *Liv-, Est- und Curländ. U.B.* vii, no. 412, p. 287.

[2] Ibid., no. 434, p. 301.

[3] Ibid., no. 107, p. 86.

[4] *H.R. 1256–1430*, vii, nos. 828, 836, pp. 590–7.

[5] *Liv-, Est- und Curländ. U.B.* vii, nos. 524, 527, pp. 358–61; *H.R. 1256–1430*, viii, nos. 82, 84, pp. 58–59.

[6] *Liv-, Est- und Curländ. U.B.* vii, nos. 448–9, p. 306.

[7] Ibid. viii, nos. 609, 614, pp. 358, 361; *Hans. U.B.* vi, nos. 1028, 1030, pp. 575–6.

[8] H. J. Smit, *De Opkomst van den Handel van Amsterdam*, 1914, p. 268.

[9] Postan, loc. cit., p. 124.

[10] *Liv-, Est- und Curländ. U.B.* ix, no. 557, pp. 409–10; *H.R. 1431–76*, ii, no. 328, p. 270.

ing that the merchant now comes thither so sickly with his trade'.[1]

In 1441 a merchant complained that his and others' honey was lying unsold at Novgorod, and that the Russians did not buy either salt or herring, unless very cheaply, but only wanted cloth.[2] At the same time the German factory informed Lübeck that its buildings were falling into ruins, as it was impossible to maintain them with the few goods coming there.[3] In the following year the Livonian towns again acknowledged the factory's poverty and its inability to pay the priest.[4] In 1444 they complained anew that the other Hanse towns, disregarding the ban on trade, sent goods into Russia along unusual routes, via Viborg and Abo, through Sweden, and via Polotsk, to the 'inexpressible detriment of the Hanseatics'.[5] Lübeck countered this with the statement that the Livonians themselves sent merchandise to Polotsk, which then went on to Novgorod, in spite of the hostilities between Livonia and Russia.[6] In the next year the Livonian towns had to admit that the Russians suffered no shortages of either salt or cloth, that they had enough money to finance the war, and thus the only thing left was to make peace.[7] The towns' customary weapon against the Russians had become obsolete. When fire destroyed part of the Novgorod factory and its fence in 1453, there was no money to rebuild it:[8] its decline had continued almost uninterruptedly since the beginning of the fifteenth century, long before its final closure by the Russians in 1494, and long before Novgorod's subjugation by Moscow.

The towns of Prussia seem to have been in even worse a plight than those of Livonia, in the first instance owing to the wars with Poland after 1410. In 1422 the towns of Braunsberg, Elbing, Königsberg, and Thorn—the only members of the Hanse apart from Danzig—declared the costs of sending delegates to

[1] *Liv-, Est- und Curländ. U.B.* ix, no. 564, p. 415; *H.R. 1431–76*, ii, no. 331, p. 273.
[2] *Hans. U.B.* vii 1, no. 720, p. 365.
[3] *Liv-, Est- und Curländ. U.B.* ix, no. 753, p. 525.
[4] *Akten und Rezesse der livländ. Ständetage*, i 4, no. 464, p. 439; *H.R. 1431–76*, ii, no. 603, p. 502.
[5] *Liv-, Est- und Curländ. U.B.* x, nos. 1, 14, pp. 1, 6; *H.R. 1431–76*, iii, no. 112, p. 54.
[6] *Liv-, Est- und Curländ. U.B.* x, no. 44, p. 35; *H.R. 1431–76*, iii, no. 155, p. 74.
[7] *Liv-, Est- und Curländ. U.B.* x, no. 184, p. 121; *H.R. 1431–76*, iii, no. 216, p. 116.
[8] *Liv-, Est- und Curländ. U.B.* xi, no. 290, p. 254; *Akten und Rezesse der livländ. Ständetage*, i 5, no. 560, p. 582; *H.R. 1431–76*, iv, nos. 179–80, p. 120.

the Hanseatic diets too heavy for them, as they had little sea-
ward trade, and Braunsberg refused altogether to participate.[1]
In the next year Thorn declined to send one of its aldermen to
the assembly at Wismar.[2] In 1424 Danzig joined in the complaints of the Prussian towns about their plight: they had suffered so much through recent events—probably referring to the
Polish wars—that they were unable to attend the meeting at
Lübeck.[3] During the following years Braunsberg and Königsberg adhered to their resolution not to participate in any meetings outside Prussia, not even by correspondence; and all the
Prussian towns stressed repeatedly that they were too poor to
bear the costs.[4] In 1428 the Grand Master granted Thorn, in
view of 'the ruin and visible decay of the town's inhabitants',
the right of staple for corn and all other goods passing by land
or water,[5] with the result that the trade sought alternative
routes and by-passed Thorn. The town of Breslau defaulted on
the payment of its life-annuities and interest, which hit the
Prussian towns: all their attempts at redress were unsuccessful.[6]
Danzig and other towns also complained about the import of
foreign beer which ruined their brewing industry.[7] In 1436
Danzig had to borrow money to finance an embassy to Flanders,
which it declared a heavy burden and beyond its strength.[8] In
1454 the town in vain tried to raise a loan of 100,000 guilders at
Lübeck.[9] Its population declined considerably during the first
half of the fifteenth century,[10] so that its complaints seem to have
been well-founded.

If Danzig undoubtedly experienced great difficulties, the
smaller Prussian towns entirely lost their importance and their
independent trade.[11] Already in the late fourteenth and early
fifteenth centuries over 70 per cent. of the Prussian trade had

[1] *H.R. 1256–1430*, vii, nos. 461, 467, 559, pp. 279, 283, 358.
[2] Ibid., no. 591, p. 394.
[3] Ibid., nos. 685, 688, pp. 461–4.
[4] Ibid., nos. 773, 790, pp. 520, 534; viii, nos. 41, 132, 295, 395, 433, pp. 29, 88, 204, 257, 290 (1425–8).
[5] *Hans. U.B.* vi, no. 753, p. 428.
[6] *H.R. 1256–1430*, vii, nos. 472, 613, 616, 687, 713; viii, no. 433; *H.R. 1431–76*, i, nos. 342, 459, 503, 507 (1422–36).
[7] *H.R. 1431–76*, i, no. 427, p. 374; ii, no. 99, p. 100 (1435–7).
[8] Ibid. i, no. 515, p. 454.
[9] Ibid. iv, nos. 270, 273–4, 278, 283–4, pp. 199–214.
[10] Abel, op. cit., p. 25.
[11] Daenell, op. cit. ii, pp. 150–1, 195.

passed through Danzig.[1] In the fifteenth century Elbing was completely overshadowed by its greater neighbour. Repeatedly the town, pointing to its decay and poverty, asked for staple and market rights and other restrictive privileges.[2] The town of Culm in 1442 even declined to attend meetings of the Prussian towns because of its poverty: this was partly granted by the other towns.[3] Braunsberg quietly dropped out of the ranks oi the Prussian towns with connexions abroad.[4] Thorn suffered badly from competition by Diebau, on the opposite bank of the Vistula, which gained from Thorn's endeavours to enforce its new staple rights.[5] In 1445 the town maintained it could only muster forty horses for military service, as against 400 in the past.[6] Its cutlery industry was ruined by the import of knives from Nuremberg which were preferred to those made at Thorn.[7] In 1450 the Prussian towns, once again emphasizing their lack of money, declined to finance an embassy to attend the Hanseatic diet at Utrecht.[8] A few years later the outbreak of the Thirteen Years War brought new severe difficulties to the Prussian towns: they had to bear the costs of the war, and their trade suffered. Especially Thorn and Elbing were severely affected by the war;[9] Danzig in 1467 was described as being about one-third deserted;[10] for many years the towns complained about their poverty and their heavy debts.[11] Danzig was unable even to pay the interest on its debts, and many of its creditors had to sell their bonds at a considerable loss.[12]

Growing Dutch competition was shown by more imports of Bay salt which caused a fall in prices. In 1443 40 Dutch ships laden with salt arrived at Danzig, 13 others having been captured by pirates; and in 1449 as many as 108 ships arrived from the Bay. Of these, only 14 were from Danzig, and only 13 from

---

[1] Hirsch, op. cit., pp. 38–39, and P. Simson, *Geschichte der Stadt Danzig*, i, 1913, pp. 100–2, giving the *Pfundzoll* figures for the years 1390 and 1396 ff.

[2] *H.R. 1431–76*, ii, nos. 379, 481, 563, pp. 303, 401, 475 (1440–2).

[3] Ibid., nos. 571, 629, 642, 653, pp. 486–552.

[4] Daenell, op. cit. ii, p. 150.

[5] *Acten der Ständetage Preussens*, iii, no. 51, p. 92; *H.R. 1431–76*, iii, no. 475, p. 365.

[6] *Acten der Ständetage Preussens*, ii, no. 398, p. 639.

[7] *H.R. 1431–76*, iii, no. 273, p. 155.

[8] Ibid., nos. 588–91, p. 444.

[9] Hirsch, op. cit., p. 187; Daenell, op. cit. ii, pp. 152–4, 191, 195.

[10] *Thunert*, no. 6, p. 30.

[11] Ibid., nos. 13, 31, 45, 178, 288, pp. 75–76, 155, 170–2, 405–8, 559 (1468–79).

[12] Simson, op. cit. i, p. 277.

Lübeck, while nearly all the others were Dutch.[1] From Riga it was emphasized several times in 1458 that salt would fetch a good price if the Dutch failed to arrive, that so much salt was brought there that prices fell, and that no business could be done if the Russians did not buy.[2] Indeed, within sixteen days the price of Bay salt dropped by one-third owing to the arrival of the Bay fleet, proving that the writers' fears were justified.[3] At Riga Bay salt was then one-third cheaper than Lüneburg salt.[4] At Königsberg in 1461 Bay salt was at least 15 per cent. cheaper than Lüneburg salt and was therefore preferred by the buyers.[5]

These imports undermined the position of Lüneburg and severely affected that of Lübeck. Lüneburg defaulted on the payment of interest on its rents in which many north-German burghers had invested, so that many found themselves in great difficulties.[6] In 1431 the town's debts amounted to 184,000 marks; by 1448 they had risen to 588,000, and by 1457 to 677,000 marks.[7] Nor did matters improve later. In 1460 a Swedish abbess, who wanted to invest money at Lübeck, was advised by her correspondent not to do so, for things looked very bleak there on account of the Lüneburgers' defaulting which had caused other towns to stop their payments.[8] Two years later it was pointed out in another letter from Lübeck that, without the Lüneburg trade, the Lübeckers might as well leave, and the fair might as well be closed.[9] In 1468 the aldermen of Lüneburg attempted to raise a loan at Lübeck, as they were neither able to pay their debts nor to sell their salt;[10] they begged to have their town's plight considered and have a deferment granted of the payments due.[11] In 1471 King Christian of Den-

---

[1] Daenell, op. cit. i, p. 322; Vollbehr, op. cit., p. 53; Ketner, op. cit., p. 119. Cf. the tables of salt prices in the Appendix.

[2] W. Stein, 'Handelsbriefe aus Riga und Königsberg', *Hansische Geschichtsblätter*, 1898, nos. 15–16, pp. 99–101.

[3] Ibid., nos. 3, 10, 15–16, pp. 78, 90–91, 99, 103.

[4] Ibid., no. 15, p. 99.

[5] Ibid., nos. 23, 25, pp. 113–16.

[6] *U.B. Lübeck*, viii, nos. 544, 550, 558–9, 565, 571, 580, 583, 587, 678, pp. 591–720 (1448–50).

[7] H. Lange, 'De Origine Belli Praelatorum Luneburgici', *Scriptorum Brunsvicensia Illustrantium*, ed. G. W. Leibniz, iii, 1711, p. 239; 'Lübecker Ratschronik', *Die Chroniken der deutschen Städte*, xxx, 1910, pp. 78–79, 173, and n. 4.

[8] *U.B. Lübeck*, ix, no. 893, p. 929.   [9] Ibid. x, no. 222, p. 231.

[10] Ibid. xi, no. 331, p. 347.   [11] Ibid. xi, no. 362, pp. 382–3.

mark prohibited the transit of Bay salt through his dominions, for many churches and monasteries, widows and orphans had invested in Lüneburg life-rents and had suffered severely for many years through the low prices of Lüneburg salt: this was only due to the Dutch shipments of Bay salt which was filling all the eastern lands.[1] In 1472 it was acknowledged anew by Lüneburg's creditors that the low salt prices prevented the town from paying its debts so that it required more financial support.[2]

Dutch activity was not confined to the import of Bay salt and other goods. From the Prussian harbours they went into the interior, and from Prussia into Poland, selling cloth and buying corn.[3] In 1438 the Prussian towns considered how to prevent this.[4] In 1456 Danzig complained about non-Hanseatics using unusual routes which ruined the trade.[5] Five years later Dorpat advocated counter-measures against the Hollanders and other foreigners who pushed aside the Hanseatics.[6] According to Lübeck, the Hanseatics were losing their livelihood to the non-Hanseatics.[7] In 1469 the Prussian towns negotiated with the Polish towns how to prevent the increasing shipments of herring and other merchandise by the Dutch to Cracow and to Breslau.[8] In the same year the Hanse even appealed to the Flemish towns for help against the Dutch, admitting that it was unable to cope with the problem: the Dutch had made such progress that all the business was in their hands.[9] New restrictions against them were adopted in 1470.[10] In 1461, however, Riga as well as the Hanse factory at Bruges declared that they were unable to apply the prohibitions against Dutch shipping, as not enough Hanseatic ships were available for loading, so that they had to use

---

[1] *Hans. U.B.* x, nos. 18, 20, pp. 10–12.

[2] *Die Chroniken der deutschen Städte*, xxxi 1, 1911, p. 97, n. 1.

[3] Hirsch, op. cit., p. 129; Vollbehr, op. cit., p. 34.

[4] *H.R. 1431–76*, ii, nos. 214, 223, pp. 173–80. It was thus not 'by the end of the century' that 'the towns of Prussia themselves began to look with dismay at the Dutch entering Poland', but much earlier than assumed by M. Postan, in *The Cambridge Economic History of Europe*, ii, 1952, p. 256.

[5] *H.R. 1431–76*, iv, no. 455, pp. 319–20.

[6] Ibid. v, no. 87, p. 50.

[7] Ibid. v, no. 70, p. 34.

[8] *Thunert*, no. 23, p. 121. See also *Hans. U.B.* ix, no. 739; x, nos. 82, 759, 801; xi, nos. 22, 349, 830, 1118, 1124 (1470–99) for imports of North Sea herring into Prussia and Poland.

[9] *H.R. 1431–76*, vi, no. 198, p. 180.

[10] Ibid., no. 356, pp. 326–7.

K

Hollanders and others out of necessity.[1] In 1471 Thorn expressed its strong opposition to the prohibition of the transit of
Bay salt and other Dutch merchandise by Denmark at the in-
stigation of the Wendish towns, for the ban would result in grave
danger to the common weal.[2] By that time the Dutch position
in the Baltic was so strong that some eastern towns themselves
demanded the admission of the foreigners; this was also demanded by the nobility and the country districts of Prussia.[3]

The Hanse did not succeed in excluding the Dutch from the
Baltic nor in imposing its restrictions upon them. An attempt to
do so by force was made in the second quarter of the fifteenth
century; but it ended in complete failure and was not repeated.
The war of the Hanse against Holland and Denmark which
broke out in 1427 and continued with some interruptions until
1441 ended in a ten years' truce: this the Hanse, owing to its
exhaustion, was glad to prolong to 1461 and beyond.[4] All the
restrictions introduced recently had to be abrogated and the
Dutch were promised the right of free intercourse as of old.[5]
During the war the volume of trade became so curtailed that
prices rose considerably, that of salt in the east to the advantage
of Lüneburg and Lübeck,[6] that of corn in the west to the detriment of Holland, which also suffered from the falling off of its
export and carrying trade. Yet the Prussian and the Livonian
towns suffered equally from the curtailment of trade and high
import prices. They no longer supported Lübeck and concluded
a separate treaty with Holland: the internal unity of the Hanse
was seriously impaired. Above all, after the restoration of peace
the ephemeral advantages, which Lübeck had enjoyed during
the war through the closing of the Sound and its control of the
land route across Jutland, disappeared again. The Dutch resumed their advance with new impetus, in spite of the re-enact-
ment of the old restrictions by the Hanse.[7] The Dutch had

---

[1] *H.R. 1431–76*, v, nos. 141, 224, pp. 77, 134; *Liv-, Est- und Kurländ. U.B.* xii, no. 112, p. 57.   [2] *H.R. 1431–76*, vi, no. 445, p. 421.

[3] *Acten der Ständetage Preussens*, ii, nos. 323–4, 396, pp. 485–8, 633–4.

[4] A. Weiner, 'The Hansa', *The Cambridge Medieval History*, vii, 1932, p. 235; K. Pagel, *Die Hanse*, 1952, pp. 256, 354.

[5] *H.R. 1431–76*, ii, nos. 491, 494, pp. 425–30; Daenell, op. cit. i, pp. 282–320; Vollbehr, op. cit., p. 45.

[6] See the tables of salt prices in the Appendix.

[7] Vollbehr, op. cit., pp. 45–47; Weiner, loc. cit., pp. 230–5; Ketner, op. cit., pp. 18–20.

gained a decisive victory which they exploited during the following decades. In 1476 Dutch shipping accounted for practically one-quarter of all ships putting into Danzig.[1] In 1497 and in 1503 about 70 per cent. of the ships coming through the Sound were Dutch.[2]

Glimpses of private correspondence between Hanseatic merchants from Riga in 1458 and from Königsberg in 1461 indicate that Dutch competition was not the only cause of trade difficulties. At Riga the trade with the Russians, the town's main activity, was still suffering badly from a glut in cloth. The Russians were only willing to buy English cloth which was cheaper than Flemish.[3] Few Russians and Latvians visited Riga; many *terling* of cloth were returned unsold from Polotsk and could not be sold at Riga either.[4] The trade in fur was equally bad, as there was no demand for it in Flanders, so that the merchants suffered heavy losses.[5] From Königsberg thirty months later merchants reported that business was bad, that it was impossible to get money, that their salt, herring, cloth, iron, lime were all unsold, that all prices were low, and that they could only sell on credit.[6] In 1459 it was similarly emphasized in a letter to Reval that it was impossible to sell salt or herring, and that the writer would have left long ago if he could have sold at a profit.[7] From Reval a merchant wrote in 1470 that he could not sell the timber which he had received and that such quantities were lying there that a hundred ships could not carry it away.[8]

The Hanse towns sought shelter from increasing competition and mounting difficulties behind a growing wall of restrictions. In 1435 Danzig forbade all foreigners to trade with other guests or to visit the interior, while hitherto its policy had been much more liberal and many foreigners had been treated like Hanseatics. In 1441 all trading between guest and guest and their

---

[1] 156 Dutch ships out of a total of 629: V. Lauffer, 'Danzigs Schiffs- und Warenverkehr am Ende des XV. Jahrhunderts', *Zeitschrift des Westpreussischen Geschichtsvereins*, xxxiii, 1894, pp. 7–8.

[2] *Bang*, i, pp. 2–3: these are the two first Sound registers which have been preserved.

[3] *Stein*, nos. 10, 13, pp. 91, 95.

[4] Ibid., nos. 11, 14, 16–18, pp. 91–92, 98, 101, 104, 106.

[5] Ibid., no. 16, p. 101.

[6] *U.B. Lübeck*, x, no. 8, p. 6; *Stein*, nos. 21, 25, pp. 110, 115–16.

[7] *Liv-, Est- und Kurländ. U.B.* xi, no. 840, p. 656.

[8] Ibid. xii, no. 749, p. 416.

participation in the retail trade were finally forbidden; guests were ordered not to import any goods but their own and the produce of their own countries, this being plainly directed against the Dutch carrying trade.[1] In 1435 Hamburg ordered all guests to offer their goods publicly for sale for three days during which they were forbidden to trade with each other. About the middle of the fifteenth century a compulsory staple for corn was established there.[2] At Lübeck it was decreed at the same time that no guest was to buy anything from a guest that had not been offered for sale for eight days, and no burgher was to buy on behalf of a guest during that time; all goods imported by guests were to be put into a closed cellar in the house of a host where they could be controlled.[3] About 1459 Riga also banned the trading of guest with guest, on account of its burghers' strong complaints about foreign competition.[4] Thereafter trade on the Dvina dwindled, and the German factory at Polotsk lost its importance, for even the inhabitants of Riga ceased to visit it.[5] Thorn's staple was confirmed in 1457 by its new master, King Casimir of Poland: all merchants travelling through Poland were to use the roads via Thorn and no others.[6] Thus the Hanse towns enforced staple rights, treated even fellow Hanseatics like foreigners, and excluded them from the privileges enjoyed by their own citizens.

This policy merely aggravated the evils it was supposed to cure. It was impossible to canalize trade through a growing number of staple towns with their rigorous restrictions: trade sought alternative routes, for many merchants did not abide by these regulations, and the Hanseatics themselves suffered under them. Such a policy was perhaps feasible at a time of trade contraction: it was bound to be fatal during a period of expansion which began in the sixteenth century.

The commercial difficulties were increased by the sharp

---

[1] Hirsch, op. cit., pp. 129, 230–1; Vollbehr, op. cit., p. 34; Hans. U.B. x, p. 608, n. 2.

[2] Stein, op. cit., p. 49; Vollbehr, op. cit., p. 33.

[3] U.B. Lübeck, vi, no. 784, pp. 763–4.

[4] Akten und Rezesse der livländ. Ständetage, ii 1, nos. 1–3, pp. 1–4; U.B. Lübeck, ix, no. 813, p. 843; H.R. 1431–76, iv, no. 764, p. 533.

[5] H. Hildebrand, 'Das deutsche Kontor zu Polozk', Baltische Monatsschrift, xxii, 1873, p. 380; H. G. von Schroeder, 'Der Handel auf der Düna im Mittelalter', Hansische Geschichtsblätter, xxiii, 1917, p. 155.

[6] Hans. U.B. viii, no. 626, p. 404: repeated in 1469, 1474, 1477, 1485, and 1496.

fluctuations of prices.[1] In Prussia, for example, prices were remarkably stable up to 1410; then they began to rise sharply and the fluctuations became very marked. The date itself points to the primary cause: the beginning of the wars against Poland. Another cause was the severe debasement of the Prussian coinage which was due to the wars and the decline of the Teutonic Order. After the sharp rise of prices in the second decade of the fifteenth century, most prices continued, with many fluctuations, at this higher level. If, however, the debasement of the coinage is taken into account, the prices of most commodities, whether imported or exported, declined gradually, so that by the mid-fifteenth century many were no higher than at the beginning of the century. If bad harvests causing high corn prices, or bad catches driving up herring prices, or trade stoppages causing high salt prices for a limited period, are neglected, the general trend of the prices of more than twenty commodities studied seems to have been roughly parallel. Thus the evidence available from Prussia does not point to falling agrarian and rising industrial and import prices, which allegedly created such great economic difficulties in the fifteenth century.[2] Although it was sometimes said at Danzig that it was difficult to get butter,[3] its prices also do not indicate any rise more marked than those of the other commodities.[4] The price of herring in 1416 was well over four times that obtaining earlier in the century because the catches in Scania were very poor after 1411;[5] but by the 1450's its price was also back at the former level if the debasement of the coinage is taken into account, probably because of better catches and the imports of North Sea herring from Holland mentioned above.

The decline of the Hanseatic towns on the Baltic has been

---

[1] For this paragraph, see the price tables in the Appendix.

[2] H. Cunow, *Allgemeine Wirtschaftsgeschichte*, iii, 1929, p. 50; Abel, op. cit., pp. 84–85, 89–91, 164, and *Agrarkrisen und Agrarkonjunktur in Mitteleuropa*, 1935, pp. 33–35; M. Postan, in *IXᵉ Congrès International des Sciences Historiques*, i, 1950, pp. 229, 231.

[3] *Veckinchusen*, no. 115, p. 139 (1416).

[4] As asserted by J. Schreiner, *Pest og Prisfall i Senmiddelalderen*, Oslo, 1948, pp. 10 ff., 82, and M. Postan, in *The Cambridge Economic History of Europe*, ii, pp. 209–10: both refer to J. Pelc, *Ceny w Krakowie w latach 1369–1600*, Lwów, 1935; but Pelc, p. 30, quotes no butter prices at all between 1420 and 1468. The few fifteenth-century butter prices which he quotes indicate sharp fluctuations rather than a general upward trend.

[5] Daenell, op. cit. i, p. 269; Postan, loc. cit. ii, p. 201.

attributed to the migration of the herring from the Baltic which is said to have ruined the Scanian trade. Some fifteenth-century chroniclers, indeed, lamented the disappearance of the herring and believed it to have been the cause of the rise of the Dutch;[1] but the Hanseatic documents do not corroborate this opinion. Catches in Scania varied from year to year.[2] In the late fifteenth century other chroniclers lamented the glut in herring there which caused prices to fall sharply, so that the fish repeatedly had to be thrown back into the sea.[3] Thus the chroniclers' statement that the herring never returned to Scania can be disproved. In 1463 more than 20,000 people are reported to have congregated there,[4] another sign that the herring catches must again have been considerable, which is also indicated by the fall in prices after 1430. In this field also the decisive factors seem to have been the successful competition of the Dutch and their improved methods of catching, gutting, and curing, rather than any natural phenomena.[5]

The decline of the Baltic towns was certainly not caused by events which occurred at the very end of the fifteenth or in the sixteenth century, such as the closing of the German factory at Novgorod by the Russians in 1494, the discoveries and the shifting of the trade routes to the Atlantic seaboard, or the rise and the successful competition of the nobility: this did not become a cause for complaint by the towns until the early sixteenth century,[6] while the trade with the Indies became important only at a much later time. The rise of the south-German towns can only have affected the northern towns indirectly, as most of their trade was seawards, and as they exported bulky commodities which could not be sent by alternative routes.

[1] 'Rufus Chronik' and 'Chronik des Dominikaners Hermann Korner', in *Die Chroniken der deutschen Städte*, xxviii, 1902, pp. 226–7. Already Hirsch, op. cit., p. 146, n. 356, and D. Schäfer, *Das Buch des lübeckischen Vogts auf Schonen*, 1887, pp. xl–xlii, have criticized this opinion, but legends are slow to die.

[2] Postan, loc. cit. ii, p. 201.

[3] *Caspar Weinreichs Danziger Chronik*, ed. T. Hirsch and F. A. Vossberg, 1855, pp. 39, 45, 80, 84–85; E. Assmann, *Stettins Seehandel und Seeschifffahrt im Mittelalter*, 1951, p. 26; Hirsch, op. cit., p. 146, n. 356.

[4] *H.R. 1431–76*, v, no. 369, p. 257.

[5] Daenell, 'Der Ostseeverkehr und die Hansestädte', *Hansische Geschichtsblätter*, x, 1903, p. 15; J. Romein, *De Lage Landen bij de Zee*, p. 132.

[6] *Akten und Rezesse der livländ. Ständetage*, iii, nos. 53–54, 89, 109–10, 136, 302, pp. 188–776; *H.R. 1477–1530*, vi, nos. 188, 522, 585, pp. 140, 485, 548; vii, nos. 370–1, 413, pp. 664–740; *H.R. 1531–60*, i, nos. 350, 413–14, pp. 363–91 (1511–35).

On the positive side, important causes of the decline of the Baltic towns were the trade contraction and the agrarian crisis of the fifteenth century, the competition of the Dutch and others, the wars, invasions, feuds, and robberies of the period, the defeat and decline of the Teutonic Knights, and last but not least their own restrictive regulations which they were unable to enforce. That this was not a general tendency of the time is proved by Nuremberg which flourished under a liberal trade policy in the fifteenth century.[1] Perhaps even more remarkable was the inability of the Baltic towns to recover in the sixteenth century, in contrast with western European towns which had equally suffered in the fifteenth. In the east decline developed into decay, and this lasted until the nineteenth century. The only exceptions were some towns outside Germany, such as Riga and Danzig, which acquired a virtual monopoly of the export and import trade of their wide hinterland. Danzig greatly benefited from its dominating position at the mouth of the Vistula and the growing corn exports of Poland;[2] and the same applied to Riga at the mouth of the Dvina. The German towns' inability to recover, even at a time of expansion and boom, also points to fundamental defects within the Hanse, rather than to extraneous events, as the ultimate cause of its decline. It was perhaps natural that the Hanse attempted to preserve a monopoly market, to restrict trade to certain places and to certain routes, to enforce privileges for the benefit of a narrow merchant aristocracy; but such attempts were bound to fail in the changing circumstances of the fifteenth and sixteenth centuries.

The decay of the eastern towns was a fact of fundamental importance for the course of German and of European history. It opened the way for the rise of the nobility, and it separated events in the east from those in the west: there the renewed rise of the towns and of the urban middle classes transformed state and society, but the east no longer participated in this development.

[1] J. Müller, 'Die Handelspolitik Nürnbergs im Spätmittelalter', *Jahrbücher für Nationalökonomie und Statistik*, xciii, 1909, pp. 599–602.

[2] Simson, op. cit. i, pp. 301–2; J. Pelc, *Ceny w Gdańsku w XVI i XVII Wieku*, Lwów, 1937, p. 172; *The Cambridge History of Poland (to 1696)*, pp. 249, 447–8.

X

The Subjugation of the Brandenburg and Pomeranian Towns

IN the fifteenth century the violent conflicts between patricians and plebeians, which were so characteristic of medieval town life, continued unabated. As trade was the most important economic activity of the eastern towns, and as they depended on their membership of the Hanse, none of the revolts against the ruling merchant aristocracies was successful for any length of time, in contrast to similar movements elsewhere. The aristocracies' rule was equally upheld by the territorial princes; they saw in the internal unrest prevalent in so many towns an opportunity to extend their sway over them, to deprive them of their privileges, and to strengthen their own power. This intervention of the rulers was a new factor which strongly influenced the outcome of the struggle and was to have grave consequences for the towns. In Brandenburg a new and ambitious ruling house, the Hohenzollerns, thus seized a chance of reasserting princely power in a territory from which it had almost disappeared in the course of the fourteenth century. From their south-German lands they were accustomed to long-drawn-out conflicts with the great Imperial city of Nuremberg; they soon transferred this anti-urban bias to Brandenburg where the towns were much younger and weaker than they were in southern Germany.

Already the son of the first Hohenzollern margrave, John, governor of the Mark in his father's place, was called upon to decide conflicts between the burghers and the aldermen in several Brandenburg towns. At Prenzlau the commons expelled the patricians from the council and attempted to rule themselves. The margrave, however, in 1426 decided that their complaints were unfounded; he appointed a new council which was to select its own successors, admonished the burghers to be obedient to it in future, and forbade oppositional meetings and alliances.[1]

---

[1] *Riedel*, xxi, nos. 219–20, pp. 260–2; 'Magdeburger Schöppenchronik', *Die Chroniken der deutschen Städte*, vii, 1869, p. 374.

Several of the leaders of the commons were executed.[1] In the following year the margrave in a similar way intervened in the Neustadt of Brandenburg: the mayors and aldermen were to retain their full powers and were to render an account of the town's income and expenditure every year to sixteen burghers selected by themselves; in case of any disagreement the ultimate decision rested with the margrave.[2] At Stendal, which had been the centre of lower-class unrest in the fourteenth century,[3] a new revolt of the lower guilds, especially the clothmakers, broke out in 1429. Margrave John had two clothmakers executed, while others were banished for ever from the town and country. The clothmakers had to promise not to hold any meetings concerned with their ruler or the town council, nor to increase their masters' number above a hundred, and only to accept their own children as guild members. All guilds and the commons had to take an oath of fealty and obedience to the margrave and the aldermen, against whom they would never make any alliance or ordinance; only the patricians and clothiers were exonerated from any blame for the revolt.[4] In the same year dissension between the aldermen and the guilds and commons occurred in the Neustadt of Salzwedel: the margrave enjoined the lower orders to remain obedient in future to the aldermen.[5] In 1438 Margrave Frederick appeared in person at Salzwedel and repeated this admonition,[6] as it seems because new unrest had broken out. Thus the first Hohenzollern margraves maintained the rule of the patricians and at the same time strengthened their own power, making the latter dependent on the rulers' support.

The struggle between the ruler and the twin towns of Berlin and Cölln broke out under Margrave Frederick II who came to the throne in 1440. It seems that already then he was envisaging the possibility of such a conflict, for when confirming the rights and privileges of the two towns, he only did so 'with simple words' and did not vow it to the saints, as the custom was, before the town rendered homage to him.[7] In 1432 the

---

[1] F. Priebatsch, *Die Hohenzollern und die Städte der Mark im 15. Jahrhundert*, 1892, p. 61.

[2] *Riedel*, ix, no. 164, p. 129.   [3] See above, pp. 86-87.

[4] *Riedel*, xv, nos. 286-8, pp. 230-3; xvi, no. 60, p. 52; Götze, op. cit., pp. 192-6.

[5] *Riedel*, xiv, no. 314, p. 245.   [6] Ibid., no. 333, p. 262.

[7] Ibid., D i, p. 304; *Fidicin*, i, pp. 252-3: note of Berlin's town clerk.

aldermen of Berlin and Cölln reunited the two towns into one with a common town hall, council and court, but without conceding to the guilds any share in the town government.[1] Over these questions friction soon arose which Frederick used to his advantage. In 1442 the guilds and commons appealed to him and begged him to revoke the amalgamation of the two towns and to reinstall separate councils in them. In February he appeared with armed might inside the town, had the keys to the town gates delivered to him, and appointed a new council, one for each town. He decreed that after twelve months each council was to select a new one, above all from the guilds and commons, and to submit the names to him for his approval: for these he could substitute others according to his pleasure. All alliances of the two towns with others inside and outside the country were declared null and void.[2] Six months later Berlin and Cölln had to cede to the margrave their common town hall, the higher and lower jurisdiction, the right of electing their own judges, their staple right, and a site at Cölln for the erection of a castle.[3] They thus lost their most important privileges, their alliances with the other Brandenburg towns and with the Hanse, and their independence. Frederick also forbade his other towns to send delegates to the Hanseatic diets.[4] In the following year Salzwedel excused its absence from the diet at Lüneburg with the 'great invasion which has overcome us'.[5]

The conflict between Frederick and Berlin, however, was not yet at an end. In 1443 the margrave laid the first stone for his new castle at Cölln.[6] This building arising before their eyes aroused the burghers' wrath: for them it was a symbol of the loss of their ancient liberty.[7] Early in 1448 they attempted to flood the foundations by opening a sluice in the town moat and refused to close it when ordered to do so.[8] They arrested and

---

[1] *Riedel*, xii, no. 38, pp. 510–11; *Das Stadtbuch des alten Köln an der Spree*, ed. P. Clauswitz, 1921, p. 43.

[2] *Riedel*, Supplement, no. 88, pp. 287–90; *Fidicin*, ii, no. 126, pp. 180–6; *Das Stadtbuch des alten Köln*, pp. 43–44.

[3] *Von Raumer*, i, no. 67, pp. 207–8.

[4] *Voigt*, p. 387, note.

[5] *Fidicin*, iv, no. 171, p. 176; *Voigt*, no. 111, p. 387.

[6] *Voigt*, no. 112, p. 388.

[7] A. Krantz, *Wandalia*, Cologne, 1519, lib. xii, cap. x; A. Angelus, *Annales Marchiae Brandenburgicae*, Frankfurt on Oder, 1598, p. 214.

[8] *Fidicin*, ii, no. 136, p. 197.

imprisoned the margrave's judge and declined to release him; other followers of the prince were expelled from the town.[1] Finally, the people's fury exploded in an attack on the princely residence: its doors were forced, the archives were ransacked, and letters and documents were destroyed or stolen.[2] Both sides then prepared for war and looked for allies. Berlin and Cölln tried to restore their old alliances with the other towns, asked them for help against Frederick and denounced him everywhere, at Lübeck, Hamburg, Lüneburg, and Magdeburg, as a violator of their liberties and rights.[3] Whether the Hanseatic towns replied at all to this request, is not known. In Brandenburg only a few small towns, Mittenwalde, Neu-Ruppin, and Perleberg, promised help; while Prenzlau offered its services in vague terms.[4] The other towns did not reply or refused help. Frederick in his turn travelled from town to town; everywhere he addressed the burghers in moving words, submitted to them his plea against Berlin, and asked for their help against the rebels. The towns of Bernau and Spandau, both near Berlin and perhaps jealous of its greater wealth and power, were the first to promise him assistance; other towns followed suit and sent men-at-arms to Frederick who was assembling his forces at Spandau.[5]

Certain of the support of the nobility and of many towns, the margrave proposed that 3 prelates, 2 noblemen, and 4 burghers should adjudicate in the quarrel between him and Berlin. The town at first refused, but in May 1448, deserted by its allies and threatened by the hostile forces, it had to accept the judgment of this court. It sat at Spandau and heard Frederick describe all the crimes of Berlin and his own forbearance and kindness.[6] Its verdict confirmed the decisions of 1442 in every point: Frederick retained the castle, the court and the jurisdiction, the staple right, the tolls and mills, the town hall, and the right of appointing the aldermen in the two towns which were again separated; they had to vow obedience to their ruler and faithful observance of the letters of 1442.[7] In addition many burghers

---

[1] Ibid., no. 141, p. 211; iii, no. 401, p. 329; *Riedel*, Supplement, no. 93, p. 294.

[2] *Fidicin*, ii, no. 140, p. 208.

[3] Ibid., nos. 140-1, pp. 206-12; *H.R. 1431-76*, vii, no. 531, p. 842.

[4] *Riedel*, iv, no. 53, p. 336; xi, no. 28, p. 245; *Fidicin*, ii, no. 138, p. 199; iii, p. 330; iv, nos. 173-4, pp. 177-8.   [5] *Riedel*, xii, no. 67, pp. 328-9.

[6] *Fidicin*, ii, nos. 140-1, pp. 200-13.

[7] *Von Raumer*, i, nos. 68-69, pp. 209-12.

were punished individually. One after the other they had to appear before the margrave at Spandau and put into his hands all their own and their wives' properties. They lost their estates and fiefs, or at least half of them, and had to pay heavy fines, ranging from 100 to 3,000 guilders; several were banished from the town.[1] In later years some of the burghers, after humble supplication, had their sentences reduced or remitted.[2] From then onwards the margrave appointed the aldermen in both towns.[3] Their opposition was finally broken; deprived of their self-government and of their commercial privileges, they became weak and unimportant, and never again opposed their ruler. In 1452 they resigned from the Hanse because it had not helped them against the margrave, and thus lost the still valuable contacts with the League.[4]

The other Hanseatic towns of Brandenburg, especially those of the Old Mark and Frankfurt, were so frightened by Frederick's victory that they did not attend the diet of 1450 either.[5] Twice more he intervened in internal conflicts in the towns, protecting the rule of the aldermen and strengthening his power. In 1467 he abolished the assessors, hitherto appointed by the commons of Potsdam to assist the aldermen, and threatened dire punishments for any attack against the latter.[6] In the next year he punished the rebellious guilds of Gardelegen and restored the authority of the aldermen over them; the guild wardens had to swear obedience to him and to the council.[7] Thus the second Hohenzollern margrave reasserted princely authority over the towns which had enjoyed almost independence, thanks to their alliances with each other and their membership of the Hanse. The League apparently did not realize the importance of the issue: from its point of view Brandenburg was of secondary interest, especially as it was faced with other and graver problems in its main field of interest at the same time.[8]

---

[1] *Fidicin*, ii, no. 142, pp. 214–17.

[2] Ibid., no. 144, pp. 219–20; *Riedel*, Supplement, no. 97, p. 296; *von Raumer*, i, no. 114, p. 243.

[3] *Fidicin*, ii, nos. 143, 145, 147, pp. 218–26; *von Raumer*, i, no. 70, p. 213; ii, no. 21, p. 19 (1449–76).

[4] *H.R. 1431–76*, vii, no. 531, p. 842; H. Rachel, *Die Handels-, Zoll- und Akzise-politik Brandenburg-Preussens bis 1713*, 1911, p. 5.

[5] *H.R. 1431–76*, iii, nos. 649, 672, pp. 485, 512.

[6] *Riedel*, xi, no. 37, p. 182.

[7] Priebatsch, op. cit., pp. 82, 105.   [8] See above, p. 130.

While Berlin had been subjugated, the leading towns of Brandenburg, those of the Old Mark, retained their independent position. The conflict between them and the margrave began under Frederick's brother and successor, Albert, who had been engaged in great struggles with the Imperial city of Nuremberg, but had been unable to reduce it.[1] Friction arose as soon as the Old Mark towns took the oath of allegiance to the new ruler in 1471: Stendal was careful enough to have its privileges confirmed first, while Salzwedel was less cautious and therefore had to pay for the confirmation.[2] The next ten years were filled by a dispute between the margrave and the towns over the payment of his debts amounting to 100,000 guilders. In 1472 Albert proposed to a diet held at Berlin to raise the sum by an excise on the brewing and sale of beer. The towns which possessed a very important brewing industry were highly indignant and opposed the plan vigorously, but the prelates and the nobility were in favour. Owing to the towns' opposition the project had to be dropped for the time being. It was then agreed that the prelates and nobility should raise 30,000, the towns 50,000, and the margrave himself 20,000 guilders, the towns contributing the lion's share and more than was customary.[3] After a few weeks Albert recalled the Estates and informed them that he would raise his share of 20,000 guilders by a new toll on merchandise from which prelates and noblemen would be exempted for their own goods and produce. The towns naturally rejected this; but early in 1473 a court of the Estates, with a large majority of assessors from the higher orders, decided in favour of the margrave.[4] A few weeks later another court, similarly composed, found against the towns of the Old Mark and the Priegnitz which now refused to contribute their share of the 50,000 guilders promised by the towns.[5]

The towns' resistance continued in spite of the verdict. In those of the Old Mark open revolts broke out when Albert attempted to install the collectors of the new toll, so that the attempt had to be abandoned. Throughout the Old Mark the

---

[1] G. Schrötter, 'Nürnbergs wirtschaftlicher und finanzieller Niedergang', *Historisch-politische Blätter für das katholische Deutschland*, cxl, 1907, p. 337.

[2] *Riedel*, xiv, no. 420, p. 349.

[3] Ibid., no. 420, pp. 350–1; C ii, nos. 63, 72, pp. 62, 73.

[4] Ibid., C ii, no. 72, pp. 72–75; xiv, nos. 420, 426, pp. 351–7.

[5] Ibid., C ii, no. 75, p. 89.

burghers stood on guard and prepared for armed resistance. At Stendal they threatened to cut off the heads of the princely councillors believed to be responsible for the toll.[1] Encouraged by this attitude several towns of the Middle Mark withdrew their promise to give the new toll. At Frankfurt, whose trade on the Oder was threatened, the commons demanded that one of their number should be sent to the margrave to re-nounce the toll. Instead of its quota of forty men-at-arms the town only sent twelve and declared it would not send any in future unless the toll were abolished. At Havelberg, in the Priegnitz, the collectors were chased away. The other Priegnitz towns equally refused and declared they would rather suffer for their refusal as God wished. In Pomerania it was rumoured that the Brandenburg towns had agreed to refuse their ruler any military aid until the toll was rescinded.[2] Only Berlin did not join the opposition. Eventually the Old Mark towns bought their freedom from the new toll for 6,000, and the Priegnitz towns for 1,500 guilders:[3] to that extent their resistance was successful.

In 1480 Albert demanded new financial support from the Estates. The prelates and the nobility again suggested an excise on beer. But the urban representatives declared that their burghers would never agree and refused anything to be put on beer.[4] The towns of the Middle Mark were willing to grant the usual *Bede*, but the Old Mark towns declined to make any grant on account of their poverty. Thereupon Margrave John, gover-nor of the Mark in his father's place, summoned them to appear before a court of the Estates of the Middle Mark and simul-taneously informed them that this court would decide even in their absence.[5] The Estates of the Old Mark then offered him half the usual *Bede* if he dropped the case.[6] This offer John refused and the case was heard, although the Old Mark towns disputed the court's competence and demanded trial before the prelates and nobility of the Old Mark. The margrave brought up all his complaints against the Old Mark towns, especially

[1] *Riedel*, xiv, no. 428, p. 359; C ii, nos. 87, 91, pp. 101, 113.
[2] Ibid., B v, nos. 1939–40, 1945–7, 1950, 1952, pp. 205–33; C ii, no. 87, p. 101.
[3] Ibid., i, no. 114, p. 194; Priebatsch, op. cit., p. 144 (1476).
[4] *Riedel*, C ii, no. 196, pp. 246–8; *von Raumer*, ii, no. 50, pp. 47–48.
[5] *Riedel*, C ii, no. 205, p. 257; *von Raumer*, ii, no. 57, p. 55.
[6] *Von Raumer*, ii, no. 60, p. 57.

against Stendal, the centre of all resistance. He accused them of minting when minting was forbidden, of prohibiting their burghers from seeking justice in his court, of holding court whenever they pleased, of trying all cases themselves, and in general of usurping judicial rights.[1] The court of the Estates, again composed of a large majority of noblemen, decided in favour of the margrave: he was empowered to confiscate the goods and property of the Old Mark towns until they paid their share of the tax.[2] The conflict continued into the following year. The prelates and nobility of the Old Mark then separated from their towns and declared their willingness to pay if the towns did so.[3] Finally these agreed to pay 13,000 of the 17,000 guilders demanded by the margrave, and this compromise was accepted by the latter.[4]

In 1486 John succeeded his father as ruler of Brandenburg, and soon the struggle between him and the Old Mark towns broke out afresh. Early in 1488 he asked the Estates for a new money grant. The prelates and nobility as well as the towns of the Middle Mark and Priegnitz consented to an excise on beer of twelve pfennigs a tun for seven years. The agreement of the higher orders was won by the provision that the beer brewed by them in their castles and houses was to be exempt; while that of the towns may have been secured by granting them one-third of the levy for their own purposes.[5] Perhaps the aldermen of the Old Mark towns would also have been won over by this promise: this was prevented by an uprising of the guilds and commons of the Old Mark towns against the margrave, the nobility, and the aldermen, against their enemies within and without the gates; they suspected them of collusion in the excise question which was vital for the economic welfare of the towns. Stendal again took the lead. The guilds of the clothmakers, furriers, shoemakers, bakers, and linenweavers, which were excluded from the council, rose and compelled the aldermen to a promise that they would resist the excise and to other concessions.[6] Then the burghers attacked and pillaged noble estates near Stendal, took several noblemen prisoners, arrested others when they rode into Stendal to redeem their property, and tried and executed three

---

[1] Ibid., nos. 59, 63, pp. 56–60. [2] Ibid., nos. 58, 63, pp. 56, 60.
[3] Ibid., no. 65, p. 62. [4] *Riedel*, C ii, no. 217, pp. 267–8.
[5] Ibid., no. 265, pp. 333–6. [6] Ibid. xv, no. 452, p. 408.

noblemen.[1] The burghers of Salzwedel also marched against the nobility, burned and looted their estates, and put several noblemen to death. Then, however, they sent messengers to the margrave asking for clemency and delivering themselves into his hands. When John was already on his way to Salzwedel, another outbreak occurred against the convent of the Holy Ghost outside the gates which was occupied with armed force.[2] Similar risings against the margrave and the aldermen took place in the other Old Mark towns, but apparently not leading to an attack on the nobility.[3]

Thus the margrave, secure of the support of the nobility, could finally reduce the towns of the Old Mark. In April 1488 he appeared with his forces before Stendal which did not attempt to resist. The town had to surrender all its ancient privileges: that of not being obliged to render military aid outside the town walls, that of being entitled to choose another ruler if oppressed by the margrave, the higher and lower jurisdiction, the unions and alliances with other towns, and the right of free election of its aldermen: from then onwards the margrave was to appoint the aldermen, exactly as at Berlin. The excise on beer had to be granted to him for fourteen instead of seven years, and its amount was also doubled. The five rebellious guilds lost their guild status and rights:[4] these were retained only by the ruling guilds of the merchants, clothiers, and butchers which had taken no part in the revolt.[5] Three ringleaders were beheaded and many burghers were banished from the town.[6] All the burghers on their knees had to swear obedience to the margrave and the aldermen, who ruled the town on his behalf, and to vow never again to plot against them.[7] A few days later Salzwedel made its submission and surrendered its privileges and the keys to the town gates. It lost its rights of jurisdiction and of free election of its aldermen; it had to grant the double excise for fourteen years; the houses standing too close to the princely castle had to be demolished, and a passage from it into the town was to be

[1] *Riedel*, xv, nos. 451–2, 477–9, pp. 407–30.
[2] Ibid. xiv, no. 496, p. 422.
[3] Ibid. vi, no. 212, p. 149; nos. 69–70, pp. 384–5; no. 52, p. 431; p. 432, n.
[4] Ibid. xv, no. 452, pp. 408–10.
[5] Ibid. xv, nos. 456–7, pp. 413–14; xxv, no. 333, p. 430.
[6] Götze, op. cit., p. 237; Priebatsch, op. cit., p. 171; *Riedel*, xv, no. 459, p. 416.
[7] *Riedel*, xv, no. 452, pp. 408–10.

built.[1] Two burghers were executed.[2] The smaller towns of the
Old Mark also had to give up their privileges and rights, to
sign similar documents of submission, and to agree to pay the
excise and, in some cases, heavy fines.[3] The political and economic strength of the Old Mark towns was broken for good; they
were cowed and soon lost their importance and their influence.

A few years later Margrave John consummated his victory of
1488 by trenchant interventions in the two towns of the Middle
Mark which stood next to Berlin in importance. In 1490 he
decreed that the guilds of the Neustadt of Brandenburg were no
longer to summon the burghers to the town hall, nor to negotiate
with the guilds of the Altstadt; for he would protect and maintain the aldermen and would not allow the guilds to dominate
them or to rule in their place.[4] In 1496 Frankfurt had to surrender the highest jurisdiction which it had acquired more than
a century earlier; in future its aldermen were to be appointed
by the margrave, and its taxes were increased.[5] In neither case
was any revolt or resistance mentioned which might have induced the margrave to intervene.

Thus the authority of the ruler was enforced in all the more
important towns of Brandenburg. The other towns were small
market towns whose main livelihood was agriculture, and many
of them were sinking down to the position of villages. In the
large towns the weak resistance against the encroachments of
the prince and of the nobility was due in the first instance to
their isolation and their internal conflicts, but also to their
general decline and their great economic difficulties in the
fifteenth century. By the early sixteenth century this decline had
progressed so far that Salzwedel, Stendal, and Berlin withdrew
finally from the Hanse and were declared non-Hanseatics in
1517; so was Frankfurt in 1525.[6] Thus the relations between the
League and the Brandenburg towns came to an end.

[1] *Riedel*, xiv, no. 496, pp. 419–23.   [2] Götze, op. cit., p. 243.
[3] Gardelegen, Osterburg, Seehausen, Tangermünde, and Werben: *Riedel*, vi,
no. 212, pp. 149–51; no. 69, p. 384; no. 52, pp. 431–2; xvi, p. 118, n.
[4] *Von Raumer*, ii, no. 87, p. 83; *Riedel*, ix, no. 314, pp. 241–2.
[5] *Riedel*, xxiii, nos. 176, 366–7, pp. 125, 305–7; Priebatsch, op. cit., pp. 173–4.
[6] *H.R. 1477–1530*, vii, nos. 39, 108, pp. 61, 176; ix, no. 132, p. 260. Berlin after
its subjugation had never again attended a Hanse diet, but had remained a member
of the League: W. Stein, 'Die Hansestädte', *Hansische Geschichtsblätter*, xxi, 1915, p.
133; E. Kaeber, 'Die Beziehungen zwischen Berlin und Cölln im Mittelalter', ibid.
liv, 1929, pp. 87–88.

Similar conflicts between the dukes and their towns occurred in Pomerania. As early as 1428 Duke Casimir used internal unrest at Stettin to enforce his will upon the town. The commons demanded that the aldermen should account for the urban revenues and for a tax levied against the Hussites at the duke's request. The two mayors, who refused to do so, had to quit Stettin and begged Casimir for help. The duke appeared with armed force in Stettin, but was driven out by the armed burghers who, 'with Hussite ferocity', threatened to kill him; but he succeeded in re-entering the town and then reinstituted the aldermen. The ringleaders were broken on the wheel; the town was fined heavily and had to leave the Hanse; a ducal castle was built which would control and hold down Stettin.[1] It thus experienced exactly the same fate which befell Berlin some years later.

In 1478 the two Pomeranian duchies were reunited by Duke Bogislav X who showed the same anti-urban tendencies as the Brandenburg Hohenzollerns and many other princes of the time. In 1486–7 he helped the dukes of Brunswick against Hildesheim and other towns and the dukes of Mecklenburg against Rostock. In 1490 he began to build a new castle at Stettin which aroused great opposition. The quarrel between him and the town was settled in his favour: Stettin had to pay higher taxes and a fine for minting debased coins, and had to give up its right of legal appeals to Magdeburg.[2] A new conflict broke out in 1502 because Stettin refused to sell the duke property required for an extension of the castle and to hand over to him one of his servants who had committed a breach of the peace within the town and thus came under its jurisdiction. Bogislav blockaded Stettin by land and water until the burghers begged for mercy on their knees. They had to give up the ducal servant, to cede the required property without compensation, to pay a fine, and to depose their mayor and jurymen.[3] All Pomeranian towns, after an initial refusal, had to agree to pay the duke tolls increased threefold in 1498, only Stralsund being successful in

---

[1] Kantzow, *Pomerania*, ed. 1908, i, pp. 347–8, 351–2; Barthold, op. cit. iv 1, pp. 83–85; Kratz, op. cit., pp. 391–2; Wehrmann, op. cit. i, p. 200.

[2] Kantzow, op. cit. ii, pp. 50–51; von Bilow, op. cit., pp. 244–6; Barthold, op. cit. iv 1, pp. 486–7; Kratz, op. cit., p. 395; Wehrmann, op. cit. i, p. 245.

[3] Kantzow, op. cit. ii, pp. 86–87; Barthold, op. cit. iv 2, pp. 32–33; Kratz, op. cit., p. 396; Wehrmann, op. cit. i, p. 245.

resisting this demand.[1] Bogislav also interfered with the towns'
jurisdiction and internal affairs, limited their independence,
and forced them to appeal to him, and not to urban courts outside Pomerania as the custom was.[2]

Encouraged by these successes and embittered by the resistance of Stralsund against the new tolls, Bogislav then took up
the fight against the leading town of Pomerania. Late in 1503
he began to blockade the town and invaded its villages and
estates; but the burghers resisted strongly, pillaged his villages,
and made noblemen and peasants alike swear fealty to them.
A few months later a peace was concluded which confirmed the
status quo.[3] Eight years later the conflict broke out anew, this
time ending in a significant defeat for Stralsund: the town was
completely isolated, while Bogislav was supported by the Estates.
Although the peace of 1504 was confirmed, Stralsund had to
pay a heavy fine, to cede the jurisdiction in seven villages to the
duke, and to permit its burghers to appeal to him in legal cases
instead of to Lübeck. Yet the ducal victory was by no means
complete, as they were still allowed to appeal to Lübeck and
retained their minting and other rights which Bogislav had
disputed.[4] To that extent the outcome of the struggle differed
from Brandenburg. One town alone, however, was unable to
withstand the changes of the time: the other Pomeranian towns
also declined and lost their old liberties, while Stralsund was
badly affected by the decline of the Hanse.

When in the sixteenth century the nobility rose to become the
ruling class in society, the eastern towns were already too weak
to resist effectively. The subjugation and the decline of the
towns fundamentally changed the medieval balance of society
and made way for the rule of one class over the others. In Prussia
the same result was achieved by the cession of all important
towns to Poland in 1466. The one important town remaining to
the Teutonic Knights, Königsberg, alone was too weak to be a

---

[1] Kantzow, op. cit. ii, p. 82; Barthold, op. cit. iv 2, pp. 21–23; von Bilow, op.
cit., pp. 244–5.

[2] Wehrmann, op. cit. i, pp. 241, 244, 246, 256.

[3] *Stralsundische Chroniken*, i, pp. 15–16, 215–16; Kantzow, op. cit. ii, pp. 88–95;
Barthold, op. cit. iv 2, pp. 38–47; Fock, op. cit. v, pp. 27–31; Wehrmann, op. cit.
i, p. 245; J. C. Daehnert, *Pommersche Bibliothek*, ii, 1753, pp. 47–52.

[4] Kantzow, op. cit. ii, pp. 99–101; Barthold, op. cit. iv 2, pp. 80–82; Fock,
op. cit. v, pp. 32–35; Wehrmann, op. cit. i, p. 245.

counterweight to the nobility, although it held its own for a considerable time and resisted more strongly than the towns of Brandenburg and Pomerania. With the decay of urban life and activity, urban self-government also declined. The aristocracies remained entrenched in power and relied on the rulers' support against the lower orders which ceased to be a danger to them. The towns gradually assumed the sleepy and dull appearance which most of them preserved until the nineteenth century. For the cities of many western countries the period from the sixteenth to the nineteenth century was their golden age, economically and politically as well as in the fields of art and culture. In eastern Germany, on the other hand, towns fostered by a ruler and dependent upon him at most might grow; but urban self-government and independence were things of the past.

XI

The Decline of the Peasantry and the Imposition of Serfdom

THE deterioration of the peasants' legal position in the fifteenth century was due to economic and political difficulties, to the wars and invasions, and to the desertion of the land, which also hit the landlords and noblemen as well as the burghers of the towns. The sixteenth century, however, was a period of peace and prosperity in north-eastern Germany. The price of corn and other goods exported rose sharply, and the landlords benefited greatly from the export of corn and other produce. If they had converted deserted peasant holdings and villages into demesnes in the fifteenth century because they could not find new tenants, these vacant lands in the sixteenth century were no longer sufficient to satisfy their hunger for larger demesnes and more profits. They thus evicted or bought out peasants, appropriated the glebe lands or the freeholds of the village mayors, and also founded new demesnes for their younger sons and nephews. The impetus of this movement was increased by the introduction of the Reformation, for the Church no longer offered suitable careers to young noblemen, and long coveted church lands could be expropriated with impunity. As early as 1490 a Pomeranian nobleman seized six monastic villages: whereupon Duke Bogislav is said to have declared that, if the Church were to be spoliated, he certainly had a better claim to do so than the nobleman.[1]

The rapid growth of demesne farming made heavier labour services necessary. The number of peasants, however, had shrunk in the fifteenth century, and was later further reduced through evictions and the buying out of peasants. For the individual peasant the burden thus became heavier and heavier, and soon his children, too, were forced into service. Therefore the tendency

---

[1] Kantzow, op. cit. ii, p. 49; Wehrmann, op. cit. i, p. 256. The best secondary authorities for the subject of this chapter are: for Brandenburg, F. Grossmann, *Über die gutsherrlich-bäuerlichen Rechtsverhältnisse in der Mark Brandenburg vom 16. bis 18. Jahrhundert*, 1890; for Pomerania, C. J. Fuchs, *Der Untergang des Bauernstandes und das Aufkommen der Gutsherrschaften nach archivalischen Quellen aus Neu-Vorpommern und Rügen*, 1888.

to abscond and to seek better conditions elsewhere increased, and in consequence the peasants with their families were tied to the soil and became serfs. Their rights were more and more curtailed, while their obligations increased and their punishments grew heavier: additional inducements to run away. It was a vicious circle, and there was no way out once the movement had set in with full force. There were, of course, local differences in the peasants' situation, but these were much less due to the individual landlords' attitude than to differences of status between different peasant groups, to the geographical position, to the quality of the soil, and to the needs of the local nobility. The position of peasants directly under the ruler was hardly better than that of peasants on private estates. Contrary to a popular assumption, it made equally little difference to the peasants' fate whether they resisted the introduction of serfdom and of the new burdens or not: in Prussia, where a real peasants' war broke out in 1525, their position became as bad as in Brandenburg or in Pomerania where no revolts occurred. Wherever the peasants rose in 1525 they were supported by the lower orders in the towns and their leaders often were of urban origin; but in Brandenburg the towns were already subjugated and the peasants could no longer expect any backing from them. In Prussia, on the other hand, there was close co-operation between the peasants and the guilds and commons of Königsberg which, together with the religious changes and the secularization of an ecclesiastical principality, facilitated the uprising.[1]

In April 1525 the Teutonic Order in Prussia was dissolved and the Reformation was introduced. The last Grand Master, Albert of Hohenzollern, became the first duke of Prussia and a liegeman of the king of Poland. The former Teutonic Knights became landlords and joined the ranks of the local nobility; a homogeneous upper class with identical economic and political interests came into being. The limited protection which the peasants had enjoyed under the Order vanished; so did the last barriers preventing the nobility from imposing its will upon the country. The new duke was in a weak position: he co-operated closely with the nobility and fulfilled its wishes so as to get money

---

[1] For details see F. L. Carsten, 'The Peasants' War in East Prussia in 1525', *International Review for Social History*, iii, Leiden, 1938, pp. 398 ff.

grants from the Estates.[1] These became the decisive factor in the government of the duchy, always ready to seek the support of the crown of Poland against their ruler and to play out the one against the other to increase their privileges. The military traditions of the Teutonic Knights, their methods of administration, their links with southern and western Europe disappeared, and Prussia became a small and unimportant duchy, almost indistinguishable from the other principalities of the area. Only the large domains of the duke still bore witness to the one-time policy of the Order of keeping most of the land in its own hands, which even the events of the fifteenth century had not entirely nullified. In the other principalities, it was only the dissolution of the monasteries which gave to the rulers substantial domains of their own, all other property having been sold in course of time.

The Prussian ordinances of 1526 reflected the growth of noble power, the defeat of the peasants in the preceding year, and the dependence of the duke upon the nobility. It was no longer mentioned that the peasant could depart freely having provided a successor to take over the holding; it was simply stipulated that no peasant or peasant's son was to be accepted by any lord or Junker without a written permit from his former lord. The peasants' children, before accepting other service, had to report to their lord and serve him for the due wages if required to do so. A peasant also needed a permit if he wanted to undertake work outside the estate. If a peasant continually neglected his holding it could be given to another peasant: 'continuous neglect' was not defined, nothing was said about what was to happen to the evicted peasant, and no legal safeguards protected the peasant against his lord.[2] German and Prussian peasants were treated alike in these ordinances, and even the Prussian freemen hardly better than the peasants: the legal position of these groups more and more approximated.[3] Thus the peasants and their sons were tied to the soil, and their hereditary right of possession was infringed for the first time. By the ordinances of 1540 the Prussian freemen's right of bequeathing their farms was severely cur-

---

[1] Breysig, introduction to *Urkunden und Actenstücke*, xv, pp. 22–23; Forstreuter, op. cit., p. 100.
[2] Plehn, loc. cit. xvii, pp. 444–5; G. Aubin, op. cit., pp. 129–31.
[3] Aubin, op. cit., p. 132.

tailed: if there was no heir, the freeman could not dispose of the farm and its stock; if there were several sons, the lord could select one of them as the heir, while the others, if they wanted to leave, had to pay a ransom and lost their rights of inheritance.[1] The Prussian peasants' right of inheritance was limited to movable goods, but the stock of the farm and what served to maintain it were excluded.[2] The condition of freemen and peasants alike was deteriorating quickly.

The same was the case in Pomerania. A Pomeranian chronicler, writing in the fourth decade of the sixteenth century, sharply distinguished between two different groups of peasants.

The peasants' position is by no means equal. Some possess the heritage of their farms, give moderate dues and have to render limited services. These are well off and rich; and if one of them wants to leave the farm with his children, he sells it with his lord's consent, gives him a tithe of the purchase price . . . and departs freely with his children and chattels whither he wants to go. But with the others it is different; for they do not possess the heritage of their holdings and have to serve their master whenever he wants them; often they cannot do their own work because of the services and thus they empoverish and abscond. There is a saying that these peasants merely have to serve six days a week, the seventh day they have to carry letters. They are thus in practice villeins, for the lord gets rid of them when he pleases. But if the peasants or their children want to leave and do so without the lord's consent, he recovers them as his villeins even if they have handed over to a good successor. The peasants' sons and daughters are not allowed to leave the estate unless by special permit. . . . Yet many run away or leave by stealth so that the holdings get deserted. Then the lord has to try to find another peasant . . . and he with his children becomes as servile as the other peasants. . . .[3]

The second group obviously were in a very bad position.[4] Yet the first group also, although well-to-do at a time of rising corn prices, could no longer leave without a permit, had to hand over

[1] Aubin, op. cit., p. 136.
[2] W. von Brünneck, 'Die Leibeigenschaft in Ostpreussen', *Zeitschrift der Savigny-Stiftung für Rechtsgeschichte*, viii, 1887, pp. 43, 55.
[3] Kantzow, *Pomerania*: ed. Kosegarten, 1817, ii, pp. 418–20; ed. Gaebel, 1908, ii, pp. 161–2.
[4] Kantzow calls them *eigen*, implying that they were the property (*Eigentum*) of their lord.

a tenth of the purchase money, and had to render labour services: their legal position, too, had become much worse.

This was confirmed by another almost contemporary source,
the old laws and customs of Rügen, collected before 1550 by its
advocatus, Matthias von Normann, 'from noblemen and peasants,
clergy and laity'. As this was the area where, according to
Kantzow, the peasants were especially well-off,[1] Normann's
legal evidence is particularly valuable, for it modifies Kantzow's
description to a considerable degree. No peasant could sell his
farm or cottage without his lord's consent, for it was for him to
decide whether he wanted to dismiss the one and to accept the
other peasant.[2] Then the peasant could leave, but there were
some exceptions: if he had settled young and poor under a lord
and had grown rich under him, the lord had to be compensated
for his loss before the peasant could depart; and a peasant without an heir could be prevented from leaving because after his
death his farm would revert to his lord.[3] Runaway peasants,
their wives and children, and absconded servants could be
recovered by their masters if they could prove that they were
theirs.[4] Heirs could be compelled to take over a farm or cottage
if they did not find a suitable successor within a year and four
weeks.[5] In principle the peasants' children could marry freely;
but nobody was allowed to marry into the farm without the
lord's consent, for which a payment was due to him; equally for
every child portioned a due had to be paid, otherwise the child
had to be returned; formerly this due amounted to twelve
shillings and four pence, but recently it had become unlimited.[6]

The peasants' children had to serve as menials if their lord
could not otherwise get enough servants; but the father could
provide a substitute if he did not want his children to go into
service.[7] The lord could evict the peasant provided he gave him
a year's notice and paid him what had been paid for the farm
according to the 'heritage letter' and for any ameliorations; if
there was no 'heritage letter', the price was to be fixed by
arbiters.[8] As all prices were rising, the payment of the price fixed
in the 'heritage letter' was in the lord's interest; in recent days,

---

[1] *Pomerania*, ed. 1817, ii, p. 433; ed. 1908, ii, p. 170.
[2] *Normann*, pp. 274, 279.
[3] Ibid., pp. 278–9, 297.
[4] Ibid., pp. 309–10.
[5] Ibid., pp. 291, 299.
[6] Ibid., pp. 283–6, 294–5.
[7] Ibid., p. 284.
[8] Ibid., pp. 274, 346.

moreover, some lords were demanding all the money the peasant received for his farm, less only the amount he himself had paid for it:[1] thus the peasant became the victim of the inflationary process. Another innovation was the introduction of a heriot, the best horse of a deceased peasant, in addition to which the heirs had to pay a due of five marks.[2] Other stipulations also seem to have been recent innovations, for example, the right to recover absconded peasants and their children which was the final clause in a chapter dealing with an entirely different subject. Thus the peasants were already tied to the soil with their children, they could be evicted and were burdened with new dues. Their children had to serve as menials and were not permitted to marry freely. The main difference between these peasants and Kantzow's lower group was that their services were limited, while the latter's were unlimited. Normann did not divide the peasantry into two distinct groups: Kantzow's distinction probably was one of wealth rather than of legal status.

Kantzow also observed some of the changes which were taking place then. The young noblemen, he related, used to seek a career at a princely court or in war, while those not bent on honours became robbers or squeezed wealthy peasants; 'in previous years the noblemen have not been industrious and interested in agriculture; but recently this has changed, and the nobility has never been so rich and powerful as now'.[3] One reason for this new interest was the boom of corn prices, another was the Reformation, introduced in 1535 against the opposition of the nobility, which was anxious to preserve the ecclesiastical positions filled by its sons and daughters.[4] To compensate themselves noblemen bought out peasants to found new residences for younger sons.[5] The monastic peasants came under the rule of ducal officials, eager to squeeze them to cover the growing needs and debts of the dukes. The new ducal domains set an example in the increase of labour services, the eviction of peasants, and the foundation of new demesnes and sheep farms.[6]

---

[1] Fuchs, op. cit., pp. 58–59.   [2] *Normann*, pp. 291–4.
[3] *Pomerania*, ed. 1817, ii, pp. 404–5; ed. 1908, ii, p. 153.
[4] Barthold, op. cit. iv 2, pp. 267, 282–3, 286–7; Fock, op. cit. v, pp. 344, 357–9; Fuchs, op. cit., pp. 65–66; Spahn, op. cit., p. 37.
[5] Spahn, op. cit., p. 124.
[6] Von Brünneck, 'Die Leibeigenschaft in Pommern', *Zeitschrift der Savigny-*

When the former monastery of Belbuk was visited in 1558, it was officially admitted that the peasants were much more burdened than they had been under the monks.[1]

In Brandenburg the nobility of the Old Mark in 1540 referred to an old custom which, they maintained, permitted them to buy out peasants to enlarge their demesnes and asked for a confirmation of this right. That this was far from ancient emerged from the ensuing argument: the nobility of the whole Mark merely reasoned that, as the peasant could sell his farm at any time and hand it over to a successor, why should the nobleman not have power to buy out an unruly peasant?[2] Margrave Joachim II fulfilled their wish and granted them the rights of buying out disobedient and unruly peasants, and of founding a new noble residence on peasant land; this last concession was at first limited to the Old Mark but later extended to the whole country.[3] Even before this date peasants were bought out by their lords, one nobleman even refusing to pay them the purchase price.[4] The noblemen also appropriated the glebe lands, and repeated admonitions to restore them were of no avail.[5] They obviously considered these lands their legitimate spoils at a time when the princes dissolved the monasteries. The peasants who had served the priest were forced to work on the noble demesne, and even the sextons were not spared.[6] Land belonging to burghers of small towns was equally added to the demesnes. As early as 1501 the von Krummensee had to promise the burghers of their town of Landsberg, near Berlin, that they would not buy out any more holdings or houses of burghers without the consent of the community so that the town would not be weakened.[7] In 1554 the von Rohr undertook not to buy out any further holdings belonging to burghers of their town

Stiftung für Rechtsgeschichte, ix, 1888, p. 136; Fuchs, op. cit., p. 66; Wehrmann, op. cit. ii, pp. 77, 81, 89–90.

[1] 'Das Kloster Belbog', Baltische Studien, ii 1, 1833, p. 58.
[2] Friedensburg, i, no. 17, pp. 94–95.
[3] Ibid., no. 18, pp. 98, 101.
[4] Riedel, vii, no. 35, p. 226; ix, no. 139, p. 453; x, nos. 82, 86, pp. 172–6; xi, no. 190, p. 144.
[5] Ibid. vii, nos. 15, 118–20, 125, pp. 255–6, 261, 285, 383–8; no. 68, p. 455; no. 26, pp. 490–501; x, no. 91, p. 179; xi, nos. 190, 260–1, pp. 144, 478, 485–6; xii, nos. 47, 65, pp. 33, 202; Friedensburg, i, no. 12, p. 55.
[6] Riedel, vii, nos. 15–16, pp. 36–37; no. 35, pp. 225–30; no. 15, pp. 273, 284–5; no. 68, p. 455; no. 26, pp. 489, 495; xii, no. 47, p. 33.
[7] Ibid. xii, no. 15, p. 62.

of Freienstein, in the Priegnitz, unless there was a pressing need and the community agreed to it.[1] In spite of this promise more burgher lands were later incorporated with the demesne.[2]

As a consequence the Junkers demanded more and more labour services from their peasants, and these in vain sought the protection of the margrave's court, the *Kammergericht* in Berlin. In 1540 the nobility complained that they found it necessary to commute quit-rents into services, but that the peasants declined and were supported by the *Kammergericht* in this attitude. The margrave decided that, if it was lawful that the peasants had to render services instead of paying quit-rents, this was to be done and their refusal was to be disregarded.[3] In the following year the *Kammergericht* decided a dispute between one von Bredow and the peasants of six Havelland villages in favour of the nobleman: the peasants were to serve him 2 or 3 days a week, according to the season, from early morning till evening, and in addition to cart wood for his kitchen and to wash and shear his sheep,[4] a total of approximately 150 days in the year. Services of 2 days weekly became customary about the middle of the century. The nobility of Lebus petitioned the margrave to impose such services on their peasants.[5] In the Priegnitz the peasants of the von Quitzow and the von Rohr served 2 days a week; and in 1555 Margrave Joachim II permitted the von Platen to commute their peasants' quit-rents into services of the same amount.[6] Yet the Junkers were not satisfied; in 1550 they protested that the *Kammergericht* was stipulating limited services and that the peasants were to receive food while serving.[7] The margrave promised to remedy this: the peasants should serve according to custom and should receive food where this had always been the practice, unless they voluntarily forwent this right.[8] He thus did not give way entirely to the nobility which was aiming at unlimited services; while the *Kammergericht* apparently

---

[1] *Riedel*, ii, no. 40, p. 297.
[2] Ibid., p. 256.
[3] *Friedensburg*, i, nos. 17–18, pp. 95–96, 102, n. 2.
[4] *Riedel*, vii, no. 20, pp. 60–61.
[5] *Friedensburg*, i, no. 101, p. 301 (1547 or 1548).
[6] *Riedel*, xxi, no. 64, p. 515.
[7] *Friedensburg*, i, no. 236, p. 687.
[8] Ibid., no. 291, p. 814.

preferred uniform regulations to varying local customs which could be changed more easily.

In Brandenburg the peasants were not yet tied to the soil, but the first steps in this direction were made in the first half of the sixteenth century. In 1518 it was stipulated that runaway peasants had to be handed over, while peasants who had found a successor could leave freely with their children and settle in any town or village inside the country.[1] In 1536 it was added that no peasant was to be received anywhere without a written proof that he had departed with his lord's consent.[2] In 1550 the regulation of 1518 was repeated, but with the significant addition that the different customs of the Ucker Mark were to be observed:[3] there the peasant apparently was no longer allowed to leave when he had found a successor. The cathedral chapter of Havelberg in 1555 decided that every departing peasant should pay according to his means.[4] The peasants' sons and daughters since 1518 were only permitted to enter other people's service after they had offered their services to their lord;[5] they were obliged to serve him before others, according to the ordinances of 1550.[6] The punishment of any infringement of these many regulations was left to the noblemen,[7] who were thus plaintiff and judge in the same person. To prevent any appeals from their jurisdiction they demanded, in 1540, that any peasant complaining without cause about his lord to the *Kammergericht* was to be put into the dungeon, and this request was granted by the margrave 'in order to deter them from complaining wantonly'.[8]

In the second half of the sixteenth century much heavier labour services were imposed upon the peasants; during the harvest they often became unlimited. In 1562 Margrave Joachim II decreed that the peasants should not be forced to perform unbearable and uncustomary services.[9] In 1574 peasants of the

[1] *Von Raumer*, ii, no. 16, p. 226.
[2] *Friedensburg*, i, no. 9, p. 36: repeated in 1538–9, 1572, and 1602.
[3] Ibid., no. 294, p. 834. Cf. the judgement of 1383, above, p. 81.
[4] *Riedel*, iii, no. 69, p. 152.
[5] *Von Raumer*, ii, no. 16, p. 225: repeated in 1534, 1536, 1538, 1550, 1572, 1602, and 1611.
[6] *Friedensburg*, i, nos. 292, 294, pp. 823–9.
[7] *Von Raumer*, ii, no. 16, p. 226; *Friedensburg*, i, no. 294, p. 835 (1518–50).
[8] *Friedensburg*, i, nos. 17–18, pp. 90, 99: repeated in 1572 and 1602.
[9] *Mylius*, ii 1, no. 9, col. 55.

von Trotha in the Ucker Mark, and often also the village mayors and millers, had to render unlimited services.[1] In 1581 the cathedral chapter of Havelberg had to admit that its peasants were so overburdened that many a village, especially at harvest time, was left with but two or three wagons or ploughs; the peasants also had to render new services to the margrave and were worn out by these doubled and trebled services.[2] The peasants of the domain of Zechlin, in the Priegnitz, in 1574 were obliged to customary but unfixed services, later fixed at three days a week plus the shearing of sheep.[3] Other peasants of the margrave in the same district had to render unlimited services, at least during the harvest.[4] The same applied to the peasants of the domain of Spandau, near Berlin, of the domain of Ruppin, and of a domain in the Ucker Mark in the late sixteenth century.[5] All these were former monastic peasants whose position had declined considerably since the dissolution. Unlimited services during the harvest were decreed by Margrave John George for the whole districts of the New Mark and of Sternberg in 1572, and again in 1593.[6] Eventually, after many disputes, the *Kammergericht* in the early seventeenth century decided that all peasants were liable to unlimited services unless they could prove the contrary.[7] Even if the peasants were in a position to do so, they nevertheless had to render carrying services in addition.[8]

The last quarter of the sixteenth and the first of the seventeenth centuries witnessed a rapid growth of demesne farming in the Middle Mark. The number of *Hufen* held in demesne increased from 3,236½ to 4,885½ or by more than 50 per cent.; while the peasant *Hufen* decreased from 21,889½ to 20,240½, or by 8 per cent.:[9] there were still 4 peasant *Hufen* to 1 held in demesne. In 1588 and in 1606 the noblemen of the Old Mark and the Priegnitz themselves complained about the frequent eviction of peasants and the many abuses: peasants were not only bought out, as legally permitted, for new noble residences,

---

[1] *Riedel*, xiii, no. 122, pp. 118–27. [2] Ibid. iii, no. 82, pp. 191–2.
[3] Ibid. ii, p. 353. [4] Ibid., pp. 325–6.
[5] Grossmann, op. cit., p. 39, n. 5; *Riedel*, iv, p. 481; xiii, no. 42, p. 518 (1590–2).
[6] *Mylius*, vi 1, nos. 32–35, 45, cols. 99–104, 133.
[7] *Scheplitz*, ii, tit. xxi, p. 15; Grossmann, op. cit., p. 39 (1607–26).
[8] Grossmann, op. cit., pp. 39, 41, n. 3 (1600–12).
[9] Ibid., pp. 111–38: figures of the *Schossregister* of 1624.

but also for widows' jointures, new dairy and sheep farms, and
extension of demesnes, and no tax was paid from the former
peasant holdings.[1] The Junkers also appropriated meadows
hitherto used for grazing by the peasants: in the New Mark this
practice was sanctioned by Margrave John George in 1572.[2]
From 1620 onwards the children of peasants and cottagers,
whose services were not needed by their parents, had to serve
their lord for three years; if they ran away they could be fetched
back, and if need be arrested and imprisoned.[3] Even the personal
freedom of the peasants in some parts of Brandenburg became
doubtful. In 1552 a local writer stated that in the Mark all
peasants were brought up in freedom and that nobody was born
a serf.[4] Fifty years later, however, a legal authority, while quoting this sentence with approval, had to add that it was impossible to say anything about the peasants of the Ucker and New
Marks;[5] and soon these were classified as *leibeigen*.[6] Thus the
peasants, in growing numbers, escaped across the frontier into
Poland, where numerous German villages were founded at that
time.[7]

In Prussia the deterioration of the peasants' status in the later
sixteenth and early seventeenth centuries was less marked than
in Brandenburg, perhaps because it was already rather bad by
that time. Some further aggravations were introduced by the
ordinances of 1577: the peasants' daughters were also tied to
the soil; before leaving they had to pay a ransom, and freedom
of marriage ceased to exist. Furthermore, the noblemen were
empowered to compel a peasant's child to serve them and to
punish parents and child if the parents withheld him without
reason, or if the child refused to serve. Neither the length of this
service nor the age of the children liable was stipulated. The
noblemen were merely admonished not to take away those
children needed by the peasants themselves.[8] The town of

[1] Ibid., p. 27, n. 5.   [2] *Mylius*, vi 1, no. 32, col. 100.
[3] Ibid. v 3, no. 5, cols. 12–13.
[4] G. Sabinus, *De Brandeburgo urbe electorali metropolitana totius Marchiae . . . Brevis*
Historia, ed. Berlin, 1611.
[5] *Scheplitz*, i, p. 384.
[6] Grossmann, op. cit., pp. 31–32; Korn, loc. cit., p. 43.
[7] Schmidt, op. cit., pp. 314, 325–31; G. Köster, 'Die Entwicklung der nordost-
deutschen Verkehrsstrassen', *F.B.P.G.* xlviii, 1936, p. 140.
[8] A. Kern, 'Beiträge zur Agrargeschichte Ostpreussens', *F.B.P.G.* xiv, 1901,
p. 156; Plehn, ibid. xvii, 1904, p. 445; G. Aubin, op. cit., pp. 133–5.

Königsberg declined to apply the ordinances, continued to receive runaway peasants and often refused to hand them over.[1] In the following year there was unrest among the peasants, so that Duke Albert Frederick exhorted the noblemen not to demand excessive labour services.[2]

New regulations for servants and menials were published in 1612 and in 1633. According to these, the peasants' children had to serve at their lord's will; if they ran away they could be imprisoned, and in case of a second offence they could be flogged.[3] Again Königsberg protested strongly, so that the regulations of 1633 had to be printed without its consent.[4] In the next year the town in a long memorandum declared: in Prussia all peasants were free and not serfs, and their children were free to go wherever they wanted to, without paying a penny to their Junker, to study or to learn a trade; yet the poor peasants, those under the duke like those under the nobility, were treated like wild beasts, and their children had to serve their Junker for little food and poor wages, with heavy work and many blows; Pharaoh also made the children of Israel into serfs and plagued them with immoderate labour services: this servitude was a hellish poison which prevented people from settling in the country and from occupying the vacant holdings.[5] On these grounds Königsberg rejected serfdom outright: they had better things to do than to search for runaway peasants and servants, an attitude which none of the Brandenburg towns dared take any longer. Like the towns of Livonia, Königsberg realized that this question was of vital importance for its well-being and strength.

While the majority of the Prussian freemen were gradually pressed down to the level of the peasantry, there remained one strong group of free peasants, an intermediate class between the peasantry and the nobility. These were the German freemen who had been invested by the Teutonic Knights with small estates from which military services had to be rendered,[6] but

---

[1] Plehn, loc. cit., pp. 448–9; Aubin, op. cit., pp. 136–7.
[2] Kern, loc. cit., p. 156.   [3] Ibid., pp. 160, 166.
[4] Plehn, loc. cit., p. 449.
[5] Resolution of the aldermen, courts, and commons of Königsberg of 8 Feb. 1634: printed as a pamphlet in 1640, pp. 8–9, 14–17: a copy in *Ostpreuss. Folianten*, vol. 653.
[6] See above, pp. 54–58.

who had not acquired the jurisdiction and the other prerogatives and had thus not entered the ranks of the nobility.[1] These
were the *Cölmische Freie*, or for short *Cölmer*, indicating that they
had been granted Culmic law. There were few of them in the
Samland with its strong Prussian population, but many in
Natangen; they owned over 15 per cent. of all the land in
Prussia.[2] They were entirely independent and often well-to-do,
employing many servants, farm-hands, and shepherds. They had
the right to submit their grievances to the diet, but were not
directly represented in it. They formed a very exceptional group
for which there was no parallel in any of the adjoining territories inside or outside Germany;[3] the best probably would be
the petty *szlachta* of Poland, only that they belonged to the
nobility.

In Pomerania, in the later sixteenth century, the dukes, now
the owners of large monastic estates, led the way in the establishment of new demesnes and sheep farms and in the eviction
of peasants for that purpose. On the island of Rügen the first
ducal demesnes were founded in the 1570's: they had to be tilled
by the peasants of the nearby villages whose quit-rents were
cancelled. They could thus be worked at small cost and brought
in comparatively high yields, so that the first examples were
soon followed by others.[4] On the mainland also many ducal
demesnes, stock- and sheep-farms were founded on former monastic lands and those founded earlier were considerably enlarged
at the cost of the peasantry.[5] The nobility soon followed this
example. In 1550 and in 1560 the towns and the duke complained
because the noblemen ceased to pay taxes from the holdings
incorporated with their demesnes; in 1563 a commission was
appointed to inquire into the matter and into the eviction of

[1] Plehn, loc. cit., p. 411; Aubin, op. cit., p. 139.
[2] 17,137 out of a total of 109,974 *Hufen*, according to an 'Extract aller des
Hertzogthumbs Preussen Huben Zahl' of the early seventeenth century in *Ostpreuss. Folianten*, vols. 647–8, 661–2, 669 iii, 682–3. Of the remaining *Hufen*, the
nobility had 39,324 and the peasants 53,513.
[3] Knapp, op. cit. i, pp. 14–15.
[4] Fuchs, op. cit., pp. 76–77; J. von Bohlen, *Geschichte des adlichen, freiherrlichen und
gräflichen Geschlechts von Krassow*, 1853, i, pp. 160–1; ii, p. 211.
[5] A. G. von Schwarz, *Einleitung zur Pommersch-Rugianischen Dörffer-Historie*, 1734,
pp. 20–21; 'Nhamen der Dorffer . . . des Klosters Belbuck', *Baltische Studien*, vi 1,
1839, pp. 166–70; E. Gohrbandt, 'Das Bauernlegen bis zur Aufhebung der Erb-
untertänigkeit . . .', ibid. xxxviii, 1936, pp. 201–5; *Kratz*, ii, p. 85: all with many
details.

peasants. In 1581 the dukes declared that peasant eviction was becoming more marked every year, causing a fall in the yield of taxation which ought to cease.[1] In 1585 the nobility admitted that its peasants had to render labour services instead of the quit-rents which had been increased several times.[2] In western Pomerania the wealthy towns of Stralsund and Greifswald rivalled with the nobility in evicting peasants, increasing their dues and services, and founding new demesnes.[3] In eastern Pomerania some peasants were already *leibeigen*, so that they, and not their holdings, were sold or handed over.[4] As in Brandenburg, the peasants fled in large numbers across the frontier into Poland to escape their plight.[5]

In the early seventeenth century the changes of the sixteenth were legalized and the peasants' status was fixed at a uniform and low level. In the duchy of Pomerania-Stettin the Estates in a resolution of 1600 declared it ought to be decided whether evicted peasants could leave freely with their chattels, or whether they and their families had to redeem themselves from serfdom first and had to leave the stock of the farm behind: significantly the term *Leibeigenschaft* was used to describe the peasants' condition.[6] The Estates were obviously pressing for the introduction of a ransom; in the following year the question was repeated, and it was further emphasized that the children remained subject to serfdom if their parents left on account of poverty.[7] In 1616 the new regulations for the peasantry of Pomerania-Stettin were finally published: all the peasants, without exception, were declared 'leibeigen, homines proprii et coloni glebae adscripti'; they and their sons were forbidden to leave without a permit and formal manumission; they were liable to unlimited labour services; their fields and meadows belonged solely to their lord so that they had no hereditary rights whatever; the lord could take the farm away or put the peasant on another farm; but if a peasant was evicted and not given a new farm, then he could ask for his and his children's release and could take the stock of

[1] Von Brünneck, loc. cit. ix, p. 129, n. 2; Fuchs, op. cit., pp. 68–69; Wehrmann, op. cit. ii, p. 90.
[2] Spahn, op. cit., p. 125, n. 2.   [3] Fuchs, op. cit., pp. 79–80.
[4] *Kratz*, i, nos. 527, 533, 536, 539, 579, pp. 337–404 (1584–1614).
[5] Wehrmann, op. cit. ii, pp. 8, 73, 91; Gohrbandt, loc. cit., p. 213.
[6] Von Brünneck, loc. cit. ix, p. 134; Fuchs, op. cit., p. 70.
[7] Von Brünneck, loc. cit. ix, pp. 134–5; Fuchs, op. cit., p. 70.

the farm with him; even the sons of free peasants, village mayors, innkeepers, and millers were liable to serfdom; everybody was strictly forbidden to accept a peasant without a writ of release from his lord.[1] In the other duchy, Pomerania-Wolgast, the Estates in 1618 demanded that the same regulations be introduced; but this was only done in 1645 when western Pomerania had become a Swedish possession.[2] In the whole of Pomerania these regulations remained in force far into the eighteenth century:[3] they stipulated a peasant law much worse than that of Brandenburg or of Prussia.

The Reformation certainly stimulated the foundation of new demesnes and the eviction of peasants by the rulers and the noblemen. In 1540 the nobility of Brandenburg declared that it had a great interest in the bishoprics, chapters, monasteries, and commanderies in which it could provide for its sons and friends.[4] Later it complained about the dissolution of the nunneries and their conversion into domains.[5] It thus felt the loss of a large number of sinecures. It must be remembered, however, that the whole movement was well advanced when the dissolution took place, and that the same development occurred in Poland which remained Catholic.[6] A much greater stimulus to increased demesne farming was provided by the rising prices and the growing demand of western European countries for corn imports. At Danzig, at the end of the sixteenth century, the price of corn was three to four times as high as it had been at the beginning of the century.[7] Heavier labour services and the tying of the

[1] Von Brünneck, loc. cit. ix, pp. 136–8, 143–6; Fuchs, op. cit., pp. 71–73; D. Gaede, *Die gutsherrlich-bäuerlichen Besitzverhältnisse in Neu-Vorpommern und Rügen*, 1853, pp. 8, 43–44.
[2] Von Brünneck, loc. cit. ix, p. 149, n. 3; Spahn, op. cit., p. 201; Gaede, op. cit., p. 42.
[3] Von Brünneck, loc. cit. ix, p. 147.
[4] *Friedensburg*, i, no. 17, p. 87.
[5] Ibid., no. 101, p. 300 (1547–8).
[6] Rutkowski, op. cit., pp. 32, 106–7.
[7] See the detailed statistics in Pelc, *Ceny w Gdańsku w XVI i XVII Wieku*, pp. 47–48, 117; but I cannot conclude from them that the price of rye, in the second half of the century only, rose by 247 per cent., that of barley by 187, and that of oats by 185 per cent., as asserted ibid., p. 169, and by H. Rosenberg, 'The Rise of the Junkers', *The American Hist. Review*, xlix, 1944, p. 233. This result they arrived at by comparing the, particularly low, average for 1546–50 with the, particularly high, average for 1596–1600. If one compares the average for 1538–55 with that for 1591–1610, the rise is only 107 per cent. in the case of rye, 90 in that of barley, and 85 in that of oats.

peasant to the soil were the corollary of extensive demesne farming which depended on peasant labour.

Everywhere the change-over from peasant to demesne farming seems to have been due to the economic requirements of a numerous and rather poor nobility which depended on agriculture for its living. Wherever this class was less numerous or more wealthy, for example, in the Old Mark to the west of the Elbe, or in the Prussian bishopric of Ermland, demesne farming was less prominent. In the Old Mark the soil was better and the nobility wealthier than elsewhere in Brandenburg: according to a contemporary estimate the yields were twice or thrice as high as in the Priegnitz across the Elbe.[1] In addition, the break-up of the manorial system had proceeded much further in the Old Mark than in the more eastern districts which had been colonized later. For the Ermland, other factors seem to have been decisive: in 1466 it was politically separated from Prussia and was not secularized later; the sale of the rulers' estates to the nobility did not take place there. The Ermland thus remained a district with few large estates and a strong peasantry: the rise of the nobility did not affect this small principality, although its natural features were exactly the same as those of its neighbours. Thus demesne farming did not everywhere become equally predominant; and wherever this was not the case, the peasants' legal and economic position remained more favourable. These districts, however, were like small islands in a sea of noble power and peasant serfdom which engulfed most of eastern Europe.

[1] *Friedensburg*, ii, no. 484, p. 565 (1567–9).

XII

The Rule of the Estates

THE rise of the nobility and the decline of the towns and of the peasantry had far-reaching consequences in the political field. The increasing impecuniousness of the territorial princes made them dependent on money grants by their Estates. In Prussia the affluence of the Teutonic Order had prevented the rise of the local Estates which took place in the other principalities in the later Middle Ages; but even there the crisis of the fifteenth century resulted in the Estates gaining control of taxation and other matters.[1] The treaties with Poland of 1422 and 1433–5 entrusted the Estates with the supervision of the peace; if the Order violated the treaties, they were entitled to refuse military aid.[2] The dissolution of the Order in 1525 made the duke finally dependent on the Estates,[3] as the government was no longer in the hands of the Teutonic Knights whose interests had differed from those of the local nobility, and who had counterbalanced its influence.

Within the Estates of each principality the declining towns were losing their power, and the nobility in the sixteenth century became the predominant factor.[4] This was partly due to the Reformation through which the clergy were eliminated from the Estates: henceforth they consisted only of the nobility and the towns, with the nobility usually divided into a higher and a lower nobility, so that the old division into three houses was formally maintained. In Prussia it was also due to the division of the country, the leading towns having been ceded to Poland in 1466. In Brandenburg the political weight of the towns since the fifteenth century was even more limited than in Prussia.

---

[1] For details see: *Acten der Ständetage Preussens*, i, nos. 162–4, 397, pp. 203–6, 531; S. Grunau, *Preussische Chronik*, ed. M. Perlbach, R. Philippi, and P. Wagner, ii, 1889, p. 42; C. Schütz, *Historia Rerum Prussicarum*, Zerbst, 1592, fols. 128–30; von Baczko, op. cit. iii, pp. 119–20, 155; M. Töppen, 'Der Deutsche Ritterorden und die Stände Preussens', *Historische Zeitschrift*, xlvi, 1881, pp. 435–8, 445–7.

[2] *Acten der Ständetage Preussens*, i, nos. 316, 476, 508, 550, pp. 398–711; von Baczko, op. cit. iii, pp. 103, 169.

[3] Forstreuter, op. cit., pp. 100–1.

[4] For Prussia, G. Aubin, op. cit., p. 109; E. Wilke, loc. cit., p. 51; Forstreuter, op. cit., p. 99.

The Reformation had another consequence: outside Prussia, the rulers became the owners of large domains, so that their interests as landlords henceforth coincided with those of the nobility and were opposed to those of the towns in matters of commerce. Exactly as in England, the dissolution of the monasteries did not make the rulers independent of the votes of credit granted by the Estates. The princes' growing need of money and the quickly rising prices forced them to sell or pawn many of the monastic estates to noblemen.[1] The Estates of Brandenburg as little as the English Parliament realized that this was the cornerstone of their power: disinclined to vote taxes, they constantly pressed their ruler to redeem the pawned domains and monasteries and even granted him money for this purpose.[2] Yet the problem always reproduced itself after a few years, so that the Estates' power remained and was even extended into new spheres. They, and not the prince, were the real rulers of the country, controlling the finances and the administration, the Church, and the universities, as well as all appointments in state and Church. Thus, contrary to a widely held opinion, the princes' power was not strengthened by the Reformation, but it continued to decline.

In Brandenburg the most important concessions to the Estates were made by Margrave Joachim II in 1540 and in 1549, directly after the dissolution of the monasteries which failed to alleviate his financial situation. Against a money grant of one million guilders to pay off his debts, he had to promise in 1540 that he would not decide nor do anything in matters affecting his country's well-being or ruin without previously consulting the Estates, and that he would not conclude any alliance without the consent of their representatives.[3] Nine years later the Estates, against a grant of two million guilders, took over the collection and administration of the tolls and taxes: henceforth their officials and their committees controlled the Brandenburg finances.[4] His successor, John George, employed native noblemen in preference to foreigners and commoners as his

[1] For Brandenburg, see *Friedensburg*, i, nos. 132, 162, 270, 275–6, 287, pp. 391–3, 463–7, 756–9, 769–75, 805; ii, no. 441, p. 427 (1549–64).

[2] Ibid. i, no. 118, p. 343, and *passim*.

[3] *Mylius*, vi 1, nos. 22–23, cols. 61, 66: repeated in 1572, 1602, and 1653.

[4] Ibid., no. 26, col. 78; Prutz, *Preussische Geschichte*, i, pp. 230–1; S. Isaacsohn, introduction to *Urkunden & Actenstücke*, x, p. 11.

officials, and was granted the sum of 800,000 guilders.[1] In 1610 this concession was extended: all offices and benefices were to go to Brandenburg noblemen; only military appointments could be given to foreigners if no suitable natives could be found.[2] When the first Brandenburg forces were mobilized in the Thirty Years War, not only were all their officers native noblemen, but they were nominated jointly by the margrave and the Estates, and the soldiers had to take the oath to both, and not only to the margrave.[3] The Estates also exercised control over the levying and the training of the army and over its finances, and every military step required their consent.[4]

Not that the Brandenburg noblemen were particularly bellicose. On the contrary, time and again they urged their rulers to pursue a peaceful policy and not to conclude any alliances lest the country should get involved in war;[5] to them their corn exports and other commercial enterprises became far more important than the feuds and robberies which had occupied them in the preceding century.[6] They thus were firmly opposed to any expansion and to any territorial claims in which the Hohenzollerns were interested. The Junkers well realized the dangers inherent in the political aspirations of the ruling house when this tried to secure from the crown of Poland the co-infeudation with the duchy of Prussia, which might easily involve Brandenburg in the many wars between Poland and Sweden over the domination of the Baltic coast. The general prosperity of the sixteenth century and the easy profits which could be made in agriculture and trade thus extinguished any military ambitions on the side of the nobility. Even the former Teutonic Knights, after 1525, settled down to the peaceful life of the country squire and quickly amalgamated with the local nobility. For northeastern Germany, in contrast with most other parts of Europe, the sixteenth century was an extraordinarily peaceful period

---

[1] Prutz, op. cit. i, pp. 247–8; G. Schmoller, introduction to *Acta Borussica, Behördenorganisation*, i, 1894, pp. 75–76.

[2] *Mylius*, vi 1, no. 69, col. 192.

[3] Ibid., no. 88, cols. 287–9 (1620).

[4] Prutz, op. cit. i, p. 326; Isaacsohn, loc. cit., pp. 23–24.

[5] Prutz, op. cit. i, pp. 266, 284; R. Koser, *Geschichte der brandenburgisch-preussischen Politik*, i, 1913, pp. 283, 330; O. Hintze, *Die Hohenzollern und ihr Werk*, 1915, pp. 135, 152; H. Croon, *Die kurmärkischen Landstände 1571–1616*, 1938, pp. 105 ff.

[6] See the comment of the Pomeranian chronicler Kantzow, above, p. 154.

which lasted until the Thirty Years War spread to the Baltic coast. Perhaps it was the policy of the Estates which was at least partly responsible for this exceptionally long peace.

The nobility of Prussia also acquired far-reaching political privileges in the course of the sixteenth century. In 1542 Duke Albert conceded that the highest officials of the duchy, the four *Oberräte*, with the possible exception of only the chancellor, had to belong to the high nobility; they were to supervise the domains and the financial administration; they were to govern in the absence of the duke as well as after his death until the accession of the next duke.[1] Associated with the *Oberräte* in the administration of Prussia were six to eight legal councillors (*Hofgerichtsräte*) and the *Hauptleute* of the four districts (*Ämter*) near Königsberg;[1] the latter also, since 1546, had to belong to the native nobility.[2] Foreigners could only be appointed legal councillors if no suitable natives could be found, and natives were to be preferred to foreigners for all offices and benefices.[2] These were the concessions which the duke had to make for a money grant and the reaffirmation of the right of succession of his house by the Estates.[3] In 1566 Duke Albert had to grant further extensive privileges to the nobility: the chancellor as well as the majority of the legal councillors also were to be native noblemen; the powers of the *Oberräte* were considerably extended; the Estates were to present candidates for the posts of rural judges; above all, the Estates were empowered, if ever a duke infringed their privileges and liberties, to ask the king of Poland to maintain them; any alliance concluded and any help promised by a duke was null and void without the consent of the crown of Poland and the Estates of Prussia.[4] The Prussian noblemen were eager to gain the liberties of the Polish nobility with which they were connected by many bonds.[5] The power of the Estates was thus firmly secured, more firmly than in any other German principality.[6]

In 1609 further steps were taken to strengthen the influence

---

[1] *Privilegia der Stände dess Hertzogthumbs Preussen*, fols. 51–56; von Baczko, op. cit. v, pp. 464–70; Breysig, loc. cit., pp. 25–26.

[2] *Privilegia . . .*, fol. 50; von Baczko, op. cit. iv, pp. 259, 463–4; Breysig, loc. cit., p. 30.   [3] Breysig, loc. cit., p. 28.

[4] *Privilegia . . .*, fols. 60–66; von Baczko, op. cit. iv, pp. 319–21, 475–83; Breysig, loc. cit., pp. 39–42, 46, 124.

[5] Aubin, op. cit., p. 104.   [6] Breysig, loc. cit., p. 45.

of the Estates. Every step affecting the status of Prussia from then onwards required the Estates' agreement; ducal orders which infringed their privileges were automatically null and void. Visitations of the domains could only be held with their consent, because such visitations 'weakened the wealth and the authority of the nobility'. Native noblemen were to occupy two-thirds of the seats in the high court and to administer most of the local districts (*Ämter*), from which posts commoners 'were not to be excluded altogether'. Noblemen were to be preferred to others if any domains were to be leased.[1] Thus commoners were in practice excluded from the last offices which had still been open to them. The noblemen treated the domains as if they were their private estates and diverted the surplus into their own pockets.[2] Only the strong opposition of Königsberg prevented the nobility from wielding absolute power. Yet duke after duke sided with the nobility and against the towns in attempting to get money grants from the Estates, an aim which might equally have been pursued by combining with the towns against the nobility; for the rulers were tied to the nobility by common views and a common way of life and thus repudiated any attempt at a conciliation made by the towns.[3] Therefore the dukes were unable to play off one Estate against the other and to strengthen their own power,[4] and they drove Königsberg into embittered opposition; while the other towns were too small and too weak to give it any support.

The dukes of Pomerania also, in 1560, had to promise not to conclude any alliances nor to start any wars without the approval of their Estates, and to consult them about the conduct and financing of any wars.[5] Only native noblemen could hold the office of a *Landrat*, while all other important offices were to be given to native Pomeranians.[6] Exceptions could only be made for very important reasons and with the consent of the most prominent of the *Landräte*.[5] These officials of the Estates had the decisive voice in the government, exactly as the *Oberräte* in Prussia. Within each principality the Estates and their officials fostered the interests of the predominant group, the nobility: in

---

[1] *Privilegia . . .*, fols. 98–109; Breysig, loc. cit., pp. 115–32.
[2] Breysig, loc. cit., pp. 52–53, 57–58.
[3] Ibid., pp. 21–24, 132, 184, 186, 221–2.   [4] Ibid., p. 24.
[5] *Schoettgen-Kreysig*, iii, no. 342, pp. 318–19; Spahn, op. cit., pp. 143–5.
[6] *Schoettgen-Kreysig*, iii, no. 361, p. 350; Spahn, op. cit., p. 25.

the field of commercial policy its interests clashed directly with those of the towns, but their protests were overruled.

When the excise on beer was introduced in Brandenburg in 1488, it was stipulated that the beer brewed by prelates and noblemen was to be exempt from this duty, if they brewed for their own consumption but not for sale.[1] As might have been foreseen, this clause proved almost useless in practice. The noblemen could now produce beer cheaper than the towns and proceeded to brew large quantities and to sell it to the peasants and village inns and ale-houses, to the detriment of the important urban brewing industry.[2] They forbade their peasants to fetch beer from the towns and forced them to buy theirs, so that the excise did not produce the expected yield and the towns lost their trade. This was recognized by Margrave Joachim I in 1513 and in 1523, and he forbade these and similar practices.[3] These orders were repeated frequently under his successor,[4] but they met with little success: for brewing was also undertaken on the margraves' domains, so that their interests were identical with those of the nobility. Nothing occurred so often in the deliberations of the Brandenburg Estates as the complaints of the towns about brewing in the countryside.[5] In 1595 the towns declared that they were no longer able to defend the country because of the closing down of the breweries.[6] Indeed, 891 ruined breweries were counted in the Brandenburg towns, giving substance to their endless complaints; while new breweries were springing up everywhere in the countryside, so that the very foundations of urban activity were undermined.[7]

Until the sixteenth century the corn exports of Brandenburg were handled by the towns and their burghers who benefited considerably from this trade.[8] When the nobility became more interested in producing corn for the market it began to invade this sphere of urban enterprise. In 1523 complaints were raised

[1] *Riedel*, C ii, no. 265, p. 336.

[2] Croon, op. cit., pp. 96–97.

[3] *Riedel*, C iii, no. 198, p. 229; *von Raumer*, ii, no. 17, p. 227.

[4] *Friedensburg*, i, nos. 9, 12–13, 16, 165–6, 184; ii, nos. 332–3, 339, 340–1 (1536–56).

[5] Ibid. i, nos. 9, 16, 103, 141–4, 146, 148, 151–4, 183, 196, 199, 238, 245; ii, nos. 303, 305, 309, 315, 322, 332, 350, 366–7, 396, 437 (1536–64).

[6] M. Hass, *Die kurmärkischen Stände im letzten Drittel des 16. Jahrhunderts*, 1913, p. 167.   [7] Ibid., pp. 166, 168; Croon, op. cit., pp. 96–97.

[8] Hass, op. cit., p. 136; Croon, op. cit., p. 91.

that noblemen were exporting corn, even when this was forbidden on account of scarcity, and that they were doing violence
to the margrave's servants who attempted to prevent this.[1] When
exports were forbidden, the peasants had to bring their corn
into the nearest town for sale; but this restriction was revoked in
1536 because of complaints by prelates and nobility.[2] The noblemen began to by-pass the towns altogether and to export for
themselves or to sell directly to foreign merchants. In this field
also the decisive point was that noblemen exporting their own
corn were granted freedom from the export duty, in spite of the
towns' opposition against a measure bound to jeopardize their
position.[3] Naturally, no distinction could be made between the
Junkers' own produce and that of their peasants, so that the
export duty was evaded on a large scale. In 1540 the noblemen
were permitted to export corn freely overland, but not by water,
even when exports were forbidden in times of scarcity.[4] In 1569
a new export duty for all corn was introduced: three years later
Margrave John George, against a money vote of the Estates,
exempted the corn of noblemen exported overland from this
duty for five years, but as the nobility assumed, for good.[5] In
the early seventeenth century prelates and noblemen were entitled to export their own produce by land or by water, although
it was not expressly stated that they were exempt from all tolls
and duties.[6] In the New Mark, however, for many years no
duty at all was paid by the noblemen for exported corn.[7] In
spite of repeated prohibitions of the margraves,[8] noblemen continued to buy up and to export corn other than their own, to
engross and forestall the market, to hold back supplies during
the winter to obtain better prices in the spring from foreign
merchants, so that there was scarcity and dearth in the towns.[9]

---

[1] *Von Raumer*, ii, no. 17, p. 228.   [2] *Friedensburg*, i, no. 9, p. 36.
[3] Hass, op. cit., p. 136; Croon, op. cit., p. 91. Both refer to an old custom per-
mitting the free export of the noblemen's own corn: but it seems to go no farther
back than to 1527: *Mylius*, vi 1, no. 13, col. 19.
[4] Ibid., no. 22, cols. 61–62.   [5] Hass, op. cit., pp. 137–9.
[6] *Mylius*, vi 1, no. 58, col. 156 (1602). Isaacsohn, loc. cit., p. 17, asserts that they
were entirely exempt from all tolls.   [7] Rachel, op. cit., p. 83.
[8] *Mylius*, vi 1, nos. 16, 36, 58, cols. 29, 106, 156; iv 1, nos. 6–7, cols. 13–14; v 2,
no. 10, col. 78; *Friedensburg*, i, nos. 9, 12, 165, 184; Hass, op. cit., pp. 163–4 (1534–
1603).
[9] Hass, op. cit., pp. 162–3; Croon, op. cit., pp. 93–95: complaints of the towns
of 1598 and 1608.

If the sale of beer and of corn were the two most important commercial activities of the Junkers, they were not their only ones. They, as well as foreign merchants, bought up and exported wool, hemp, flax, cattle, hides, butter, cheese, suet, tallow, honey, fish, poultry, and eggs.[1] Furthermore, the noblemen were entitled to import, free of duty, wine, salt, and millstones for their own use, and misused this privilege to undersell the burghers of the towns. All the decrees against noble trading and forestalling and against similar practices[2] met with little success. The feudal knights thus became merchants and entrepreneurs. In contrast with the English gentry, they had a strong anti-urban bias: they did not need the towns and flourished at their expense. The Brandenburg towns declined further: their monopoly of trade and industry was broken and they no longer dominated the countryside. Stendal, in the Old Mark, in 1556 declared itself unable to pay its share of the margrave's debts: all its once flourishing trade with Antwerp, Amsterdam, and other places had come to an end; houses were decaying in all its streets, and poverty prevented their rebuilding.[3] The towns of the Priegnitz refused to take over part of Stendal's share of taxation because, so they declared, they felt the towns' ruin much stronger than Stendal.[4] Indeed, a few years later almost a quarter of their houses was deserted.[5] In 1564 it was estimated that all the towns of electoral Brandenburg together had only about 16,000 houses.[6] The largest town, Berlin, had just over 1,300; and only Brandenburg, Frankfurt, Prenzlau, and Neu-Ruppin, and, in the Old Mark, Salzwedel, Stendal, and Tangermünde had more than 500 houses.[7] The remaining towns, with an average of less than 300 houses each, hardly deserved the name of towns. In spite of their decline and the prosperity of the nobility, the towns had to continue to pay two-thirds of

---

[1] *Friedensburg*, i, nos. 140, 155, pp. 409–41; Hass, op. cit., p. 162; Croon, op. cit., p. 94.

[2] *Mylius*, iv 4, no. 4, col. 13; v 2, nos. 4–6, cols. 8–13; no. 4, col. 210; Hass, op. cit., pp. 163–4; Croon, op. cit., p. 95 (1549–1607).

[3] *Friedensburg*, ii, nos. 345 *f* and *k*, pp. 111–17.

[4] Ibid., no. 345 *h*, p. 114.

[5] Ibid., no. 484, p. 564: 317 out of a total of 1,373 houses in five towns (1567–9).

[6] Ibid., no. 412, pp. 309–11, 473, n. 4; Götze, op. cit., pp. 250–1.

[7] Götze, op. cit., pp. 250–1. Somewhat different figures for the Middle and Ucker Mark towns are given by A. F. Riedel, in *Märkische Forschungen*, ii, 1843, pp. 191–2; for the Old Mark towns by W. Zahn, *Die Altmark im dreissigjährigen*

all taxes,[1] while the noblemen were tax-free although their feudal obligations were no longer in force. The towns were too weak to resist constant encroachments by the nobility or to influence the rulers in any way. Their part in the deliberations of the Estates was a merely negative and complaining one.

In Prussia and in Pomerania the development was exactly the same. The Prussian nobility was exempted from the obligation to offer all their corn for sale in the nearest town which applied to the other producers. The noblemen used this privilege to buy up corn and to sell it directly abroad or to foreign merchants.[2] The noblemen and the noble administrators of the domains equally were exempt for their personal consumption from the excise on beer; thus they brewed beer in large quantities and sold it to the peasants who used to be supplied by the towns.[3] In vain did Königsberg protest strongly against these activities: it had to admit in 1634 that, in spite of many complaints, nothing whatever had changed.[4] The Pomeranian noblemen also exported corn, some from their own harbours and in their own ships, or sold it directly to foreign traders; they transported their cattle and other produce to Poland, Saxony, or other countries for sale.[5] The towns of Pomerania in vain protested against the trading of foreign merchants, especially Dutchmen, Scotsmen, and Frenchmen.[6] Thus the towns continued to decline in spite of the expansion and the general prosperity of the sixteenth century.

While the towns of Pomerania–Stettin had already been reduced to a state of obedience,[7] the stronger towns of Pomerania–Wolgast, especially Stralsund and Greifswald, had been able to withstand their dukes' attacks and encroachments.[7] In the early seventeenth century they also were finally subjugated by the dukes. In 1601 Stralsund refused to render homage to Duke Philip Julius because he was a minor and thus unable to confirm

Kriege, 1904, pp. 58–59. The towns themselves estimated six inhabitants per house: *Friedensburg*, ii, no. 412, p. 311 (1564).

[1] *Friedensburg*, ii, no. 391, p. 237; Isaacsohn, loc. cit., p. 15 (1562–94).

[2] M. Töppen, 'Zur Geschichte der ständischen Verhältnisse in Preussen', *Historisches Taschenbuch, Neue Folge*, viii, 1847, pp. 313–14; Breysig, loc. cit., p. 22.

[3] Breysig, loc. cit., pp. 21–22; Töppen, loc. cit., viii, p. 315; and 'Der lange königsberger Landtag', ibid. x, 1849, pp. 557, 577–9.

[4] From a Königsberg pamphlet printed in 1640: a copy in *Ostpreuss. Folianten*, vol. 653, p. 6.   [5] Spahn, op. cit., p. 164.

[6] Ibid., p. 173.   [7] See above, pp. 146–7.

the town's privileges; it only withdrew its objections after
lengthy negotiations in which it firmly stood out for its rights.[1]
During the following years the conflict was renewed. The duke
attempted to apprehend aldermen of Stralsund returning from
a Hanseatic diet and attacked and pillaged urban lands. Stralsund sued him in the Imperial court, the *Reichskammergericht*,
which issued a sharp mandate of prohibition. Yet the duke used
internal dissensions in the town to win over the guilds of the
bakers, shoemakers, tailors, and smiths, and thus secured the
opening of the gates to his forces. In 1615 the Estates finally
mediated a treaty between him and Stralsund by which the
town granted him the right of entry and sojourn, and in case of
war the right of maintaining a garrison there.[2] Greifswald was
reduced to obedience in a similar way a few years before. In
1604 Philip Julius intervened as a mediator between the aldermen and the burghers and reorganized the urban administration, the court, and the election of the aldermen.[3] Four years
later there was another conflict: the burghers forcibly seized a
murderer, who had sought the protection of the ducal bailiff at
Eldena, and executed him. For this deed they had to seek the
ducal pardon by humble supplication and had to pay a fine of
5,000 guilders.[4] The towns' opposition was broken for good, and
their political influence waned accordingly.

Throughout north-eastern Germany and the non-German
countries farther east, the nobility was the ruling class. At the
beginning of the seventeenth century the ruler himself was
nothing more than a *primus inter pares*, the largest landowner in
a society dominated by the landowners' interests, a society in
which the production and the sale of corn was the most important enterprise. There was nothing to indicate that Brandenburg or Prussia would ever play a major part in German or in
European affairs.

---

[1] *Memorialbuch* of Joachim Lindemann, Stralsund's town clerk, in *Baltische
Studien*, viii 2, 1842, pp. 79–115; Barthold, op. cit. iv 2, pp. 438–40; Fock, op. cit.
vi, pp. 35–37.

[2] *Erb-Vertrag, zwischen dem Durchleuchtigen und Hochgebornen Fürsten und Herrn,
Herrn Philippo Julio, regierendem Hertzogen zu Stettin, Pommern etc. an einem und S. F. Gn.
erbunterthänigen Stadt Stralsund am andern Theil . . . anno 1615. in Stralsund auffgerichtet*,
Stralsund, 1654, pp. 28–29; Lindemann, loc. cit., pp. 131–5; Barthold, op. cit. iv
2, pp. 449–50, 465–7; Fock, op. cit. vi, pp. 38–41, 51–68.

[3] Lindemann, loc. cit., pp. 119–20; Barthold, op. cit. iv 2, p. 450; Fock, op.
cit. vi, p. 47.   [4] Barthold, op. cit. iv 2, p. 463.

It is true that Brandenburg was one of the larger German principalities and that, as one of the seven electorates, it was of some importance in Imperial affairs. In general, however, the Palatinate, Saxony, Bavaria, and the ecclesiastical electorates were of greater weight than Brandenburg. Prussia, being outside the Empire and a Polish fief, was even less important than Brandenburg. This was cut off from the sea and from all important trade routes; its two most vital highways, the Elbe and the Oder, reached the sea outside Brandenburg territory, and their traffic was encumbered by numerous tolls and conflicts between the riparian powers. Most of Brandenburg's soil was poor, either sandy or waterlogged: not for nothing was the electorate derisively called 'the sand-box of the Holy Roman Empire'. Its towns and industries were negligible and decaying. Its military strength was non-existent, for the feudal services had fallen into desuetude during a long period of peace, and the hiring of mercenaries was prevented by the margraves' impecuniousness and the pacific tendencies of the ruling aristocracy which refused to grant the necessary means. Thus Brandenburg was almost bound to become the helpless victim in any conflict in which it might become involved at a time when great struggles for power were raging in western as well as in eastern Europe.

The likelihood of this was growing owing to the Hohenzollerns' political ambitions and carefully planned policy of marriages which was reaping its first rewards at the beginning of the seventeenth century. For a long time the Brandenburg Hohenzollerns had cast longing eyes on the territories along the Baltic coast, especially Pomerania, which commanded the mouth of the Oder, and Prussia, which belonged to another branch of their family. In 1529 Margrave Joachim I concluded a treaty with the dukes of Pomerania by which he renounced his claims to the feudal overlordship over it and received in exchange a guarantee of the right of succession of his house if the ducal family of the Greifen were to fail.[1] With regard to Prussia, the Brandenburg Hohenzollerns in 1568 and 1578 secured the co-infeudation by the king of Poland.[2] The ties with Prussia were strengthened in 1591 by the marriage of John Sigismund, the eldest grandson of the Elector John George, to Anne, the eldest

[1] Prutz, op. cit. i, p. 188; Koser, op. cit. i, p. 227.
[2] Prutz, op. cit. i, pp. 238, 256; Koser, op. cit. i, pp. 266–8.

daughter of the duke of Prussia who had no male heirs. Anne, moreover, was a double heiress: she was also a niece of the last duke of Cleves and Jülich, John William, who died childless in 1609. Upon his death the husbands of the two nieces, John Sigismund of Brandenburg and Wolfgang William of Palatinate-Neuburg, occupied the rich duchies on the lower Rhine and held them against the claims of the Emperor. A general European war was only avoided by the murder of Henry IV in 1610. After long quarrels between the different claimants the Cleves inheritance was divided and Brandenburg received the duchy of Cleves itself and the counties of Mark and Ravensberg, thus acquiring its first foothold in western Germany. A few years later, after the death of Duke Albert Frederick of Prussia in 1618, the Prussian inheritance fell in, but Prussia remained a Polish fief.

Brandenburg thus acquired territories of great strategical and economic importance, coveted by many European states, but separated from the Mark by many other territories. From this time onwards the Hohenzollerns were bound to be drawn into the power conflicts on the lower Rhine, where the struggle for Dutch independence was not yet terminated, and into those on the Baltic coast, as the Swedish and the Polish branches of the house of Vasa, in their struggle for Baltic supremacy, were eager to gain control over Prussia with its valuable tolls and harbours. In the Thirty Years War, however, Brandenburg's part was that of a passive spectator, and its territory was invaded by friend and foe alike. In 1631 Gustavus Adolphus forced his brother-in-law, George William of Brandenburg, onto the Swedish side;[1] but already in 1635 the elector made his peace with the Emperor, which did not alleviate the plight of his country, most of which was occupied by Swedish troops. When the last duke of Pomerania died in 1637, George William was in no position to enforce his hereditary claims, and the duchy remained in Swedish hands. It was only thanks to French support in the peace negotiations that Brandenburg, in 1648, received eastern Pomerania, the more backward and less valuable half of the duchy, without Stettin and the mouth of the Oder; as a compensation for western Pomerania, she was then given the three secularized bishoprics of Cammin, Halberstadt, and Minden,

---

[1] See Koser, op. cit. i, pp. 439–46.

and the expectancy of the important archbishopric of Magdeburg on the Elbe.[1] Thus Brandenburg became the largest north-German principality, second in size and rank within the Empire only to the Habsburg territories, not on account of its strength and military prowess, but owing to fortuitous circumstances and to the good services of France.

Small territories scattered between the Meuse and the Niemen, however, did not make a strong state: in each of them the ruler was equally powerless, and the real power was wielded by the Estates. Too many scattered possessions might easily divert the ruler's energies and attentions. The real problem therefore was whether the Hohenzollerns would succeed in welding their many territories into one state with a uniform bureaucracy and similar institutions, and whether they would be able to overcome local resistance and particularism. That such a unifying policy was by no means bound to succeed was shown by the example of the Habsburgs whose centralizing policy was only partially successful in some of their possessions and who never established a unitary state. Probably their task was made more difficult by the many languages spoken in their dominions and their entirely different traditions: but the latter also applied to the Hohenzollern territories. The Hohenzollerns, on the other hand, did not have to cope simultaneously with the problems of the Empire, the Low Countries, the Balkans, Italy, and Germany and could thus concentrate on one main task.

That the Hohenzollerns realized the need for creating new institutions, capable of dealing with the problems of their new acquisitions, was shown by the foundation of the *Geheimer Rat*, or privy council, by the Elector Joachim Frederick in 1604. In his instruction for the new council he specially emphasized the pending 'highly important and difficult matters, in particular those of Prussia and Jülich' for which he 'needed good and sound advice by faithful people'.[2] Thus even before the deaths of the last dukes of Cleves and of Prussia the Hohenzollerns began to adapt their policy to their new responsibilities. Furthermore, the elector clearly aimed at the creation of a council not

---

[1] Ibid., pp. 494–5, 499–501.
[2] Instruction of Dec. 1604 in C. A. L. Klaproth and C. W. Cosmar, *Der Königl. Preussische und Churfürstl. Brandenburgische Wirklich Geheime Staats-Rath an Seinem zweihundertjährigen Stiftungstage*, 1805, pp. 299–309.

subject to the influences of the Brandenburg Estates with their purely local and anti-expansionist tendencies. He himself appointed the councillors: among them was not a single nobleman from Brandenburg, but one from Jülich and one from Prussia, to emphasize the link with these principalities, as well as several noblemen from other parts of Germany and some commoners, most of them from Brandenburg.[1] Naturally, the Brandenburg Estates protested loudly against this infringement of one of their most cherished privileges, the *jus indigenatus*.[2] This protest was successful: under the next ruler, John Sigismund, only one foreigner and one commoner seem to have been appointed to the privy council; while the large majority of its new members were noblemen from Brandenburg and from Prussia, usually belonging to leading Junker families, such as the Gans von Putlitz, the von Bellin, von Dohna, and von Schlieben.[3] Thus the native nobility succeeded in conquering an organ which had been created to circumvent its influence. The privy council gradually became a local council for the Brandenburg Mark only and quite unsuitable for the purpose for which it had been founded. Even the *Hauptleute* of two small districts of Brandenburg, both purely local officials, received the title of privy councillors.[4]

When the Thirty Years War engulfed Brandenburg and the other Hohenzollern possessions, no progress at all had been made towards their unification and the creation of common institutions. Inside each small principality the power of the Estates was too strong to be affected by a mere change of the ruling house. The new ruler of Cleves and Mark and of Prussia was normally residing in far-away Berlin and could but occasionally visit his new lands on the Rhine and Ruhr and on the Baltic. In his absence the Estates ruled through their councils and officials as they had done of old. There was not one Hohenzollern state, but only a number of principalities which happened to have the same ruler but had no other bond between them. The weakness of the ruler was the corollary of the Estates' power: there was no sign of any future absolute government.

[1] See the names, in Klaproth and Cosmar, op. cit., pp. 313–16; Prutz, op. cit. i, pp. 286–7.

[2] Schmoller, introduction to *Acta Borussica, Behördenorganisation*, i, p. 76.

[3] Klaproth and Cosmar, op. cit., pp. 317–39 (1608–19).

[4] Ibid., p. 339, assuming that they were only *Geheime Räte von Hause aus*.

THE FOUNDATION OF THE HOHENZOLLERN DESPOTISM

XIII

The Great Elector's Victory over the Estates of Brandenburg

D URING the Thirty Years War Hohenzollern power in Brandenburg reached its nadir: from 1627 onwards the country was occupied by foreign troops, so that the elector for long years had to reside in far-away Prussia which was less affected by the war and less at the mercy of foreign troops. Yet the war at the same time weakened the political power of the Estates and sapped their economic strength. The Imperial and the Swedish troops which in turn occupied Brandenburg did not wait for the Estates' consent before levying taxes, but they put forward definite demands and resorted to force and collection by the soldiery when their orders were not speedily complied with. When the Estates tried to negotiate and to have the demands reduced, they were told from the Swedish headquarters that they could try such bargaining with their elector: the Swedes were using the right of the sword and were not interested in their privileges.[1] These factors were used by the energetic minister of the Elector George William, Count Schwartzenberg, who was not a native of Brandenburg but came from the Rhineland and had been in the service of the Emperor and of the last duke of Cleves before entering that of Brandenburg. He pushed aside the privy council which was dominated by the native nobility and ruled despotically with the help of non-noble councillors.[2] He levied contributions without consulting the Estates and used military force to extort

---

[1] Koser, op. cit. i, p. 507.
[2] Schmoller, loc. cit. i, p. 77.

taxes for the maintenance of the Brandenburg troops.[1] In 1627 he had the councillor von Winterfeldt, a Brandenburg noble-man, arrested on a charge of high treason: two other privy councillors were implicated in the trial so as to discredit them.[2] Soon the privy council ceased to play an important part in the government of Brandenburg.[3]

Count Schwartzenberg increasingly concentrated all matters in his own hands. In 1630 a special war council, or *Kriegsrat*, was formed: it soon became his favourite organ of government and expanded into the non-military sphere.[4] According to Schwartzenberg himself, the other departments acquired the habit of handing on all business which they disliked to the war council.[5] After 1635 all its members, with one exception, were either foreign noblemen or commoners.[6] When the Elector George William died in 1640 the personnel of the Brandenburg government consisted of sixteen councillors ten of whom were commoners, as were all the lower officials.[7] By that time the privy council had ceased to function: as Schwartzenberg wrote to the elector a few weeks before his death, for a long time only he himself and Striepe had acted as members so that it seemed advisable to find another suitable privy councillor.[8] In practice the whole council consisted of Count Schwartzenberg alone, for Striepe was mainly employed with judicial matters.[9] The former was strong enough to forbid unruly army officers to argue, dispute, and criticize and to tell them curtly to obey his orders.[10]

This policy met with the furious opposition of the Estates. When the diet met in 1636 they strongly attacked the war council and refused to vote any taxes unless its accounts were submitted to them. The government, however, merely replied that the

[1] Koser, op. cit. i, pp. 467, 472, 507; Hintze, op. cit., p. 176; F. Wolters, *Die Zentralverwaltung des Heeres und der Steuern* (*Geschichte der brandenburgischen Finanzen in der Zeit von 1640 bis 1697*, ii), 1915, pp. 38, 47, 51.

[2] Klaproth and Cosmar, op. cit., pp. 173–9; Prutz, op. cit. i, p. 341.

[3] According to Prutz, op. cit. i, p. 338, the privy council was dissolved altogether, but there is no documentary evidence for this.

[4] Wolters, op. cit., pp. 26–29, 33–34, 44–46.

[5] *Protokolle & Relationen*, i, p. 74 (Dec. 1640).

[6] Their names are given by Wolters, op. cit., p. 33, and B. von Bonin, 'Der kurbrandenburgische Kriegsrat', *F.B.P.G.* xxv, 1912, pp. 60–61.

[7] *Urkunden & Actenstücke*, i, pp. 398–9 (Dec. 1640).

[8] Letter of Nov. 1640 quoted by Klaproth and Cosmar, op. cit., p. 155.

[9] Ibid., pp. 155–6.

[10] O. Meinardus, in *Protokolle & Relationen*, i, p. xliii (Sept. 1640).

Estates had been invited to send a representative to the war council which they had not done.[1] The diet then was dissolved, and Count Schwartzenberg continued to levy taxes without the Estates' consent. He even introduced a completely new tax by a mere decree.[2] His triumph became apparent in 1639 when selected representatives of the Estates met and adopted an entirely conciliatory attitude.[3] He had gained an important victory over the Estates and simultaneously eliminated the Junkers' influence upon the government: he believed that the one was not possible without the other, and as a 'foreigner' he had no tender feelings towards the native nobility.

At the end of 1640 the Elector George William died and was succeeded by his twenty-year-old son, Frederick William. As happened so frequently in princely families, there had been a strong conflict between father and son, and this conflict had important political consequences. The Estates' hopes revived, and they immediately petitioned the young elector not to subject them any longer to an *absoluto dominatui*, as unfortunately had been the case, but either to let them govern themselves or be governed by sensible and loyal patriots:[4] a taunt at the person of the all-powerful Count Schwartzenberg. It is unlikely that the Estates would have used such language if they had not known on whose side the new ruler's sympathies were. Already as electoral prince he had maintained close connexions with the Estates: this had been one of the causes of the conflict with his father.[5] The quarrel probably made Frederick William critical of his father's policy, or rather of that of Count Schwartzenberg who was its soul.[6] The Estates' hope that the *absolutum imperium* would come to an end was echoed by the ex-councillor von Winterfeldt, one of Schwartzenberg's victims.[7] The issue was thus absolutely clear and fully understood at the time. The question was whether Frederick William would continue the policy of ruling against the Estates and of excluding the Junkers from

[1] Ibid. ii, pp. xiv–xv; Wolters, op. cit., pp. 37–38.
[2] Wolters, op. cit., p. 47 (Aug. 1637).
[3] Meinardus, loc. cit. ii, pp. xxiii–xxiv.
[4] *Urkunden & Actenstücke*, x, p. 88 (Jan. 1641).
[5] Meinardus, loc. cit. ii, p. xxxiii; Prutz, op. cit. i, p. 383.
[6] In later years Frederick William went so far as to accuse Schwartzenberg of attempts at poisoning and assassinating him: Prutz, op. cit. i, pp. 384–5; Koser, op. cit. i, p. 479.
[7] *Protokolle & Relationen*, i, p. 44 (Dec. 1640).

a government which was becoming absolute, or whether a reaction in favour of the Estates would take place.

The young elector acted swiftly. The timely death of Schwartzenberg in March 1641 made it unnecessary to dismiss him or to proceed against him. A few weeks later the main instrument of his strong government, the war council, was dissolved.[1] Instead, the privy council was restored to its former place and even made responsible for military affairs.[2] With the power of the privy council that of the Brandenburg Estates revived: they again levied and administered the taxes and even distributed the money to the individual companies.[3] Some of the officials prominently associated with the former régime were dismissed or retired.[4] By preference noblemen from Brandenburg and Pomerania were appointed to the privy council. Among 16 councillors appointed between 1641 and 1651 only 3 were commoners, and only 4 were foreign noblemen. The majority were Junkers: 6 from Brandenburg, and 3 from Pomerania, from the well-known families of the Gans von Putlitz, von Burgsdorf, von dem Knesebeck, von Platen, von Ribbeck, and von Sparr, von Horn, von Kleist, and von Schwerin.[5] In the elector's absence representatives of the Estates were to deliberate upon matters of state with the privy councillors.[6] Even in small matters Frederick William was anxious to respect the Estates' wishes: although they had not yet expressed any opinion, he declared that he could not see his way to admit the Jews into Brandenburg because it would give the Estates cause for complaint.[7] The change of policy could hardly have been more complete.

The elector soon had an opportunity to intervene in the old quarrel between the nobility and the towns over the repartition of taxes. In 1594 a distinction had been introduced between ordinary and extraordinary taxation: to the former the towns

---

[1] *Protokolle & Relationen*, i, p. 226 (Apr. 1641).

[2] Ibid. i, p. 552; Wolters, op. cit., pp. 39, 62.

[3] Wolters, op. cit., p. 62; Prutz, op. cit. i, p. 393; *Protokolle & Relationen*, i, pp. 224, 557.

[4] Wolters, op. cit., pp. 57–58; Koser, op. cit. i, p. 483; *Protokolle & Relationen*, i, p. 290: dismissal of von Blumenthal in July 1641 because of his prominent part in the former régime.

[5] See the names in Klaproth and Cosmar, op. cit., pp. 346–56.

[6] *Protokolle & Relationen*, ii, p. 594 (Sept. 1644).

[7] *Urkunden & Actenstücke*, i, p. 479 (July 1641).

had to contribute two-thirds, but the latter taxes, for example, those levied for war against the Turks, were shared equally between the two groups.[1] The nobility itself was exempted from all taxes so that the share of the countryside was borne by the peasantry. During the Thirty Years War the problem arose whether the contributions levied by the foreign troops were to be treated as ordinary or as extraordinary taxes. From 1625 to 1637 the towns were only assessed for half of their amount, for they were treated like taxes levied against the Turks: intended to stay a calamity of the Empire. But after 1638 Count Schwartzenberg allocated two-thirds of the Brandenburg contributions to the towns as he considered them ordinary taxes. Year after year the towns protested against this repartition, but their protests were of no avail.[2] After lengthy negotiations a compromise was arrived at in 1643: henceforth the towns were to pay 59, and the countryside 41 per cent. of all contributions; the towns had to promise that they would not introduce *modi generales*,[3] an excise on production and sales after the example of the United Provinces, but would adhere to the antiquated and stereotyped contribution, a uniform land- and poll-tax levied in towns and country alike. This concession worked against the towns which had lost a large part of their population before and during the war and still had to continue to pay their fixed quota. Prenzlau, for example, had only 107 out of 787 houses occupied, the Altstadt of Brandenburg 65 out of 365, Frankfurt 272 out of 1,029, and the smaller towns had suffered even worse.[4] The heavy taxation thus proved a severe obstacle to their recovery, while the nobility remained exempt, in spite of its many commercial activities which weakened the towns.[5]

Yet any attempt of Frederick William to remedy this situation would have seriously affected the good understanding between him and the Estates: in 1648 the privy councillors still emphasized that it was their main endeavour to maintain this relationship.[6] In the long run, however, it was impossible to

---

[1] Isaacsohn, loc. cit., p. 42.

[2] Ibid., pp. 42–43; *Protokolle & Relationen*, i, p. 654.

[3] *Urkunden & Actenstücke*, x, p. 120; *Protokolle & Relationen*, ii, p. 125.

[4] *Protokolle & Relationen*, ii, pp. 113–15: detailed calculation of the towns, with many figures, June 1643.

[5] *Urkunden & Actenstücke*, x, p. 115: the towns in Mar. 1643.

[6] *Protokolle & Relationen*, iv, p. 104: relation of May 1648.

reconcile the electoral policy with that of the Estates. Frederick William's possessions stretched from the Meuse to the Niemen and, although Brandenburg geographically and politically remained the centre of his dominions, he had to consider the problems and dangers facing his other territories. Peace was concluded in 1648, but new power conflicts were likely to break out in the west as well as in the east. In that case the elector was determined not to play the part his father had played in the Thirty Years War, that of a helpless victim of the warring parties, but to use these conflicts to strengthen his own position and to gain new lands: above all Stettin and the mouth of the Oder which had eluded him in 1648, and Jülich which had gone to the rival claimant of the Cleves' inheritance. The Brandenburg Estates, on the other hand, were not interested in the conflicts on the lower Rhine and on the Baltic. They wanted peace and quiet to recuperate from the ravages of the war. They did not care for the rights of the persecuted Protestants of Jülich which Frederick William tried to champion by force of arms, nor for the delimitation of the frontier between Swedish and Brandenburg Pomerania along the Oder. Above all, they were impoverished and thus considered that with the cessation of hostilities the Brandenburg forces should be disbanded as had been the custom in the past: in any case, they would not contribute anything towards any military enterprise to extend the electoral possessions.

Frederick William, on the other hand, looked upon his scattered lands as parts of one whole. As early as 1649, while his relations with the Brandenburg Estates were still quite friendly, he instructed his privy councillors to take into account not only the Brandenburg Mark, but all his lands and subjects and the whole state, and the Estates were to do the same.[1] The issue emerged more clearly in the following year during a controversy between the privy council and the Brandenburg Estates about a question where the latter had strong feelings. The Estates were urged to grant the elector some money for the Pomeranian frontier dispute with Sweden: as Brandenburg and Pomerania were now like *membra unius capitis*, the Estates should act as if a part of Brandenburg were endangered.[2] The Estates,

---

[1] *Protokolle & Relationen*, iv, p. 274 (Sept. 1649).
[2] *Urkunden & Actenstücke*, x, p. 194 (Dec. 1650).

however, replied it was unlikely that Pomerania, Prussia, or Cleves would help them in a similar contingency: therefore Brandenburg should not get mixed up in the quarrels of foreign provinces.[1] There the matter had to rest for the time being.

The next round also went in favour of the Estates. Hard pressed for money as he was, the elector in 1651 introduced a stamp-duty without consulting the Estates. They protested vigorously against this innovation, stating that nothing like it had ever been done in the whole history of Brandenburg; taxes had always been granted by them, after mature deliberation with their ruler, and it had always been left to them to decide upon the *modus* of a tax and the way of levying what they had granted. This protest the privy councillors considered not to be *de nihilo* and advised the elector to suspend the duty. He eventually had to agree that it should not be taken where the Estates' consent was required, e.g. in the *Kammergericht*.[2] The Estates obviously were determined to preserve intact their power of the purse.

It thus became clear that such paltry attempts and mere exhortations would never bring any success to Frederick William. Early in 1652 he decided to call a general diet, attended by the entire nobility and all the towns: such a diet had not been held for thirty-seven years, and it was to be the last of its type.[3] Normally, only 'deputation diets' were called, which were attended by two representatives of the nobility from each *Kreis*, by deputies of the leading towns and of the ecclesiastical foundations. In addition, every year the thirty to forty members of the 'large committee' of the Estates met to transact current business and to administer the Brandenburg finances.[4] The elector apparently still believed in co-operating with the Estates and hoped to find this general assembly more amenable than the smaller meetings. His instruction to the privy councillors and the summons to the diet showed his main aim. Instead of the antiquated contribution, he suggested the reintroduction of *modi generales*, to be taken from each measure of seed-corn, from cattle, merchandise, craftsmen, and each inhabitant, so that rich as well as poor would pay,[5] whereas the noblemen and their

[1] Ibid., p. 196.   [2] Ibid., pp. 207–10 (Apr.–May 1651).
[3] Isaacsohn, ibid., p. 174; G. Schmoller, *Preussische Verfassungs-, Verwaltungs- und Finanzgeschichte*, 1921, pp. 34, 37.
[4] Schmoller, op. cit., pp. 34–35. Cf. above, p. 166.
[5] *Urkunden & Actenstücke*, x, pp. 222–5 (Jan.–Mar. 1652). *Modi generales* had been

demesnes were exempt from the contribution. This was precisely the reason why the nobility declared that the proposed new tax would bring with it *maximam speciem servitutis* and would make them the equals of the lowest in the country and *in ipsa patria deterioris conditionis* than elsewhere; *modi generales* originated in times of war and emergency, and the example of the Netherlands was not valid for Brandenburg. They hit the nail on the head by adding that such a modus once introduced was rarely abolished, would make a hole in the old institutions, and would establish equality between the Estates.[1] Some towns, indeed, came out in favour of *modi generales*; but they met with the strongly expressed disapproval of the noble members of the privy council who stated that the old institutions should not be totally changed or overthrown,[2] thus echoing the opinion of the representatives of their class. Significantly the only commoner among the four councillors responsible for this statement dissented strongly from the majority and often got involved in disputes with his noble colleagues on that account.[3]

The Estates countered the electoral proposition by submitting a long list of their grievances. They asked for a confirmation of all their privileges: their rights of jurisdiction over their peasants, of imprisoning them if they complained and could not prove their case, of evicting disobedient peasants if they had cause to do so, of buying out peasants according to custom, and of doing as they pleased with the holdings of peasants who were *leibeigen*; escheated fiefs should be conferred upon native noble families and should not be added to the electoral domains, so that the nobility would be maintained.[4] The Estates added that they would only grant supply after these grievances had been met: in that case they promised the comparatively large sum of 500,000 talers payable over six years and a smaller amount for two years,[5] while it was more usual to grant money for a shorter period only. The negotiations dragged on, and the diet which

adopted by the Estates of the Middle and Ucker Marks in 1641: *Mylius*, iv 3, no. 1, cols. 77–82; Rachel, op. cit., pp. 511–12.

[1] *Urkunden & Actenstücke*, x, pp. 230–1 (Mar. 1652).

[2] *Protokolle & Relationen*, iv, pp. 556–7: relation of privy councillors Gans Edler von Putlitz, von dem Knesebeck, von Platen, and Tornow, June 1652.

[3] Ibid. v, p. 73: letter of Tornow to Jena, Dec. 1655.

[4] *Urkunden & Actenstücke*, x, pp. 238–41: gravamina of Apr. 1652.

[5] Ibid., pp. 246, 249 (Apr.–May 1652).

had first met early in 1652 was adjourned seven times, the last time with the proviso that the Estates should not appear *in corpore* in Berlin but should send deputies with full powers. When these assembled in May 1653 they asked for a general diet, so that the diet was once more adjourned.[1] Frederick William had resolved not to repeat the experiment of a general diet but to negotiate with the deputies who were more tractable.

The result of the prolonged negotiations was the famous *Recess* promulgated on the dissolution of the diet of 1653, which not only confirmed the old privileges of the Brandenburg nobility, but also added important new rights to them.[2] The elector achieved one of his aims, the grant of 530,000 talers, payable in small instalments over six years, and could thus raise a small standing army;[3] but he had to forgo his other aim, the introduction of the excise and the reform of the antiquated system of taxation. It was a compromise solution, and on paper at least the Estates got the better of the bargain. Most of their grievances were met. Frederick William promised to preserve their private jurisdictions;[4] peasants who complained wantonly could be imprisoned by their masters; peasants could be bought out if the nobleman in question had no demesne or house, and they could be evicted *ob grave et enorme delictum*, but only after due inquisition and judgement,[5] presumably by their lord himself, as he was the owner of the *jus primae instantiae*. These clauses merely confirmed the old privileges of the nobility. But a new clause was added which was to prove fatal to many peasants: *Leibeigenschaft* was to remain in force wherever it had been introduced and was customary; if a peasant against this custom wanted to prove his freedom, it would require bona fides and title on his side, or the knowledge and forbearance of his lord.[6] In other words, the peasant had to prove that he was not *leibeigen*, either by documents which he was unlikely to possess, or through the even more unlikely co-operation of his master. Henceforth the legal presumption was that he was *leibeigen*, at least in certain districts.[7] The very fact that these were not specified opened up possibilities of future extension into new areas.

---

[1] Ibid., pp. 252–4, 260–5.
[2] Fully printed in *Mylius*, vi 1, no. 118, cols. 425–66.
[3] See below, p. 270.   [4] Ibid., col. 436.
[5] Ibid., col. 437.   [6] Ibid., col. 438.
[7] See W. von Brünneck, 'Die Aufhebung der Leibeigenschaft durch die Gesetz-

Prelates and noblemen were to be allowed, as they had been of old, to export their corn, cattle, wool, and other produce free of duty by land or water—with the exception of the new duty on corn which everybody had to pay[1]—and to import likewise their requirements of wine, victuals, salt, and millstones,[2] so that the noblemen could continue to bring in large quantities and to undersell the burghers. If a nobleman's estate had to be sold, a member of his class should be preferred as buyer to a commoner; but if it could not be helped at all and the estate had to be knocked down to a burgher because no one else was willing to satisfy the creditors, then the contract should only be made with the right of redemption, and for a few rather than for many years.[3] In other words, noble land was to remain noble land, and commoners should not become the equals of the nobility by acquiring an estate. Only with regard to escheated fiefs the wishes of the nobility were not entirely fulfilled: the elector merely promised to confer them on noblemen, especially native ones, in preference to others; but he reserved his right to add them to one of his domains.[4] As bailiffs (*Hauptleute*) for these domains he would appoint none but native noblemen, as had been done of old.[5] In the filling of other benefices and offices he promised that he would prefer native noblemen to foreigners; yet commoners should not be excluded altogether, and he reserved his right to appoint them as well as foreigners, whether they had already rendered memorable and useful services or were merely likely to do so in future: he expressly refused to have his hands tied in this respect.[6] In other political matters, however, he had to give way. He had to repeat the promise of his predecessors[7] not to conclude an alliance affecting his subjects without the consent of the Estates and to hear their advice in all important matters touching the country's well-being or ruin; he further undertook to summon them in such *gravioribus causis* and to include his propositions in the summons to the diet,[8] so that the deputies could be instructed. What must

---

gebung Friedrichs des Grossen . . .', *Zeitschrift der Savigny-Stiftung für Rechtsgeschichte*, x, 1889, pp. 42–44.

[1] See above, p. 171.

[2] *Mylius*, vi 1, no. 118, cols. 448, 451.   [3] Ibid., col. 461.

[4] Ibid., col. 441.   [5] Ibid., col. 440.

[6] Ibid., col. 432.   [7] See above, p. 166.

[8] Ibid., col. 434.

have been even more galling, he had to undertake not to introduce the *modi generales* without the consent of the Estates.[1]

Frederick William had got his money grant, but he had to
buy it with concessions which not only confirmed the social
privileges of the nobility but also the political power of the
Estates. From their point of view the granting of supply,
although for six years, probably weighed lightly compared with
the important points which they had scored, in particular as
the noblemen themselves did not contribute towards the grant.
Nor does it seem at all likely that the elector made these concessions with the idea of revoking them as soon as he was strong
enough to do so. It was very doubtful whether he would ever
be able to turn the scales against the nobility, and it was only
thanks to the war between Sweden and Poland from 1655 to
1660 that he could gain the upper hand against the Estates:
otherwise his position would have been the same as before when
the six years' grant expired in 1659. By internal evidence also
it seems unlikely that Frederick William at this juncture had
any plan of making himself absolute and of ruling against the
Estates. It was much more circumstances which forced him onto this road, above all the impact of foreign affairs on internal
developments. It was much more the war of 1655–60 than the
diet of 1653 which marked the turning-point in the relations
between the elector and the Estates in all his territories. Thanks
to his military preparations he was able to play an active part
in this war. He considered it the obvious duty of the Estates, not
only of Prussia, which was directly involved in the war, but
equally of Brandenburg and of Cleves, to grant him the money
for the conduct of the war. When they failed to do so, he raised
it without their consent. At the end of the war he had gained
great strength and a standing army, capable of breaking any
resistance against the collection of taxes required for its maintenance. Thus the Estates were never able to regain the ground
which they had lost: it seems very likely that the same would
have been the case twenty years earlier, if Frederick William
had then continued Count Schwartzenberg's policy.

At the beginning of the war, indeed, the elector continued
his policy of co-operation with the Estates. In 1656 he instructed
his privy councillors to treat them leniently wherever possible

[1] Ibid., col. 460.

and to see that they granted him in an amicable way 40,000 talers for four months.[1] He was even somewhat annoyed that the privy councillors had permitted the town of Frankfurt to raise its heavy contribution through *modi generales*, because the nobility was so strongly against this tax, so that preparations for its introduction in Berlin were stopped.[2] As late as 1658 he decided to postpone its introduction at Frankfurt until the Estates had been heard,[3] and the excise was not sanctioned there.[4] In Berlin it was introduced in 1658, but abolished again, after a few months, because of strong pressure by the merchants and retailers as well as by the local nobility.[5] The Estates, however, refused to grant the large sums required for the war, beyond the 530,000 talers they had voted previously, so that the attitude of Frederick William hardened perceptibly. In 1657 he informed the privy councillors that, for the defence of the country, he considered himself entitled to levy taxes without the Estates' consent if they could not be moved by any remonstrations.[6] Accordingly, in addition to the instalments of the 530,000 talers, from the outbreak of war in 1655 to May 1657, 517,766 talers were levied in Brandenburg, a total of 717,766 talers in just over two years.[7] Yet this sum did not include supplies in kind which, according to one estimate, reached nearly the same amount.[8] In 1656 40,000 to 50,000 talers were levied monthly, and the burden grew until, for some time in 1659, 110,000 talers were raised in a month.[9] Complaints never ceased, and even the privy councillors reported as early as 1657 that the towns would become completely deserted if the burden were not alleviated; military force, they continued, had to be used on a large scale to extort the money, and the poor had to give up everything, even their beds; afterwards it was often impossible to sell the seized goods, so that the cost of such measures was often higher than the amount of tax due.[10] In the

---

[1] *Protokolle & Relationen*, v, p. 159 (Aug. 1656).
[2] Ibid., p. 73 (Dec. 1655).   [3] Ibid., p. 439 (Nov. 1658).
[4] Rachel, op. cit., p. 518.
[5] Ibid., p. 518; *Mylius*, iv 3, no. 3, cols. 85–90; *Protokolle & Relationen*, v, pp. 439, 449, 477, 492–3 (June 1658–Feb. 1659).
[6] *Urkunden & Actenstücke*, x, p. 335 (Jan. 1657).
[7] Ibid., pp. 337–9.   [8] Isaacsohn, ibid., p. 478.
[9] Wolters, op. cit., p. 292; K. Breysig, 'Der brandenburgische Staatshaushalt...', *Jahrbuch für Gesetzgebung, Verwaltung und Volkswirthschaft im Deutschen Reich*, xvi, 1892, p. 452.   [10] *Protokolle & Relationen*, v, pp. 323–4 (May 1657).

towns of the New Mark more than half of all the houses were unoccupied in 1660.[1]

The peasants suffered equally, and many fled abroad.[2] In the Priegnitz a veritable rising broke out at Easter 1656 to prevent the collection of the contribution, if necessary by armed force, so that very little could be levied.[3] Four ringleaders were arrested, but until the summer the movement continued to grow so that troops had to be held in readiness.[4] Thereafter it seems to have subsided.

The period of peace after 1660 brought a certain lightening of the burden, but not a return to the condominium of the Estates; nor was the army dissolved. The towns continued to complain bitterly. In 1661 the small town of Vierraden petitioned for relief, as there were only a few burghers left, and as they had been ruined by the recent troop movements.[5] When the Altstadt of Brandenburg did the same, the privy councillors admitted that its petition was well founded, but could see no way of helping it, as almost all the towns were in a similar plight.[6] Soon after they reported that the towns were declining from day to day and were mere shadows of what they had once been.[7] In 1662 Spandau petitioned: before the wars it had had 400 burghers, and now only 70 to 80 were left.[8] In 1663 the town of Pritzwalk was granted a moratorium for three years because it had lost, through wars and fires, five-sixths of its inhabitants; the trade of the remaining sixth, mainly clothmakers, was ruined and the town almost deserted.[9] In 1666 the privy councillors admitted that the contribution could only be levied by force, the people being totally impoverished and many absconding.[10] Several towns complained that, instead of one N.C.O. and two private soldiers, officers with many more other ranks were sent in to enforce the payment of taxes and that they were compelled to pay them double fees in addition.[11]

The Estates lamented that 22,000 talers a month was now apparently considered *pro ordinario onere*, although they had

---

[1] G. Franz, *Der Dreissigjährige Krieg und das deutsche Volk*, 1943, p. 23.
[2] *Protokolle & Relationen*, vi, pp. 114, 295.
[3] *Mylius*, vi 1, no. 126, cols. 493–6.
[4] *Protokolle & Relationen*, v, p. 145 (July 1656).
[5] Ibid. vi, p. 325 (Apr. 1661).   [6] Ibid., p. 435 (Aug. 1661).
[7] Ibid., p. 441 (Sept. 1661).   [8] Ibid., p. 643 (Oct. 1662).
[9] Ibid., p. 809.   [10] Ibid. vii, p. 434.   [11] Ibid., p. 495 (May 1666).

never, either *expresse* or *tacite*, agreed to it but had often protested against it. They also complained that Frederick William had not kept his promise of 1653 to consult them in important matters, and that they were exhorted to continue with these heavy and unbearable burdens solely *per modum praecepti*.[1] The elector was now strong enough to reply curtly that it was not always possible to call a general diet, for political matters had to be treated discreetly.[2] In reality no general diet was ever held after 1652, and even deputation diets became rare: the Estates had clearly lost ground heavily.

It became obvious that Brandenburg was unable to bear the cost of a growing army if the antiquated and uneven contribution was maintained. Therefore Frederick William, as early as 1661, submitted to the Estates a new proposal to introduce *modi generales*, taking care to instruct the privy councillors that as few deputies as possible should be invited.[3] In spite of this precaution they declined, arguing that any measure introduced previously had always become a *causa continua* and that noblemen would have to pay this tax like the lowest *plebeji*.[4] The elector gave way;[5] but five years later he returned to the subject. A deputation diet was called and it was proposed that, in view of the prevailing misery, a *modus contribuendi* should be adopted to which everybody would contribute.[6] The result might again have been negative, had not Frederick William's hand been strengthened by a popular movement in the towns, especially in those of the Old Mark which had a long tradition of popular uprisings and social unrest. The economic plight of the towns caused a revival of the age-old conflict between the aldermen and the guilds and commons. The burghers began to look at the excise as their only hope of relief from the crushing taxation and to suspect the aldermen, who were the urban deputies to the diets, of collusion with the nobility. In the Old Mark and the Priegnitz the ruling patrician families were often interested in beer brewing and feared that the excise would fall on this industry as that of 1488 had done.[7] For this reason, and also because they paid comparatively little contribution,[8] most

---

[1] *Urkunden & Actenstücke*, x, pp. 389–91 (July 1666).   [2] Ibid., p. 393.
[3] Ibid., p. 489 (Oct. 1661).   [4] Ibid., p. 493 (Nov. 1661).
[5] Ibid., p. 504 (Jan. 1662).   [6] Ibid., p. 510 (Jan. 1667).
[7] *Protokolle & Relationen*, vii, p. 466 (Apr. 1666).
[8] *Urkunden & Actenstücke*, x, p. 571 (Feb. 1670).

mayors and aldermen were opposed to the introduction of the excise. The lower classes, on the other hand, only saw their plight and wanted to escape the contribution and its forcible levying by the soldiers.

The conflict in the Old Mark towns broke out openly in 1663. A burgher of Stendal, Jacob Deetze, and two burghers of Salzwedel established contacts with the lesser towns of the Old Mark and of the Priegnitz and held secret *conventicula*; the mayors and aldermen begged the privy council to prohibit these activities.[1] Deetze and his confederates by-passed the privy council with its majority of noblemen by putting their case directly to Frederick William who was then at Königsberg. He at first severely frowned upon any attempts at undermining the authority of the aldermen and supported the privy council's efforts to uphold it; but when the deputation arrived at Königsberg and submitted a petition for the adoption of the excise, he realized that this coincided with his own intentions and gave them a friendly hearing.[2] The friction between burghers and aldermen continued, above all at Salzwedel, and frequently called for the attention of the privy council.[3] Finally, the elector appointed a commission to investigate the many complaints of the burghers and to reform the urban administration in the Old Mark.[4] It seems unlikely that this commission achieved much, for in 1667 the old state of affairs still obtained there.

When the diet was summoned in that year to deliberate upon the introduction of the excise, unrest broke out anew. The burghers feared that their deputies would again side with the nobility and resolved to take matters into their own hands. Jacob Deetze of Stendal once more took the initiative and was supported by the guilds of his town. They got into touch with those of Salzwedel and other towns and suggested sending a deputation to Frederick William to support the excise. The guilds of many towns decided to participate, while the aldermen feared a general uprising which might become a peasants' war.[5] The

[1] *Protokolle & Relationen*, vii, p. 35 (May 1663).
[2] Ibid., pp. 35–36, 48 (June 1663).
[3] Ibid., pp. 18, 23, 101, 142, 149, 194, 197–9, 238, 350, 417 (1663–6).
[4] Ibid., p. 530 (Aug. 1666).
[5] *Urkunden & Actenstücke*, x, pp. 512–18: the deputies of the Old Mark towns to the elector, Mar. 1667.

deputation went to Berlin and found the elector highly displeased with the Old Mark towns because he had been informed that they were against the excise. For the same reason their burghers were branded as 'plotters and preventors of this highly meritorious undertaking' in the Brandenburg towns through which the deputation had to pass on its way to Berlin. When it submitted its petition the electoral disfavour was changed into grace.[1] In the Old Mark the movement against the aldermen grew so that they feared for their safety unless they gave way; the burghers had to be enjoined to obedience by electoral decrees.[2] But they achieved their aim: the urban deputies to the diet were instructed to vote for the speedy introduction of the excise.[3] The nobility, however, resisted tooth and nail. Its deputies repeated the old arguments that this *onus* would last for ever, and that it would make the noblemen in their own *patria multo deterioris conditionis* than elsewhere and make many high ministers and valiant generals the equals of peasants and burghers.[4] They then offered 24,000 talers on condition that the excise would be dropped.[5]

The towns got frightened and begged repeatedly for the introduction of the excise in the whole country, without any exemption, if only on trial. They emphasized that, if it were only adopted for the towns and not for the country, this would lead to fraud and losses, while the noblemen would brew, buy, and sell without paying excise and thus ruin the towns.[6] Yet Frederick William, always short of money, was won over by the nobility's offer. He once more gave way and decided that the *modus contribuendi* was not to be altered: as he chose to put it, on account of the many weighty arguments of the nobility concerning the interests of the whole country, especially its commerce.[7] Popular pressure, however, increased. In many towns the guilds and commons combined against the aldermen. In the Old Mark the burghers pledged themselves not to pay any contribution and to wring the necks of those who would try to levy

---

[1] *Urkunden & Actenstücke*, x, p. 520: the guilds of Stendal to those of Salzwedel, Mar. 1667.

[2] Ibid., p. 515; Rachel, op. cit., p. 521 (Mar.–Apr. 1667).

[3] *Urkunden & Actenstücke*, x, p. 520 (Mar. 1667).

[4] Ibid., p. 524 (Mar. 1667).   [5] Ibid., p. 532 (Apr. 1667).

[6] Ibid., pp. 529–30, 538.

[7] Ibid., p. 535, and *Mylius*, iv 3, no. 17, col. 23 (Apr. 1667).

its arrears by military force. The agitation began to spread to the peasants who also refused to pay.[1]

The result of popular pressure on the one hand, and of noble pressure on the other, was a decree which proved that the towns' fears were fully justified. It introduced an excise on beer, wine, spirits, salt, seed-corn, cattle, slaughtering, baking, artisans, journeymen, and labourers, but only for the towns, and only for three years, from 1 June 1667; so as not to harm the urban brewing industry, the excise was also to be levied in the towns under the nobility and from beer brewed outside the towns. There followed a clause, however, apparently added as an afterthought, which left each town free to adopt the new tax or not, and to abolish it again even before 1670.[2] And when the nobility protested strongly against this breach of Frederick William's promise of 1653, he replied that he had left it to each town to decide whether it would introduce the excise: therefore the noblemen were free to adopt it for their towns and inns or to leave it.[3] This, of course, meant that they would not adopt it and thus be able to brew more cheaply than the towns. Another privilege was added to their ancient exemptions from most tolls and taxes: the victory was theirs.

In most towns the excise was adopted *tumultuario modo* through popular pressure;[4] but it did not prove a great success. The government's intention was not that the total quantum of the towns should be raised by the excise: it was merely conceived as an aid towards their share of the contribution.[5] Thus most towns soon abandoned the scheme; only Berlin and—after 1671— Frankfurt retained it permanently.[6] The bad effect of this half-measure soon began to show. In 1680 it had to be admitted that the brewing industry moved more and more into the country-side, and that the Junkers brewed larger and larger quantities which they sold directly or through the village inns and ale-houses.[7] After the end of the wars against France and Sweden Frederick William, who was by then strong enough to act

---

[1] *Urkunden & Actenstücke*, x, p. 543 (Apr. 1667).
[2] *Mylius*, iv 3, no. 5, cols. 91–95 (Apr. 1667).
[3] *Urkunden & Actenstücke*, x, pp. 552–7 (June 1667).
[4] Ibid., p. 569; for details see: A. Zimmermann, *Versuch einer historischen Entwicke-lung der märkischen Städteverfassungen*, iii, 1840, pp. 99–105.
[5] Rachel, op. cit., p. 524: electoral resolutions of Dec. 1668.
[6] Ibid., p. 525.   [7] *Mylius*, iv 3, no. 9, col. 110.

without the Estates, decided to terminate the ambiguous situation which had existed since 1667. By a decree of 1680 the excise was made obligatory, but only for the electoral towns; it was to be levied on many more articles and goods; detailed regulations sought to prevent fraud and more brewing by noblemen, either on their estates or in their towns and villages.[1] This decree apparently met with small success, so that in 1682 the excise was extended from the electoral towns to those under the nobility, again without the Estates' consent.[2] This, however, did not stop the brewing and distilling of the noblemen and the other inhabitants of the country.[3]

After 1680 the excise was further modified in detail and applied to more articles, but after 1684 there were few alterations.[4] No attempt was made to introduce it in the whole country: as long as the old Prussia existed, up to the early nineteenth century, the system, or rather two systems, remained in force: the excise in the towns and the contribution in the countryside. From Brandenburg the excise was gradually extended into the other principalities, under Frederick William into Pomerania, Magdeburg, Halberstadt, and Minden, and under his successor into the other provinces; but everywhere it was only introduced in the towns.[5] If they had wanted to do so, the Hohenzollerns certainly could have introduced a general excise, as it existed in the United Provinces, but they seem to have preferred the separation between town and country and the maintenance of the social privileges of the nobility.

At the beginning the municipal authorities administered the excise independently. The aldermen from their midst appointed an 'excise director' and exercised the jurisdiction in excise matters.[6] Soon, however, because of many complaints about incorrect administration and incessant wrangles of the interested groups, the government demanded the right of supervision and

---

[1] *Mylius*, iv 3, no. 9, cols. 101–16.

[2] *Urkunden & Actenstücke*, x, p. 581 (Nov. 1681).

[3] L. von Orlich, *Geschichte des preussischen Staates im siebzehnten Jahrhundert*, i, 1838, pp. 456–8: urban complaint of 1683.

[4] G. Schmoller, *Umrisse und Untersuchungen zur Verfassungs-, Verwaltungs- und Wirtschaftsgeschichte, besonders des preussischen Staates im 17. und 18. Jahrhundert*, 1898, p. 152.

[5] Schmoller, *Preussische Verfassungs-, Verwaltungs- und Finanzgeschichte*, p. 96; Rachel, op. cit., pp. 538–46, 560–70; Wolters, op. cit., pp. 160–1.

[6] Rachel, op. cit., p. 533; C. Bornhak, *Geschichte des preussischen Verwaltungsrechts*, i, 1884, p. 418.

control. In Berlin, as early as 1674, a state official was entrusted with the supervision of the administration and was formally installed as 'excise director' in 1677, against strong urban protests.[1] For other towns a *commissarius loci* was appointed by the government to supervise the municipal administration, usually in several towns. He had to see to it that the regulations were observed, to audit and to revise the accounts, and to decide minor disputes. After 1680 he began to interfere in administrative details and steadily to extend his sphere of influence. The municipal administrators became his subordinates; eventually they were appointed by him and no longer by the town in question.[2] He also began to intervene in other fields of urban administration and to curtail the powers of the aldermen. He became responsible for all matters of 'police' and the intermediate authority between the towns and the government.[3] State officials were appointed to urban offices; the aldermen were told whom to appoint as mayor, or were forbidden to choose certain candidates.[4] Thus within a few decades the remnants of urban self-government disappeared. The towns became subordinate to a new body of officials who were their 'all-powerful guardians', the most typical representatives of the 'police state interfering with everything'.[5] And these officials were appointed by, and responsible to, the elector himself: they were the cornerstone of a new bureaucracy which was entirely at the disposal of the ruler.

The fact that the excise was only introduced in the towns had other equally important consequences. The nobility remained free from taxation. Noblemen merely had to render feudal services in case of war, and these were no longer useful from the military point of view. Therefore Frederick William permitted those noblemen who had to send a *Lehnpferd* in case of hostilities to pay forty talers instead. This was done in 1663 and in 1665,[6]

---

[1] Rachel, op. cit., pp. 533–4.

[2] Bornhak, op. cit. i, pp. 419–20, and *Preussische Staats- und Rechtsgeschichte*, 1903, p. 120; Schmoller, op. cit., p. 96; von Orlich, op. cit. i, p. 453.

[3] *Mylius*, ii 1, no. 56, cols. 175–6; vi 1, no. 157, col. 560; iv 3, no. 17, cols. 171–2 (1683–4); Schmoller, introduction to *Acta Borussica, Behördenorganisation*, i, p. 103.

[4] Zimmermann, op. cit. iii, pp. 17–20.

[5] Schmoller, loc. cit., p. 104 ,and in *Umrisse und Untersuchungen . . .* , p. 300; Wolters, op. cit., p. 159.

[6] *Mylius*, iii 2, no. 36, cols. 61–62; Bornhak, *Geschichte des preussischen Verwaltungsrechts*, i, p. 327; F. Hirsch, 'Die Armee des Grossen Kurfürsten und ihre Unterhaltung während der Jahre 1660–66', *Historische Zeitschrift*, liii, 1885, pp. 242, 248.

but the response seems to have been small so that the permission was not repeated in later decrees which ordered the *Lehnpferde* to assemble.[1] Thus for the time being the noblemen and their growing demesnes did not contribute anything towards the burden of taxation. Even former peasant holdings farmed by noblemen, although in theory liable to the contribution, in practice were exempt. Twice Frederick William attempted to change this and threatened the nobility with an inquiry into the eviction of peasants and the concealed peasant *Hufen*:[2] but these attempts met with complete failure, although local investigations yielded rich results.[3] To give but a few examples: in the small district of Beeskow alone, by 1652 all the peasants in 12 out of a total of 26 noble villages had either left or been bought out and evicted; at least 281 peasant *Hufen* had been added to the demesnes, not counting many deserted and many cottagers' holdings; many peasants had become cottagers, and many cottagers servile labourers (*Hausleute*).[4] In the New Mark district of Arnswalde 263 *Hufen* were held in demesne at the beginning of the seventeenth century; by 1652 their number had grown to 615; up to 1714 the number of peasants in noble villages fell from 420 to 80.[5] In eight districts of eastern Pomerania the number of peasants under the nobility was almost exactly halved between 1600 and 1670.[6] Thus the noblemen continued to evict peasants without much interference by the government, and former peasant land as a rule ceased to be taxable, which meant that the remaining peasants became all the more heavily burdened.

The excise became a permanent urban tax, but the towns did not benefit from a yield higher than their allotted monthly quantum, for such a surplus was not credited to them but to the countryside.[7] They were even more victimized because urban trade and industry were taxed, while those carried on in the countryside remained free. The excise thus became a barrier to the economic development of the towns: to prevent fraud its

[1] *Mylius*, iii 2, nos. 40, 55, cols. 65–66, 87–88 (1669–78).

[2] *Urkunden & Actenstücke*, x, pp. 417–18, 424, 428, 536–7 (1667 and 1670).

[3] Breysig, loc. cit., p. 477.   [4] Franz, op. cit., p. 113.

[5] Ibid., p. 24.

[6] Ibid., p. 124: it decreased from 6,463 to 3,242 peasants; on the domains of the same districts the number only fell from 1,937 to 1,658.

[7] *Urkunden & Actenstücke*, x, p. 581 (Nov. 1681).

payment was checked at the gates of each town by minor officials who inspected everything going in and out.[1] The towns thus became separated by customs barriers from the surrounding country, another obstacle to economic progress. The division between town and country, already very marked, was accentuated[2] by the completely different institutions and financial and economic systems which separated them from the late seventeenth to the early nineteenth century. The urban middle and lower classes remained weak and obedient to the authorities, and the state controlled the towns. The movement in favour of the excise was the last popular movement which occurred in the Brandenburg towns until the nineteenth century.

As the Estates had prophesied, the excise had come to stay. Thus the towns were no longer summoned to the diets which, in the eyes of the ruler, were mainly concerned with the assignment and the repartition of the rural contribution and with the administration of the country's debts and loans. These functions could now be fulfilled equally well by the *Kreistage*, which were attended only by the nobility resident in the small district in question: in the elector's opinion it was no longer necessary to hold diets which would only cost money and raise grievances.[3] The backbone of the Estates was broken through the introduction of the excise. Frederick William used their conflicting interests to split the Estates, and he could then deal with each separately. During his later years this indeed became the main aim of his policy in Prussia and elsewhere: there he used the experiences gained in Brandenburg to the full.

Whatever power was left to the Brandenburg Estates after 1680 was further curtailed by another new authority, the *Generalkriegskommissariat*, which was responsible for the taxes destined for the growing army.[4] Its officials were active and ruthless, more willing to execute the electoral wishes against opposition than the privy council or other old-established authorities. The new officials assigned their share of the contribution to the rural *Kreise* and arranged for the billeting of troops, tasks which had hitherto been undertaken by the local Estates. They interfered

---

[1] *Mylius*, iv 3, no. 9, col. 116 (May 1680); Rachel, op. cit., p. 633.
[2] Hintze, op. cit., p. 208; Schmoller, *Umrisse und Untersuchungen* . . . , p. 157.
[3] G. A. H. Stenzel, *Geschichte des preussischen Staats*, ii, 1837, pp. 424, 449.
[4] See below, pp. 259–64.

with the administration of taxes, while previously the Estates had negotiated directly with the privy council. They issued orders to the Estates and dealt with their petitions and grievances, former functions of the privy council.[1] These points were discussed by the deputies of the nobility in 1683. Those of the Old Mark complained that the total ruin of the country and its institutions was threatening, and that the Estates' privileges would be totally annihilated if these tendencies were not opposed in time, *et quidem mascule*.[2] Those of the Middle Mark, however, advised a humble petition to the elector to let only the privy council deal with their solicitations, but to omit, for modesty's sake, the name of the *Generalkriegskommissariat* and to remain *in terminis generalioribus*.[3] Those of the Ucker Mark agreed with the complaints against the 'insufferable usurpations' of this body and advocated to decline, as far as possible, its *judicium*; but they thought it almost hopeless to avoid it, as the privy council itself consisted of nothing but *Kriegsräte*, who presumably all thought of the *Generalkriegskommissariat* as the soul of the state.[4] The final *votum generale* of the nobility duly avoided the obnoxious word and merely stated in general terms that the ancient privileges were 'almost annulled and emaciated so that no *umbra libertatis* seemed to be left'; the grievances of the Estates should be discussed and settled by no other authority than the privy council.[5]

There could hardly be a better proof for the decline of the Estates' strength within the short period of thirty years. They meekly petitioned against something which they dared not name; they did not hope that they would achieve anything; they knew that they had lost their influence, yet they would not fight to regain it; they were the helpless victims of a development which they did not understand. The separation of the Estates, brought about by their own disunity, was fatal to their power. The absolute rule of the elector and of his new bureaucracy was firmly established.

The burden of taxation was steadily mounting. After 1662 an annual tax of 264,000 talers was levied in electoral Brandenburg; this rose to 324,000 in 1666, but fell to 288,000 in 1674. During the war years of 1678–9 it rose steeply to 448,000 and

[1] *Urkunden & Actenstücke*, x, pp. 586–96 (1683).
[2] Ibid., p. 587.   [3] Ibid., p. 588.
[4] Ibid., p. 595.   [5] Ibid., p. 600.

549,000 talers respectively. After the conclusion of peace it was reduced, but never below 340,000; and in the last years of Frederick William's reign it rose again above 400,000 talers,[1] as much as had been levied during the war of 1655–60.[2] This burden fell on a population of perhaps 270,000 people, or even less.[3] This taxation ensured the maintenance of a sizable standing army which saw to it that the taxes were paid. Yet this had not been achieved without making important concessions to the class on whose support the ruler depended. The nobility remained free from taxation, its social position and economic privileges were reinforced, and it remained the absolute ruler over its peasants and the burghers of its small towns. The absolute government of Frederick William stopped short outside the private estates. The nobility with its strong corporate spirit was always able to bring strong pressure to bear upon a prince who shared its opinions and its prejudices. The result was the conclusion of the compromises of 1653 and 1667 which, for a long period to come, remained the basis of the Hohenzollern despotism.

[1] Hirsch, loc. cit., p. 273; Breysig, loc. cit., pp. 456–7; Wolters, op. cit., pp. 292–3.

[2] See above, p. 190.

[3] If one multiplies the average death figures for 1688–96—the earliest known ones—by 33, the result is 271,300 inhabitants for electoral Brandenburg (Kurmark): O. Behre, *Geschichte der Statistik in Brandenburg-Preussen*, 1905, p. 447. Working backwards from the census figures of 1740, Behre estimated the population of the Kurmark as 207,000 in 1688: ibid., p. 198: thus 270,000 may be too high a figure.

XIV

The Defeat of the Estates of Prussia[1]

THE duchy of Prussia was somewhat smaller than Brandenburg;[2] but it had a larger population,[3] and owing to its
geographical position, the better quality of its soil, and
the energetic policy of the Teutonic Order it was more developed and more prosperous than Brandenburg. It seems
likely that in the late seventeenth century Prussia had a population of about 400,000,[4] while Brandenburg was well below that
figure. Above all, Prussia had one really important commercial
centre, the town of Königsberg, which overshadowed all the
towns of Brandenburg. Its trade was more important than that
of the whole Mark; in the south-eastern corner of the Baltic its
importance was second only to Danzig's, in competition with
which it had risen since the mid-sixteenth century.[5] Königsberg mainly exported the products of Prussia, Lithuania, and
White Russia, such as rye and other corn, hemp, flax, malt,
tallow, wax, and ashes; and it imported especially salt, and to a
lesser degree herring, wine, tobacco, sugar, and spices.[6] It had

[1] The subject of this chapter is much better documented than that of the last
one, in *Urkunden & Actenstücke*, xv–xvi, which print many extracts from *Ostpreuss.
Folianten*, vols. 647–722, and from other sources. Much interesting material, however, has been omitted, and the editors seem to have overlooked vol. 723 of the
Ostpreuss. Folianten.

[2] Prussia comprised 672 Prussian square miles, electoral Brandenburg 459, and
the New Mark 238, together 697 square miles.

[3] In 1688, the year of the death of Frederick William, the figures for births,
marriages, and deaths for Prussia were all higher than those for the Kurmark and
the New Mark taken together: 17,423 against 16,735; 5,095 against 4,081; and
10,880 against 9,854. These are the earliest figures available: Behre, op. cit.,
pp. 133–4.

[4] Using the death figures from 1688 to 1699, the earliest known ones, F. W. C.
Dieterici, 'Über die frühere und die gegenwärtige Bevölkerung . . .', *Mittheilungen
des statistischen Bureau's in Berlin*, iv, 1851, p. 230, estimated the population of
Prussia as over 500,000 at the end of the seventeenth century. But this figure is
almost certainly too high, as he multiplied the average death figures by 37. If
multiplied by 33, the result is 405,000 for the years 1688–92 and 448,000 for the
years 1688–99. Behre, op. cit., p. 198, working backwards from the census figures
of 1740, estimated the population as 358,000 in 1688.

[5] Rachel, op. cit., pp. 364–5, 375. Cf. the numbers of ships from Königsberg
sailing through the Sound after 1557 in: *Bang*, i, pp. 19–387.

[6] Rachel, op. cit., pp. 365, 370. In 1670 Königsberg exported 6,190 *lasts* of rye
and 5,322 of other corn, 2,650 of hemp ,1,134 of malt, and 840 of flax, and im-

numerous guilds, strictly separated into the aristocratic ones of the merchants and brewers which possessed a monopoly of trade and commerce,[1] and the lesser crafts which, according to a list of 1671, numbered no less than 82. There were then 85 shoemakers, 72 tailors, 56 butchers, 47 skinners, 36 coopers, 35 linenweavers, and 14 goldsmiths.[2] The large majority of these guilds, however, had but a few masters; the list indicated comparatively little industry, but a high degree of specialization and of wealth. Königsberg had about 30,000–40,000 inhabitants and was thus much larger than Berlin but smaller than Danzig;[3] it was divided into the three towns of Altstadt, Kneiphof, and Löbenicht which had their separate councils and institutions.

Politically, Königsberg was organized on a fairly democratic basis, the three colleges of aldermen, the three courts, and the guilds and crafts or commons of the three towns all participating in important decisions. The ultimate decision was reached by a majority vote, but the minority had the right of contradiction and could bring its dissentient voice before the diet.[4] The aldermen often referred matters back from the diet to the guilds and commons.[5] The burghers were proud of their privileges, conscious of the wealth and power of their town, and did not hesitate to oppose the duke and the nobility as if they were an independent Estate.[6] Constitutionally this was not the case, for the third Estate was formed by Königsberg and the small towns together, and these participated in the deliberations when a diet was held.[7] Yet their importance was small; they were

ported as many as 5,475 *lasts* of salt, mainly from the Bay: *Urkunden & Actenstücke*, xvi, p. 677.

[1] H. Rachel, 'Handel und Handelsrecht von Königsberg', *F.B.P.G.* xxii, 1909, p. 113, and op. cit., p. 444. They alone were called *Zünfte*, the other guilds *Gewerke*.

[2] The list is in *Ostpreuss. Folianten*, vol. 702, no. 114.

[3] Schmoller, *Preussische Verfassungs-, Verwaltungs- und Finanzgeschichte*, p. 47. Simson, op. cit. ii, p. 463, estimates the population of Danzig at 50,000 in the early seventeenth century. Berlin had at most 10,000–12,000: Zimmermann, op. cit. iii, pp. 93, 118; Schmoller, op. cit., p. 45.

[4] H. Rachel, *Der Grosse Kurfürst und die ostpreussischen Stände*, 1905, pp. 89–91. For an example see: *Urkunden & Actenstücke*, xvi, p. 508 (1666).

[5] Cf. the diet summons of 1640 and 1655 in *Ostpreuss. Folianten*, vols. 647, 660.

[6] Rachel, op. cit., p. 89, and *Die Handels-, Zoll- und Akzisepolitik Brandenburg-Preussens bis 1713*, p. 377.

[7] The small towns voted together with Königsberg, the decisions within the third Estate being reached *per majora*, so that they were often overruled; but they also, on occasion, dissented from the majority: *Ostpreuss. Folianten*, vol. 686, fol. 284 (1661).

treated with scant respect by the government and were helpless in the great struggles between Königsberg and the nobility. They soon became the first victims of the increasing strength of the monarchy.[1]

This applied equally, and perhaps even more strongly, to another group which was not even part of an Estate, the free peasants or *Cölmer*, together with the village mayors and inn-keepers.[2] In contrast to the ordinary peasants, these higher sections of the peasantry attended the local meetings held in each *Amt* prior to the meeting of the diet; there the proposition was read and the deputies were elected; their instructions were debated and drawn up, as was the list of grievances submitted separately by the local nobility and by the *Cölmer*. After the conclusion of the diet both groups were summoned again to hear the relation of the deputies.[3] The deputies themselves, however, had to be members of the local nobility, usually one or two from each of the forty districts or *Ämter* into which Prussia was divided, and they represented only the nobility.[4] Thus the *Cölmer* were not an Estate, and not even part of the Estate of the nobility; yet they were reckoned to belong to the Estates, they were only liable to pay taxes voted by the Estates, and their privileges were confirmed together with those of the Estates.[3] In common with the nobility they had to render horsemen's services in case of war, as they had done for centuries.[5]

If the nobility formed the second Estate, the first Estate, since the disappearance of the bishops and prelates, consisted of the twelve *Landräte*, local officials who were appointed for life by the ruler at the government's suggestion from the ranks of the native nobility.[6] Thus the latter formed two Estates, against the one of the towns, but this did not imply that the first and second Estates could outvote the third, as all three had to reach agreement: only certain limited matters could be referred to the *complanatio* of the government.[7] Yet the nobility occupied the

---

[1] Rachel, *Der Grosse Kurfürst und die ostpreussischen Stände*, pp. 94–96.

[2] See above, p. 161.

[3] These points were stated repeatedly by the *Cölmer* and by the nobility: *Urkunden & Actenstücke*, xvi, pp. 39–40, 598, n. 2; *Ostpreuss. Folianten*, vol. 675, pp. 905–7; vol. 676, pp. 21–22; vol. 699a, fol. 39 (1662–70).

[4] Rachel, op. cit., pp. 86–87.   [5] Ibid., pp. 84–85.

[6] *Urkunden & Actenstücke*, xvi, p. 429, n. 2; Rachel, op. cit., pp. 76–77.

[7] Rachel, op. cit., pp. 206–7; Schmoller, op. cit., p. 62: the dissenting Estate claimed the right of appeal to Poland.

highest constitutional position and dominated the general and the local administration.[1] From its ranks were chosen the four *Oberräte*, the highest officials of the duchy,[2] as well as the *Landräte* who were also the *Hauptleute* of the most important *Ämter*, and the *Hauptleute* in general.[3] In the absence of a diet, important decisions were taken by the 'small consilium', which consisted of the four *Oberräte*, the *Hauptleute* of the four principal *Ämter*, and the three mayors of Königsberg.[4] In this *consilium* all decisions were taken by a majority vote, giving a clear majority to the representatives of the nobility.[5] Equally, when a Prussian court of appeal was constituted in 1657, the nobility received two-thirds of the posts, including that of the president.[6] The voting by majority within all the colleges of the Estates was a characteristic of Prussia, which distinguished it from Poland where all matters were decided *per unanimem omnium ordinum consensum*.[7] Another difference was the relative weight and influence of Königsberg which prevented Prussia from becoming a noblemen's republic.[8] In addition, the Prussian nobility was not exempt from taxation, as was the nobility of Brandenburg and so many other countries.

In contrast with Brandenburg and with Cleves, Prussia was not affected by the Thirty Years War. In the contemporary war between Sweden and Poland, however, Gustavus Adolphus in 1626 landed in Prussia and soon conquered its most important fortresses. Memel and Pillau, which commanded the entrance to Königsberg, remained in Swedish hands. Heavy tolls and dues were imposed by the new masters, and the country suffered badly from the forcible levying of taxes and the depredations of the military.[9] The number of ships putting into Pillau

---

[1] Rachel, op. cit., p. 76; *Urkunden & Actenstücke*, xvi, p. 1058.
[2] See above, p. 168. The *Oberratsstube* was dominated by a few great families: *Urkunden & Actenstücke*, xvi, p. 1057; Klaproth and Cosmar, op. cit., pp. 347–72.
[3] See above, pp. 168–9.
[4] *Urkunden & Actenstücke*, xvi, p. 463, n. 2; p. 760, n. 1.
[5] Rachel, op. cit., p. 126.
[6] *Urkunden & Actenstücke*, xv, pp. 432–3.
[7] Ibid. xvi, p. 522 (letter of Jan. 1667).
[8] O. Hintze, 'Die Hohenzollern und der Adel', *Geist und Epochen der Preussischen Geschichte*, 1943, p. 45, states that Prussia had become 'eine förmliche Adelsrepublik . . . ähnlich wie Polen. . .'.
[9] Von Baczko, op. cit. v, pp. 75–76, 86; Breysig, in *Urkunden & Actenstücke*, xv, p. 185.

declined sharply on account of the new tolls. As in Brandenburg, the example of the Swedes was quickly followed by the officers of the Elector George William. Königsberg and the other towns complained bitterly that he surrounded himself with men who made the burghers pay for everything, that the new tolls ruined their trade, that the officers usurped the urban jurisdiction and demanded bribes from the burghers.[1] On the other hand, the relationship between the ruler and the nobility was comparatively close: the first and second Estates granted him considerable amounts of money and did not press for the abolition of their grievances. They granted taxes on merchandise, drinks, and interest which mainly hit the towns, and the nobility also benefited from the stipulation of maximum prices for the services and wares of craftsmen. This was the price George William had to pay, only that it did not come out of his pocket.[2]

The towns firmly opposed this policy and appealed to Poland; but their resistance was broken. They were further aggravated by the maintenance and increase of the Swedish tolls in the Prussian harbours after their evacuation by the Swedish forces. The approval of Poland was bought by the cession of a share in the administration and yield of the tolls.[3] The towns repeatedly demanded their abolition, but without success.[4] They also complained that beer was brewed in the villages and ducal domains, that the peasants were forbidden to fetch beer from the towns, that urban beer was confiscated in the villages, and that the urban trade was impeded.[5] The small towns and the *Cölmer* equally strongly complained about the depredations of the soldiers, the enforced contributions not granted by the Estates, the damages and the violence they were suffering through billeting and forced labour.[6] These two groups were least able to resist and thus suffered most, while Königsberg and the nobility were better able to defend their privileges. In 1642 Königsberg went so far as to refuse to swear fealty to the new

---

[1] Von Baczko, op. cit. v, pp. 75, 78; Breysig, loc. cit., pp. 184–6.

[2] Von Baczko, op. cit. v, p. 148; Breysig, loc. cit., pp. 197–9, 218; Rachel, op. cit., p. 21.

[3] Von Baczko, op. cit. v, pp. 125–6; Breysig, loc. cit., pp. 216, 219, 222.

[4] *Urkunden & Actenstücke*, xv, pp. 245–6, 278, 333; i, pp. 194, 335 (1640–9).

[5] Ibid. xv, pp. 255, 262, 316–20; *Ostpreuss. Folianten*, vol. 660: complaint of the small towns of 1655, all with many details.

[6] *Urkunden & Actenstücke*, xv, pp. 251, 259–60, 266–7, 270–1, 340 (1640–7).

elector until its grievances were removed, and it took the oath only after long and tedious negotiations.[1]

During the following short period of peace the Estates recovered most of the ground which they had lost. In 1655 they granted the elector an excise on all food and drink consumed in the country, on cloth, manufactures, corn, and cattle, but only for one year, and only against important concessions: the administration and levying of the excise was left to the Estates, it was to be paid into their chest, the *Landkasten*, and noblemen were exempt for their personal consumption.[2] Frederick William also had to give a formal assurance that the grant would in no wise prejudice the privileges and liberties of the Estates, that it would cease after twelve months, that all damages caused by the troops would be repaired and would be deducted from the officers' pay.[3] Thus the elector was enabled to raise some troops for the impending new war between Sweden and Poland, although Brandenburg, by the money vote of 1653, contributed much more than Prussia which alone was directly affected by the war.[4]

It was this war of 1655 to 1660 which decisively influenced the course of Prussian history in several ways. In the first instance, Frederick William, by first combining with Sweden and later with Poland, managed to get his sovereign possession of Prussia guaranteed by both sides, in the treaties of Labiau and Wehlau respectively, which were confirmed at the conclusion of peace at Oliva in 1660. Henceforth it would not be possible for the Estates to play out the elector against the king of Poland and to seek support in Poland if their privileges were threatened. The power and prestige of Frederick William and of his army had grown considerably, and he need no longer fear foreign intervention in the internal affairs of Prussia. Poland furthermore recognized the electoral sovereignty without consultation with the Estates, and the treaties of Labiau and Wehlau were not submitted to them for approval.[5] Their position was also

---

[1] Von Orlich, op. cit. i, pp. 78–79.

[2] *Urkunden & Actenstücke*, xv, p. 359, n. 1.

[3] Ibid., pp. 363–4; *Ostpreuss. Folianten*, vol. 661: 'geeinigtes Bedenken' of 3 Aug. 1655, and *loco protocolli*, 1 Sept. 1655.

[4] According to a note in *Ostpreuss. Folianten*, vol. 669 ii, p. 872, and vol. 682, p. 87, the excise of 1655 yielded only about 70,000 talers; but it was continued until 1661.   [5] Breysig, loc. cit., p. 235.

weakened by the many contributions levied and by the introduction of troops without their consent, by the military rule,
and by the elector's complete disregard for the conditions
which they attached to their grants.[1] The tolls were increased
by him as well as by the Swedes, and new taxes on trade
were imposed by unilateral action.[2] The financial administration was taken out of the Estates' hands by the newly
founded military Commissariat which simply assigned monthly
contingents to the country and proceeded to forcible levying
by soldiers if the money was not forthcoming.[3] For many
years the Estates could only groan about these and similar
practices.[4]

Above all, Prussia was terribly devastated by the marches of
ill-disciplined troops, by looting, burning, and foreign invasion.
According to an old estimate, the Tartars, who invaded Prussia
during the winter of 1656–7, burned 13 towns and hundreds of
villages, killed 23,000 people and carried 34,000 away into
slavery, while the plague killed another 80,000.[5] Dearth and
famine aggravated the plight of the country. In the summer of
1657 only about 20,000 *Hufen*, or hardly more than one in six, were
considered to be able to pay taxes.[6] Königsberg also suffered
badly and its trade declined sharply, partly because of the new
tolls.[7] The excise was continued with a supplement against the
town's protests and to the indignation of the burghers: their
trade had to bear the main burden and food prices rose, while
the countryside escaped much more lightly owing to difficulties
of levying and control.[8] In 1659 Königsberg refused to continue
the excise and to admit Brandenburg troops sent from the

[1] Breysig, loc. cit., pp. 235, 367, n. 2.
[2] Rachel, *Die Handels-, Zoll- und Akzisepolitik . . .* , pp. 389–91.
[3] *Urkunden & Actenstücke*, xv, p. 403; Wolters, op. cit., pp. 164–6.
[4] *Urkunden & Actenstücke*, xv, pp. 372–4, 400–1, 403, 412, 452; von Baczko, op.
cit. v, pp. 233–4.
[5] Von Baczko, op. cit. v, p. 206. Franz, op. cit., p. 27, n. 57, thinks that for
Prussia the war of 1656–7 had the same effects which the Thirty Years War had
for many parts of Germany.
[6] *Urkunden & Actenstücke*, xv, pp. 409, 412. The total number of *Hufen* was about
110,000–115,000.
[7] Von Baczko, op. cit. v, p. 227; Rachel, op. cit., p. 391.
[8] Rachel, op. cit., p. 547. According to an account of 1662 in *Ostpreuss. Folianten*,
vol. 692, no. 153, Königsberg during the war years paid 294,910 talers in excise,
and the remainder of the country only 295,022 talers, or about the same as the one
town: but see p. 209, n. 9, below.

Rhineland, but threatened with force it had to give way.[1]
Frederick William was even more irate when he heard that
Königsberg intended to send a delegation to attend the peace
conference: if they persisted in this preposterous plan they would
live to regret it.[2]

After the conclusion of peace Prussia had to continue to
feed the troops and to pay heavy taxes, which caused renewed
bitter complaints and passive resistance in many places.[3] The
Oberräte reported that noblemen as well as burghers had the
tiles from the roofs seized by the soldiers if they did not pay,
which was quite unheard-of.[4] The years 1660–2 were years
of great dearth in Prussia: the harvest failed several times in
succession, and corn prices soared to unprecedented heights.[5]
Opposition against Brandenburg rule grew. Frederick William
was pilloried as the greatest tyrant and enemy of the people.[6]
Some noblemen as well as burghers of Königsberg declared
that they could not go on living under this yoke, that not even
Turks and Tartars were treated as they were, and that they
were ready to rise if Poland would support them.[7] As the
Estates had not yet recognized the electoral sovereignty, they
considered that their ancient rights were still in force and that
they could seek protection in Warsaw against the violation of
their privileges.[8] According to their accounts, the load of taxation from 1655 to 1661 amounted to nearly seven million
talers, or one million per year;[9] this figure did not include the
tolls and customs: a truly formidable burden for a country with

---

[1] Von Orlich, op. cit. i, pp. 282–3; von Baczko, op. cit. v, p. 242: letters of
Mar.–Aug. 1659.

[2] Von Orlich, op. cit. iii, p. 61: letter of Frederick William to the *Oberräte* of
Aug. 1659.

[3] *Urkunden & Actenstücke*, xv, pp. 461, 470–2, 658–9; von Baczko, op. cit. v,
pp. 312–14, 480.

[4] Von Baczko, op. cit. v, p. 479 (Sept. 1660).

[5] *Urkunden & Actenstücke*, xv, pp. 573, 575, 743, 763 (Aug. 1661–Mar. 1662);
Pelc, op. cit., p. 49.

[6] *Urkunden & Actenstücke*, ix, p. 139, n. 1 (Oct. 1660).

[7] *Urkunden & Actenstücke*, ix, pp. 183, 234, 309: Hoverbeck's letters to Frederick
William from Warsaw, Jan.–Aug. 1661; Rachel, *Der Grosse Kurfürst und die ostpreussischen Stände*, p. 27.

[8] Rachel, op. cit., p. 26; *Urkunden & Actenstücke*, xv, p. 702 (Dec. 1661).

[9] Of these seven millions, 4,565,000 were levied by contribution from the land,
1,472,000 were levied in kind, and 868,000 talers by the excise and its supplement,
the *Anlage*: *Ostpreuss. Folianten*, vol. 692, no. 153; vol. 695, pp. 492–3; vol. 698,
fols. 25–26.

P

a few hundred thousand inhabitants, ravaged by war, plague, and famine.

It was thus obvious that the Estates would not simply recognize the changes resulting from the war and the electoral sovereignty, but that they would use the opportunity of a diet called for this purpose to demand, the recognition of their privileges and the abolition of their grievances: the continued presence of troops and the heavy taxes exacted for their maintenance, and, as far as Königsberg was concerned, the continuation of the tolls and excise which impeded its trade. This diet was called in May 1661 and lasted exactly two years. It was only concluded after a long struggle and after the arrival of Frederick William himself with military strength. This long diet of 1661–3 compared in importance with the long Brandenburg diet of 1652–3, and its result also was a compromise between the ruler and the Estates. Their resistance and the important concessions they gained, in spite of the war which had weakened them considerably, proved the firm roots and the vitality of the institution.

At the opening of the diet the Estates were treated to a long sermon: the preacher stressed that changes in empires and principalities were made by God because of the sins of their inhabitants and would cease with them; a kind ruler was like a shepherd of his people who was entitled to take the wool of his flock but not their skins; it was for the powers that be alone to make laws and to rule, to grant privileges and liberties and to maintain them; this the subjects had to recognize and had to honour and obey the powers, for they were God's image; who honoured them honoured God Himself, and who despised them despised God Himself; who resisted the powers resisted the ordinance of God and would not escape His judgement, while privileges were but private laws.[1] This homily did not improve the mood of the Estates and only contributed to earn its author their undying hatred. The doctrine of the Divine Right certainly had few adherents in Prussia at that time. The Estates, according to custom, then proceeded to formulate their grievances, most prominent among which were the forcible levying

---

[1] 'Landtags-Predigt, Bey der Zusammenkunfft der Gesambten Löblichen Stände des Hertzogthumbs Preussen . . . gehalten Durch Christian Dreiern . . .', Königsberg, 1661, pp. 19, 23–26: a copy in *Ostpreuss. Folianten*, vol. 672. Cf. *Romans*, xiii. 1–2.

of taxes and demands for the disbanding of the troops and for the cessation of all military measures.[1] They also showed that, beyond negative demands, they fully understood the issue, for they asked for biennial diets lasting a definite number of weeks and for notification of the subjects to be discussed a fortnight in advance, so that the deputies could be properly instructed after due discussion.[2]

A few days later the Estates officially renounced the excise and the new tolls, as they had only granted them for a limited time and for definite purposes.[3] It became increasingly difficult to collect the excise: the noblemen forbade their tenants to pay it, and all mills, except the electoral ones, ceased to charge it, so that the ruler lost his mill dues as well.[4] The government was forced to make concessions: the number of troops and of the officials employed in the obnoxious Commissariat was severely reduced;[5] the contribution, the levies in kind, the new tolls, and the excise supplement, but not the excise itself, were rescinded, and the excise was reduced to the pre-war rates.[6] These concessions, however, were insufficient to pacify the opposition. Königsberg in particular felt aggrieved because the excise was continued: it could not escape it as easily as the countryside.[7] The burghers especially were strongly opposed to it, while the aldermen were more conciliatory.[8] The latter often complained to the authorities about the suspicion and the popular pressure under which they suffered.[9]

This cleavage inside Königsberg equally emerged with regard to the cardinal issue, the recognition of the electoral sovereignty by the Estates. Already before the diet met the commons were urging that a deputation should go to Warsaw and seek support there against Brandenburg. The aldermen opposed this and

[1] *Urkunden & Actenstücke*, xv, pp. 461, 472, 529, 658–9.
[2] Ibid., pp. 526, 638 (July and Nov. 1661).
[3] Ibid., p. 532 (July 1661).
[4] Ibid., pp. 461, 547, 626, 760: letters to the elector of Aug. and Nov. 1661 and Mar. 1662.
[5] Ibid., p. 562: electoral decree of Aug. 1661; but see Wolters, op. cit., pp. 167–8: the whole Commissariat was paid for another year, and some of its officials until the autumn of 1663.
[6] Electoral patent of 8 Aug. 1661: copies in *Ostpreuss. Folianten*, vols. 672, 677.
[7] See above, p. 208, n. 8.
[8] *Urkunden & Actenstücke*, xv, pp. 585, 611; xvi, p. 163 (Oct. 1661–June 1662).
[9] Ibid. xv, pp. 509, 552, 763; xvi, pp. 93, 119, 138, 153: letters of von Schwerin to the elector, July 1661–June 1662.

asked them to wait at least until the diet had met, but the commons persisted and held their own meetings to discuss the matter. The aldermen were dismayed, the more so because the urban courts sided with the commons, although they were considered a *pars magistratus*.[1] The mayor of the Altstadt, when appealed to by von Schwerin, the electoral representative, said that they and their descendants would lose all their freedom if they did not send the deputation.[2] The burghers, we are told, believed that only the king of France was sovereign: when he needed money, he could ask his subjects to declare their property; if anyone then made a false declaration, he lost his head as well as all his possessions to the king: this was the power the elector would wield if he became sovereign.[3] After lengthy negotiations, in November 1661, the first and second Estates, the aldermen and the courts of Königsberg, and the small towns recognized Frederick William's sovereignty under certain conditions; but the commons of Königsberg dissented and refused to give way, unless their consent were asked in a general Sejm of Poland.[4] They thus felt strong enough to oppose their aldermen as well as the government and the nobility.

The man who emerged during these months as the leader of the popular opposition was the *Schöppenmeister* (foreman of the jury) of the Kneiphof court, Hieronymus Roth. He was the son of a well-known and wealthy Königsberg family; his ancestors had been ducal councillors and judges, and his father had been the mayor of the Kneiphof. He himself was a member of the aristocratic merchants' guild and owned considerable property.[5] The *Schöppenmeister* was the natural spokesman of the burghers, as he had to report their decisions to the aldermen: as Roth put it himself, he was 'the burghers' mouth'.[6] Roth's influence was so strong that Frederick William's representative, von Schwerin, requested his presence and tried to argue with him. Roth, however, stood his ground: the Prussians were free men and had

---

[1] *Ostpreuss. Folianten*, vols. 674 and 686, fol. 1261: 'Ex Protocollo der Erbahren Räthe der dreyen Städte Königsbergk . . . den 13 May Anno 1661.'

[2] *Urkunden & Actenstücke*, xv, pp. 519–20 (July 1661).

[3] Ibid., p. 552: von Schwerin to the elector in Aug. 1661.

[4] Ibid., pp. 621–3, 631–2.

[5] O. Nugel, 'Der Schöppenmeister Hieronymus Roth', *F.B.P.G.* xiv, 1901, pp. 395–7, 399–400.

[6] Ibid., p. 404.

never been any ruler's direct subjects; the king of Poland could not cut off a free people from the crown without their consent; nobody could object to his speaking for the freedom of his country, and he was prepared to repeat his words to the elector.[1] Von Schwerin insisted that Roth should be arrested and tried.[2] Early in 1662 the town of Kneiphof received an order to hand him over, but decided to appeal against it.[3] The burghers were further embittered by the construction of new fortifications on urban land by the commander of the electoral fortress near Königsberg. They rightly perceived that the new works were planned against their town;[4] they tried to disturb the work and to destroy it, but were repulsed by the soldiers.[5] Frederick William fully upheld the action taken by his forces.[6] The Kneiphöfers were so incensed that they daily pressed the aldermen to send the deputation to Warsaw; the latter told von Schwerin that their lives would be in danger if they attempted to arrest the ringleaders.[7]

During the following months the pressure on the aldermen to withdraw their recognition of the electoral sovereignty continued unabated, and their side was weakened by the defection of the courts of the Kneiphof and Löbenicht which made common cause with the burghers. These declared that a few noble deputies could not grant what was opposed by so many thousand burghers, and that an appeal to the king of Poland was no rebellion.[8] Finally the two disaffected courts and all the commons of Königsberg appealed to King John Casimir for help: they had been separated from Poland by force and would never consent to it, for the transfer of sovereignty was legally void.[9] In July 1662 Roth proposed to the assembled burghers a solemn oath against 'the foreign councillors' who wanted to cut off the

---

[1] *Urkunden & Actenstücke*, xv, pp. 595–6, 614–19.

[2] Ibid., pp. 597, 611, 715 (Oct. 1661–Jan. 1662).

[3] Ibid., p. 750 (Feb. 1662).

[4] *Ostpreuss. Folianten*, vol. 669 ii, pp. 136–7: 'Der Städte Königsberg Unterthänigste Bittschrift umb demolirung der Schantze Friederichsburg.'

[5] *Protokolle & Relationen*, vi, pp. 537–9; *Urkunden & Actenstücke*, xv, p. 726; von Baczko, op. cit. v, p. 325.

[6] *Protokolle & Relationen*, vi, p. 541 and n. 1; von Orlich, op. cit. iii, pp. 125–7, 139.

[7] *Urkunden & Actenstücke*, xv, p. 747: von Schwerin to the elector in Feb. 1662.

[8] Ibid. xvi, pp. 93, 137–8, 153 (Apr.–June 1662).

[9] Ibid. xvi, pp. 155–62 (June 1662).

free Prussians from the Polish crown; they were to defend their freedom with their lives and not to rest until the old state of affairs was restored.[1] The authorities enforced a blockade against Königsberg, while the Kneiphöfers mobilized the burgher guard, manned the town walls and mounted cannon to defend themselves against any attack.[2] Roth's oratory dominated the burgher assemblies which were held against the prohibition of the aldermen.[3]

The situation was, however, dramatically changed by the arrival of Frederick William and by the subsequent arrest of Roth through a military *coup de main* in October: he was taken by soldiers from his house, put into a carriage and brought to the castle; troops stood in readiness outside the town, but no resistance was offered.[4] Roth was then interrogated at length by the privy councillors, but they were unable to establish any definite guilt.[5] He was taken away to a Brandenburg fortress and imprisoned there for the rest of his life without ever being brought to trial.[6] With the arrest of their leader the burghers' resistance collapsed. A year after his arrival in Prussia Frederick William could write from there that everything was quiet in Königsberg and everybody content.[7] Faced with strong military force and unsupported by Poland and by the Estates the burghers had to recognize the electoral sovereignty.

Meanwhile the diet dragged on. In March 1662 the first and second Estates granted the elector the desired excise for three

---

[1] Von Baczko, op. cit. v, pp. 483–4; *Urkunden & Actenstücke*, xvi, p. 173, n. 4.

[2] *Ostpreuss. Folianten*, vol. 669 ii, pp. 990, 1058–9; vol. 690 ii, fols. 265–6, 284; *Urkunden & Actenstücke*, xvi, pp. 192–3, 196 (18–25 July 1662).

[3] *Urkunden & Actenstücke*, xvi, pp. 196, 226, 235: reports of July and Sept. 1662.

[4] Slightly different versions of the arrest in *Ostpreuss. Folianten*, vol. 668 ii, p. 407; vols. 674, 676, 679, pp. 1583–4; vols. 686, 689 i, fol. 31 (while Breysig, loc. cit., p. 250, n. 1, says that he was unable to find any report about the arrest).

[5] *Urkunden & Actenstücke*, xvi, pp. 253 ff.; *Ostpreuss. Folianten*, vol. 689 i, fols. 32–33 (Nov. 1662). There is no evidence whatever for the statement that Roth was tried, found guilty, and sentenced for high treason: thus W. Platzhoff in B. Gebhardt, *Handbuch der deutschen Geschichte*, 7th ed., i, 1930, p. 806, and F. Schevill, *The Great Elector*, 1948, p. 211.

[6] It does not seem justified to say that Roth 'represented reactionary ideas' (Nugel, loc. cit., p. 477) or that he was 'hopelessly and everlastingly in the wrong' (Schevill, op. cit., p. 210). Roth certainly was no champion of modern democracy, as little as were Peter and Paul Wentworth or Sir John Eliot; but he stood out for the same ideas which they defended: with the difference that he was defeated, while their ideas ultimately triumphed.

[7] *Urkunden & Actenstücke*, ix, p. 864 (Oct. 1663); cf. ibid., pp. 843–5.

years, but only under stringent conditions: its administration was to remain in the hands of the Estates; after three years a diet was to be summoned to hear the accounts; no other tax or imposition was to be levied during that time; three-quarters of the money was to be used to redeem pawned domains; the Estates were not to be obliged to pay the electoral debts nor to feed the troops; the grant was not to prejudice in the least degree the country's privileges or their posterity.[1] Most of these conditions, but not the allocation of supply, were accepted by Frederick William.[2] Königsberg, however, continued to object to the excise which it disliked particularly and insisted that grievances must be abolished first.[3] The government tried to use its right of *complanatio* against the town;[4] but it remained firm, although the aldermen did their best to win over the burghers.[5] For five months the electoral mills remained closed and the burghers' corn was ground without a payment of excise, so that the *complanatio*, although published by decree, was invalidated.[6] Instead Königsberg offered to pay 66,000 talers, but the offer was declined.[7] After his arrival in Prussia Frederick William made further important concessions: he promised not to start an offensive war concerning Prussia, nor to levy any tax, either in peace or war, without the Estates' consent.[8] These, however, replied that, if their consent was alone required for offensive wars but not defensive ones, their influence would be excluded for ever, and that anyhow the difference was merely one of words.[9]

The Estates then came back to their demand for biennial or triennial diets. Frederick William was willing to summon a diet every six years, but the Estates insisted on three.[10] No wonder that he wrote several times during these months that he was tired of these negotiations, that he would use other means and

[1] Ibid. xvi, p. 18, n. 2.   [2] Ibid., p. 94, n. 4.
[3] Ibid., pp. 56–57, 87.
[4] *Ostpreuss. Folianten*, vols. 687, 690 ii, 683: electoral patent of 1 June 1662; *Urkunden & Actenstücke*, xvi, pp. 120–1.
[5] *Ostpreuss. Folianten*, vol. 682, pp. 290–4; *Urkunden & Actenstücke*, xvi, p. 163 (June 1662).
[6] *Urkunden & Actenstücke*, xvi, p. 290, n. 1.
[7] Von Baczko, op. cit. v, p. 333 (June 1662).
[8] *Urkunden & Actenstücke*, xvi, p. 290 (Nov. 1662).
[9] Ibid., pp. 338–9 (Jan. 1663).
[10] Ibid., pp. 303, 352–3 (Dec. 1662–Mar. 1663).

show his teeth, that the Prussians were bad people, and worse than those of Cleves.[1] In the end most of the demands had to be granted. He promised to maintain the Estates' privileges, not to levy any taxes without their consent, to wage war without their agreement only *in casibus necessitatis*, to hear and heed their advice in all important matters affecting Prussia, and to hold triennial diets.[2] Even Königsberg was permitted to raise its share of the sum granted, 100,000 out of 280,000 talers, by taxes of its own choosing and thus escaped the excise; it was to employ its own collectors and to have its separate financial administration, while the nobility and the small towns administered the excise.[3] Nor was the elector more successful in furthering the cause of his co-religionists, the Calvinists: they were excluded from all important offices, which remained reserved·to Lutherans, and were only conceded two posts in each of the higher courts and four posts as *Hauptleute* of the *Ämter*, exclusive of the four principal ones.[4] Thus any attempts to foster an electoral faction among the higher officials in opposition to the strictly Lutheran majority were not likely to meet with much success. About 1690 Frederick William's successor was still advised by a Prussian supporter to protect the Reformed religion with more vigour than had been done in the past, so that the Calvinists would to some extent at least be able to hold the balance against the Lutherans.[5] Obviously no headway had been made in this respect in twenty-seven years.

In spite of all electoral concessions, however, the diet of 1661–3 marked the beginning of the end of the Estates' political power and the commencement of monarchical government,[6] like the Brandenburg diet of 1652–3. The Prussian Estates had granted the money with which a small army could be maintained in peace-time, and against this cardinal fact privileges

---

[1] *Urkunden & Actenstücke*, ix, pp. 846–7, 851–2 (Jan.–Mar. 1663).

[2] It is usually stated (e.g. by Schmoller, op. cit., p. 64) that the request for triennial diets was not granted, but Prince Radzivill, the governor of Prussia, *Urkunden & Actenstücke*, xvi, p. 480, n. 1, expressly stated the opposite.

[3] Von Baczko, op. cit. v, pp. 489–503; *Urkunden & Actenstücke*, xvi, pp. 103, 418–25, 480, n. 1 (Mar.–May 1663).

[4] Von Baczko, op. cit. v, p. 503 (July 1663). Hintze, *Geist und Epochen der Preussischen Geschichte*, p. 45, and Schmoller, op. cit., p. 64, wrongly assert that the Calvinists were admitted 'to the offices'.

[5] *Urkunden & Actenstücke*, xvi, p. 1058; cf. M. Spahn, ibid., p. 1084.

[6] Breysig, ibid. xv, p. 469.

were of no avail. As an alderman of Königsberg put it a few years later, they had suspected at the beginning of the elector's sovereignty that he would be unable to exist without an army: in itself they did not object to this, if only their privileges could be preserved.[1] Yet the struggle between the ruler and the Estates was by no means over. In contrast with Brandenburg and with Cleves, it continued to the end of the reign, and even then Frederick William was by no means as absolute in Prussia as he was in Brandenburg, another sign of the vitality of the Prussian Estates. The years after 1663 were comparatively peaceful. For the time being the elector was satisfied with the taxes granted, as he was not involved in war until 1672. The Estates insisted on their power of the purse and on triennial diets, which they considered the cornerstone of their liberties.[2] But they did not prove too difficult about the extension of the excise when it was due to expire. It was prolonged for two years in 1666 and in 1668, against a formal assurance that it would automatically cease after that time unless it was extended by the Estates.[3] Even Königsberg accepted the excise, but only after renewed strife inside the town.[4]

Frederick William himself thought the excise the most suitable modus, for the nobility contributed little, and the towns and the peasants most.[5] And this opinion was fully shared by the towns.[6] Indeed, during the first year of the common excise Königsberg alone paid 32 per cent. of the amount collected.[7] Thus the old conflicts inside the town and between the town and the nobility over the modus of taxation were bound to break out anew. This happened in 1670 with the expiration of the excise granted in 1668. The elector threatened to continue it without a grant and even to impose a land-tax by force unless the Estates reached agreement.[8] The government enjoined speed and promised the elector's thousandfold thanks for a favourable vote, which caused derisive gestures among the Königsberg deputies.[9] Two months

[1] Ibid. xvi, p. 645, n. 1 (Nov. 1670).
[2] Ibid., p. 480, n. 1: Prince Radzivill to the elector in Mar. 1666.
[3] Ibid., pp. 515–19, 541 (Sept. 1666 and July 1668).
[4] Ibid., pp. 506–9 (July 1666).
[5] Ibid., p. 504, n. 1: the elector to the government in July 1666.
[6] Ibid., p. 506, n. 1; p. 544; *Ostpreuss. Folianten*, vol. 692, no. 123 (1666–8).
[7] *Urkunden & Actenstücke*, xvi, p. 543, n. 1; cf. above, p. 208, n. 8.
[8] Ibid., p. 613, n. 1: electoral rescript of Aug. 1670.
[9] Ibid., p. 635, n. 1 (Sept. 1670).

later Frederick William ordered the levy of a land-tax, but a few days later he cancelled this order on condition that the Estates granted him an excise for three years.[1] It took several more months of negotiations before the Estates made any grant. Not only the commons of Königsberg, but also the nobility now strongly objected to the excise and made common cause against its renewal.[2] The nobility then granted only 42,000 talers for four months, which Frederick William at first wanted to reject, but eventually accepted; while Königsberg granted a poll-tax.[3] It was only in September 1671 that the excise was granted anew for two years, under the conditions that it would be administered by the Estates and would be paid into their chest, that it would automatically expire after the stipulated time, and that no other taxes would be levied except in a case of emergency. The small towns' protest against the excise was overridden.[4]

Again Königsberg was considered the core of the opposition. How hostile the mood against the town was among the electoral officers and officials emerged from the examination of the captain of horse, Hugh Montgomery, and some inhabitants of the town of Fischhausen in January 1671. The former electoral representative in Warsaw, von Brandt, while staying at Fischhausen, had indulged in wild talk against Königsberg. The witnesses testified under oath that he had said: Königsberg was not worthy to have such a gracious master; if he were the elector, he would drive many out of the town and put honest people into it, and then he would levy contribution by force throughout the country.[5] The towns demanded that von Brandt should be punished,[6] but nothing more was heard about the affair. During the following years the excise was regularly paid, to the amount of nearly 100,000 talers each year; up to 1676 it accounted for over 60 per cent. of all Prussian taxes.[7]

From 1672 onwards Brandenburg was again involved in war, this time on the Rhine against Louis XIV. The war decisively

---

[1] *Urkunden & Actenstücke*, xvi, p. 646, n. 2: electoral rescripts of Nov. 1670.

[2] Ibid., p. 637, n. 1; p. 685 (Aug. 1670–Feb. 1671).

[3] Ibid., pp. 692–4 (Mar. 1671).

[4] Ibid., pp. 708–9, 711, n. 2; pp. 712–13, 716 (Sept. 1671).

[5] *Ostpreuss. Folianten*, vol. 701, nos. 122–4; vol. 702, nos. 44 a–c.

[6] Ibid., vol. 701, no. 112; vol. 702, pp. 1059–60 (Feb. 1671).

[7] *Urkunden & Actenstücke*, xvi, p. 836: the remaining 40 per cent. came from poll-taxes. Cf. ibid., p. 938, n. 1: the annual yield of the excise was fairly even up to 1679.

affected the relations between Frederick William and the Prussian Estates, although Prussia was only touched by the war when the Swedes invaded the duchy at the end of 1678: exactly as the Estates of Brandenburg and of Cleves were deprived of their power by the war of 1655–60, which took place far away from these principalities. As the Prussian Estates showed no interest in German or Imperial affairs, the government used an opportune threat from the Turks to induce them to vote money.[1] The Estates, however, proved as difficult as ever. They disbelieved in the Turkish danger and declared that the French threat to Cleves did not affect them: they need not participate in all wars in Europe.[2] The towns argued that they were so impoverished that they could not even pay the expenses of their deputies to the diet; Memel had to maintain a garrison of 500, not counting wives and children, and some burghers had 3 to 4 soldiers billeted upon them; other small towns stated that their garrisons had grown from 25 to 90 men.[3] The government and the *Landräte* emphasized the poverty and dearth in the country which caused numerous holdings to become deserted.[4] Fourteen months later the governor, the Duke of Croy, reported that the poverty was very great and daily growing, and that want made any action impossible.[5] In the spring of 1674 he sent to Berlin a sample of the bread eaten by the peasants, which mainly consisted of chaff and ground bark, to underline his statements; the cattle were dying from disease and the people were escaping into Poland.[6]

Frederick William, however, hardened perceptibly. He was preoccupied with the war and considered this a case of emergency overriding all privileges. Early in 1673 he wrote that, according to experience, the costly diets and deliberations with the Estates did not help, that the present highly dangerous junctures did not admit such lengthy procedures, and that he was forced to take different measures.[7] Soon after he ordered

---

[1] Ibid., p. 746, n. 1: the Duke of Croy to the elector in May 1672 regretting that the Turkish danger had ceased.
[2] Ibid., pp. 797–8 (Mar. 1674).
[3] Ibid., pp. 737, 751, n. 1 (Apr.–June 1672).
[4] Ibid., pp. 723–4; von Orlich, op. cit. i, pp. 354, 362 (1672).
[5] Von Orlich, op. cit. i, p. 360 (Apr. 1673).
[6] Ibid. i, p. 363.
[7] *Urkunden & Actenstücke*, xvi, pp. 770–1 (Jan. 1673).

the government to impose a land-tax without a grant by the Estates.[1] In the summer he threatened the same, because no privilege or assurance could oblige him to abandon his state and the welfare of the country: in such emergencies *salus provinciae* must be the supreme law.[2] The poll-tax, which was eventually granted, was immediately levied by the military, and the excise was forcibly continued.[3] The land-tax was decreed by the government, but it had to report that not even the hardest military measures could bring it all in, for there was nothing left to be seized of the peasants and the impounded cattle found no buyers.[4] Early in 1674 the nobility assembled in strength in Königsberg and the governor feared a revolution: yet the feared alliance between nobility and burghers did not materialize.[5] Königsberg resolutely opposed all taxes it had not consented to: General von Görtzke, the military commander, pressed strongly for the use of force against it, but Berlin could not reach a decision.[6]

In May 1674 Königsberg was finally occupied by the army. Early in the morning several thousand men marched quietly into the town; they found the gates open, occupied the streets and squares, unhinged the gates, and cut down the poles. The burghers were completely taken by surprise and put white handkerchiefs out of the windows. The aldermen under tears affirmed their loyalty and devotion and offered the payment of 12,000 talers.[7] The Duke of Croy advocated clemency and the acceptance of this offer; but General von Görtzke was in favour of much stronger measures and against acceptance and had frequent conflicts with the governor. It took him and the government considerable time before their more moderate counsels prevailed with Frederick William.[8] Königsberg had to agree to pay 2,000 talers of contribution per month; the damage resulting from the military occupation was put at well over 20,000

---

[1] Von Baczko, op. cit. v, pp. 429–30 (Jan.–Feb. 1673).

[2] *Urkunden & Actenstücke*, xvi, p. 782 (July 1673).

[3] Ibid., p. 785, n. 2 (Oct. 1673).

[4] Ibid., p. 790, n. 3; von Baczko, op. cit. v, p. 436 (Dec. 1673).

[5] *Urkunden & Actenstücke*, xvi, p. 793, n. 1; Rachel, *Der Grosse Kurfürst und die ostpreussischen Stände*, p. 103 (Jan. 1674).

[6] *Urkunden & Actenstücke*, xvi, p. 793, n. 1; p. 795, n. 2; p. 801, n. 1 (Jan.–May 1674).

[7] Ibid., pp. 801, 803, 805, n. 1; an undated report in *Ostpreuss. Folianten*, vol. 706.

[8] *Urkunden & Actenstücke*, xvi, p. 805, n. 1 (May–June 1674).

talers.[1] Its trade suffered and goods could not be sold for want of buyers.[2] The town's resistance was broken for good and it consented to the excise.[3] The days of burgher independence were over.

During the following years the opposition against the forcible levying of taxes came mainly from the nobility, while the electoral position had become much stronger. In 1676 a diet was summoned and told to take supply first and to finish its deliberations within a fortnight without a discussion of grievances.[4] Two years later Frederick William demanded 50,000 talers a month, then reduced his demand to 20,000, but after a few months he asked for 35,789 talers a month.[5] From October 1677 to the end of 1679 the Estates paid more than 4 million talers into the *Kriegskammer*,[6] or 150,000 talers a month, sums which they had never paid before.[7] The country was reduced to a terrible plight: the common people had to still their hunger 'with chaff, rotten draff, and other horrible and inhuman things', as an eye-witness reported early in 1678.[8] The nobility protested against the levying by military force before there was any time to collect the money and against the soldiers' looting: why should its blood be drained for the sake of the Empire with which it had nothing to do?[9] The elector again referred to the *casus necessitatis* which entitled him to levy taxes if his subjects hesitated to grant money for the defence of the country.[10]

Even after the peace of Nymegen Frederick William repeated this argument, again alluding to the Turkish danger and the unsettled state of affairs in general.[11] The sum levied in Prussia after 1680 was still over 300,000 talers per year;[12] yet this was considerably less than the sum levied in electoral Brandenburg which had a smaller population.[13] The Estates in vain asked for

[1] Ibid., p. 809; von Baczko, op. cit. v, p. 448 (Aug.–Sept. 1674).
[2] Von Baczko, op. cit. v, p. 445.
[3] *Urkunden & Actenstücke*, xvi, p. 809.
[4] Von Baczko, op. cit. v, p. 517 (proposition of May 1676).
[5] Ibid. v, pp. 468, 472 (May–Nov. 1678).
[6] Von Orlich, op. cit. i, p. 392.
[7] Cf. the payments during the war of 1655–60, above, p. 209.
[8] Rachel, op. cit., p. 235.
[9] *Urkunden & Actenstücke*, xvi, pp. 846–7, 850, 901, n. 2 (June 1678–Sept. 1679).
[10] Ibid., p. 901 (Aug. 1679).   [11] Ibid., p. 928 (June 1680).
[12] Stenzel, op. cit. ii, p. 421; Rachel, op. cit., p. 289; Breysig, in *Jahrbuch für Gesetzgebung, Verwaltung und Volkswirthschaft im Deutschen Reich*, xvi, 1892, p. 458.
[13] See above, p. 201.

a general diet to discuss their grievances:[1] they had to be content with small and short 'convocations'. They had to recognize that the elector formulated his requirements not according to the country's capacity to pay, but according to his military needs: this made assemblies of the Estates and their councils unnecessary and useless and cancelled their privileges.[2] After the end of the reign it was feared that Prussia might find herself in the same position as Brandenburg where a tax quantum was prescribed by the authorities and the Estates had nothing to do but to collect it according to a fixed repartition.[3] In practice Prussia had nearly reached the same stage.[4]

During the war years the levying and administration of the taxes passed into the hands of the revived *Kriegskommissariat* or, as it was usually called, the *Kriegskammer*. This office had its origin in the war of 1655-60, but had almost disappeared in the ensuing period of peace, when the Estates were again in charge of the financial administration.[5] Already in 1669, however, the dismissed officials were reappointed and began an investigation of the taxable land and the financial administration in general.[6] The majority of them were not natives of Prussia; they were appointed by, and received their orders directly from, the elector.[7] Gradually the Commissariat extended its sphere of influence at the cost of the older authorities, especially in matters of taxation. It unilaterally fixed the amount of contribution to be paid by the *Cölmer* and by the electoral peasants.[8] It tried burghers of the small towns in cases of conflicts with soldiers, as well as peasants who had enlisted if their masters demanded them to be returned.[9] Above all, it pushed aside the officials of the Estates charged with the administration of the taxes, itself ordered their levy and repartition, pressed for forcible levies if no grants were made, and issued the necessary orders to the

---

[1] *Urkunden & Actenstücke*, xvi, pp. 925, 956, 996, 1017; von Baczko, op. cit. vi, p. 276 (1680-7).
[2] *Ostpreuss. Folianten*, vol. 715, fol. 300; similarly ibid., fol. 892, and vol. 718, fol. 1127.
[3] *Urkunden & Actenstücke*, xvi, p. 1059.
[4] Rachel, op. cit., pp. 289, 295.
[5] See above, pp. 208, 211.
[6] Wolters, op. cit., p. 169.
[7] Rachel, op. cit., p. 300; Wolters, op. cit., pp. 166-72.
[8] *Urkunden & Actenstücke*, xvi, pp. 597-8 (1670).
[9] Ibid., pp. 627, 666 (1670).

local officials.[1] When this proved not effective, special local tax-collectors were appointed who were subordinate only to the Commissariat.[2] Its officials and the higher officers of the army were the bitter enemies of the Estates, the protagonists of an absolute régime, and always the advocates of the sharpest measures: thus during the war an autocratic and military rule was established in Prussia.[3]

After the war the Commissariat was not reduced again, nor did it give up the position it had gained. From Berlin one of its most able and ruthless officials, Colonel von Barfuss, a Branden-burg nobleman, was sent to lead the Prussian Commissariat.[4] He and other of its officials were appointed commissioners to audit the accounts of the *Landkasten*, against the custom and the Estates' protests.[5] When their deputies proposed that the tax-collectors should pay the money into the *Landkasten*, the governor was willing to agree, but von Barfuss objected and carried his point.[6] He forced the *Oberräte* to impose higher taxes and to order their collection without a grant by the Estates.[7] Officials of the Commissariat refused to take orders from the civil govern-ment and were upheld in this attitude by von Barfuss, for he and they were only responsible to the elector.[8] The local officials, the *Hauptleute*, on the other hand, refused to execute the orders of the *Kriegskammer*, as they were only responsible to the civil government.[9] Confusion became worse when the latter ordered the levy of taxes granted by the Estates, while General Count Dönhoff proceeded to levy another without such a grant and demanded from the government the electoral seal for the pur-pose.[10] Frederick William even tried to use army officers to in-vestigate local fraud and deficiencies in the poll-tax; but the Prussian government, without querying his order, entrusted the

---

[1] Ibid., pp. 780, 806-9, 841-2, 851, n. 2; pp. 903-4, 909-10, 923-4, 933-4, 941; von Baczko, op. cit. v, pp. 448-9; vi, pp. 24-25, 271-2 (1673-80).

[2] *Urkunden & Actenstücke*, xvi, pp. 838, 936, 937, n. 4 (1878-80); Rachel, op. cit., p. 307.

[3] Rachel, op. cit., pp. 300-1; von Baczko, op. cit. vi, pp. 12-13.

[4] Wolters, op. cit., pp. 170, 425-8.

[5] *Urkunden & Actenstücke*, xvi, p. 940 (Aug.–Sept. 1680).

[6] Ibid., p. 939, n. 1 (Sept. 1680).

[7] Ibid., p. 957, n. 1; p. 963, n. 2 (June–Oct. 1681).

[8] Ibid., p. 889, n. 1; p. 935, n. 1; p. 946 (July 1679–Dec. 1680).

[9] Ibid., p. 933, n. 1; p. 948, n. 2 (Aug.–Dec. 1680).

[10] Ibid., pp. 933, 948; von Baczko, op. cit. vi, pp. 24-25 (July–Dec. 1680).

task to the *Hauptleute*, although the elector at first upheld his first order.[1]

The *Landkasten* and the financial administration of the Estates were finally emasculated by a decree which ordered all taxes for the army to be paid directly into the *Kriegskammer* and all assignations for army needs to be made directly by it.[2] In vain did the Estates protest against this order and against military interference with their negotiations.[3] Thus the real power was no longer vested in the civil government, although it strenuously resisted all military encroachments, but in the new military authorities which co-operated closely with the army.

The power of the Commissariat also decided a question of great constitutional importance. Up to 1680 the elector and the government always tried to persuade the Estates to levy the taxes granted by a uniform modus and only reluctantly agreed to the separations of Königsberg, after all attempts at conciliation had failed. During the war, however, the *Cölmer* and the electoral peasants were in practice separated from the Estates, as they could be burdened much more easily than the others. Nothing occurred so frequently in the negotiations of the Estates as the complaints of the *Cölmer* about new and heavy burdens, and of the small towns about the billeting and the insolences of the troops. These two classes became the first victims of the rising military state. Possibly inspired by this success, or by the example of Brandenburg where a complete separation of town and country existed since 1680,[4] Frederick William then changed his policy: he used the separatist tendencies of Königsberg and, from 1681 onwards, allowed it to raise its share by taxes of its own choice, while decreeing himself the modus of contribution for the *Cölmer* and peasants. In this way the Estates were split into four parts and the negotiations with them in reality became negotiations with the nobility alone.[5] The *Oberräte*, the Estates, and the *Cölmer* all protested against this separation and against the latter's deprivation of their privilege of attending the *Amts-*

---

[1] *Urkunden & Actenstücke*, xvi, p. 927, n. 1 (Feb.–Mar. 1680).
[2] Ibid., p. 951, n. 1; p. 966 (Mar.–Oct. 1681); Rachel, op. cit., p. 310.
[3] *Urkunden & Actenstücke*, xvi, pp. 983–4, 987, 990 (July 1683–Sept. 1684).
[4] See above, p. 196.
[5] Rachel, op. cit., pp. 286, 289; R. Bergmann, *Geschichte der ostpreussischen Stände und Steuern von 1688–1704*, 1901, pp. 5, 172.

tage and participating in the negotiations;[1] but the elector remained firm and declared that the separation was absolutely fair.[2] Colonel von Barfuss and the subsequent head of the Prussian Commissariat, von Viereck, were specially instructed to make all efforts to maintain the separation which had been brought about with such great pain.[3]

From 1681 Königsberg raised its taxes through the excise, while the country was forced to adopt the land-tax.[4] The nobility countered this by a proposal to raise its share equally by the excise so that the separation would cease; but Frederick William forbade the use of the excise for the whole country.[5] The question played an important part during the convocation diets of 1683 and 1685. In 1683 the *Landräte* and the nobility voted an excise, but were told that they must give it up, as the elector would not accept it; when the Estates persevered the *Kriegskammer* threatened to impose the land-tax without a grant; in the end Colonel von Barfuss *cum adhaerentibus* terminated the diet prematurely.[6] In 1685 the Estates heard, at first informally, that the *Kriegskammer* was opposed to the excise; then von Viereck informed them that he had orders to foster the separation and to prevent the general excise; the small towns were threatened with dire consequences if they continued to adhere to it and *nolentes volentes* eventually voted against it.[7] These reports about the proceedings of 1683 and 1685 show the great powers of the Commissariat which had almost superseded the civil authorities and made the diets a farce. A few years later a Prussian writer declared that, if Frederick William by such methods intended to reduce the Estates to obedience, he had erred because they could effect nothing useful.[8] At the end of his reign the elector thus gave up one of his major political aims, the introduction of the general excise, by which alone the country would have

---

[1] *Urkunden & Actenstücke*, xvi, pp. 962, 986, n. 2; pp. 995, 999, 1004, 1015; *Ostpreuss. Folianten*, vol. 715, fol. 801; vol. 717, pp. 222-3; vol. 718, fols. 1210-12; vol. 723, nos. 2, 142.

[2] *Urkunden & Actenstücke*, xvi, pp. 1001, 1002, n. 1; p. 1007, n. 2 (1686).

[3] Wolters, op. cit., pp. 426, 436: instructions of June 1683 and July 1685.

[4] Bergmann, op. cit., p. 5.

[5] Rachel, op. cit., p. 293.

[6] *Urkunden & Actenstücke*, xvi, pp. 983-4; *Ostpreuss. Folianten*, vol. 723, nos. 2, 5 (*in dorso*).

[7] *Ostpreuss. Folianten*, vol. 723, nos. 60, 106 (31 July, 14 and 17 Aug. 1685).

[8] *Urkunden & Actenstücke*, xvi, p. 1060.

Q

benefited economically, in favour of a policy of *divide et imperabis*.[1]

Prussia suffered severely from a policy which had its eye on short-term financial advantages and neglected all long-term measures for the country's recovery, so that the inhabitants would be able to pay the taxes demanded from them.[2] The peasants suffered most; their taxes were heavier even than the *Cölmer*'s;[3] war, plague, and dearth aggravated their plight; many of them fled, if possible across the frontier, so that the villages became deserted.[4] According to one estimate, in 1685 every tenth holding was still deserted.[5] The small towns had to bear the burden of the billeting of the troops. At the end of the reign the Commissariat, without consulting the towns, imposed upon them the much heavier Brandenburg urban excise as a permanent tax: every month they had to notify the Commissariat of its yields and to make all payments according to its assignations.[6] Königsberg escaped the Brandenburg excise, but its trade was steadily declining. Its tolls and other duties remained much higher than those of Danzig and Riga and were further increased during the war without any relief after its end,[7] so that the trade sought alternative routes. During the first three decades of the seventeenth century an average of well over 400 ships from Königsberg had sailed westwards through the Sound every year; during the second half of Frederick William's reign the average was less than 200.[8] It seems very likely that the town's obedient attitude after 1674 was connected with its economic decline; and this applied even more strongly to the small towns.

[1] Instead of such a policy the nobility in July 1683 enjoined the elector to adopt a policy of 'conjunge et conservabis, et sic feliciter imperabis': *Ostpreuss. Folianten*, vol. 718, fol. 1212.

[2] Cf. Rachel, op. cit., p. 312, and M. Philippson, *Der Grosse Kurfürst*, ii, 1902, p. 202.

[3] *Urkunden & Actenstücke*, xvi, p. 982, n. 1 (taxes per *Hufe* in 1683–4); *Ostpreuss. Folianten*, vol. 722 (taxes per *Hufe* in 1685–6): in each instance a peasant *Hufe* paid more than a *Cölmer*'s, at times much more.

[4] *Urkunden & Actenstücke*, xvi, pp. 438, 516, 561, 582–3, 586, 627, 733–4, 768, 988, 1020, 1026 (1663–88).

[5] Von Baczko, op. cit. vi, p. 45; Stenzel, op. cit. ii, p. 422.

[6] *Urkunden & Actenstücke*, xvi, p. 1027 (Feb. 1688); von Baczko, op. cit. vi, p. 61; Rachel, *Die Handels-, Zoll- und Akzisepolitik* . . . , pp. 576–7.

[7] Rachel, op. cit., pp. 392, 394–5, 419; *Urkunden & Actenstücke*, xvi, pp. 540, 565, 993 (1668–85).

[8] *Bang*, i, pp. 167–387; N. E. Bang and K. Korst, *Tabeller over Skibsfart og Varetransport gennem Øresund 1661–1783*, i, 1930, pp. 2–29.

The nobility lost its political independence and some of its political privileges; but it retained its social position and its dominant role in the government. It was not tax-free, but it paid much less than the other classes.[1] Soldiers were not billeted in noble houses.[2] The government made no effort to check the buying out of *Cölmer* and peasants by noblemen: only the towns sometimes asked them to be more moderate in this respect.[3] In 1663 the privy councillors discussed how to prevent the leasing of domains by noblemen from which they reaped enormous profits,[4] but nothing was done. The same applied to another plan, although the Commissariat was entrusted with its execution: to find out the 'concealed' *Hufen* from which no taxes were paid, and of which there were very large numbers.[5] From 1669 onwards periodical attempts to investigate the *Hufen* were made, and a special commission was appointed for the purpose, but nothing was achieved.[6]

The nobility was equally successful in retaining practically all important offices in its hands. This point it pressed frequently; even the conferment of the post of a local country judge upon a commoner aroused angry protests.[7] This case seems to have been the only attempt of its kind. In the military sphere, only the two commandants of the key fortresses of Memel and Pillau were 'foreigners',[8] as were some of the leading officials of the Commissariat. The local government remained entirely in the hands of the Prussian nobility. As a Prussian himself pointed out about 1690: 'if somebody in Prussia manages to become *Landrat*, or *Hauptmann*, that helps him and all his cousins and brothers-in-law, and the small dependent Junkers must worship the *Herr Hauptmann* and the *Herr Landrat* like an idol'. The writer went on

---

[1] *Urkunden & Actenstücke*, xvi, p. 982, n. 1; Spahn, ibid., p. 1077; Rachel, *Der Grosse Kurfürst und die ostpreussischen Stände*, p. 206.

[2] *Urkunden & Actenstücke*, xvi, p. 876; p. 899, n. 1; p. 959, n. 1; p. 970 (1679–82).

[3] Ibid., p. 534 (1668).

[4] *Protokolle & Relationen*, vi, pp. 860–1; Schmoller, op. cit., p. 62; Breysig, in *Jahrbuch für Gesetzgebung, Verwaltung und Volkswirthschaft*, xvi, 1892, pp. 9–10.

[5] Eventually, under Frederick William I, as many as 34,000 concealed *Hufen* were discovered, or exactly one-third of those paying taxes.

[6] Von Orlich, op. cit. i, p. 397; *Urkunden & Actenstücke*, xvi, pp. 599, 786, n. 3; p. 937, n. 4; pp. 965, 1000, 1019, 1023, 1026 (1669–88); Spahn, ibid., p. 1084.

[7] *Ostpreuss. Folianten*, vols. 699, 704, no. 219; vols. 705–6, 707, fol. 433; vol. 713, p. 226 (1670–7).

[8] L. Tümpel, *Die Entstehung des brandenburgisch-preussischen Einheitsstaates*, 1915, p. 65.

to advise the new elector that he should deprive the nobility of some of its far too great powers and restore the burghers to the position they had held prior to 1605 when they had possessed much more authority,[1] a fitting comment on over seventy years of Hohenzollern rule.[2]

Politically speaking Frederick William had gained a remarkable success against strong opposition. The Estates were never again to rule Prussia. Their own disunity was the main cause of their downfall: this the nobility realized too late, after the firm establishment of the electoral power and the defeat of Königsberg, which was above all due to its complete isolation. Yet the spirit of opposition remained strong in Prussia. The young Frederick II was told as late as 1740 by the spokesman of the Prussian nobility that it was an error of statecraft to call the refusal of a diet a triumph and an accretion of unlimited power.[3] It was only in the course of the eighteenth century that Prussia became reconciled to be ruled from Berlin as a province of a centralized Hohenzollern state.

[1] *Urkunden & Actenstücke*, xvi, p. 1058.
[2] Cf. Spahn, ibid., p. 1078.
[3] *Acta Borussica, Behördenorganisation*, vi 2, p. 44; Hintze, ibid., vi 1, p. 8.

XV

The Conflict with the Estates of Cleves and Mark

THROUGH a successful policy of marriages the Hohenzollerns not only acquired territories which were very similar in character to their native Brandenburg; they also gained two principalities on the lower Rhine which had reached a level of development far ahead of that of eastern Germany. The more important of these was the duchy of Cleves, stretching across the Rhine close to the frontiers of the United Provinces and linked with them by many political and economic ties. Farther to the south-east, in the valley of the Ruhr, there lay the county of Mark where the production and the sale of coal and iron already played an important part in the economic life. Towards the end of the seventeenth century these two small principalities had perhaps 140,000–150,000 inhabitants, while electoral Brandenburg, although much larger, had at most 270,000.[1]

The social structure of Cleves and Mark was completely different from that of Brandenburg with its predominant Junker class, its subservient burghers, and its servile peasants who depended on the whims of their masters. In the Rhenish territories there also was a native nobility which formed the first Estate in the diet of both principalities. The nobility, however, neither dominated the diet as the Junkers did in the east, nor did it possess their privileges: in particular it was not exempt from all taxes and customs duties. There were other important differences: demesne farming had declined since the Middle Ages and had become very unimportant. The nobleman received dues from the peasants who had leased his land and therefore he did not require labour services. The estates had not been consolidated as they had been in the east, but consisted of widely

---

[1] See above, p. 201. Cleves comprised 33 and Mark 46 Prussian square miles, while electoral Brandenburg had 459. Using the death figures from 1698 to 1708 Dieterici, in *Mittheilungen des statistischen Bureau's in Berlin*, iv, 1851, p. 245, estimated the population of Cleves and Mark as about 180,000. But this figure is almost certainly too high, as he multiplied the average death figures by 37. If one multiplies the average death figures for the years 1688–96 (printed by Behre, op. cit., p. 451) by 33, the result would be 153,000 for Cleves and Mark. Working backwards from the census figures of 1740 Behre, op. cit., p. 198, estimated the population to have been 138,500 in 1688, the year of the death of Frederick William.

scattered holdings and rights; manorial jurisdiction was un-known.[1] In the early seventeenth century there were only 106 noble estates in Cleves and only 135 in Mark.[2] The same characteristics applied to the electoral domains which were small and lay scattered among private estates and holdings.[3]

The strength of the nobility was more than equalled by that of the towns. The general decline of the German towns in the sixteenth and seventeenth centuries had indeed affected the once flourishing towns of Mark, such as Bochum, Dortmund, Hamm, Soest, Solingen, and Unna, some of which had once been prominent members of the Hanse: their trade and industry were declining and they were becoming impoverished.[4] The towns of Cleves, however, still retained their old importance and prosperity. The Rhine trade had made them rich; the produc-tion of cloth, linen, and leather were important local industries.[5] The burghers participated in the growing wealth of the Nether-lands by selling Dutch merchandise in the neighbouring terri-tories. The leading town of Cleves, Wesel on the right bank of the Rhine, was an important trading centre[6] and the home of proud burghers. These had played an important part in the rise of Calvinism[7] and considered themselves the equals of any noble-man. Only the principal towns, seven in Cleves and eight in Mark, sent deputies to the diet where they formed the second Estate. Wesel naturally took a leading part in the Estates' deliberations, and its burghers looked with longing eyes at the newly-won free-dom of the Dutch with whom they were closely associated.

Compared with the situation of the peasants in eastern Germany that of the peasants of Cleves and Mark was very favourable. A minority was entirely free, living in villages on the left bank close to the frontier of Guelderland.[8] The large major-

---

[1] O. Hötzsch, 'Stände und Verwaltung von Cleve und Mark in der Zeit von 1666 bis 1697' (*Urkunden und Aktenstücke zur Geschichte der inneren Politik des Kurfürsten Friedrich Wilhelm von Brandenburg*, ii), 1908, pp. 248, 326–7; Hintze, *Geist und Epochen der Preussischen Geschichte*, 1943, p. 375; M. Lehmann, *Freiherr vom Stein*, i, 1902, pp. 89, 93.   [2] Hötzsch, op. cit., p. 255, n. 1.

[3] Ibid., pp. 69, 327; Lehmann, op. cit. i, pp. 89–90.

[4] Rachel, *Die Handels-, Zoll- und Akzisepolitik . . .*, p. 465; A. von Haeften, in *Urkunden & Actenstücke*, v, p. 97; Hötzsch, op. cit., pp. 330–1.

[5] Hötzsch, op. cit., p. 329; Schmoller, op. cit., p. 49.

[6] Rachel, op. cit., p. 464; von Haeften, loc. cit., p. 95.

[7] The Jesuits in a famous doggerel maintained that 'Geneva, Wesel, and La Rochelle are the devil's other hell'.

[8] Von Haeften, loc. cit., pp. 6, 359, n. 144.

ity, the so-called *Hausleute*, had to give dues to their landlords and held their farms on a lease which was in practice hereditary.[1] In Mark there were some serfs (*Eigenbehörige*) who had to pay certain special dues, but whose obligations were as closely circumscribed as those of the other peasants.[2] An even more distinctive feature was the rural self-government in which the peasants participated side by side with the noblemen resident in the district and with the local officials. Every year in the summer an *Erbentag* was held in each small district, attended by the local nobility, the bailiffs of the domains, and peasant deputations. Its main business was the local allotment of the taxes granted by the diet[3] and the granting of taxes for local requirements, such as the upkeep of roads and bridges, salaries of local officials, jails, and poor relief. The accounts for the past year were audited and approved.[3] In the districts close to the Rhine and the Meuse the construction and upkeep of dikes and sluices were discussed and settled. The local officials, namely the tax-collectors who were also responsible for police matters, and the dike-reeves, were elected. The lists of fines which had been imposed were read.[4] Below these *Erbentage* the same matters were transacted on the village level by *Kirchspieltage* which were also attended by noblemen and peasants alike.[5] This vigorous local self-government provided a strong basis for the diets. Although the peasants were not represented there, the diets were firmly linked with the practical political activities of the population and had a more representative character than they possessed elsewhere.

Furthermore, in Cleves and Mark there was neither the strict division between town and country nor between the social classes which had become so strongly marked in the east. Noble estates could be, and were, bought by commoners.[6] The industries

---

[1] *Urkunden & Actenstücke*, v, p. 563: report of Oct. 1651. The most usual form of lease was the *Leibgewinnspacht*, valid for the lives of two to three persons; when one of them died another person was normally admitted to the contract against a money payment: Hötzsch, op. cit., p. 69, n. 11; von Haeften, loc. cit., p. 6, n. 5.

[2] Hötzsch, op. cit., pp. 325–6; Lehmann, op. cit. i, p. 90.

[3] *Scotti*, i, pp. 314–15, 419 (1653–64).

[4] Hötzsch, op. cit., pp. 66–67; Lehmann, op. cit. i, pp. 100–1; Tümpel, op. cit., pp. 142–3.

[5] Lehmann, op. cit. i, p. 102.

[6] Ibid., p. 89; *Scotti*, i, p. 273, clause 33: *Recess* of 1649 expressly referring to the non-noble possessors of noble estates.

were not confined to the towns but were often established in the countryside.[1] Finally, the dukes of Cleves, following the example of their Burgundian neighbours, had created a modern bureaucracy and had successfully tried to eliminate the remnants of feudalism.[2] Considering the conditions existing in seventeenth-century Germany, Cleves and Mark were thus extraordinarily advanced; their social structure was very similar to that of the United Provinces, but almost the reverse of that obtaining in Brandenburg. When these territories fell into the hands of the Hohenzollerns, a chance of far-reaching importance offered itself to them. The question was how they would react to these western conditions: would they try to make use of them to influence and reform conditions in Brandenburg; or would they, on the contrary, try to introduce Brandenburg institutions and methods of government into the Rhineland; or would they leave conditions as they had existed of old?

During the first thirty years of Hohenzollern rule on the Rhine it seemed as if the last of these possibilities would be adopted. The authorities in Berlin hardly interfered with the accustomed state of affairs; the Estates continued to govern the country as best they could. Their position was strengthened because the Jülich-Cleves inheritance was not finally divided until 1666 between the two chief claimants, Brandenburg and Palatinate-Neuburg. At first the two claimants administered the principalities jointly, and in 1614 they divided them provisionally, at the same time guaranteeing and extending the privileges of the Estates. In addition, foreign troops began to intervene in the struggle between the claimants. In 1614 Spanish troops under Lisola took Wesel, whereupon Dutch troops occupied other towns of Cleves; they were called in by Brandenburg as support against Spain and Palatinate-Neuburg.[3] The possession of Cleves and its fortified towns was of great strategical importance to Spain as well as to the United Provinces, for their struggle was bound to be renewed on the expiration of the twelve years' truce of 1609. Brandenburg, far distant and weak, was unable to intervene and to strengthen its hold on its

[1] Hötzsch, op. cit., pp. 324–5; Rachel, op. cit., p. 629; Lehmann, op. cit. i, p. 90.
[2] Lehmann, op. cit. i, p. 93.
[3] L. von Aitzema, *Saken van Staet en Oorlogh, in ende omtrent de Vereenigde Nederlanden*, ed. 1669, i, pp. 106–8; iii, pp. 182–4.

Rhenish territories, but had to leave them a prey to the warring parties.

Matters became worse with the actual outbreak of the Thirty Years War in which the command of the lower Rhine was a vital issue. Most of Cleves was occupied by the Dutch. Imperial and Spanish troops advanced down the Rhine to gain access to the United Provinces but were forced to retreat. In 1639 Imperial troops took Calcar, on the left bank of the Rhine, enforced heavy contributions and pillaged the country; within a few years 300,000 talers were extorted from the population of the left bank, not counting the cost of forcible levy by the military, enforced tolls, and deliveries in kind.[1] In 1640 Hessian troops expelled the Imperialists from Calcar, with the result that contributions were levied by both armies. The same applied to Mark where the Imperialists held Hamm and the Hessians Lippstadt.[2] The amount levied in Cleves from 1616 to 1641 by the Dutch alone was calculated at 1,553,783 talers by a Cleves official.[3] Most of these contributions were imposed without the Estates' consent, and military force was used when the money was not forthcoming. The Estates never ceased to complain about this infringement of their rights and about the exhaustion of the country.[4] Exactly as in Brandenburg and Prussia, the example of the foreign armies was followed by the Cleves government: it levied contributions without consulting the Estates and used military force to collect the money.[5]

The economic consequences of the long struggle differed considerably in the various districts. The county of Mark was longer occupied by foreign troops than Cleves and suffered much more. Its trade and industry declined further, especially mining and the manufacture of cloth and linen; the towns became almost totally impoverished.[6] In Cleves also the Rhine trade was badly hit and the once flourishing manufacture of cloth and leather was nearly destroyed.[7] The transit trade to Holland, however, continued uninterruptedly, and one great commercial advantage

---

[1] Von Haeften, loc. cit., p. 76.
[2] Ibid., pp. 105, 191.
[3] Urkunden & Actenstücke, v, p. 137: report of Feb. 1641.
[4] Ibid., pp. 131, 151, 174, 182, 203, 219, 222, 291, 303-4, 332, 375 (1641-9).
[5] Ibid., pp. 97, 131, 182, 219, 222, 283, 291, 304, 332, 338, 375 (1622-47).
[6] Von Haeften, loc. cit., pp. 97, 952-3; Hötzsch, op. cit., p. 330.
[7] Von Haeften, loc. cit., pp. 952-3; Hötzsch, op. cit., p. 329.

accrued from the war: the occupation of the most important towns by Dutch garrisons brought Dutch capital into Cleves and strengthened the ties with Holland. As the Meuse was closed through the major part of the war, the towns of Cleves on the right bank of the Rhine became the chief depots for the export of Dutch goods into the Rhenish and Westphalian lands and into the Spanish Netherlands.[1] While the towns on the right bank flourished in spite of the war, those on the left bank suffered considerably.[2]

With the end of the war, however, the advantageous position of the towns on the right bank came to an end; but Dutch garrisons remained at Wesel, Emmerich, Rees, and four smaller towns, so that the close commercial and political relations with Holland continued. In Brandenburg the results of the Thirty Years War were a general impoverishment and a weakening of the Estates' power, parallel with the first successful experiment in absolute government.[3] In Cleves and Mark the results were far more complex: in Cleves at least the Estates' strength was not sapped and their opposition against Berlin was as strong as ever. In Mark, on the other hand, owing to the general decline the opposition against Frederick William was far weaker, and the impoverished nobility showed a far stronger inclination to enter his service.[4]

The first clashes between the young elector and the Estates of Cleves occurred while the Thirty Years War was still in progress. To improve his position against Palatinate-Neuburg Frederick William recruited troops and in 1646 invaded the duchy of Berg which belonged to his rival's share of the Cleves inheritance. The Estates did not confine themselves to protests against this action and against the forcible levying of taxes: they decided to publish a bill of contradiction calling on all inhabitants to refuse the payment of taxes.[5] This bill was duly posted at Wesel, Emmerich, and Rees and, under the protection of the Dutch garrisons, in the villages of the right bank.[6] Then the Estates of Cleves and Mark renewed their old hereditary

---

[1] Von Haeften, loc. cit., pp. 94–95; Rachel, op. cit., pp. 464–5.
[2] See above, p. 233.
[3] See above, pp. 179–81.
[4] Von Haeften, loc. cit., p. 97.
[5] *Urkunden & Actenstücke*, v, pp. 284–6 (Aug. 1646).
[6] Ibid., p. 287.

alliance with those of Jülich and Berg to assist each other and to resist jointly all oppression and curtailment of their liberties and privileges, whether by their ruler or any other person.[1] According to the elector, some leaders of the Estates compared themselves with the Parliamentary party in England and threatened publicly to treat him as the English had treated their king.[2] Thanks partly to the Estates' strong opposition, his military venture ended in complete failure. Frederick William was naturally embittered by this resistance which emanated from mere commoners. When the diet met in 1647 he indignantly interrupted the speech of Dr. Isinck and exclaimed that the learned doctors were rascals and that the matter could soon be settled if he had to deal with gentlemen only, pointing to the deputies of the nobility.[3]

The towns' strong opposition to the electoral policy was a new factor. From 1641 onwards they repeatedly declared their willingness to grant money if the taxes were repartitioned between the Estates according to that old modus (*Matrikel*) to which the nobility also had to contribute.[4] The dispute between the nobility and the towns over the nobility's exemption from taxation was of long standing. Until 1639 the noblemen contributed to the taxes raised for defence purposes and for wars against the Turks.[5] This obligation was implicitly recognized by the nobility itself as late as 1648.[6] According to an expert's opinion expressed forty years later, the nobility contributed regularly up to 1644 or 1645.[7] In Mark also a special 'knight's tax' was still mentioned in regulations of 1640, but not after this date.[8] If Frederick William wanted to gain the support of the towns and to induce them to vote taxes, he could have taken their side in the conflict over the participation of the nobility. As early as 1641, however, his councillor von Blumenthal,

[1] Aitzema, op. cit. iii, pp. 191–2 (Feb. 1647).
[2] Thus a pamphlet published in 1647 at the elector's behest: *Cleefsche Patriot, Verthoonende de intentie van de Missive, gesonden aen hare Ho. Mogende Heeren Staten Generael der Vereenighde Nederlanden, van wegens de Cleefsche Landt-Stenden*, p. 23.
[3] *Urkunden & Actenstücke*, v, p. 316 (protocol of the diet, 16 Apr. 1647).
[4] Ibid., pp. 157, 159, 160, 167, 204 (Mar. 1641–Mar. 1643).
[5] Von Haeften, loc. cit., pp. 21, 27, 45–46, 77, 952, 996, mentioning twenty instances from the years 1557–1639.
[6] *Urkunden & Actenstücke*, v, p. 361.
[7] Hötzsch, op. cit., p. 215, n. 1: letter of the Estates' *Syndikus* Schmitz of 1689.
[8] Ibid., p. 215, n. 1.

a Brandenburg nobleman, without even mentioning the problem of the noblemen's exemption, advised him strongly against the use of the old *Matrikel*, because then the towns would escape too lightly with just over 15 per cent. of the burden, while the countryside and the clergy would be unable to bear the remainder,[1] implicitly assuming that the nobility would be tax-free. Thus the opportunity to win the towns' allegiance passed.

Other questions led to increased friction between towns and noblemen and offered to the government an opportunity to win the adherence of the one as against the other. One dispute concerned the proportion of noblemen and commoners in the government and in other posts. In 1648 the Cleves nobility promised 1,000 talers to Dr. Isinck if he could obtain from the elector a written assurance that, among other concessions, the government (*Regierungsrat*) would contain 8, and the high court (*Justizrat*) 5 native noblemen.[2] This demand was later modified: the nobility would be satisfied with a written promise granting it a majority in both councils.[3] The following month their ruler duly undertook that for ever 6 noblemen and 3 commoners would sit in the *collegia* of the government, and equal numbers of both classes in *collegio justitiae*.[4] Accordingly 6 noble and 3 non-noble *Regierungsräte* and 5 noble *Justizräte* were appointed or confirmed in office.[5] Wesel protested strongly against this favour bestowed upon the nobility; it refused to contribute to the taxes granted by the diet, and it pledged its allegiance not unconditionally as did all the others, *sed salva protestatione* against the composition of the councils.[6] The other towns, however, acquiesced.

All the towns were driven into embittered opposition by another step of the government. To win supporters and to reward his adherents Frederick William, from 1645 onwards, began to grant 'jurisdictions' to certain noblemen. The grantees were to exercise police authority and civil and criminal juris-

---

[1] *Protokolle & Relationen*, i, p. 364.
[2] *Urkunden & Actenstücke*, v, p. 361.
[3] Ibid., p. 361, n. 146 (Oct. 1649).
[4] Ibid., pp. 397–8 (Nov. 1649).
[5] Von Haeften, loc. cit., p. 398, n. 163, not giving the names of the non-noble *Justizräte*.
[6] *Urkunden & Actenstücke*, v, p. 396 (Nov. 1649).

diction of the first instance and to receive the fines and *corvées* hitherto due to the prince.[1] In eastern Germany the Junkers exercised these rights and thus maintained their authority over their peasants; as they owned compact and fairly large estates, ownership of land and exercise of public authority were thus combined in one hand, relieving the state of the burden of local administration. In the Rhineland, however, there were no compact estates and no manors, but only a jumble of holdings belonging to the ruler, to ecclesiastics, noblemen, burghers, or peasants.[2] Thus the noblemen, through the grant of 'jurisdictions', not only acquired rights over their peasants, but over many others as well, including those on the domains.[3] At the same time the universal character of the rural self-government was destroyed, for it ceased to function where 'jurisdictions' were established. The practical advantages of private jurisdiction which existed in the east were entirely lacking, and the result was great confusion, especially in legal matters, and a weakening of public authority.[4] In spite of strong protests from the towns, 'jurisdictions' over sixty villages and estates were granted between 1645 and 1652.[5] There was a financial reason for this policy: the grantees had to pay a considerable sum on the spot and a yearly fee later.[6] Yet there were other and more important motives: Frederick William wanted to make the nobility the bearer of state authority;[7] he also wanted, as with the appointment of noblemen to government offices, to create a party willing to support his policy.

In opposing this policy the towns of Cleves in 1648 argued quite correctly that the 'jurisdictions' diminished the income and the authority of the prince, that his subjects were deprived of his protection, and that the lands and the peasants of their burghers thus came under the authority of noblemen and could be exploited by them.[8] Simultaneously they offered to recompense the grantees for what they had paid; they begged that at

[1] Von Haeften, loc. cit., p. 351; Hötzsch, op. cit., pp. 177–8.
[2] See above, pp. 229–30.
[3] Tümpel, op. cit., p. 144; Hötzsch, op. cit., p. 177.
[4] As admitted by Frederick William himself in 1655: *Urkunden & Actenstücke*, v, p. 806, n. 1.
[5] A full list is given by von Haeften, loc. cit., p. 351, n. 133.
[6] Hötzsch, op. cit., p. 177.
[7] Thus von Haeften, loc. cit., pp. 117, 952.
[8] *Urkunden & Actenstücke*, v, p. 350.

least the 'jurisdictions' should not be extended beyond the noble estates. If no such promise could be obtained, they appealed to the towns of Mark not to take part in any diets and to start proceedings *in camera imperiali* to achieve revocation.[1] The elector agreed to give the desired promise if the towns consented to pay him 30,000 talers, a demand later lowered to 22,000: in future no 'jurisdictions' would be granted.[2] Another written assurance to this effect was handed to the towns a few months later, this time on condition of a grant of 56,000 talers.[3] Encouraged by this success the towns went further and demanded that the 'jurisdictions' already granted should be rescinded, which caused great consternation among the nobility.[4] Eventually an agreement was reached that in future 'jurisdictions' were only to be granted with the Estates' consent; this was confirmed by Frederick William in the *Recess* promulgated at the dissolution of the diet of 1648.[5] Against this declaration the nobility in its turn protested to the Imperial Chamber. Pending its decision, not only did those noblemen who had been granted 'jurisdictions' continue to exercise them, but many new ones were granted during the following years: as late as 1664 the Imperial Chamber had not reached a decision.[6]

Meanwhile the quarrel continued. Early in 1649 the towns of Wesel and Rees instructed their deputies in the diet not to enter into any deliberations until the 'jurisdictions' had been rescinded and the number of non-noble councillors demanded by the towns had been conceded.[7] In July Frederick William promised that the 'jurisdictions' would be revoked as soon as the towns paid the money to indemnify the grantees.[8] Two months later he was reported to have signed this order.[9] After a further two months, however, he informed his officials that the towns had obtained his signature surreptitiously, as they had concealed the inhibition mandates of the Imperial Chamber vetoing any change: the officials should not execute his previous order but leave everything as it was.[10] The towns naturally were infuriated.

---

[1] *Urkunden & Actenstücke*, v, p. 350.   [2] Ibid., p. 354: report of Feb. 1648.
[3] Ibid., p. 355: report of May 1648.
[4] Ibid., p. 356: reports of June 1648.
[5] Ibid., pp. 358–9: agreement of 19 July and *Recess* of 23 July 1648, clause 2.
[6] Von Haeften, loc. cit., p. 351, n. 133; p. 360.
[7] *Urkunden & Actenstücke*, v, p. 373.   [8] Ibid., p. 384.
[9] Ibid., p. 386.   [10] Ibid., p. 397 (Nov. 1649).

As Rees wrote to Wesel, they could no longer trust their ruler's signature and seal.[1] During the following years they continued to complain,[2] but all to no effect. At the diet of 1666 a settlement was finally negotiated by the privy councillors and confirmed by Frederick William, according to which eighteen noblemen— all those who were qualified and natives of Cleves—were to retain their 'jurisdictions', while the grant of a new one required the Estates' consent and was to be invalid without it.[3] In spite of this, however, more 'jurisdictions' were granted, by the elector as well as by his successors: seven such grants were made between 1666 and 1722.[4]

The peasants themselves were not represented in the diets and as a rule had no means of voicing their opposition. Only when Frederick William gave away the 'jurisdiction' over four villages of free peasants they offered him 3,000 talers to remain independent, whereupon he promised them graciously that they should remain for ever under his direct authority.[5] In the county of Mark the conflict never reached the sharpness it assumed in Cleves. In 1650 the elector undertook, with certain reservations, to revoke the 'jurisdictions' he had granted, whereupon the Estates consented to raise 40,000 talers.[6] Five years later he again promised that he would 'immediately and completely' rescind the 'jurisdictions' granted because, as he had to admit himself, they encroached upon his rights, aggravated his subjects, and created great confusion in legal matters.[7] In spite of all these disadvantages, in Mark also the 'jurisdictions' were not revoked, and eleven more were granted between 1666 and 1716.[8]

Frederick William indeed reaped one definite advantage from the favours bestowed upon the nobility. A party came into being which supported him, and the Estates were no longer

---

[1] Ibid., p. 397, n. 162 (Jan. 1650).

[2] Ibid., pp. 583, 624, 659, 717–18, 971, 1010 (1652–64).

[3] *Scotti*, i, pp. 479–81 (electoral confirmation of 23 Oct.); *Urkunden & Actenstücke*, v, p. 1024 (negotiations of 21 and 23 Oct.); von Haeften, loc. cit., pp. 954–5.

[4] *Acta Borussica, Behördenorganisation*, iv 1, no. 229, pp. 491–2 (report of the Cleves government of Mar. 1724); Hötzsch, op. cit., pp. 12, 181.

[5] *Urkunden & Actenstücke*, v, p. 359 (July 1648).

[6] Ibid., p. 400.

[7] Ibid., p. 806, n. 1; *Acta Borussica, Behördenorganisation*, iv 1, p. 491, n. 1; no. 256, pp. 532–3.

[8] *Acta Borussica, Behördenorganisation*, iv 1, no. 229, pp. 492–3 (government report of Mar. 1724).

united in their opposition. This was shown clearly when he undertook a new military enterprise against Palatinate-Neuburg in 1651. Again the Estates of Cleves, Jülich, Berg, and Mark declared that they were not interested in the quarrels of their rulers. They renewed their hereditary alliance and published a bill of contradiction warning the inhabitants not to participate in the hostilities and, if any had taken service on either side, to leave it at the earliest opportunity.[1] A few days later, however, 14 Cleves noblemen—about one-third of those entitled to attend the diet—protested against this step, for it was derogatory to their master and they had not consented to it.[2] Of these 14, 5 were councillors, 2 held other official posts, and 1 was an army officer; while 9 of them had been granted 'jurisdictions' or were to receive them in the near future.[3] The united front was broken. Yet the Estates of Cleves went further: they cautioned all officials against levying taxes to which they had not agreed and threatened to hold them and their possessions responsible and to indict them before the Emperor.[4] They refused to grant any money and insisted on the cessation of the forced contributions and on the removal of the troops.[5] They appealed to the States General as well as to the Emperor for support against their prince.[6]

These protests did not prevent the continuation of strong military measures. Cavalry from the regiment of Colonel von Wilich-Lottum, a Cleves nobleman, during the night drove away cattle belonging to burghers of Emmerich and Rees; some towns began to waver, in particular those on the left bank which were not protected by Dutch garrisons.[7] In the end, however, the Estates were again victorious. The intervention of the Emperor forced the belligerent parties to conclude peace in October 1651, another humiliating defeat for Frederick William.[8] As he demanded a considerable sum to pay off his troops, the conflict with the Estates persisted, and with it the forced

---

[1] *Urkunden & Actenstücke*, v, pp. 509–10 (July 1651).
[2] Ibid., p. 512 (July 1651).
[3] See the names, ibid., p. 351, n. 133; p. 398, n. 163; p. 500, n. 1.
[4] Ibid., p. 534 (Aug. 1651). The Emperor Ferdinand III had forbidden to support the elector in any way in his enterprise against Palatinate-Neuburg.
[5] Ibid., p. 541 (Sept. 1651).
[6] Ibid., pp. 544–5, 551–3 (Sept.–Oct. 1651).
[7] Ibid., pp. 548, 550–1 (Sept.–Oct. 1651).
[8] Von Haeften, loc. cit., p. 602.

contributions and the levying by the military.[1] The reduction of
the troops took a long time. In November 1652 the Estates of
Cleves and Mark decided to send a deputation to the Emperor
to complain about their ruler's measures; but some towns,
Cleves, Duisburg, and Rees, opposed this step,[2] and the towns
of Mark dissociated themselves altogether.[3] As two years earlier,
the pro-electoral faction among the nobility, assembled by
Colonel von Wilich-Lottum,[4] protested publicly against the
deputation to which they had not consented.[5] This protest was
signed by twelve noblemen, seven of whom were councillors,
officers, or government officials.[6] Soon after Cleves and Xanten
associated themselves with their protest.[7] The Estates were now
split beyond repair. They met in two rival assemblies, and the
leaders of both groups tried to win over the waverers.[8] The
loyal faction revoked the mandate of the deputation which had
meanwhile left for Ratisbon, while the other party disputed
their power to do so and instructed the deputation to proceed
with the complaint.[9]

The government's difficulties were increased by the widespread opposition. The tax-collectors were threatened with
imprisonment and were openly resisted so that very little money
was collected.[10] The garrison of Lippstadt could not be paid:
'they suffered hunger and were almost naked'.[11] Government
salaries were in arrears for four to eight years, and there was not
enough money to pay the messengers and other daily expenses.[12]
Frederick William resolved on the use of force. He ordered
Colonel von Spaen, another Cleves nobleman, to arrest the
deputies on their return from Ratisbon.[13] As von Spaen had no
soldiers available with whom to execute the order, he had to
ask the commandant of the Dutch garrison of Rheinberg for an

---

[1] *Urkunden & Actenstücke*, v, pp. 561, 565–6 (Oct.–Nov. 1651).
[2] Ibid., pp. 622, 624–5 (Nov. 1652).
[3] Ibid., pp. 649–51 (June–July 1653).
[4] Ibid., p. 667 (Aug. 1653).
[5] Ibid., p. 662 (July 1653).
[6] Ibid., p. 398, n. 163; p. 500, n. 1; p. 669.
[7] Ibid., p. 663 (Aug. 1653).
[8] Ibid., pp. 665, 667–8 (Aug. 1653).
[9] Ibid., pp. 668–9 (Aug. 1653).
[10] Ibid., p. 727: report of the tax-collector Valk of Apr. 1654.
[11] Ibid., p. 726: report of the *commissarius* Ludwig of Apr. 1654.
[12] Ibid., p. 708: government report of Dec. 1653.
[13] Ibid., pp. 733–4 (July 1654).

escort of horsemen, pretending that he had to transport valuable jewellery and documents, and thus was able to effect the arrest of von Wilich, a noble member of the deputation;[1] but the others escaped. On hearing this news some infuriated Cleves noblemen pursued von Spaen to rescue the prisoner; they only desisted when von Spaen threatened to cut down his captive. The chase continued from Cleves across the Ruhr into Mark, but without success.[2] The Estates protested sharply against the arrest:[3] Wesel advocated another complaint to the Emperor; but again the towns of Mark as well as Cleves and Duisburg, followed by the loyal members of the nobility, dissociated themselves from the protest which thus lost its effectiveness.[4]

The two military enterprises against Palatinate-Neuburg had ended in failure, as had the attempts to curtail the power of the Estates. In the *Recesse* of 1649 and 1653 they obtained far-reaching concessions from their ruler. He had to confirm all their old privileges, including those of free assembly on their own initiative and of negotiation with foreign powers.[5] If their privileges or the stipulations of the *Recesse* were violated, the Estates could refuse the payment of the taxes they had granted.[6] Yearly accounts of the revenue and expenditure were to be rendered to them.[7] Any surplus from the domains was not to be used outside the principalities.[8] No troops were to be introduced or recruited there and no taxes were to be levied without the Estates' consent.[9] Frederick William had to recognize the *jus indigenatus* (reserving all offices to natives of Cleves and Mark) and to dismiss all 'foreign' officials.[10] All officials had to swear to maintain the stipulations of the *Recesse*.[11] Under these conditions the diet eventually voted a tax of 50,000 talers, and even this against the opposition of some towns which aimed

---

[1] *Urkunden & Actenstücke*, v, p. 745: the States General to the elector in Aug. 1654.
[2] Ibid., pp. 738–9, 756.
[3] Ibid., p. 740 (July 1654).
[4] Ibid., pp. 745–6, 764 (Aug.–Nov. 1654).
[5] Ibid., p. 390: *Recess* of 1649, clause 1; Schmoller, op. cit., p. 59.
[6] *Urkunden & Actenstücke*, v, p. 395: *Recess* of 1649, clause 73.
[7] Ibid., pp. 392, 395: clauses 27–28, 65 of 1649.
[8] Ibid., p. 689: *Recess* of 1653, clause 7.
[9] Ibid., pp. 392, 690: *Recess* of 1649, clause 33; *Recess* of 1653, clause 10.
[10] Ibid., pp. 391, 393, 690.
[11] Ibid., pp. 391, 691: *Recess* of 1649, clause 7; *Recess* of 1653, clauses 4–6.

at the abolition of the 'jurisdictions'.[1] The Estates' victory seemed complete.[2] They had secured privileges far surpassing those which the elector granted to the Brandenburg Estates in 1653,[3] and were strengthened rather than weakened by the events of the past forty years.

New military preparations, however, began only a few months later, this time not for a war on the Rhine but on the Baltic coast. The war between Sweden and Poland of 1655-60 was to influence fundamentally the relations between the ruler and the Estates of Cleves and Mark, although these had no interest in the war and were not touched by it. As early as December 1654 the elector demanded a decision on defence measures and recruiting.[4] The Estates were willing to raise 50,000 talers, but on the condition that they would in future be free from recruiting, billeting, and similar burdens; and the towns insisted that the nobility was to participate as it was a tax for defence, which was opposed by the latter.[5] The government declined to accept these conditions and levied 35,000 talers in Cleves: 7,000 from the towns, but nothing from the nobility.[6] It thus sided with the nobility and at the same time raised the towns' share from one-sixth to one-fifth of the total.[7]

Wesel and other towns then refused to pay, as the conditions attached to their grant had not been fulfilled, and the government again resorted to forcible levying. The regiments of von Spaen and von Wilich-Lottum were billeted on the burghers' farms and estates, horses and cattle were driven away, and the burghers were treated 'as if they were open enemies'.[8] The Estates renewed their complaints to the Emperor and to the States General: within six to seven months, they declared, over 300,000 talers had been levied without their consent, and large numbers of troops had been recruited and billeted upon them so that they were utterly exhausted.[9] The policy of the Dutch,

---

[1] Ibid., pp. 717-18 (Feb. 1654).
[2] Hintze, *Die Hohenzollern und ihr Werk*, p. 209; Schmoller, op. cit., p. 59.
[3] See above, pp. 187-9.
[4] *Urkunden & Actenstücke*, v, p. 765.
[5] Ibid., pp. 768-70 (Dec. 1654).
[6] Ibid., p. 770, n. 1.
[7] Since 1612 the towns had only paid one-sixth of each tax, instead of one-fifth as before: von Haeften, loc. cit., p. 46.
[8] *Urkunden & Actenstücke*, v, pp. 807-8, 811: reports to the States General, June 1655. [9] Ibid., pp. 816-18 (Aug. 1655).

however, had changed to one of friendship with Frederick William, and the commandants of their garrisons no longer protected the towns against the Brandenburg troops.[1] The governor of Cleves, Prince John Maurice of Nassau, attempted to intervene on behalf of the overburdened principalities with the elector;[2] but the latter, early in 1656, asked him to continue recruiting, for he had great designs and could 'consider neither friend, nor enemy, nor Estates'.[3] The governor ordered the levy of another 70,000 talers without consulting the Estates: military force had to be used, and several officials, referring to their oath, refused to proceed with it.[4]

Other electoral officials, however, were only too pleased with the course of events. Thus Daniel Weimann considered the construction of a fortress at Calcar 'an inestimable work for His Electoral Highness, whereby he would gain a footing in the country and would in future have to fear neither the Estates nor the States General. These junctures cannot be paid with money. ... One must proceed with arrests against the deputies and with trials against the Estates ...'; but he was careful enough to ask the addressee to return this letter.[5] He also told the diet that 'subjects must not grumble but pray when their prince was fighting ... and must remember that kings and princes encountered danger and war for the sins of the people ...'.[6] The opinions of the new school of officials could hardly be expressed more candidly. These opinions were not shared by the inhabitants of Cleves. Prince John Maurice thought that any further levy would bring matters to a head; people were refusing to pay another penny and would oppose the tax-collectors with armed might.[7] At the end of 1656 the government informed the elector that in the past two years 522,979 talers had been levied in Cleves and Mark, not counting food, fodder, and extorted presents; the peasants were leaving their farms and resisting the collections forcibly; 'more complications, if not a general uprising of desperate subjects', were to be expected.[8] During 1657 taxes continued to be raised by military force, and new com-

---

[1] *Urkunden & Actenstücke*, iv, p. 138; Aitzema, op. cit. iii, p. 1204.
[2] *Urkunden & Actenstücke*, v, p. 820, n. 1 (Aug. 1655).
[3] Ibid., p. 840 (Feb. 1656).
[4] Ibid., p. 860, n. 1 (Sept.–Oct. 1656).
[5] Ibid., pp. 877–8 (Nov. 1656).
[6] Ibid., p. 891 (Mar. 1657).
[7] Ibid., p. 884 (Nov. 1656).
[8] Ibid., p. 885 (Dec. 1656).

panies were recruited without consulting the Estates.[1] Another of their privileges was violated by an order that they were not to assemble without the authorities' permission.[2]

Until July 1658 17,000 talers were levied monthly; owing to the repeated and pressing remonstrances of the government the amount was then lowered to 12,000 talers.[3] Prince John Maurice declared it an absolute impossibility to collect the money and again was apprehensive of a general uprising.[4] Even Weimann was concerned about the 'complete ruin' of the country 'from which so many tons of gold have already been squeezed'; the vice-chancellor Diest publicly refused to sign the warrants as being against his conscience and the *Recess*.[5] Between 1655 and 1660 altogether more than 1,500,000 talers were raised in Cleves and Mark, not counting deliveries in kind.[6] Yet the feared rising did not occur: the Estates' strength was sapped through their own disunity and the rule of military force.

The war of 1655–60 strengthened Frederick William's position both externally and internally. After the end of the war he was strong enough to revoke some of the concessions he had been forced to make in 1649 and 1653. Instead of negotiating with the Estates he sent a new *Recess* already signed and sealed to Prince John Maurice and informed the Estates that he would not come to Cleves until they had accepted it unconditionally.[7] The Estates, however, although inclined to concessions, decided to return the *Recess*, whereupon John Maurice secretly left Cleves, followed by the Estates.[8] They were summoned again and threatened with the arrival of their ruler with a large military force who would treat them 'somewhat harshly'.[9] They still attempted to defer a decision until the elector's arrival, but eventually the majority gave way and accepted the new *Recess*; only the deputies of Wesel, Rees, and Hamm and several noblemen objected and left the assembly.[10] Some weeks later even they apologized

---

[1] Ibid., pp. 892, 895, 899, 907 (Mar.–Sept. 1657).
[2] Ibid., pp. 902, 907 (Aug.–Sept. 1657).
[3] Von Haeften, loc. cit., pp. 788, 915.
[4] *Urkunden & Actenstücke*, v, p. 907 (Sept. 1657).
[5] Ibid., p. 908, n. 2 (Sept. 1657).
[6] Ibid., p. 970 (Jan. 1661).
[7] Ibid., p. 960 (Aug.–Sept. 1660).
[8] Ibid., pp. 960–1 (Oct. 1660).
[9] Ibid., p. 964 (Oct. 1660).
[10] Ibid., pp. 965–8 (Oct.–Nov. 1660).

and accepted: as John Maurice put it, 'apparently those of Cleves and Mark all want to be good children . . .'.[1]

By the *Recess* of 1660 and its supplement of 1661 Frederick William gained a number of important points. No longer mentioned were the rights of the Estates to negotiate with foreign powers and to refuse the payment of taxes if the stipulations of the *Recess* were violated.[2] Also omitted were the promise that no troops would be introduced without the Estates' consent, as well as the oath of all officials to preserve the stipulations of the *Recesse*; the appointment and dismissal of all officials was now left to the elector.[3] On the other hand, the *jus indigenatus* was maintained for all posts in the government and in the courts;[4] furthermore, the Estates retained their most important privileges, the voting and auditing of taxes, and the right of free and unfettered assembly on their own initiative, after due notification of the meeting place and the agenda to the government.[5] The solution was essentially a compromise, exactly as the Brandenburg *Recess* of 1653 and the Prussian *Recess* of 1663. In contrast with Brandenburg and Prussia, however, very few changes occurred in Cleves and Mark after 1661. The *Recesse* remained in force throughout the seventeenth and eighteenth centuries, and with them the Estates retained their constitutional position and some political influence.[6] That much their resistance had achieved.

The *Recesse* of 1660–1 settled the relations between the ruler and the Estates. They did not settle the various points at issue between the Estates themselves, in particular the conflict about the tax-exemption of the nobility. In the past it had not denied its obligation to contribute to taxes raised against the Turks. In 1664, however, when the towns of Cleves appealed to this custom and asked how much the nobility was willing to contribute, it refused to pay anything whatever, either then or in the future. Thereupon the towns, declaring they would not

---

[1] *Urkunden & Actenstücke*, v, p. 969 (Nov. 1660).

[2] Hintze, op. cit., p. 210; von Haeften, loc. cit., p. 959, n. 3; p. 960, n. 4.

[3] Von Haeften, loc. cit., p. 959, n. 1–2; *Scotti*, i, pp. 337–8, 340, 351, 382: *Recess* of 1660, clauses 4, 7, 11, 14, 34; *Recess* of 1661, clause 36.

[4] *Scotti*, i, pp. 337–8, 340–2, 346–7, 350, 382: *Recess* of 1660, clauses 4, 7, 11, 14, 18, 31, 34; *Recess* of 1661, clause 36.

[5] Ibid., pp. 342–3, 346, 374–5: clauses 19, 21, 29 of the *Recess* of 1660, and clause 17 of that of 1661.

[6] Lehmann, op. cit. i, p. 98; Schmoller, op. cit., pp. 60–61.

grant anything as long as the noblemen persisted in their attitude, took legal action against them.[1] Frederick William was told
by Prince John Maurice that this dispute offered an opportunity which had not occurred for many years to put the nobility under an extreme obligation to himself and his house: it
was well known, he thought, that everything for the elector's
advantage and contentment had always been effected by the
nobility, while the towns daily tried to interfere as much as
possible with his high authority, 'as it were the apple of his eye'.[2]
Frederick William in his reply expressed his annoyance that
some towns dared to make the nobility participate 'against the
old custom and their immunity', and thus caused disunity.[3]
John Maurice again assured him that the noblemen, in contrast
to the towns, had always granted money most liberally and that
they were highly delighted to hear that their prince would maintain their rights and customs.[4] Frederick William decided that
the nobility was not to contribute and that the tax was to be
raised by a hearth-money; this he declared least unfair because
'hitherto the countryside has been notoriously overburdened'.[5]

In July 1664 Frederick William graciously acceded to the
request of the nobility and solemnly promised to maintain it for
ever in its *privilegio nobilitatis et immunitatis*: not a jot should be
exacted from, or imposed upon it.[6] Yet the towns were not defeated. They met and resolved not to agree to the hearth-money
but rather to suffer military force.[7] The survey of hearths throughout the country, with the exception of those of noblemen, met
with strong protests from the towns, and those occupied by
Dutch garrisons resisted it openly. The towns accused the nobility of usurping the government, of occupying not only all
officers' posts, but also those of most government councillors.
They declared that the illegal usurpation of 'jurisdictions' was
continuing against all electoral promises; soon all villages would
be under noble authority; the few remaining free peasants had
to sell their farms to the owners of 'jurisdictions', and all the
peasants were burdened with illegal services and dues and
various additional taxes. The towns further accused the noble

[1] *Urkunden & Actenstücke*, v, p. 995 (Apr. 1664).
[2] Ibid., p. 998 (Apr. 1664).   [3] Ibid., p. 1003 (Apr. 1664).
[4] Ibid., p. 1004 (Apr. 1664).
[5] Ibid., pp. 1004, 1006, n. 1 (Apr.–July 1664).
[6] Ibid., pp. 1006–7 (July 1664).   [7] Ibid., p. 1008 (Aug. 1664).

councillors of partisanship, while the nobility brought the same charge against the commoners on the council. The towns offered to the elector 10,000 talers if the hearth-money were dropped; but Prince John Maurice and Alexander von Spaen urgently advised against this, as the ruler's authority would suffer and the nobility would be alienated, and insisted on the hearth-money.[1]

In December 1664 all preparations were complete and the assessments were published,[2] according to which each clergyman, burgher, and peasant had to pay over two talers each, and labourers and the poor half that amount. The towns appealed to the Imperial Chamber against the 'pretensions of the nobility'. Therefore the non-noble members of the government advised the elector to delay the levy of the hearth-money; but he sharply reprimanded them 'for their one-sided attitude' and ordered the imposition to proceed.[3] During 1665 the conflict continued unabated. The government was split into noblemen and commoners who very nearly came to blows with each other.[4] Only the small towns paid the hearth-money, while the others refused. According to John Maurice, they wanted 'in their pride and disobedience' to follow 'the maxims of the towns of Holland and Guelderland'; he summoned troops from Lippstadt and was determined to use force.[5] Frederick William agreed. Cleves, Xanten, and Duisburg paid their quota when troops marched in at the beginning of July. Where the troops had to remain outside the walls because of the Dutch garrisons, the burghers' cattle and their peasants' corn were seized so that even Wesel eventually paid its quota.[6]

The towns had lost the battle. During the diet of 1666 they finally had to obey the electoral orders and to recognize that the nobility was exempt from all taxation, and that they themselves would contribute one-fifth, instead of one-sixth, of all taxes.[7] The quota of the towns of Mark was also raised.[8] The towns still escaped very lightly, for the much poorer towns of

[1] *Urkunden & Actenstücke*, v, pp. 1010–11 (autumn 1664).
[2] Ibid., pp. 1013–14 (Dec. 1664).   [3] Ibid., p. 1014 (Jan. 1665).
[4] Ibid., p. 1015 (report of Feb. 1665).
[5] Ibid., p. 1018 (report of June 1665).   [6] Ibid., pp. 1018–19.
[7] Ibid., p. 1024; *Scotti*, i, pp. 478–9: protocol of the diet and electoral confirmation of Oct. 1666.
[8] *Urkunden & Actenstücke*, v, p. 1013 (Dec. 1664).

Brandenburg had to bear 59 per cent. of all taxes, and more than this after the introduction of the excise.[1] They had to give way on all important issues, that of taxation, that of the 'jurisdictions', and that of posts in the government and in the army. On all these points Frederick William and his officials supported the claims of the nobility: the towns alone were too weak to defeat this alliance. A few days later the noblemen were granted, after the example of Brandenburg, freedom from customs for their own requirements of wine, millstones, and building materials.[2]

Very few political and constitutional changes occurred in Cleves and Mark after 1666. No attempt was made to employ 'foreign' officials: the *jus indigenatus* was strictly observed,[3] in striking contrast with Brandenburg and Prussia. There was no tendency to curtail the Estates' rights any further, and they even regained some of the ground which they had lost. As long as they granted the taxes required the power of the purse formally remained in their hands. After 1683 they exercised a form of budget right: at the request of a deputation sent to Berlin it was decreed that in future the estimates were to be communicated to them together with the financial requirements so that they could express their opinions.[4] If in any one year more was levied than had been granted by the diet, the government subsequently had to account for the difference.[5] Every year, with few exceptions, Frederick William was able to draw well over 100,000 talers from Cleves and Mark, and after 1675 the sum at times passed the 200,000 mark.[6] On an average the two principalities contributed about one-half to two-thirds of what Brandenburg paid; per head of the population they paid almost the same and sometimes a little more:[7] but in reality,

---

[1] See above, pp. 183, 198; M. Lehmann, *Historische Aufsätze und Reden*, 1911, p. 105.

[2] Von Haeften, loc. cit., p. 1023, n. 1; Rachel, op. cit., p. 484.

[3] Hötzsch, op. cit., p. 48.

[4] Ibid., p. 694 (Mar. 1683).

[5] Ibid., pp. 351, 750 (Nov. 1685).

[6] Ibid., pp. 341–2, the detailed figures for every year from 1667 to 1697. Cf. von Haeften, loc. cit., p. 943, n. 5.

[7] During the years 1688–96 births in Cleves and Mark averaged 52·9 per cent. of those in Brandenburg; marriages averaged 56·1, and deaths 56·4 per cent. of those in Brandenburg, according to the figures printed by Behre, op. cit., pp. 447, 451. Thus Cleves and Mark seem to have had about 55 per cent. of the population of electoral Brandenburg.

considering their far greater wealth, they were much less burdened than Brandenburg. To that extent the resistance of Cleves and Mark had borne fruit.

Nine times Frederick William attempted the introduction of the excise, each time without success.[1] Equally fruitless were almost all other attempts at reform.[2] An exception was the foundation of the provincial Commissariat in the last years of the reign. In 1684 von Wilich-Bötzlar, a Cleves nobleman, was appointed *Obercommissar* for Cleves and Mark; two years later a collective Commissariat was formed consisting of him and four native commoners.[3] It was an independent authority, responsible for the administration, assessment, and repartition of the taxes.[4] Exactly as in Brandenburg and Prussia, friction soon developed between the old-established and the new authorities. The Commissariat extended its activities at the cost of the government; the Estates complained that the latter had no power left.[5] Frederick William had to intervene and, interestingly enough, did so against the expansionist tendencies of the Commissariat. He expressed his displeasure and forbade the Commissariat any interference with, or adjustment of, the taxes granted by the Estates, any dismissal of their deputies, and any dispatch of tax demands.[6] The Commissariat equally failed to investigate and to reform the urban administration and tax systems. Although inquiries into these matters were among its functions,[7] the towns were successful in achieving a transfer of the negotiations to Berlin, and thereby frustrated von Wilich's intentions. In 1687 Frederick William ordered the investigations to cease and fulfilled most of the towns' wishes. The Commissariat had been defeated.[8] It did not become all-powerful as it did in Brandenburg and in Prussia.

The towns of Cleves retained their own administration and their self-government. The government and the Estates of Cleves continued to function side by side with the new authorities. Through the period of despotism the Estates preserved their

---

[1] Hötzsch, op. cit., p. 346 (in the years 1667–8, 1671, 1674–5, 1677, 1679, 1686–7).

[2] Ibid., pp. 13, 76, 202–3, 206, 208, 379, 387, 570, 773, 896.

[3] Ibid., pp. 155–60, 870–3 (Sept. 1686).

[4] Ibid., pp. 166, 756–7, 870–1 (Sept. 1686).

[5] Ibid., pp. 157, 160, 166, 760.   [6] Ibid., pp. 875–6 (Mar. 1687).

[7] Ibid., p. 168.   [8] Ibid., pp. 768–73, 1022–8 (Sept. 1687).

basic rights of periodic meetings when and where they pleased, of granting taxes, and of participating in legislation.[1] In this respect they stood alone in the Hohenzollern monarchy and almost alone in the whole Empire.

The contrast between the development in Brandenburg and Prussia and that in Cleves is very striking. It is difficult to say why Frederick William, after 1666, did not continue the struggle against the Estates and did not enforce any reforms, but left matters as they were and even allowed the Estates to regain some of their influence. He may not have been very much interested in the happenings in the far-distant Rhineland as long as he got his will in Brandenburg, his central and, from his point of view, most important possession. But this seems unlikely because in the equally distant Prussia the Estates were pushed back much more energetically than in the west, even in the last years of the reign. Nor was it the strength of the Estates which prevented Frederick William from eliminating their influence in Cleves and Mark. By 1666 they had lost their power, and the French wars after 1672 further sapped their strength, while in Prussia the Estates continued to resist until the end of the reign. The towns of Cleves and the whole country were declining owing to the wars and the withdrawal of the Dutch garrisons which caused a cessation of the intimate relations with the United Provinces.[2] The Estates would have been unable to render any further resistance to a centralizing and absolutist policy: perhaps the elector, having achieved certain concessions in the *Recesse* of 1660–1 and finding the Estates willing to grant considerable amounts, did not see the necessity of going any further. His policy towards the Estates was perhaps less absolutist and consistent than has often been assumed, and more adapted to the different circumstances existing in his territories.

There is one aspect, however, where Frederick William's policy was quite consistent throughout: it was in favour of the nobility and it was directed against the towns. In Brandenburg an alliance between the elector and the towns was probably impossible because they were too weak to be used as a counterbalance against the Junkers. In the Rhineland, however, the

[1] Lehmann, *Freiherr vom Stein*, i, p. 98.
[2] *Urkunden & Actenstücke*, v, p. 948, n. 12; p. 997; Hötzsch, op. cit., p. 336, n. 1; p. 553, n. 2; p. 761 (1664–87).

towns were strong, although declining towards the end of the reign; in addition, between them and their ruler there was the bond of a common religion, that of Calvinism. Yet these factors did not deter him from siding against them on each controversial issue and from allying himself with the local nobility. Frederick William could only conceive of local government as being conducted by the landlords, and of state authority as being maintained through an alliance between the prince and the nobility. In his western principalities, however, this policy was only partly successful. It proved impossible to transplant the Brandenburg structure of society to the Rhineland, and local institutions and self-government survived although they were weakened. Only some of the outward appearances of the Junker predominance were established, for example the 'jurisdictions' and the tax-exemption of the nobility. The large estates, however, and the dominant role of the Junkers, the serfdom of the peasants, and the subservience of the burghers could not be transferred. The changes introduced did not fundamentally affect the structure of society in Cleves and Mark: the two principalities continued to live in their own way, little influenced by the central authorities and by the Hohenzollern state as a whole.

XVI

The State of the Great Elector

WHEN the young Frederick William came to the throne in 1640, there was no Brandenburg state: he merely owned a number of scattered principalities, each with its own government and institutions. When he died in 1688, there was a fairly centralized state which was governed from Berlin and was held together by several uniform institutions. The firm establishment of these institutions was the elector's life-work; the basis on which he founded the Hohenzollern state remained unchanged throughout the eighteenth century. Frederick William's achievements had a negative as well as a positive side. The negative one consisted of his struggle against the Estates of his different possessions: they were deprived of the power of the purse and of their influence over many civil and all military appointments; they were no longer consulted in foreign affairs and hardly in internal matters; they no longer dominated the local governments, and the latter lost much of their power to new organs. In the creation of these Frederick William showed his positive aims. It was partly force of circumstances, partly the impact of foreign affairs, partly his own external and internal ambitions, which gradually made the elector adopt a policy directed against the Estates and in favour of military centralization. In this policy he was naturally influenced by the example of Louis XIV; but it did not consist of a mere copying of foreign institutions and had important features of its own.

At the beginning of the seventeenth century the privy council was founded to advise the ruler in questions arising from the impending territorial acquisitions and to prepare the way for them. During the Thirty Years War, however, the privy council almost ceased to exist and its importance became purely local.[1] It was revived by Frederick William soon after his accession, but even then it remained in practice the local government for the Brandenburg Mark rather than an organ for all the electoral territories. Of the 16 councillors appointed during the first 12 years of the reign, 8 were natives of Brandenburg and

---

[1] See above, pp. 177–80.

3 of Pomerania, but none came from Cleves or from Prussia.[1] Obviously local Brandenburg influences were paramount in this council, and this often meant those of the local Estates. Thus in 1645 the privy councillors suggested the names of three Brandenburg noblemen for appointment as councillors, adding that this would also please the Estates which had petitioned for the appointment of more noble councillors to the *Kammergericht*.[2] Some attempts were made to discuss the affairs of Cleves and Prussia in the privy council, at least when Frederick William himself was present, but these attempts were soon given up again.[3] When he was absent from Berlin, the privy councillors were expressly forbidden to debate questions relating to Prussia, Cleves, and Ravensberg.[4] When the elector nevertheless asked for their opinion about the grievances of the Cleves Estates, they replied that most of them were not familiar with these matters and that the others had forgotten them, as they had not been discussed by them for several years.[5] In 1649 Frederick William again admonished the privy councillors to take into account not only the Brandenburg Mark, but all his lands and subjects and the whole state:[6] obviously because they had failed to do so.

Gradually, however, the privy council emerged as the central organ for all the electoral territories, at the same time remaining the government for the Brandenburg Mark, the most central and most important principality. As the Brandenburg government the privy council also wielded judicial powers, especially if the parties to a case agreed to accept its decision. This occurred very frequently, for justice could thus be obtained more speedily and more cheaply than from the *Kammergericht*, so that the privy council became overburdened with legal business. Therefore a committee of the privy council was constituted in 1658 as the highest court for the Mark: the parent body was to retain the supervision over judicial matters, but no longer to adjudicate itself.[7] Even in later years, however, the privy council itself dealt with many legal cases and was frequently

---

[1] Klaproth and Cosmar, op. cit., pp. 346–56.
[2] *Protokolle & Relationen*, iii, pp. 213–14.
[3] Tümpel, op. cit., pp. 75–76.   [4] Ibid., p. 73.
[5] *Protokolle & Relationen*, iii, p. 338 (Dec. 1645).
[6] Ibid. iv, p. 274 (Sept. 1649).
[7] Stenzel, op. cit. ii, p. 76; Bornhak, *Geschichte des preussischen Verwaltungsrechts*, i, p. 315.

appealed to,[1] especially by peasants and burghers who complained about their superiors, or about new burdens, or petitioned for alleviation of taxes. Its business throughout remained a mixture of minor cases with important matters of state, whether internal or external; there does not seem to have been any order of precedence, nor any committees dealing with certain specified matters: all this reminding us strongly of the Tudor privy council.

In 1651 an attempt was indeed made to divide the affairs into 19 departments which were distributed among 10 effective councillors.[2] Among these departments, 8 dealt with foreign and Imperial affairs and 7 with the various electoral territories: the electoral Mark, the Old Mark, the New Mark, Pomerania, Prussia, Halberstadt and Minden, and Cleves, Mark and Ravensberg, each forming one department. Apart from the supervision of the archives, there were but three functional departments: one comprising the postal services and the Jews; the second feudal matters, the mint, and the salt monopoly;[3] and the third and only important one, the army, in so far as Frederick William did not reserve military matters to himself.[4] Clearly the territorial aspect of internal affairs still predominated, and only certain minor matters and the army were considered tractable for the state as a whole. The relationship between the privy council and the local governments was not affected by the instruction of 1651, nor did it mark any progress towards greater centralization. Even in later years the bulk of the business discussed by the privy council still consisted of local Brandenburg affairs, and the division into departments soon disappeared again.[5] At the end of the reign there were not yet any proper departments, and the councillors were continuously transferred from one task to another.[6]

Military affairs were the exception from this rule. In 1651 they were to some extent still within the purview of the privy

[1] Stenzel, op. cit. ii, pp. 76, 450.

[2] Bornhak, op. cit. i, pp. 316–17; Protokolle & Relationen, iv, pp. 394–8 (Dec. 1651).

[3] From 1 Jan. 1652 the import of salt was made a state monopoly: Rachel, Die Handels-, Zoll- und Akzisepolitik . . . , p. 658.

[4] Protokolle & Relationen, iv, pp. 396–7; Tümpel, op. cit., p. 80.

[5] Tümpel, op. cit., pp. 79–81; Hintze, in F.B.P.G. xviii, 1905, p. 294; K. Breysig, Geschichte der brandenburgischen Finanzen in der Zeit von 1640 bis 1697, i, 1895, p. 20.

[6] Breysig, op. cit., p. 16.

council. When Frederick William in that year left Berlin for a campaign in the Rhineland, he left instructions for his officers, so as to relieve the privy councillors from responsibility and labour; if anything happened *in militaribus*, the privy councillors should summon certain officers and hear their advice.[1] During the war of 1655–60, however, when the elector departed for the war the governor of Brandenburg and the commandant of Küstrin, Count Dohna, were left in charge of defence and other military matters, while the privy councillors were no longer mentioned.[2] When the governor soon after fell ill and died, the *pura militaria* were entrusted to Count Dohna alone.[3] This soon caused friction between him and the privy councillors who complained that he issued orders to them and treated them as his dependants.[4] Two years later Count Dohna was appointed governor of Brandenburg in the absence of the elector: this time the *pura militaria* were left entirely to him; only questions of billeting could in his absence be decided by the privy council which had to keep him informed of its decisions.[5] The privy councillors thanked Frederick William for their exemption from the *pure militaribus*, but asked for a definition, as they had to issue orders in matters which in their opinion came within that category.[6] Thereupon the elector replied that he could not remember having exempted them from military matters and that he trusted they would faithfully discharge them, especially in the absence of the governor and in case of *periculum in mora*.[7] After the peace of 1660 all *militaria* and security matters were definitely remitted to the field-marshal and war councillor von Sparr. In matters of state touching upon the army the privy councillors had to use his and other generals' counsel; in cases of military law they had to weigh the decisions of court-martials and to communicate their opinions to von Sparr for further orders.[8] Thus military affairs were step by step withdrawn from the cognizance of the privy council.

Within the privy council there reigned, during the war, 'frightful confusion' and 'unheard-of licence' of the officials who

---

[1] *Protokolle & Relationen*, iv, p. 332.
[2] Ibid. v, pp. 200, 239, 266 (Nov. 1656–Jan. 1657).
[3] Ibid. v, pp. 306, 339, n. 1 (Apr.–June 1657).
[4] Ibid. v, pp. 339, 385, 397 (June–Oct. 1657).
[5] Ibid. v, p. 636 (Sept. 1659).   [6] Ibid. v, p. 639.
[7] Ibid. v, p. 640 (Oct. 1659).   [8] Ibid. vi, pp. 232–3 (Nov. 1660).

spoke very contemptuously about their master.[1] This seems to
have been one reason for the appointment, in 1658, of von
Schwerin as its president;[2] he held this office until his death in
1679. He was to hold rank above all other officials and to see to
it that all incoming and outgoing mail was distributed among
the councillors, to introduce matters for discussion, and to pro-
mote their early expedition.[3] Frederick William then wanted
'to put his *Etat* into a somewhat better condition'; but this
wish did not indicate any centralizing tendency, nor was it an
attempt to push the local governments down to the position of
subordinate executive organs.[4] Nor did von Schwerin's appointment bring to an end the friction and confusion in the privy
council. On the contrary, after 1662 there were two well-defined
factions, one led by von Schwerin, and the other by Jena and
later by Meinders, both commoners.[5] In 1663 von Schwerin
complained bitterly to the elector about Jena who denigrated
his loyal services and pretended he could do everything alone.[6]
In later years von Schwerin attacked Meinders sharply in letters
to the Duke of Croy, thanking the latter for his patronage of the
nobility which allegedly was persecuted by the other faction.[7]

This conflict between noblemen and commoners was of old
standing. In 1655 it flared up over the question of the excise, the
noble councillors opposing its introduction into Brandenburg
and the commoners advocating it. The former accused the latter
of being 'noblemen's foes', and the latter believed 'that one
intended, secretly and publicly, to suppress, insult, and destroy
the burgher class'. The commoners resorted to confidential
correspondence with each other and formed a common front
against the noble councillors.[8] In the struggle with the Estates
the noble councillors usually were in favour of milder measures,

---

[1] Philippson, op. cit. i, pp. 380–1: letter of von Schwerin to Weimann of Jan.
1658.
[2] Klaproth and Cosmar, op. cit., pp. 206–7, referring to the growing confusion.
[3] Ibid., p. 207; Bornhak, op. cit. i, p. 319; S. Isaacsohn, *Geschichte des preussischen Beamtenthums*, ii, 1878, pp. 137–8, 362–5.
[4] Both has been alleged by Tümpel, op. cit., p. 86. In my opinion the sentence
quoted above refers to the confusion mentioned. Tümpel himself admits that this
is the only documentary proof for his assertion, indicating that the tendency was
'noch nicht besonders kräftig'.
[5] Von Orlich, op. cit. i, p. 248.   [6] Isaacsohn, op. cit. ii, p. 157, n. 1.
[7] Von Orlich, op. cit. i, pp. 252, 256 (Oct. 1677–Apr. 1679).
[8] *Protokolle & Relationen*, v, pp. 73–75: letter of Tornow to Jena, Dec. 1655.

while the commoners advocated a more ruthless policy, especially against the nobility which dominated the Estates in the east.[1]

In this conflict inside the privy council the commoners were in a permanent minority. In 1651 they numbered 3 among 12, and in 1657 3 among 11:[2] in either year 6 councillors were native noblemen. During the remaining 30 years of the reign 22 noblemen were appointed and only 5 commoners: the proportion remained about the same. The majority of these 22 were Junkers, 6 from Brandenburg, 4 from Pomerania, and 4 from Prussia. The other 8 were foreigners who came from other German principalities.[3] Of 18 privy councillors holding this title at the end of the reign, 10 were Junkers, 4 foreign noblemen, and only 4 were commoners. In each instance the native nobility was in the majority. Although the opposite has been asserted frequently,[4] Frederick William never showed any preference for foreigners or commoners, but preferred to bestow high offices upon native noblemen, thus preparing the way for the policy of the Prussian kings of the eighteenth century. The elector himself explained in 1654 to the Estates of Pomerania: it was customary in the whole world that the nobility had preference over the commoners *in collatione officiorum*, and even if this was not so, it was a matter pertaining to his own power and free unlimited disposition.[5] This policy enabled him to reward his supporters among the Estates, especially the Calvinists,[6] and to associate them with the interests of the whole state, as they were often employed outside their native principality. In particular noblemen from Brandenburg and Pomerania were used

[1] *Protokolle & Relationen*, v, p. 73; *Urkunden & Actenstücke*, x, p. 304; xvi, p. 695, n. 2.

[2] *Protokolle & Relationen*, iv, pp. 394–8; Klaproth and Cosmar, op. cit., p. 201; A. Stölzel, *Brandenburg-Preussens Rechtsverwaltung und Rechtsverfassung*, i, 1888, p. 370, n. 2.

[3] The names and the countries of origin are given by Klaproth and Cosmar, op. cit., pp. 360–73.

[4] E.g. by Schmoller, in *Acta Borussica, Behördenorganisation*, i, pp. 130–1, and in *Umrisse und Untersuchungen...*, p. 309; Philippson, op. cit. i, pp. 379, 384; iii, p. 111; C. Bornhak, *Deutsche Verfassungsgeschichte*, 1934, p. 161; D. Ogg, *Europe in the Seventeenth Century*, 1946, p. 444; Schevill, op. cit., pp. 375–6; a hundred and fifty years ago Klaproth and Cosmar, op. cit., p. 95, held quite a different opinion.

[5] Isaacsohn, op. cit. ii, p. 140, n. 5.

[6] Klaproth and Cosmar, op. cit., p. 137; G. Schmoller, 'Der preussische Beamtenstand unter Friedrich Wilhelm I.', *Preussische Jahrbücher*, xxvi, 1870, p. 151.

in the more distant lands, and equally in the army and the diplomatic service.[1]

On the other hand, Frederick William did not exclude commoners from the higher appointments in his state, as Frederick the Great did later. There were always some commoners among the privy councillors, usually trained lawyers whose knowledge was indispensable: at the beginning of the reign Seidel, Tornow, and Jena; later Meinders, the younger Jena, and Fuchs. Most of them were ennobled for their services, but even then they continued to be classified as commoners.[2] In this respect Frederick William anticipated the policy of his grandson, Frederick William I. This was a conscious policy, for the ennobled commoners were a useful counterbalance to the great power of the native nobility. When the Prussian nobility in 1670 protested against the conferment of noble offices upon commoners, the elector adroitly replied: at all times nobility had been a reward for virtue and brave actions; as his times were also producing virtuous subjects, it would not only be to their denigration and against the origin and fundament of the whole nobility, but also against the temporal majesties if those who merited a higher estate through their virtue and actions were not to glory in it, or were not to pretend to what they had honestly acquired: this the nobility, whose first ancestors had had no other origin, itself would consider just and fair.[3] The latter continued to look down upon the newcomers. Gradually, however, the ennobled commoners acquired estates and intermarried with the local nobility so that they became assimilated to it: a *noblesse de robe* never developed in Brandenburg and Prussia.

If the privy council lost its control over military affairs during or soon after the war of 1655–60, it also lost, during the following years, its control over finance and taxation. This matter of primary importance passed to new military authorities, the *Generalkriegskommissariat* and its subordinate organs in the various principalities, which pushed aside the local governments and Estates and their control over taxation and finance. This office originated during the war of 1655–60 which had such

---

[1] Isaacsohn, op. cit. ii, pp. 208–9.

[2] Ibid., p. 207; Stölzel, op. cit., i, p. 370, n.2.

[3] 'Churfürstl: Abolitio Gravaminum', 24 Dec. 1670: *Ostpreuss. Folianten*, vol. 701, copies in vols. 698, 699, 700, 702, 705, and 706. Strangely enough, this passage of principal importance has been omitted in *Urkunden & Actenstücke*, xvi, pp. 682–4.

great importance for the internal history of Brandenburg. A Brandenburg nobleman, von Platen, was appointed *Generalkriegskommissar* with the electoral army in 1655; there was also an *Oberkriegskommissar* for Cleves (since 1647) and another one for Prussia. As von Platen represented the entire military administration on the general staff, his office from the outset assumed a central character. It was the beginning of a unified military and financial administration for the whole state. It was responsible for the assembling, equipping, remounting, victualling, and billeting of the army, its payment, stores, and magazines, the raising of money, and the imposition of contributions at home and abroad. The number of officials was small but increasing during the war years; and subordinate Commissariats came into being in most of the electoral territories, although many of them disappeared again even before the end of the war. After its end the personnel of the *Generalkriegskommissariat* was severely reduced, but von Platen and several *Kriegskommissare* remained in office, as did some of the subordinate Commissariats.[1] They thus became permanent institutions, ready to expand at the next opportunity. As von Platen was a privy councillor, the office formally remained connected with, and under the supervision of, the privy council.[2] But there was much friction between the privy councillors and the officials of the Commissariats who got their orders directly from von Platen,[3] and the functions of both offices overlapped in many fields.

During the following years of peace the *Generalkriegskommissariat* did not develop further. Von Platen remained at its head until 1667 and was mainly occupied with attempts to reform the urban finances in the Brandenburg Mark. Von Platen's successor was Meinders who was appointed a war councillor; but he did not receive the title of *Generalkriegskommissar*, nor did he become a member of the privy council while the peace lasted.[4] Meinders' instruction of 1669 clearly showed the reduced im-

---

[1] Wolters, op. cit., pp. 80–91, with many details; K. Breysig, 'Die Organisation der brandenburgischen Kommissariate', *F.B.P.G.* v, 1892, pp. 137–8.

[2] Tümpel, op. cit., p. 92.

[3] *Protokolle & Relationen*, v, pp. 362–3, 647; Wolters, op. cit., pp. 208–11.

[4] Wolters, op. cit., pp. 93–96, 208; A. Strecker, *Franz von Meinders, ein brandenburgisch-preussischer Staatsmann im 17. Jahrhundert*, 1892, p. 57. Meinders was appointed a privy councillor in Aug. 1672, i.e. after the outbreak of war: Klaproth and Cosmar, op. cit., p. 365.

portance of his office. He was to see that the soldiers received their proper pay, food, and clothing, that the officers sent in complete rolls of each company at least once every three months, that the troops were mustered more frequently to find out any deficiencies, that proper accounts were sent in by the tax-collectors from each principality, that billeting and contributions fell as evenly as possible on the different lands and places. He was to transmit any complaints about excesses of soldiers against civilians, so that the culprits could be punished, and to relate any shortages of weapons or supplies in fortresses and magazines: he was to report on all these and other points belonging to military affairs, to be present and to vote on such occasions in the privy council, and to expedite the replies and decisions therein.[1] Thus the Commissariat was reduced to an executive organ of the privy council and its head to a subordinate position,[2] without any real influence on the vital issues of army finance and taxation, and even without a seat on the privy council.

The war of 1672–9 radically changed this position. A separate treasury was set up, into which were paid the foreign subsidies, above all of the United Provinces, the contributions of the Empire, and some loans. Since 1674 it was called the *Generalkriegskasse*, the first central chest of the Hohenzollern state. It soon became the most important department of the *Generalkriegskommissariat*, pressing strongly for more centralization. At first it only collected certain extraordinary taxes from the electoral territories, for example the poll-taxes of 1677 and 1679; but soon fixed monthly contributions had to be paid into the *Generalkriegskasse* from most of these principalities. From 1683 onwards the provincial chests had to send in all vouchers and receipts for army pay to the *Generalkriegskasse* to be accounted and audited there, so that it became their superior authority and a proper central treasury.[3]

In 1675 von Gladebeck was appointed *Generalkriegskommissar*, a post which he had previously held in Brunswick; but Meinders continued to do most of the work under him.[4] Although von

[1] Strecker, op. cit., pp. 127–30: instruction of June 1669.
[2] Ibid., p. 57.
[3] Wolters, op. cit., pp. 98, 275–9, 303–4; Tümpel, op. cit., pp. 94–95; F. Freiherr von Schroetter, *Die brandenburgisch-preussische Heeresverfassung unter dem Grossen Kurfürsten*, 1892, p. 44.　　　　[4] Wolters, op. cit., pp. 101–3, 403–9.

Gladebeck was made a privy councillor on entering the electoral service, any influence of the privy council on the new central chest was carefully excluded.[1] The most important period in the development of the *Generalkriegskommissariat* began with the appointment, in 1679, of a new head in the person of von Grumbkow, a Pomeranian nobleman and a professional officer: the first one to hold this post. Under him the functions and the personnel of the office were considerably expanded, and a hierarchy independent of the other authorities was established with regard to its subordinate officials in the different principalities.[2] Especially the field of economics was brought under the control of the *Generalkriegskommissariat*. It was entrusted with the supervision of trade and manufactures and with the financing of new enterprises.[3] Through the introduction of the urban excise, first in Brandenburg and later in other territories, it began to supervise and to control the entire municipal administration.[4]

In 1685 von Grumbkow was charged with the settlement of the immigrating Huguenots. Special Commissars were appointed, responsible for bringing the newcomers into the country and settling them there, as well as for the starting of new enterprises by them. To facilitate their entry into the guilds and to reform abuses in the government of the guilds, these also were brought under the control of the *Generalkriegskommissariat*.[5] The same applied to naval and colonial enterprises and the taxes raised to finance them.[6] One of its principal tasks became the reform of the whole system of taxation. As the taxes were destined for the army, and as all the activities mentioned were to produce more taxes for the army, their control by a military administration was perhaps less strange than would appear at first sight. In this way the *Generalkriegskommissariat* lost its subordinate position and developed into a central authority directly under the ruler; and 'the maintenance, victualling, and enlargement of the army more and more became the central point of all state activity'.[7] The

[1] Wolters, op. cit., pp. 208, 212.
[2] Ibid., pp. 104–9; Philippson, op. cit. iii, pp. 214–15.
[3] Wolters, op. cit., pp. 234–9; Rachel, op. cit., p. 774.
[4] See above, p. 197.
[5] Wolters, op. cit., pp. 109, 143, 238–9; Philippson, op. cit. iii, p. 109; Schmoller, 'Das brandenburgisch-preussische Innungswesen,' *F.B.P.G.* i, 1888, p. 83; M. Meyer, *Geschichte der preussischen Handwerkerpolitik*, i, 1884, pp. 91–93.
[6] Philippson, op. cit. iii, p. 218; Wolters, op. cit., pp. 135–6, 284–8.
[7] Schmoller, *Preussische Verfassungs-, Verwaltungs- und Finanzgeschichte*, p. 88.

Generalkriegskommissariat became the most important and the most typical authority of the nascent Hohenzollern state, and it soon overshadowed the parent body from which it had sprung, the privy council.

There is no evidence that the privy council, during the later years of the reign, resisted these momentous changes; but there was much friction between high army officers and the Commissariat. From the outset its civilian officials interfered with military affairs and acted very independently of the army command. About these and other 'confusions' the commander-in-chief, von Sparr, complained in strong words as early as 1657.[1] Under von Gladebeck the conflict revived: Field-Marshal Derfflinger declared that the military were being suppressed in everything and that he was sick and tired of these methods.[2] Under von Grumbkow the position of the Commissariat grew even stronger. On his appointment Derfflinger tried to safeguard his authority by the insertion of a clause that von Grumbkow's orders always had to be communicated to him first. But this had little effect, and under their successors the influence of the Commissariat grew further. In practice the *Generalkriegskommissar* combined the functions of chief of the general staff with those of the ministers for war and for finance and thus held a key position in the whole state.[3]

A collegiate Commissariat or an individual Commissar, responsible to the central authority in Berlin, was appointed for each electoral territory, while the central office remained responsible also for the Brandenburg Mark.[4] The provincial Commissariats were particularly active in pushing back the local Estates and depriving them *de facto* of the power of the purse, and in curtailing the independence of the local governments. The privy council never possessed the tools required for these tasks, even if it had been prepared to tackle them. The *Generalkriegskommissariat* was much better suited for the purpose; many of its officials did not serve in their native principality and had no ties with the local Estates. The provincial Commissariats had the same functions, and at times the same conflicts

---

[1] Isaacsohn, op. cit. ii, pp. 170–1; Wolters, op. cit., pp. 218–20, 228, 391–4.
[2] Wolters, op. cit., p. 223; Philippson, op. cit. iii, p. 49 (Mar. 1678).
[3] Wolters, op. cit., pp. 224–6; von Schroetter, op. cit., p. 26.
[4] Breysig, in *F.B.P.G.* v, 1892, pp. 143–6; Wolters, op. cit., pp. 164–203.

with army officers, as the central authority in Berlin;[1] among
their tasks matters relating to taxation were the most prominent.
The most important local official of the Commissariat was the
commissarius loci, or *Steuerkommissar*, whose office owed its origin to
the urban excise in Brandenburg, and was transferred from there
to other territories.[2] Matters of trade and industry, the guilds,
and the settlement of the Huguenots came under his supervision.[3]
Somewhat higher in rank was the *Kriegskommissar* who might be
responsible for the victualling and billeting of an army, or might
be sent to muster a regiment, to levy contributions, or to transmit orders regarding taxation or the troops to local authorities.[4] In
addition, there were special Commissars and offices for military
stores and victualling, for the artillery, the guards, the garrisons of
the fortresses, for commercial, and for naval matters.[5] A large
bureaucracy with numerous subordinate officials came into being:
its functions were in many ways similar to those of the French
Intendants, but with a special military emphasis. The Prussian
bureaucracy developed out of these military Commissariats.[6]

The leading positions in the Commissariats were held almost
exclusively by noblemen. Of 34 *Kriegsräte* and *Geheime Kriegsräte*
appointed by Frederick William, 29 were noblemen, most of
them native Junkers; of 18 more appointed under his successor,
15 were noblemen: less than one-sixth were commoners.[7] The
heads of the provincial Commissariats also usually were noblemen, sometimes even natives of the principality in question.
Below these ranks, however, the personnel mainly consisted of
commoners; for noblemen disliked the office of *Kriegskommissar*
which brought them into frequent conflicts with the Estates,
or with army officers whom they had to supervise.[8] The office of
Steuerkommissar was almost exclusively held by commoners.[9] The

---

[1] For details see *Urkunden & Actenstücke*, v, p. 994; Isaacsohn, op. cit. ii, p. 174.
[2] See above, pp. 196–7.
[3] Rachel, 'Der Merkantilismus in Brandenburg-Preussen', *F.B.P.G.* xl, 1927,
p. 227; Schmoller, ibid. i, 1888, p. 83; Meyer, op. cit. i, p. 91; Wolters, op. cit.,
pp. 159–63.
[4] Wolters, op. cit., pp. 125–7; von Schroetter, op. cit., pp. 42, 92, 132.
[5] Wolters, op. cit., pp. 128–38, 142–3.
[6] Schmoller, in *Umrisse und Untersuchungen . . .*, p. 303.
[7] See the list of names in Wolters, op. cit., pp. 372–4. More than three-quarters
of the twenty-nine noblemen appointed by Frederick William were Junkers.
[8] Von Schroetter, op. cit., pp. 92–93.
[9] Wolters, op. cit., p. 159; Schmoller, op. cit., p. 300.

corresponding offices in the countryside, however, those of *Landrat* and *Marschkommissar*, were always held by a nobleman resident in the district in question. Both officials were appointed at the suggestion of the local nobility from their midst; they were responsible for billeting, the marching of troops, and the levying of taxes in their district. In the eighteenth century the two offices, the functions of which were very similar, were finally amalgamated. They were particularly important in the central provinces, above all in Brandenburg, Pomerania, and Magdeburg. These officials were nominated by the *General-kriegskommissariat* and were supervised by it; yet their position was different from that of its other officials: for they only served within their small districts, and they were at the same time the representatives of the local nobility,[1] in this way corresponding to the contemporary local government officials in England. In the towns, however, this combination of the old order with the new did not exist: their administration was brought completely under the control of the state.

The bulk of the revenue of the *Generalkriegskasse* came from taxation. It has been calculated that the military expenditure during the years 1655–88 amounted to almost 54 million talers, only 10 of which were not levied in the electoral territories. Of these 10 millions, almost 4 came from the electoral domains, the mint, the post, the tolls, and other regalia; while foreign and Imperial subsidies accounted for about the same amount. Another 800,000 talers also came from foreign sources, so that over 90 per cent. of the military expenditure derived from internal resources.[2] This considerable burden was very unevenly distributed between the different classes and territories. At the end of the reign, in 1688, Brandenburg, Prussia, and Cleves and Mark together contributed 1,024,000 talers, while the other five small principalities paid 595,000,[3] and thus seem to have been much more heavily burdened. The tiny principality of Halberstadt, for example, every year paid about 100,000 talers;

---

[1] Wolters, op. cit., pp. 146–56; Schmoller, op. cit., p. 300, and in *Acta Borussica, Behördenorganisation*, i, pp. 100–2; Hintze, 'Der Ursprung des preussischen Landrats-amts', *Geist und Epochen der Preussischen Geschichte*, pp. 172 ff., with extracts from many sources.

[2] Wolters, op. cit., pp. 578–80, gives the detailed figures.

[3] Breysig, in *Jahrbuch für Gesetzgebung, Verwaltung und Volkswirthschaft im Deutschen Reich*, xvi, 1892, p. 458.

while electoral Brandenburg, which was sixteen times its size and had about ten times its population, paid at most 430,000.[1] The territories in which there was least resistance were taxed most heavily: in Halberstadt the Estates lost their power with the introduction of the excise in 1674.[2] Equally, Prussia as well as Cleves, although more wealthy and more populous than Brandenburg, paid less,[3] undoubtedly because of the strength of their resistance and opposition to Brandenburg rule.

The total revenue of the state trebled in the course of the reign. At Frederick William's accession in the midst of the Thirty Years War the revenue amounted to little more than 1 million talers, about 60 per cent. of which came from the domains, tolls, forests, and other regalia, the remainder being levied by taxation. At the time of Frederick William's death the domains and regalia contributed 1,705,000 talers, and other sources, mainly taxation, 1,677,000: a total of well over 3 million talers.[4] The amount of foreign subsidies varied greatly: from less than 10,000 talers in 1686 to as much as 224,000 in 1685; in 1688 they amounted to 64,000 talers.[5] Of the total revenue more than half, and at times considerably more, was spent on the army, excluding the foreign subsidies and substantial deliveries in kind to the forces.[6] The burden fell on a population of perhaps one million,[7] which was impoverished by the Thirty Years and the subsequent wars, and on territories which were mostly backward and declining. The total revenue of France with her roughly 20 million inhabitants, or more, amounted in 1688 to about 36,666,000 talers;[8] while the electoral territories with their one million inhabitants in the same year had to raise about 3,382,000 talers, or nearly twice as much per head, although the wealth of France was much greater. On the other hand, in Brandenburg the taxes were not farmed, but collected by state

[1] Wolters, op. cit., pp. 292–6. Halberstadt had 28 Prussian square miles, and electoral Brandenburg 459. In 1688 Halberstadt had 1,053 births and 750 deaths, against 11,698 and 6,676 respectively in electoral Brandenburg: Behre, op. cit., p. 134.

[2] Tümpel, op. cit., p. 102.   [3] See above, pp. 200–1, 221, 249.
[4] Breysig, loc. cit., pp. 6–7, 520.   [5] Wolters, op. cit., pp. 578–9.
[6] Breysig, loc. cit., p. 520; Philippson, op. cit. iii, pp. 80–81.
[7] This is the estimate of Schmoller, *Preussische Verfassungs-, Verwaltungs- und Finanzgeschichte*, p. 112. This is borne out by the death figures for 1688: 32,135 in the whole state (Behre, op. cit., p. 134): if multiplied by 33, the result is just over one million.   [8] Philippson, op. cit. iii, p. 75: 110,000,000 livres.

officials, and this may in part account for the difference. The centralization of the military and financial administration was the most important result of Frederick William's reign: without it he would have been unable to maintain a sizable standing army.

The excise more and more became the favourite instrument of this centralizing policy. The Commissariats had to employ very many subordinates, inspectors, and snoopers. Over seventy excise officials were employed in the tiny principality of Halberstadt in 1677, not counting the village jurymen who had to collect and hand over the tax; their salaries varied from 8 to 1,200 talers p.a., and the total annual wage bill was 7,242 talers.[1] The lower officials were badly paid, always eager to receive tips and bribes and to play the master in a brutal manner. All goods brought into a town were checked and listed at the gates; whatever went outside was only allowed to pass if an excise receipt could be produced; anything not declared could be confiscated. Naturally, there were innumerable attempts at evasion and fraud, and trade tended to circumvent Brandenburg.[2] The excise was mainly a tax on consumption, sales, and the movement of goods, the latter being very similar to transit or market tolls; the most important parts, and the easiest to levy, were dues on milling, brewing, and slaughtering.[3] The rates in the different territories and on different goods varied considerably. Not only the inhabitants of the countryside, but also the institutions and servants of the Church, and in practice many officers and officials, were exempt from the excise.[4] Before Frederick William's death it was introduced in the towns of Prussia (without Königsberg), Pomerania, Magdeburg, Halberstadt, and Minden,[5] with the same, or worse, effects which it had in Brandenburg.

As the revenue increased with any higher consumption or greater commercial activity, the government became vitally interested in the protection of urban enterprise. It tried to prohibit all trade and industry in the countryside and to concentrate them in the towns; but in the seventeenth century most of these efforts were in vain, and the towns suffered from the

---

[1] Rachel, op. cit., pp. 637–8.   [2] Ibid., pp. 633–7.
[3] Ibid., pp. 507–8.   [4] Ibid., pp. 589–618.
[5] Ibid., pp. 538–46, 560–70; Wolters, op. cit., pp. 160–1.

competition of places in which there was no excise.[1] The starting
of new manufactures and their protection were undertaken by
the military Commissariats which attempted to use the electoral
monopolies and regalia and the local raw materials for the
purpose.[2] In accordance with the tendencies of the time the
import of foreign glass, iron and steel, tin and tin ware, copper and
brass wares, sugar, tobacco, cheap cloth, leather, salt was forbidden, as was the export of raw wool, leather, skins, and furs.
The local industries, however, were so little developed that they
could not absorb these raw materials; nor was Brandenburg
able to do without the import of manufactured articles. Thus
the prohibitions and monopolies had to be rescinded, only to be
reimposed after some time, whereupon the same difficulties re-
appeared. Even if certain articles could be produced locally,
the foreign products were usually cheaper and better; the local
factories and works hardly ever made any profits, and many had
to close down after a short time.[3]

The skill of the Huguenots, however, introduced many new
industries and was equally profitably employed in the existing
electoral iron, copper, and brass works. The immigrants started
or revived the manufacture of candles, soap, linseed-oil, paper,
mirrors, watches, optical articles, tobacco, buttons, gloves, hats,
wigs, and above all of a large variety of textiles, such as finer
cloth, silk, velvet, gauze, ribbons, lace, stockings, tapestries,
gobelins, the dyeing and printing of linen and cotton, gold and
silver braiding, and embroideries.[4] They were granted numerous
privileges and monopolies, but they suffered many disappoint-
ments and setbacks.[5] There was no market for many of their
products in Brandenburg, and labour and raw materials were
scarce. It was only in the eighteenth century that manufactures
were more firmly established on the barren soil of Brandenburg
which the immigrants found as uncongenial as that of Moab.[6]
In Prussia, Pomerania, and Cleves no new manufactures at all
were founded at that time by them.[7] Thus Frederick William's

---

[1] Rachel, op. cit., pp. 623–7, 700.   [2] Ibid., pp. 502, 643–4.
[3] Ibid., pp. 645–727, with many details for each industry.
[4] Ibid., pp. 729–31.   [5] Ibid., pp. 732–44.
[6] Hence they gave the name of *Moabit* to the area near Berlin where they tried
to cultivate the mulberry tree.
[7] Rachel, op. cit., pp. 747–49, and *Das Berliner Wirtschaftsleben im Zeitalter des
Frühkapitalismus*, 1931, pp. 6, 40–41.

aim of keeping the money in the country[1] was only very im-
perfectly realized. The Huguenots settled mainly in the towns,
especially in Berlin. But Protestants from Holland, Switzerland,
Piedmont, and the Palatinate were brought into Brandenburg
to populate the countryside and to farm the domains and deserted holdings.[2] In these fields also Frederick William initiated the
policy of the Prussian kings of the eighteenth century. Their
policy of religious toleration coincided with their own interests:
their Calvinist creed had but few followers in Brandenburg and
Prussia, and all their lands stood badly in need of more inhabitants, which meant more taxpayers and more recruits for the
army. Indeed, about one-sixth of the Huguenot immigrants
were professional soldiers.[3]

The reforms in the fields of taxation and administration, as
well as many other reforms, were caused by the creation of the
standing army.[4] When Frederick William came to the throne
in 1640, the strength of the Brandenburg forces was only
4,650 men, and in the following year they were further reduced
to 2,300 in Brandenburg and 800 men in Prussia,[5] a very small
force considering that the Thirty Years War was still in progress.
These troops were mercenaries whose discipline and behaviour
were no better than those of the Swedish and Imperial troops
which held the country to ransom. It is true that many of the
officers were native noblemen whose estates could not maintain
them; but when appeals were made to their patriotism, they
declared that they could not live from it.[6] The military value of
these ill-disciplined hosts was small, and little was lost by their
reduction. As early as 1644, however, a Brandenburg nobleman,
who had held a high post in the Swedish army, submitted to the
elector a plan for the creation of a standing army of 11,000 men
which was to be recruited partly from the country population
and the native nobility; and this plan made a lasting impression

---

[1] Thus *Protokolle & Relationen*, iv, p. 578, and von Orlich, op. cit. i, p. 461
(1652–83).
[2] Franz, op. cit., pp. 96–98.
[3] R. Freiherr von Schrötter, 'Das preussische Offizierkorps unter dem ersten
Könige von Preussen', *F.B.P.G.* xxvii, 1914, p. 110.
[4] Schmoller, in *Umrisse und Untersuchungen* . . . , p. 303; Strecker, op. cit.,
p. 64.
[5] C. Jany, *Geschichte der königlich preussischen Armee bis zum Jahre 1807*, i, 1928,
pp. 91, 100–1.
[6] *Protokolle & Relationen*, i, p. 690 (Mar. 1643); cf. Jany, op. cit. i, pp. 95–96.

on Frederick William.[1] Yet he did not have the means to put it into practice, and for more than a decade the Brandenburg forces remained very small, only increased at times of military enterprises on the Rhine against Palatinate-Neuburg, and reduced as soon as these were over. In 1653, after the conclusion of the long Brandenburg diet, the troops there numbered only 1,800 men,[2] hardly deserving the name of a standing army.

It was only during the war of 1655–60, which had such great importance for the history of Brandenburg, that a sizable army came into being. In September 1655 von Sparr, the commander-in-chief, conducted 8,000 men to Prussia where the war had started in the summer, and where another 11,000–12,000 men were recruited. By the summer of 1656 the army had grown to 22,000, about half of which were cavalry and dragoons.[3] This force was sufficient to play an important part in the war and to gain for its master the sovereign possession of Prussia from the two chief belligerents, Poland and Sweden. The officers came from all parts of the Empire, from Poland, Holland, and France, but the large majority were Brandenburgers; from the rank of captain upwards most belonged to the nobility.[4] After the peace of Oliva this army had to be severely reduced, but it was not disbanded as had been the custom with mercenary forces. Frederick William was now strong enough to levy considerable taxes from his territories, so that in 1661 he still commanded an army of about 12,000 men.[5] It had to be further reduced during the following years, but never below 7,000; already in 1666 its numbers were brought back to 12,000 and remained at about that figure until 1672.[6] The wars against France, and the Dutch and other subsidies connected with them, brought another substantial increase to over 45,000 men. With the conclusion of peace in 1679 the army was reduced to 25,000:[7] twice

---

[1] *Protokolle & Relationen*, ii, pp. 349–78; Meinardus, ibid., p. xc; Wolters, op. cit., p. 8.

[2] Jany, op. cit. i, pp. 103–10, with the detailed figures for every year and unit.

[3] Ibid., pp. 116–22; Breysig, loc. cit., p. 510. Dragoons were mounted but fought as infantry.   [4] Jany, op. cit. i, p. 158.

[5] Ibid., pp. 195–200; F. Hirsch, 'Die Armee des Grossen Kurfürsten und ihre Unterhaltung während der Jahre 1660–66', *Historische Zeitschrift*, liii, 1885, pp. 232–4.

[6] Hirsch, loc. cit., pp. 253, 262, 266; Jany, op. cit. i, pp. 203–8; P. Haake, in *Historische Zeitschrift*, cliii, 1936, p. 319.

[7] Stenzel, op. cit. ii, pp. 222, 452; Breysig, loc. cit., p. 511; Wolters, op. cit., p. 530; Jany, op. cit. i, pp. 213–74.

or thrice its size during the 1660's. Thanks partly to the subsidies of Louis XIV, it could be maintained at about this level and even somewhat increased. At Frederick William's death the standing army numbered over 30,000 men, mainly infantry.[1] It could boast important victories over the renowned Swedish army and was a force to be reckoned with even by the major military powers of Europe.

The officers' corps of this army consisted very largely of native noblemen. There were some commoners, but their promotion was usually slow, and after more than twenty years' service they might not have risen above the rank of lieutenant.[2] In the early 1690's commoners held only 12 per cent. of the commissions in four regiments for which figures are available, German noblemen 78 per cent., and Huguenots 10 per cent.[3] Only the officers of the artillery and the engineers were almost exclusively commoners.[4] On the other hand, some commoners rose to very high ranks, the most famous being Field-Marshal Derfflinger, or Colonel Ditmär who became the commandant of the important fortresses of Kolberg and Pillau: both were ennobled for their services.[5] But these were exceptions; especially among the higher ranks the native nobility predominated absolutely.[6] The few ennobled commoners were gradually assimilated, as were the more numerous Huguenots who, if noblemen, were treated as the equals of the Junkers.[7] Most Junker families were poor and found it difficult to provide for their younger sons. The army, and to a lesser extent the civil service, solved their problem. This applied above all to the Brandenburg Mark with its poor soil and its numerous nobility. But even in Cleves with its so different social structure so many noblemen entered the army that the towns complained that the nobility claimed all the officers' posts.[8] In Prussia many impoverished noblemen begged for permission to enlist either in the electoral or in a foreign army;[9] in 1701 nearly one-fifth of

---

[1] Breysig, loc. cit., p. 511; Jany, op. cit. i, pp. 300–1.
[2] Jany, op. cit. i, pp. 310, 357: two examples from 1695 in n. 447.
[3] R. von Schrötter, in *F.B.P.G.* xxvii, p. 105.
[4] Ibid., pp. 104, 116.   [5] Jany, op. cit. i, p. 310.
[6] F. von Schroetter, op. cit., p. 117, n. 4.
[7] R. von Schrötter, loc. cit. xxvii, pp. 107–11.
[8] *Urkunden & Actenstücke*, v, p. 1010 (1664).
[9] Von Baczko, op. cit. vi, p. 40 (Mar. 1684). In 1674 and 1680 the nobility

the Prussian nobility was classified as 'poor'.[1] At the death of Frederick William the strength of the officers' corps was about 1,030,[2] providing attractive openings for the members of the nobility.

In this way Frederick William compensated the nobility for the loss of its political 'liberties' and accustomed its members to serve his state.[3] The officers' corps became a reliable, strictly monarchical corporation, animated by common ideas; its members began to feel themselves not as Pomeranians or Prussians, but as owing loyalty to a wider entity, the Hohenzollern state.[4] Thus they could be, and were, used against the local Estates, even if they were natives of the same principality and thus themselves members of the same Estates. The policy of preferring noblemen as officers also was continued by Frederick William's successors. Only young noblemen were admitted into the cadet companies and schools which he founded,[5] and noble non-commissioned officers were listed by name in the quarterly returns made to his son: indicating that noblemen were *eo ipso* considered to be officer aspirants. Although many commoners were commissioned under the stress of the war of the Spanish Succession, they were purged soon after its end.[6] Thus the nobility became a service nobility; it identified its interests with those of the state which gave them positions of honour and profit.

This factor gave to the army a character quite different from that of the mercenary armies of the Thirty Years War which owed loyalty to nobody. Although it was an army of hired professional soldiers, the national element in it gradually increased, not because one did not want foreigners, but because one could not get them.[7] The foreigners who enlisted were usually of a doubtful character. During the war of 1655–60 many soldiers enlisted who had previously served Spain or the United Provinces, but many deserted after having been clad and fed for some weeks: by the time they reached the Brandenburg

---

complained that its members were forced to enter foreign armies because of their poverty: *Ostpreuss. Folianten,* vol. 707, fol. 156; vol. 715, fol. 322.

[1] Bergmann, op. cit., p. 209: 378 out of 1,930 noblemen.

[2] R. von Schrötter, loc. cit. xxvii, p. 98.   [3] Isaacsohn, op. cit. ii, p. 208.

[4] R. von Schrötter, loc. cit. xxvi, p. 437.   [5] Ibid. xxvii, pp. 119–23.

[6] Ibid., pp. 100, 107: exactly as Frederick the Great was to do after the Seven Years War.   [7] F. von. Schroetter, op. cit., p. 97; Jany, op. cit. i, p. 317.

Mark the units had melted away to a fraction of their nominal strength.[1] In 1678 Prussian officers and soldiers deserted to the Swedes, and in 1683 many soldiers deserted from Frankfurt because other states offered them better pay.[2] Many people were enticed or forced into the army by the recruiters who found it difficult enough to fill the ranks, so that they often made their victims drunk first or beat them up if they refused to join.[3] In all these matters the Brandenburg army does not seem to have been much different from other armies of the time. There were also the same harsh punishments,[4] the same rapaciousness of the officers and other ranks, the same ill-discipline of a soldiery whose pay was often in arrears, and consequently the never-ending complaints of the population, especially of the towns, against the troops and their officers, exacerbated by the fact that most officers were noblemen.[5] Frederick William was unable to prevent his officers at Frankfurt, Spandau, and other places from imposing dues of their own on ships, carts, and travellers, and on people bringing their goods to market.[6]

Through the army the native nobility became firmly linked with the Hohenzollern state. It shouldered the burden of serving the dynasty and became dominant in the higher positions of the state. The alliance between the throne and the nobility and the serfdom of the peasantry remained the basis of the Prussian state in the eighteenth century. The nobility's political power was not destroyed with that of the Estates: it revived in a new form. The relationship between Junker and serf was reproduced in the army in the relationship between officers and men. The officials and the officers became the ruling class of Prussia;[7] and most of them came from one and the same social group. In France, on the other hand, Louis XIV deliberately excluded the nobility from the administration. In Brandenburg war and

---

[1] *Urkunden & Actenstücke*, v, pp. 885, 895, 993, n. 1; *Protokolle & Relationen*, v, pp. 170, 189, 208, 222–3 (1656–7).

[2] Von Orlich, op. cit. iii, pp. 297–8; F. von Schroetter, op. cit., p. 99; Jany, op. cit. i, p. 317.

[3] *Protokolle & Relationen*, v, pp. 83, 659; *Urkunden & Actenstücke*, xvi, p. 742, n. 1; pp. 1006, 1020; F. von Schroetter, op. cit., p. 100.

[4] *Mylius*, iii 1, no. 57, cols. 177–8; Jany, op. cit. i, p. 316; F. von Schroetter, op. cit., p. 103. [5] F. von Schroetter, op. cit., pp. 102, 111–12, 122–3.

[6] Ibid., p. 123; Rachel, op. cit., p. 178, n. 2.

[7] Schmoller, 'Der preussische Beamtenstand unter Friedrich Wilhelm I.', *Preussische Jahrbücher*, xxvi, 1870, p. 551.

the needs of the army were the prime movers of internal changes. Frederick William certainly did not act according to a pre-conceived plan: circumstances and the needs of the moment shaped his policy at every turn, so that the observers noticed its indecisiveness and tortuousness. His own officials often com-plained in a similar vein when awaiting a decision from Berlin which did not come, and there were many rumours about the frequent changes of opinion at the electoral court, and about the influences exercised upon the ruler.

Frederick William carried through a 'revolution from above',[1] the first, but not the last, in the history of Prussia. The Estates gradually disappeared altogether as a factor in the state: the possibility of their transformation into a more modern repre-sentative assembly ceased to exist. It has been assumed that Brandenburg and Prussia would have gone the way of Poland if the Estates' power had not been broken and if their centrifugal tendencies had not been subordinated to a larger whole. But this is by no means certain. In Brandenburg and Prussia there was no *liberum veto* and the towns formed part of the Estates. Any growth of the towns and any rise of the urban middle classes would naturally have become noticeable within the Estates if they had survived. The Estates in the seventeenth century were certainly strong and full of vitality, quite different from their French counterpart, and they often showed good political sense and a grasp of problems much superior to that of the electoral officials. Any attempts to fit the Estates into a wider framework would have necessitated the formation of States General for the whole monarchy, and this attempt was never made. In other countries parliaments or States General helped to consolidate the state or to preserve its unity against internal and external dangers:[2] in this respect the history of Brandenburg and Prussia differs fundamentally from that of many European countries. Thus the question whether the Estates could ever have played the part of the Dutch or the French States General cannot be answered. This much, how-ever, is certain: the development of the Hohenzollern despotism cut off even the possibility of the gradual emergence of a modern

---

[1] Hintze, *Die Hohenzollern und ihr Werk*, p. 204.
[2] Ibid., p. 202, pointing especially to England, France, Sweden, Poland, and Hungary which all differed from Brandenburg and Prussia in this respect.

representative institution, as it happened elsewhere in Germany, above all in Württemberg, and in other countries.

The comparative ease with which the Hohenzollerns succeeded in establishing a centralized and absolute form of government was partly due to the after-effects of the Thirty Years War and of the war of 1655–60 which impoverished and weakened their lands, partly to the general backwardness and the economic decline. The peasant serfs were too down-trodden to revolt, and anyhow they were more oppressed by their masters than by the government. The towns, especially those of Cleves, of the Old Mark, and Königsberg, were declining and unable to provide the leaders of a rising. The nobility was won over, or split, by many concessions and the alluring prospects of official and military careers; the army was loyal and could be used against any local opposition or resistance. The size and the weight of the army also ensured that the country remained poor and backward. At the end of Frederick William's reign the French ambassador reported from Berlin that the country was so exhausted that money could only be found by the debasement of the coinage and by a cut in the pay of the troops:[1] and that was after eight years of peace.

At the end of the seventeenth century the density of the population in electoral Brandenburg and in Prussia was still less than one-third of that in Saxony and Württemberg, in Holland and France; while that in the New Mark and Pomerania was less than a quarter of that in those countries. Even Hanover and Schleswig-Holstein had a much greater density of population than the Hohenzollern territories.[2] This backwardness nobody realized more clearly than the founder of the Hohenzollern state who had been brought up in Holland and thus knew the importance of commerce and industry. Yet such were the methods and the policy which he adopted that they could only enhance the social and economic evils which he found in existence. No prosperous towns and no prosperous peasantry could develop under the shadow of the Junkers and of the standing army: they continued to dominate the country far into the nineteenth century. On the other hand, as the Hohenzollern

---

[1] H. Prutz, *Aus des Grossen Kurfürsten letzten Jahren*, 1897, p. 398: report of Aug. 1687.

[2] Schmoller, in *Umrisse und Untersuchungen* . . . , p. 570; Franz, op. cit., p. 100, n. 135, with somewhat differing figures.

despotism developed comparatively late, it showed certain modern traits: for example, the taxes were not farmed, and the officials were comparatively efficient and incorrupt. In the history of the Prussian state and of the Prussian army Frederick William, 'the Great Elector', certainly played a decisive part: he laid the foundations on which his successors built. During his lifetime he was dwarfed by the enormous power of Louis XIV; yet his work outlasted that of the French king by generations.

The most important factor in the social history of Brandenburg and Prussia, and of many other eastern European countries, was the decline of the towns and the subsequent rise of the nobility: it definitely separated the developments in the east from those in the west and created a boundary line between two different social systems. If western institutions had advanced far into eastern Europe at the time of the colonization, some centuries later an east-European society with its own distinctive features established itself in most of the districts colonized. In spite of wide differences of historical development between Mecklenburg, Pomerania, Brandenburg, Prussia, Poland, Bohemia, Moravia, Hungary, Russia, and the Baltic states, one basic fact applied to all of them: the nobility remained the ruling class, and an urban middle class did not come into being until the later nineteenth century. The nobility preserved serfdom as the condition of the majority of the population, it monopolized the key positions in state and army, and it effectively prevented the carrying through of any reforms which would have curtailed its power and influence. The remainder of the inhabitants had to obey and to pay, without being able to influence the course of events. The result was a complete division between the rulers and the ruled and between the different social classes. The Hohenzollern rulers of the seventeenth and eighteenth centuries not only accepted the existing social structure, but through a determined policy of associating the nobility with the state they strengthened and preserved its position. Reforms thus became impossible, until they had to be introduced because the old Prussia was destroyed by Napoleon on the battlefield, and even then against the fierce resistance of the ruling aristocracy.

In many ways the struggle between Frederick William and the

Estates was very similar to that between crown and parliament in England. The Estates used all the weapons of the Commons, such as grievances before supply, allocation of supply, periodical meetings, attacks against unpopular officials; in Cleves they even met without a summons by the government. In general they were much stronger than the States General and the provincial Estates in France and no weaker than the English parliament in the late sixteenth or early seventeenth centuries; but then the latter went from strength to strength, while the Estates lost their power. This was partly due to objective factors, above all the wars, but also to their own divisions and lack of a common policy. Fundamental differences separated the nobility from the towns: in England, on the other hand, the gentry and the urban middle classes were linked by strong religious, social, economic, and political ties, and both were driven into a united opposition by the policy of the Stuarts. In the Hohenzollern territories these links were lacking, and this proved the vital chink in the armour of the Estates. Instead of their forming an alliance against the crown, the crown was able to use the Junkers' class interests to win them over to an alliance with the crown. In this field also the decisive event was the rise of the nobility and the decline of the towns, otherwise this policy could never have succeeded. If in England the crown had attempted an alliance with the Lords against the Commons, this could have been defeated easily by the Commons. They and the classes which they represented were the strongest force in the England of the seventeenth century. In north-eastern Germany it was the Junkers who dominated state and society: it was therefore natural that the rulers should seek their support for the establishment and the maintenance of the state.

In Poland and some other east-European countries no strong government and no standing army came into being, and the nobility did not become a service nobility, but it retained its political powers unaltered until the nineteenth century. In Brandenburg and Prussia, on the other hand, its political powers were modified and subordinated to the needs and requirements of a state which the Junkers influenced and which influenced the Junkers. From the days of Frederick William onwards the two began to form parts of one whole; its traces can be followed through the course of German history.

APPENDIX

Prices in Prussia between 1395 and 1461

The following sources have been used for the compiling of this appendix:

Ordensfolianten 142–7, 149, 153–5, 161*a*, 200*b* in the Königsberger Staats-archiv, now at Göttingen.

C. Sattler, *Handelsrechnungen des Deutschen Ordens*, Leipzig, 1887.

Das Marienburger Tresslerbuch der Jahre 1399–1409, ed. E. Joachim, Königsberg, 1896.

Das Ausgabebuch des Marienburger Hauskomturs für die Jahre 1400–1420, ed. W. Ziesemer, Königsberg, 1911.

Das Marienburger Konventsbuch der Jahre 1399–1412, ed. W. Ziesemer, Danzig, 1913.

Hildebrand Veckinchusen — Briefwechsel eines deutschen Kaufmanns im 15. Jahrhundert, ed. W. Stieda, Leipzig, 1921.

'Handelsbriefe aus Riga und Königsberg von 1458 und 1461', *Hansische Geschichtsblätter*, Jahrgang 1898, Leipzig, 1899, pp. 57 ff.

Scriptores Rerum Prussicarum, vols. iii and v, Leipzig, 1866–74.

Hansisches Urkundenbuch, vols. v, vii 1, viii, and ix, Leipzig and Weimar, 1899–1939.

Hanserecesse von 1431–1476, ed. G. Freiherr von der Ropp, vols. i and ii, Leipzig, 1876–8.

Liv-, Esth- und Curländisches Urkundenbuch, ed. F. G. von Bunge, H. Hildebrand, P. Schwartz, and others, vols. iv, vii, viii, and x, Reval, Riga, and Moscow, 1859–96.

Urkunden-Buch der Stadt Lübeck, ed. C. Wehrmann, vol. x, Lübeck, 1898.

F. A. Vossberg, *Geschichte der Preussischen Münzen und Siegel von frühester Zeit bis zum Ende der Herrschaft des Deutschen Ordens*, Berlin, 1843.

T. Hirsch, *Danzigs Handels- und Gewerbsgeschichte unter der Herrschaft des Deutschen Ordens*, Leipzig, 1858.

Year	Rye (1 Last)			Rye Flour (1 Last)			Wheat (1 Last)		
	Number of readings	*Price in shillings**		*Number of readings*	*Price in shillings**		*Number of readings*	*Price in shillings**	
1395	1	180	180	..	..	..	1	180	180
1396									
1397									
1398	1	300	300						
1399	..	..	..	4	390	390	3	307	307
1400	32	275	275	89	361	361	38	423	423
1401	1	231	231	..	..	..	1	372	372
1402	10	314	314	17	415	415	13	506	506
1403	7	272	272	..	..	..	3	408	408
1404	21	295	295	10	372	372	13	453	453
1405	8	223	223	1	420	420	1	360	360
1406	7	203	203	2	263	263	2	386	386
1407	5	240	240	2	383	383	1	352	352
1408	9	390	369	2	365	345	2	447	423
1409	9	379	358	1	420	397	3	592	560
1410	5	362	342	2	320	303			
1411	13	302	163	..	..	..	4	401	216
1412	2	490	264	..	..	..	1	463	249
1413									
1414	1	345	115						
1415	1	900	300				1	900	300
1416	3	2,620	870	..	..	..			
1417	2	353	258						
1418									
1419									
1420									
1421	1	638	466						
1422									
1423	2	233	163	..	..	..	1	780	546
1424									
1425	..	..	..	..	..	..	1	1,020	714
1426	4	503	352	..	..	..	1	413	289
1427	3	560	392	1	810	567			
1428	2	870	609	1	900	630			
1429	3	630	441	..	..	..	1	840	588
1430	1	660	462	..	..	..	2	1,050	735
1431	1	360	252						
1432	1	513	359						
1433	1	900	630	..	..	..	1	1,080	756
1434	2	765	536	..	..	..	2	1,365	956
1435	..	..	..	..	..	..	4	364	255
1436	1	600	420						
1437	5	840	588	2	2,640	1,848			
1438	..	..	..	1	2,640	1,848	1	2,160	1,512
1439	1	533	373	..	..	..	3	1,763	1,234
1440									
1441									
1442	2	480	336						
1443	1	300	210	..	..	..	1	420	294
1444									
1445	1	195	137	1	1,160	812	1	564	395
1446									
1447									
1448									
1449	..	..	..	2	680	476			
1450									
1451	1	445	188	2	550	233			
1452									
1453	..	..	..	1	960	406			
1454									
1455	..	..	..	1	1,529	459			
1456									
1457									
1458	3 (Riga)	1,093	328						
1459									
1460									
1461	1	1,200	360	1	1,800	540	1	1,500	450

* For each commodity, column two gives the average price in Prussian shillings, column three discounts the debasement of the Prussian coinage which set in after 1407.

Year	Barley (1 Last)			Oats (1 Last)			Butter (1 Tonne)		
	Number of readings	Price in shillings*		Number of readings	Price in shillings*		Number of readings	Price in shillings*	
1395									
1396									
1397									
1398									
1399	6	246	246	1	150	150	4	122	122
1400	12	219	219	6	128	128	2	128	128
1401	12	247	247	51	100	100			
1402	25	277	277	2	110	110	1	120	120
1403	7	312	312	18	152	152			
1404	20	254	254	13	122	122	1	120	120
1405	14	249	249	5	89	89			
1406	9	223	223	4	77	77	1	150	150
1407	7	227	227	3	103	103	5	130	130
1408	2	300	284	3	100	95	6	140	132
1409	3	360	341	4	170	161	1	230	218
1410				4	175	166	1	156	148
1411	25	348	187	17	196	106	1 (Reval)	150	81
1412	4	348	187	3	220	118			
1413									
1414									
1415							2	420	307
1416	..	..	..	..	..	..	3	311	227
1417	..	..	..	..	..	..	1	303	221
1418	..	..	..	..	..	..			
1419									
1420									
1421									
1422	..	..	..	1	360	252			
1423									
1424									
1425									
1426	..	..	..	4	285	200	4	360	252
1427	..	..	..	..	..	..	2	360	252
1428	..	..	..	..	..	..	1	360	252
1429	..	..	..	..	..	..			
1430									
1431									
1432	..	..	..	..	..	..	1 (Lübeck)	225	158
1433									
1434	1	660	462	2	260	182			
1435	..	..	..						
1436									
1437	..	..	..	..	..	..	1 (Reval)	375	263
1438									
1439									
1440									
1441									
1442									
1443	1	210	147	1	150	105			
1444									
1445									
1446									
1447									
1448									
1449	..	..	..	1	300	210	3	320	224
1450									
1451									
1452	..	..	..	..	..	..	2	360	152
1453									
1454									
1455							1	600	180
1456	..	..	..	..					
1457	..	..	..	3	977	293			
1458	2 (Riga)	1,440	432						
1459									
1460									
1461	1	1,050	315	1	420	126			

* For each commodity, column two gives the average price in Prussian shillings, column three discounts the debasement of the Prussian coinage which set in after 1407.

Year	HONEY (1 Tonne)			WAX (1 Schiffspfund)			ASHES (1 Last)		
	Number of readings	Price in shillings*		Number of readings	Price in shillings*		Number of readings	Price in shillings*	
1399	4	195	195	1	275	275			
1400	4	174	174	5	1,031	1,031	1	285	285
1401	2	180	180						
1402	4	173	173	1	960	960			
1403	2	180	180						
1404	6	173	173	3	955	955	7	227	227
1405	3	170	170	1	960	960	3	210	210
1406	3	150	150				1	270	270
1407	3	167	167	1	1,080	1,080			
1408	4	200	189	2	924	874	1	300	284
1409	8	182	172						
1410	1	150	142				1	240	227
1411	11	167	90	2	968	521	2	165	89
1412	2	223	120						
1413									
1414									
1415									
1416	..	..	..	2	3,000	2,190			
1417	..	..	..	13	3,067	2,239	1	240	175
1418	..	..	..	7	2,681	1,957			
1419									
1420	..	..	..	4	2,235	1,632			
1421	..	..	..	1	1,920	1,402			
1422	..	..	..	2	2,010	1,533			
1423									
1424									
1425	..	..	..	2	2,258	1,581			
1426	..	..	..	1	2,130	1,491			
1427	..	..	..	..	..	..	4	630	441
1428									
1429	..	..	..	3	1,820	1,274	2	930	651
1430	..	..	..	1	1,740	1,218	4	960	672
1431									
1432	..	..	..	1	1,740	1,218			
1433	..	..	..	1	1,920	1,344			
1434	..	..	..	4	1,875	1,313	1	870	609
1435	2	410	287	2	1,853	1,297			
1436	..	..	..	4	1,935	1,354			
1437	..	..	..	1	1,950	1,365			
1438	..	..	..	3	2,020	1,414			
1439	..	..	..	1	2,640	1,848			
1440	..	..	..	3	2,690	1,883			
1441	2	608	426	2	3,060	2,142			
1442	1	380	276	4	2,895	2,027			
1443	1	75	53	1	2,280	1,596			
1444	..	..	..	2	2,370	1,659			
1445	..	..	..	7	2,753	1,857			
1446	..	..	..	4	2,550	1,785			
1447	..	..	..	4	2,415	1,691			
1448	..	..	..	4	2,450	1,715			
1449	..	..	..	5	2,466	1,726			
1450	..	..	..	4	2,299	972			
1451	..	..	..	..	..	..	1	495	209
1452	..	..	..	2	2,340	990	2	416	176
1453	..	..	..	..	..	..	1	420	178
1454									
1455									
1456									
1457									
1458	..	..	..	9 (Riga)	2,722	817	10 (Riga)	332	100
1459									
1460	..	..	..	..	..	..	1	525	158
1461	..	..	..	..	..	..	2	270	81

* For each commodity, column two gives the average price in Prussian shillings, column three discounts the debasement of the Prussian coinage which set in after 1407.

Year	Hops (1 Schiffspfund) [100 Scheffel]**			Beer (1 Last)			Iron (1 Last)		
	Number of readings	Price in shillings*		Number of readings	Price in shillings*		Number of readings	Price in shillings*	
1399	..	..	..	19	318	318			
1400	..	..	..	8	338	338	1	860	860
1401	..	..	..	9	342	342			
1402	..	..	..	10	327	327	1	680	680
1403	(1)	(250)	(250)	21	294	294	2	1,450	1,450
1404	(1)	(250)	(250)	14	274	274	3	1,067	1,067
1405	..	..	..	12	303	303	1	1,140	1,140
1406	..	..	..	9	324	324			
1407	..	..	..	17	282	282			
1408	1 (2)	178 (135)	169 (128)	18	246	233			
1409	(1)	(300)	(284)	29	378	359			
1410	(1)	(127)	(120)	2	445	421			
1411	(3)	(119)	(64)	7	365	197	3	1,237	666
1412	..	..	..	..	..	..	2	720	388
1413	(1)	(150)	(81)						
1414									
1415	(1)	(148)	(49)						
1416	(3)	(260)	(190)				1	2,340	1,708
1417	(1)	(150)	(110)	4	390	285			
1418	(1)	(132)	(96)						
1419	(1)	(150)	(110)						
1420	(1)	(188)	(137)						
1421									
1422									
1423	..	..	..	..	..	..	1	2,400	1,680
1424									
1425									
1426									
1427	1	135	95						
1428	..	..	..	..	..	..	3	1,880	1,316
1429	1	240	168						
1430	2	240	168						
1431	..	..	..	..	..	..	4	1,740	1,218
1432	..	..	..	..	..	..	1 (Lübeck)	1,900	1,330
1433									
1434									
1435	1	210	147						
1436									
1437	1	270	189						
1438	..	..	..	2	1,365	956			
1439	..	..	..	..	..	..	2	2,340	1,638
1440	2	315	221						
1441	1	590	413	..	..	..	1	2,520	1,764
1442	1	430	301	..	..	..	2	2,280	1,376
1443									
1444	..	..	..	4 (Reval)	890	623	1	2,400	1,680
1445	..	..	..	1	1,920	1,344	1	2,280	1,376
1446	..	..	..	..	..	..	1	2,160	1,512
1447	..	..	..	2	720	504	1	2,000	1,400
1448	..	..	..	2	728	510	1	2,280	1,376
1449	..	..	..	4	420	294			
1450									
1451	3	360	152	3	472	200	1	1,560	660
1452	1	600	254	..	..	..	2	1,709	723
1453									
1454	..	..	..	3	690	292			
1455	..	..	..	1	750	225			
1456	..	..	..	..	..	..	3	1,760	528
1457	..	..	..	1	1,500	450			
1458	3 (2 in Riga)	583	175	1 (Reval)	720	216	2 (Riga)	1,440	432
1459									
1460	..	..	..	..	..	..	3	1,860	558
1461	3	205	62	..	..	..	1	3,000	900

* For each commodity, column two gives the average price in Prussian shillings, column three discounts the debasement of the Prussian coinage which set in after 1407.
** Figures in brackets are those for 100 Scheffel.

Year	HERRING (1 Last)			SALT (1 Last)			TRAVEN SALT		
	Number of readings	Price in shillings*		Number of readings	Price in shillings*		Number of readings	Price in shillings*	
1395	1	920	920						
1396									
1397	2	600	600						
1398	1	750	750						
1399	7	620	620	3	480	480			
1400	14	569	569	20	612	612	6	840	840
1401	2	730	730	2	450	450			
1402	6	597	597						
1403	8	534	534	1	480	480			
1404	9	582	582	25	621	621	9	668	668
1405	2	850	850						
1406	7	812	812	5	602	602			
1407	8	774	774	4	675	675			
1408	9	759	718	5	294	278			
1409	6	764	723	4	780	738	4	780	738
1410	..	..	..	9	400	378	1	480	454
1411	4	1,300	700	21	540	281	4	705	380
1412	5	1,572	846	1	480	248			
1413	2	1,680	905						
1414	1	2,400	792						
1415	2	2,425	800						
1416	1	5,400	3,942	1	600	438			
1417	..	..	..	3	420	307			
1418									
1419	..	..	..	1	1,260	920	1	1,260	920
1420	..			10	624	455			
1421	2	3,690	2,694						
1422	..	..	..	1	1,380	966			
1423	..	..	..	1	1,380	966			
1424									
1425									
1426	2	4,305	3,014						
1427	1	3,000	2,100	5	2,304	1,613			
1428	..			2	1,530	1,071	1	2,220	1,554
1429	1	3,780	2,646	3	1,386	970	2	1,395	977
1430	1	3,060	2,142	1	840	588			
1431									
1432	2	2,155	1,509						
1433	..	..	..	2	1,170	819	1	1,260	882
1434	..	..	..	3	873	611			
1435	..			1	900	630			
1436	2	2,100	1,470	4	1,228	860	1	1,620	1,134
1437	1	2,520	1,764						
1438	..			1 (Reval)	1,920	1,344			
1439	3	4,020	2,814	2	1,890	1,323	1	2,160	1,512
1440	..	..	..	1	2,040	1,428	1	2,040	1,428
1441	..	..	..	3	1,300	910	3	1,300	910
1442	..			3	975	683	1	1,290	903
1443	1	720	504	3	960	672	1	1,920	1,344
1444	..	..	..	1	780	546			
1445									
1446									
1447									
1448	1	3,420	2,394	1	720	504			
1449	..	..	..	2	848	594			
1450	..			3	965	408			
1451	5	2,852	1,206	2	1,095	463	1	1,230	520
1452	..	..	..	3	1,042	441	1	1,200	508
1453	..	..	..	1	690	292			
1454	..			1	782	331			
1455	1	1,800	540	2	1,082	325	1	1,248	374
1456									
1457									
1458	..	..	..	11 (Riga)	913	274	1 (Riga)	1,220	366
1459									
1460	1	2,520	756						
1461	5	3,024	907	17	4,871	1,461	13	5,109	1,533

* For each commodity, column two gives the average price in Prussian shillings, column three discounts the debasement of the Prussian coinage which set in after 1407.

Year	FLEMISH SALT			BAY SALT			LISBON SALT		
	Number of readings	*Price in shillings**		*Number of readings*	*Price in shillings**		*Number of readings*	*Price in shillings**	
1395									
1396									
1397									
1398									
1399	1	480	480	1	480	480			
1400	13	521	521						
1401									
1402									
1403	1	480	480						
1404	11	582	582	1	960	960			
1405									
1406									
1407	1	600	600						
1408	2	360	341	2	195	184			
1409									
1410	2	435	412	1	225	213	1	315	298
1411	11	512	276						
1412	1	480	258						
1413									
1414									
1415									
1416									
1417	1	435	317						
1418									
1419									
1420	1	660	482	3	590	431	2	630	460
1421									
1422	..	..	..	1	1,380	966			
1423	..	..	..	1	1,380	966			
1424									
1425									
1426									
1427	..	..	..	3	1,080	756			
1428	..	..	..	1	840	588			
1429									
1430	..	..	..	1	840	588			
1431									
1432									
1433	..	..	..	..	..	..	1	1,080	756
1434	..	..	..	3	873	611			
1435	..	..	..	1	900	630			
1436	..	..	..	2	1,045	732			
1437									
1438	..	..	..	1 (Reval)	1,920	1,344			
1439	..	..	..	1	1,620	1,134			
1440									
1441									
1442	..	..	..	2	818	573			
1443	..	..	..	2	480	336			
1444	..	..	..	1	780	546			
1445									
1446									
1447									
1448	..	..	..	1	720	504			
1449	..	..	..	2	848	594			
1450	..	..	..	2	915	387	1	990	419
1451	..	..	..	..	..	..	1	960	406
1452	..	..	..	2	963	407			
1453	..	..	..	1	690	292			
1454									
1455	..	..	..	1	915	275			
1456									
1457									
1458	..	..	..	9 (Riga)	887	266			
1459									
1460									
1461	..	..	..	4	4,095	1,229			

* For each commodity, column two gives the average price in Prussian shillings, column three discounts the debasement of the Prussian coinage which set in after 1407.

	ALMONDS (1 Stein)			CINNAMON (1 Stein)			FIGS (1 Korb)		
Year	Number of readings	Price in shillings*		Number of readings	Price in shillings*		Number of readings	Price in shillings*	
1399	..	..	..	..	..	..	1	120	120
1400	1	45	45	..	..	..	1	105	105
1401									
1402	3	67	67	2	480	480	3	90	90
1403	1	45	45	2	540	540	5	84	84
1404	2	48	48	7	424	424	16	67	67
1405	1	90	90	3	540	540	4	57	57
1406	4	80	80	5	588	588	1	75	75
1407				2	600	600			
1408	3	60	57	3	720	680	4	90	85
1409	3	49	47	..	..	..	4	90	85
1410	..	..	..	1	720	680	1	105	99
1411	..	..	..	1	480	258	1	90	48
1412									
1413									
1414									
1415									
1416									
1417	1	300	219	..	..	..	1	210	153
1418	..	..	..	..	..	..	1	173	126
1419									
1420	..	..	..	..	..	..	4	140	102
1421									
1422									
1423	1	133	93						
1424									
1425									
1426									
1427									
1428									
1429									
1430									
1431									
1432									
1433									
1434	2	75	53	..	..	..	1	83	58
1435									
1436									
1437									
1438									
1439									
1440									
1441									
1442									
1443									
1444									
1445	1	75	53	1	660	462	1	90	63
1446									
1447									
1448									
1449									
1450									
1451									
1452									
1453									
1454									
1455									
1456									
1457									
1458									
1459									
1460									
1461									

* For each commodity, column two gives the average price in Prussian shillings, column three discounts the debasement of the Prussian coinage which set in after 1407.

Year	PEPPER (1 Stein) Number of readings	Price in shillings*		RAISINS (1 Stein) Number of readings	Price in shillings*		RICE (1 Stein) Number of readings	Price in shillings*	
1399	3	207	207						
1400	1	245	245	1	60	60	1	30	30
1401									
1402	..	..	..	2	47	47	3	25	25
1403	2	173	173	4	53	53	2	30	30
1404	22	207	207	9	33	33	2	28	28
1405	7	206	206	6	31	31	1	40	40
1406	5	217	217	2	132	132	3	27	27
1407	3	201	201	1	45	45	1	15	15
1408	2	186	176	6	64	61	2	18	17
1409	1	192	182	1	90	85	1	18	17
1410									
1411	6	255	137						
1412									
1413									
1414									
1415									
1416									
1417	..	..	..	4	131	96	3	51	37
1418									
1419									
1420	..	..	..	7	61	45			
1421									
1422									
1423					1	30	21	1	73	51
1424	..	..	..	..	..	..	1	65	46
1425									
1426	..	..	..	1	120	84			
1427									
1428									
1429									
1430									
1431									
1432									
1433									
1434	1	472	330	1	66	46	1	53	37
1435									
1436									
1437									
1438									
1439									
1440									
1441									
1442									
1443									
1444									
1445	1	510	357	1	90	63	1	50	35
1446									
1447									
1448									
1449	2	690	483						
1450									
1451									
1452									
1453									
1454	..	..	..	..	..	..	1	43	18
1455	1	480	144						
1456									
1457									
1458									
1459									
1460									
1461	1	840	252						

* For each commodity column two gives the average price in Prussian shillings, column three discounts the debasement of the Prussian coinage which set in after 1407.

Year	SAFFRON (1 Pfund)			SUGAR (1 Stein)		
	Number of readings	Price in shillings*		Number of readings	Price in shillings*	
1399	5	125	125			
1400	9	116	116	2	540	540
1401	3	107	107			
1402	2	108	108	3	450	450
1403	4	101	101	2	360	360
1404	2	89	89	2	300	300
1405	2	80	80	3	460	460
1406	1	70	70	9	615	615
1407	4	68	68	6	460	460
1408	..	..	..	2	360	341
1409	1	65	61	4	265	251
1410						
1411						
1412						
1413						
1414	1	85	28			
1415						
1416						
1417						
1418						
1419						
1420						
1421						
1422						
1423						
1424						
1425						
1426	1	135	95			
1427						
1428						
1429						
1430						
1431						
1432						
1433						
1434	1	173	121	1	390	273
1435						
1436						
1437						
1438						
1439						
1440						
1441						
1442						
1443						
1444						
1445	1	135	95			
1446						
1447						
1448						
1449	1	180	126			
1450						
1451						
1452						
1453						
1454	..	..	..	1	420	178
1455	1	360	152			
1456						
1457						
1458						
1459						
1460						
1461	1	480	144			

* For each commodity, column two gives the average price in Prussian shillings, column three discounts the debasement of the Prussian coinage which set in after 1407.

BIBLIOGRAPHY

I. SOURCES

Acta Borussica, Behördenorganisation: Die Behördenorganisation und die allgemeine Staatsverwaltung Preussens im 18. Jahrhundert, ed. by G. Schmoller and O. Hintze, vols. i, Berlin, 1894; iv 1, 1908; vi 1 and 2, 1901.

Acten der Ständetage Preussens: Acten der Ständetage Preussens unter der Herrschaft des Deutschen Ordens, ed. by M. Toeppen, 5 vols., Leipzig, 1874–86.

Akten & Rezesse der Livländ. Ständetage: Akten und Rezesse der Livländischen Ständetage, ed. by L. Arbusow and others, 3 vols., Riga, 1907–38.

Bang: Tabeller over Skibsfart og Varetransport gennem Øresund 1497–1660. vol. i: *Tabeller over Skibsfarten*, ed. by Nina Ellinger Bang, Copenhagen, 1906.

Cod. Dipl. Anhaltinus: Codex Diplomaticus Anhaltinus, ed. by O. von Heinemann, 6 vols., Dessau, 1867–83.

Cod. Dipl. Pruss.: Codex diplomaticus Prussicus, Urkunden-Sammlung zur älteren Geschichte Preussens, ed. by J. Voigt, 6 vols., Königsberg, 1836–61.

Cod. Dipl. Warm.: Codex Diplomaticus Warmiensis oder Regesten und Urkunden zur Geschichte Ermlands, ed. by C. P. Woelky and J. M. Saage, 3 vols., Mainz, Braunsberg, and Leipzig, 1860–74.

Cod. Pom. Dipl.: Codex Pomeraniae Diplomaticus, oder Sammlung der die Geschichte Pommerns und Rügens betreffenden Urkunden, ed. by K. F. W. Hasselbach, J. G. L. Kosegarten, and F. Baron von Medem, Greifswald, 1843–62.

Fabricius: Urkunden zur Geschichte des Fürstenthums Rügen unter den eingebornen Fürsten, ed. by C. G. Fabricius, 4 vols., Stralsund, Stettin, and Berlin, 1841–62.

Fidicin: Historisch-Diplomatische Beiträge zur Geschichte der Stadt Berlin, ed. by E. Fidicin, 5 vols., Berlin, 1837–42.

Friedensburg: Kurmärkische Ständeakten aus der Regierungszeit Kurfürst Joachims II., ed. by W. Friedensburg, 2 vols., Munich and Leipzig, 1913–16.

Gollmert: Urkundenbuch zur Geschichte des Geschlechts von Schwerin, ed. by L. Gollmert, Berlin, 1875.

Handfesten der Komturei Schlochau, ed. by P. Panske, Danzig, 1921.

Hans. U.B.: Hansisches Urkundenbuch, ed. by K. Höhlbaum, K. Kunze, W. Stein, and H. G. von Rundstedt, 11 vols., Halle, Leipzig, and Weimar, 1876–1939.

H.R. 1256–1430: Die Rezesse und andere Akten der Hansetage von 1256–1430, ed. by K. Koppmann, 8 vols., Leipzig, 1870–97.

H.R. 1431–76: Hanserecesse von 1431–1476, ed. by G. Freiherr von der Ropp, 7 vols., Leipzig, 1876–92.

H.R. 1477–1530: Hanserecesse von 1477–1530, ed. by D. Schäfer, 9 vols., Leipzig, 1881–1913.

H.R. 1531–60: Hanserecesse von 1531–1560, ed. by G. Wentz, vol. i, Weimar, 1941.

Kantzow: Des Thomas Kantzow Chronik von Pommern in hochdeutscher Mundart, ed. by G. Gaebel, 2 vols., Stettin, 1897–8.

—— *Pomerania oder Ursprunck, Altheit und Geschicht der Völcker und Lande Pomern, Cassuben, Wenden, Stettin, Rhügen*, ed. by H. G. L. Kosegarten, 2 vols., Greifswald, 1816–17.

—— *Pomerania, eine Pommersche Chronik aus dem 16. Jahrhundert*, ed. by G. Gaebel, 2 vols., Stettin, 1908.

Krabbo: Regesten der Markgrafen von Brandenburg aus askanischem Hause, ed. by H. Krabbo, 11 vols., Leipzig, Munich, and Berlin, 1910–33.

Kratz: Urkundenbuch zur Geschichte des Geschlechts von Kleist, ed. by G. Kratz, 2 vols., Berlin, 1862–73.

Landbuch 1337: Die Neumark Brandenburg im Jahre 1337 oder Markgraf Ludwig's des Älteren Neumärkisches Landbuch, ed. by G. W. von Raumer, Berlin, 1837.

Landbuch 1375: Kaiser Karl's IV. Landbuch der Mark Brandenburg, ed. by E. Fidicin, Berlin, 1856.

There is a more recent edition by J. Schultze, Berlin, 1940, but not containing the *Schossregister* of the fifteenth century.

Lisch: Urkunden und Forschungen zur Geschichte des Geschlechts von Behr, ed. by G. C. F. Lisch, 4 vols., Schwerin, 1861–8.

Liv-, Est- & Curländ. U.B.: Liv-, Est- und Curländisches Urkundenbuch, vols. iv–xii, ed. by F. G. von Bunge, H. Hildebrand, P. Schwartz, and others, Reval, Riga, and Moscow, 1859–1910; Zweite Abteilung, vols. i–iii, Riga and Moscow, 1900–14.

Mon. Germ. Hist., Script.: Monumenta Germaniae Historica, Scriptorum, vols. iii, xii, xiv, xvi, xix, xxi, xxv, xxix, Hanover, 1839–92.

Mylius: Corpus Constitutionum Marchicarum, oder Königl. Preussis. und Churfürstl. Brandenburgische in der Chur- und Marck Brandenburg, auch incorporirten Landen publicirte und ergangene Ordnungen, Edicta, Mandata, Rescripta, &c., ed. by C. O. Mylius, 6 vols., Berlin and Halle, 1737–51.

Normann: Matthiae Normanni Iudicis Provincialis Rugiae Codex Antiquissimi Iuris Vandalico-Rugiani ex vetustissimis observantiis Rugianis, consuetudinibus et iuribus Germanorum praecipue Septentrionalium compilatus, ed. by I. C. H. Dreyer, Lübeck and Altona, 1760.

Oelrichs: Verzeichniss der von Dregerschen übrigen Sammlung Pommerscher Urkunden zur Fortsetzung dessen Codicis Pomeraniae vicinarumque terrarum diplomatici, ed. by J. C. C. Oelrichs, Stettin, 1795.

Ostpreuss. Folianten: Ostpreussische Folianten, vols. 647–723: these are the documents of the Prussian Estates from 1640 to 1888 in the Königsberger Staatsarchiv, now at Göttingen.

Pomm. U.B.: Pommersches Urkundenbuch, 7 vols., Stettin, 1868–1936.

Preuss. U.B.: Preussisches Urkundenbuch, 3 vols., Königsberg, 1882–1944.

Privilegia der Stände dess Hertzogthumbs Preussen, darauff das Landt fundiert und biss jtzo beruhen. Auff verordnung der Herren Königlichen Commissarien nach innhalt dess Anno 1612. Recesses den Ständen in den Druck gefertiget, Braunsberg, 1616.

Protokolle & Relationen: Protokolle und Relationen des Brandenburgischen Geheimen Rathes aus der Zeit des Kurfürsten Friedrich Wilhelm, ed. by O. Meinardus, 7 vols., Leipzig, 1889–1919.

Von Raumer: Codex diplomaticus Brandenburgensis continuatus. Sammlung unge-druckter Urkunden zur Brandenburgischen Geschichte, ed. by G. W. von Raumer, 2 vols., Berlin, 1831–3.

Regesta Historico-Diplomatica: Regesta Historico-Diplomatica Ordinis S. Mariae Theutonicorum, 1198–1525, ed. by E. Joachim and W. Hubatsch, 3 vols., Göttingen, 1948–50.

Riedel: Codex diplomaticus Brandenburgensis, Sammlung der Urkunden, Chroniken und sonstigen Quellenschriften für die Geschichte der Mark Brandenburg und ihrer Regenten, ed. by A. F. Riedel, 36 vols., Berlin, 1838–65.

Sachsenspiegel: Sassenspegel mit velen nyen Addicien san dem Leenrechte unde Richtstige, Augsburg, 1516.

—— *Des Sachsenspiegels erster Theil oder das Sächsische Landrecht*, ed. by C. G. Homeyer, 3rd ed., Berlin, 1861.

Scheplitz: Joachimi Scheplitz Consuetudines Electoratus et Marchiae Brandenburgen-sis, 2 vols., Berlin, 1744–40.

Schoettgen-Kreysig: Diplomataria et Scriptores Historiae Germanicae Medii Aevi, ed. by C. Schoettgen and G. C. Kreysig, vol. iii, Altenburg, 1760.

Scotti: Sammlung der Gesetze und Verordnungen, welche in dem Herzogthum Cleve und in der Grafschaft Mark über Gegenstände der Landeshoheit, Verfassung, Verwaltung und Rechtspflege ergangen sind, ed. by J. J. Scotti, vol. i, Düssel-dorf, 1826.

Scriptores Rerum Prussicarum: Scriptores Rerum Prussicarum. Die Geschichtsquellen der preussischen Vorzeit bis zum Untergange der Ordensherrschaft, ed. by T. Hirsch, M. Töppen, and E. Strehlke, 5 vols., Leipzig, 1861–74.

Stein: 'Handelsbriefe aus Riga und Königsberg von 1458 und 1461', ed. by W. Stein, *Hansische Geschichtsblätter, Jahrgang 1898*, Leipzig, 1899, pp. 57 ff.

Stralsundische Chroniken: Stralsundische Chroniken, erster Theil, ed. by G. C. F. Mohnike and E. H. Zober, Stralsund, 1833.

Thunert: Acten der Ständetage Preussens Königlichen Anteils, ed. by F. Thunert, vol. i, Danzig, 1896.

U.B. Culm: Urkundenbuch des Bisthums Culm, ed. by C. P. Woelky, Danzig, 1884–7.

U.B. Lübeck: Urkunden-Buch der Stadt Lübeck, ed. by C. Wehrmann, vols. vi–xi, Lübeck, 1881–1905.

U.B. Samland: Urkundenbuch des Bisthums Samland, ed. by C. P. Woelky and H. Mendthal, Leipzig, 1891–8.

Urkunden der Komturei Tuchel, ed. by P. Panske, Danzig, 1911.

Urkunden & Actenstücke: Urkunden und Actenstücke zur Geschichte des Kurfürsten Friedrich Wilhelm von Brandenburg, vols. i, iv, v, ix, x, xv, and xvi, ed. by B. Erdmannsdörffer, A. von Haeften, T. Hirsch, S. Isaacsohn, K. Breysig, and M. Spahn, Berlin, 1864–99.

Veckinchusen: Hildebrand Veckinchusen — Briefwechsel eines deutschen Kaufmanns im 15. Jahrhundert, ed. by W. Stieda, Leipzig, 1921.

Voigt: Urkundenbuch zur Berlinischen Chronik, 1232–1550, ed. by F. Voigt, Berlin, 1880.

II. SECONDARY AUTHORITIES

There is no book covering the whole subject of this volume, but the author has found the following secondary works especially helpful, and the reader may find the following selection from a very large German literature useful for a study of one or the other aspect of early Prussian history.

ABEL, W., *Die Wüstungen des ausgehenden Mittelalters*, Jena, 1943.

AUBIN, G., *Zur Geschichte des gutsherrlich-bäuerlichen Verhältnisses in Ostpreussen von der Gründung des Ordensstaates bis zur Steinschen Reform*, Leipzig, 1911.

AUBIN, H., 'The lands east of the Elbe and German colonisation eastwards', *The Cambridge Economic History of Europe*, i, 1941, pp. 361 ff.

*BACZKO, L. VON, *Geschichte Preussens*, 6 vols., Königsberg, 1792–1800.

BARTHOLD, F. W., *Geschichte von Rügen und Pommern*, 5 vols., Hamburg, 1839–45.

BORNHAK, C., *Geschichte des Preussischen Verwaltungsrechts*, vol. i, Berlin, 1884.

—— *Preussische Staats- und Rechtsgeschichte*, Berlin, 1903.

BREYSIG, K., 'Der brandenburgische Staatshaushalt in der zweiten Hälfte des siebzehnten Jahrhunderts', *Jahrbuch für Gesetzgebung, Verwaltung und Volkswirthschaft im Deutschen Reich*, xvi, Leipzig, 1892, pp. 1 ff., 449 ff.

—— 'Die Organisation der brandenburgischen Kommissariate in der Zeit von 1660–1697', *F.B.P.G.* v, 1892, pp. 135 ff.

—— 'Die Entwicklung des preussischen Ständethums von seinen Anfängen bis zum Regierungsantritt Friedrich Wilhelms', *Einleitung zu Urkunden & Actenstücke*, xv, 1894.

*—— *Geschichte der brandenburgischen Finanzen in der Zeit von 1640 bis 1697*. vol. i: *Die Centralstellen der Kammerverwaltung, die Amtskammer, das Kassenwesen und die Domänen der Kurmark*, Leipzig, 1895.

CROON, H., *Die kurmärkischen Landstände 1571–1616* (Veröffentlichungen der Historischen Kommission für die Provinz Brandenburg und die Hauptstadt Berlin, ix), Berlin, 1938.

DAENELL, E., *Die Blütezeit der Deutschen Hanse*, 2 vols., Berlin, 1905–6.

F.B.P.G.: *Forschungen zur Brandenburgischen und Preussischen Geschichte*, 48 vols., Leipzig, Munich, and Berlin, 1888–1936.

*FOCK, O., *Rügen'sch–Pommersche Geschichten aus sieben Jahrhunderten*, 6 vols., Leipzig, 1861–72.

FORSTREUTER, K., *Vom Ordensstaat zum Fürstentum. Geistige und politische Wandlungen im Deutschordensstaate Preussen unter den Hochmeistern Friedrich und Albrecht (1498–1525)*, Kitzingen/Main, 1951.

FRANZ, G., *Der Dreissigjährige Krieg und das deutsche Volk*, 2nd ed., Jena, 1943.

FUCHS, C. J., *Der Untergang des Bauernstandes und das Aufkommen der Gutsherrschaften nach archivalischen Quellen aus Neu-Vorpommern und Rügen*, Strasbourg, 1888.

GLEY, W., *Die Besiedelung der Mittelmark von der slawischen Einwanderung bis 1624*, Stuttgart, 1926.

GÖTZE, L., *Urkundliche Geschichte der Stadt Stendal*, Stendal, 1873.

*GROSSMANN, F., *Über die gutsherrlich-bäuerlichen Rechtsverhältnisse in der Mark Brandenburg vom 16. bis 18. Jahrhundert* (Staats- und socialwissenschaftliche Forschungen, ix 4), Leipzig, 1890.

GUTTMANN, B., 'Die Germanisierung der Slawen in der Mark', *F.B.P.G.* ix, 1897, pp. 395 ff.

HASS, M., *Die kurmärkischen Stände im letzten Drittel des sechzehnten Jahrhunderts,* Munich and Leipzig, 1913.

*HEINEMANN, O. von, *Albrecht der Bär,* Darmstadt, 1864.

HINTZE, O., *Geist und Epochen der Preussischen Geschichte. Gesammelte Abhandlungen,* ed. by F. Hartung, Leipzig, 1943.

HIRSCH, T., *Danzigs Handels- und Gewerbsgeschichte unter der Herrschaft des Deutschen Ordens,* Leipzig, 1858.

*HÖTZSCH, O., *Stände und Verwaltung von Cleve und Mark in der Zeit von 1666 bis 1697,* Leipzig, 1908.

ISAACSOHN, S., *Geschichte des preussischen Beamtenthums vom Anfang des 15. Jahrhunderts bis auf die Gegenwart,* vols. i and ii, Berlin, 1874–8.

JANY, C., *Geschichte der Königlich Preussischen Armee bis zum Jahre 1807,* vol. i, Berlin, 1928.

KASISKE, K., *Die Siedlungtätigkeit des Deutschen Ordens im östlichen Preussen bis zum Jahre 1410* (Einzelschriften der Historischen Kommission für ost- und westpreussische Landesforchung, v), Königsberg, 1934.

—— *Das Deutsche Siedelwerk des Mittelalters in Pommerellen* (Einzelschriften der Historischen Kommission . . . , vi), Königsberg, 1938.

*KLAPROTH, C. A. L., and COSMAR, C. W., *Der Königl. Preussische und Churfürstl. Brandenburgische Wirklich Geheime Staats-Rath an Seinem zweihundertjährigen Stiftungstage den 5ten Januar 1805,* Berlin, 1805.

KÖTZSCHKE, R., and EBERT, W., *Geschichte der ostdeutschen Kolonisation,* Leipzig, 1937.

KRATZ, G., *Die Städte der Provinz Pommern,* Berlin, 1865.

KROLLMANN, C., 'Die Herkunft der deutschen Ansiedler in Preussen', *Zeitschrift des Westpreussischen Geschichtsvereins,* liv, Danzig, 1912, pp. 1 ff.

—— 'Zur Besiedlungs-Geschichte und Nationalitätenmischung in den Komtureien Christburg, Osterode und Elbing', ibid. lxiv, Danzig, 1923, pp. 3 ff.

—— 'Die Besiedlung Ostpreussens durch den Deutschen Orden', *Vierteljahrschrift für Sozial- und Wirtschaftsgeschichte,* xxi, Stuttgart, 1928, pp. 280 ff.

LOHMEYER, K., *Geschichte von Ost- und Westpreussen,* 3rd ed., Gotha, 1908.

MORTENSEN, H., and G., *Die Besiedlung des nordöstlichen Ostpreussens bis zum Beginn des 17. Jahrhunderts.* vol. i: *Die preussisch-deutsche Siedlung am Westrand der Grossen Wildnis um 1400* (Deutschland und der Osten, vii), Leipzig, 1937.

NIESSEN, P. von, *Geschichte der Neumark im Zeitalter ihrer Entstehung und Besiedlung* (Schriften des Vereins für Geschichte der Neumark), Landsberg a. W., 1905.

*ORLICH L. von, *Geschichte des Preussischen Staates im siebzehnten Jahrhundert,* 3 vols., Berlin, 1838–9.

PHILIPPSON, M., *Der Grosse Kurfürst Friedrich Wilhelm von Brandenburg,* 3 vols., Berlin, 1897–1903.

PLEHN, H., 'Zur Geschichte der Agrarverfassung von Ost- und Westpreussen', *F.B.P.G.* xvii, 1904, pp. 383 ff.; xviii, 1905, pp. 61 ff.

294 BIBLIOGRAPHY

PRUTZ, H., *Preussische Geschichte*, vol. i, Stuttgart, 1900.

RACHEL, H., *Der Grosse Kurfürst und die ostpreussischen Stände 1640–88* (Staats- und socialwissenschaftliche Forschungen, xxiv 1), Leipzig, 1905.

—— *Die Handels-, Zoll- und Akzisepolitik Brandenburg–Preussens bis 1713* (Acta Borussica, Handels-, Zoll- und Akzisepolitik, i), Berlin, 1911.

RIEDEL, A. F., *Die Mark Brandenburg im Jahre 1250 oder historische Beschreibung der Brandenburgischen Lande und ihrer politischen und kirchlichen Verhältnisse um diese Zeit*, 2 vols., Berlin, 1831–2.

ROUSSELLE, M., 'Die Besiedlung des Kreises Preussisch-Eylau in der Ordens-zeit', *Altpreussische Forschungen*, iii 2, Königsberg, 1926, pp. 5 ff.

—— 'Das Siedlungswerk des Deutschen Ordens im Lande Gerdauen', ibid. vi, Königsberg, 1929, pp. 220 ff.

Schmoller, G., *Umrisse und Untersuchungen zur Verfassungs-, Verwaltungs- und Wirtschaftsgeschichte besonders des Preussischen Staates im 17. und 18. Jahr-hundert*, Leipzig, 1898.

—— *Preussische Verfassungs-, Verwaltungs- und Finanzgeschichte*, Berlin, 1921.

SCHROETTER, F. FREIHERR VON, *Die brandenburgisch-preussische Heeresver-fassung unter dem Grossen Kurfürsten* (Staats- und socialwissenschaftliche Forschungen, xi 5), Leipzig, 1892.

SCHRÖTTER, R. FREIHERR VON, 'Das preussische Offizierkorps unter dem ersten Könige von Preussen', *F.B.P.G.* xxvi, 1913, pp. 429 ff.; xxvii, 1914, pp. 97 ff.

SOMMERFELD, W. VON, *Geschichte der Germanisierung des Herzogtums Pommern oder Slavien bis zum Ablauf des 13. Jahrhunderts* (Staats- und socialwissen-schaftliche Forschungen, xiii 5), Leipzig, 1896.

—— *Beiträge zur Verfassungs- und Ständegeschichte der Mark Brandenburg im Mittelalter*, Leipzig, 1904.

SPAHN, M., *Verfassungs- und Wirtschaftsgeschichte des Herzogtums Pommern von 1478 bis 1625* (Staats- und socialwissenschaftliche Forschungen, xiv 1), Leipzig, 1896.

STENZEL, G. A. H., *Geschichte des preussischen Staats*, vols. i and ii, Hamburg, 1830–37.

STÖLZEL, A., *Brandenburg-Preussens Rechtsverwaltung und Rechtsverfassung*, vol. i, Berlin, 1888.

TÖPPEN, M., 'Die Zins-Verfassung Preussens unter der Herrschaft des deutschen Ordens', *Zeitschrift für Preussische Geschichte und Landeskunde*, iv, Berlin, 1867, pp. 207 ff., 345 ff., 611 ff., 742 ff.

—— 'Der Deutsche Ritterorden und die Stände Preussens', *Historische Zeit-schrift*, xlvi, 1881, pp. 430 ff.

—— *Geschichte Masurens*, Danzig, 1870.

TÜMPEL, L., *Die Entstehung des brandenburgisch-preussischen Einheitsstaates im Zeitalter des Absolutismus (1609–1806)*, Breslau, 1915.

VOLLBEHR, F., *Die Holländer und die deutsche Hanse* (Pfingstblätter des Hansischen Geschichtsvereins, xxi), Lübeck, 1930.

WEBER, L., *Preussen vor 500 Jahren in culturhistorischer, statistischer und mili-tärischer Beziehung*, Danzig, 1878.

WEHRMANN, M., *Geschichte von Pommern*, 2 vols., Gotha, 1904–6.

*WOLTERS, F., *Geschichte der brandenburgischen Finanzen in der Zeit von 1640 bis

1697. vol. ii: *Die Zentralverwaltung des Heeres und der Steuern*, Munich and Leipzig, 1915.

*ZIMMERMANN, A., *Versuch einer historischen Entwickelung der märkischen Städteverfassungen*, 3 vols., Berlin, 1837-40.

The books marked with an asterisk (*) contain important documents which have been used in the text.

INDEX

Bernstein, nunnery of, 15; town of, 96 n. 3, 109.

Biesenthal, town of, 108.

Bischofsburg, district of, 56, 57; town of, 56, 57.

Bismarck, noble family of, 74.

Black Death, the, 70, 76, 80, 101, 113.

Blumberg, district of, 11; town of, 11.

Blumenthal, Joachim Friedrich von, 182 n. 4, 235.

Bochum, town of, 230.

Bötzow, town of, 96 n. 3.

Bogislav, duke of Pomerania, 8.

Bogislav X, duke of Pomerania, 146–7, 149.

Bohemia, 1, 2, 105, 276.

Bohemians, 50.

Boitzenburg, castle of, 96 n. 3, 97.

Boleslav III, duke of Poland, 8.

Boleslav, duke of Silesia, 45.

Borke, noble family of, 22.

Brandenburg, army of, *see* Army of Brandenburg; bishops of, 4, 12, 30, 35; bishopric of, 2–4, 11, 28, 35; burgraves of, 20, 46; cathedral chapter of, 11, 12; Estates of, 92, 93, 94, 141, 142, 166–8, 170–1, 173, 178, 179–200, 219, 234, 243, 254; industries of, 268; margraves of, *see* Margraves; nobility of, 92, 139, 141–4, 155–9, 167, 170–3, 178–89, 194–201, 229, 270–1, 273; towns of, 91, 92, 93, 138, 139, 141–2, 145, 148, 150, 160, 170–3, 182–3, 185, 190–9, 202, 249.

— town of, 4, 11, 49, 137, 145, 172, 183, 191; law of, 45 n. 4, 47.

— Mark, the, 2, 3, 4, 7, 8, 11, 12, 13, 14, 15, 17, 18, 20, 21, 23, 27, 28, 29, 31, 34, 35, 36, 38, 40, 43, 45, 46, 47, 48, 49, 54, 59, 71, 73, 75, 76, 78, 80, 86, 87, 89, 91, 93, 94, 95, 96, 97, 98, 99, 100, 102, 106, 108, 110, 113, 114, 136, 140, 145, 147, 150, 155, 157, 159, 162–4, 165–7, 169, 174–202, 205, 217, 221–2, 224, 229, 232–3, 246, 249–51, 253–60, 262–77.

Brandt, Eusebius von, 218.

Braunsberg, town of, 50, 61, 125, 126, 127.

Bredow, noble family of, 96, 156.

Breslau, town of, 121, 126, 129.

Brest Litovsk, town of, 121.

Brietzen, town of, 49.

Bruges, city of, 49, 50, 117, 119, 120, 121, 122; Hanse factory at, 119, 122, 129.

Brunswick, dukes of, 146, 261.

Brusewitz, noble family of, 18 n. 1, 25.

Bublitz, district of, 12, 26; town of, 12.

Buch, Johann von, 38 n. 3, 81 n. 3, 82 and n. 8; noble family of, 109.

Buckow, monastery of, 16, 99 n. 4.

Bütow, district of, 7.

Bugewitz, castle of, 90.

Burgsdorf, noble family of, 182.

Burgundian, 232.

Butchers, 86, 144, 203.

Butter, 133, 172; prices of, 133 and n. 4, 281.

Buying out of peasants, *see* Eviction.

Calcar, town of, 233, 244.

Calvinists, the (Calvinism), 216 and n. 4, 230 and n. 7, 252, 258, 269; *see also* Huguenots.

Cammin, bishops of, 12, 18 n. 1, 25, 32, 44; bishopric of, 11, 12, 35, 176; cathedral chapter of, 11; district of, 12; town of, 12.

Casimir IV, king of Poland, 132.

Casimir, duke of Pomerania, 146.

Census (peasant due), 35, 63, 65, 69.

Charlemagne, 2.

Chorin, monastery of, 14, 16, 33, 34, 74, 76, 79 n. 2, 80, 97.

Christ (*Teutonicus deus*), 2.

Christburg, commandery of, 58.

Christian I, king of Denmark, 128.

Christian, 3, 32, 33.

Christianity, 2, 5, 6, 8, 9, 18.

Christian names, 18 and n. 5, 69.

Cistercians, Order of, 14, 15, 16, 17, 33, 34, 41, 74, 76, 97.

Cleves, duchy of, 176, 178, 184–5, 205, 216, 217, 219, 229–52, 254–5, 260, 265–6, 268, 271; dukes of, 176–7, 179, 232; Estates of, 189, 219, 230, 233–51, 254, 277; nobility of, 229–31, 235–43, 246–9, 251–2, 271; peasants of, 230–1, 239, 247; towns of, 230, 232–43, 246–51, 271, 275.

— town of, 241–2, 245, 248.

Cloth, 125, 131, 230, 233, 268.

Clothiers (clothdealers), 47, 86, 137, 144.

Cloth industry, 230, 233, 268.

PRINTED IN GREAT BRITAIN
AT THE UNIVERSITY PRESS, OXFORD
BY VIVIAN RIDLER
PRINTER TO THE UNIVERSITY